D0267580

ALSO BY RALPH G. MARTIN

JENNIE: The Life of Lady Randolph Churchill—
The Romantic Years: 1854–1895
JENNIE: The Life of Lady Randolph Churchill—
The Dramatic Years: 1895–1921
SKIN DEEP—*a novel*
BOY FROM NEBRASKA
THE BEST IS NONE TOO GOOD
THE BOSSES
BALLOTS AND BANDWAGONS
WORLD WAR II: A Photographic Record of the War in
Europe from D-Day to V-E Day—*with Richard Harrity*
WORLD WAR II: A Photographic Record of the War in
the Pacific from Pearl Harbor to V-J Day
THE WIZARD OF WALL STREET
THE GI WAR
A MAN FOR ALL PEOPLE
LINCOLN CENTER FOR THE PERFORMING ARTS
PRESIDENT FROM MISSOURI—*a juvenile*

with Ed Plaut:
FRONT RUNNER, DARK HORSE

with Morton D. Stone:
MONEY, MONEY, MONEY

with Richard Harrity:
ELEANOR ROOSEVELT: Her Life in Pictures
THE HUMAN SIDE OF FDR
MAN OF THE CENTURY: Churchill
MAN OF DESTINY: DeGaulle of France
THE THREE LIVES OF HELEN KELLER

THE WOMAN
HE LOVED

Ralph G. Martin

W. H. ALLEN· LONDON
A division of Howard & Wyndham Ltd, 1974

COPYRIGHT © 1973, 1974 BY RALPH G. MARTIN
FIRST BRITISH EDITION, 1974

This book or parts thereof may not be reproduced in any form
whatsoever without permission in writing

The author wishes to thank the following for permission to
reprint material in this book. Any inadvertent omission will be
corrected in future printings if notification is sent to the publisher.

Atheneum Publishers, Inc., and Collins Publishers for material from *Harold Nicolson: Diaries & Letters 1930–1939*, edited by Nigel Nicolson, copyright © 1966 by William Collins Sons & Company, Ltd. V. Sackville-West's letters copyright © 1966 by Sir Harold Nicolson. Introduction and notes to this volume copyright © 1966 by Nigel Nicolson.

Atheneum Publishers, Inc., and David Higham Associates Ltd. for material from *The Abdication of Edward VIII* by Lord Beaverbrook, ed. by A. J. P. Taylor, copyright © 1965, 1966 by Beaverbrook Newspapers, Ltd. Preface copyright © 1966 by A. J. P. Taylor.

James Brown Associates, Inc., and Curtis Brown Ltd. for material from *Daughters and Rebels* (published in Great Britain as *Hons and Rebels* by Jessica Mitford., copyright © 1960 by Jessica Mitford.

Mrs Norma Ellis for "The First Fig" by Edna St Vincent Millay, from *Collected Poems* published by Harper & Row, Publishers copyright 1922–1950 by Edna St Vincent Millay.

Harper & Row, Publishers, Inc., and Andre Deutsch Ltd. for material from *The Labyrinth* (published in Great Britain as *The Schellenberg Memoirs*) by Walter Schellenberg, trans. by Lewis Hagen, copyright © 1956 by Harper & Row, Publishers, Inc.

Rupert Hart-Davis for material from *The Light of Common Day* by Lady Diana Cooper, copyright © 1959 by Rupert Hart-Davis.

Blake Higgs for lyrics from "Love Alone" by Blake Higgs.

David Higham Associates Ltd. for material from *Geoffrey Dawson and Our Times* by Sir Evelyn Wrench, published by Hutchinson & Company Ltd., copyright © 1955 by Sir Evelyn Wrench.

Little, Brown and Company and George Weidenfeld and Nicolson Ltd. for material from *The Wandering Years* by Cecil Beaton, copyright © 1961 by Cecil Beaton.

Macmillan Publishing Company, Inc., and Hodder and Stoughton Ltd. for material from *Abdication* by Brian Inglis, copyright © 1966 by Brian Inglis.

Newbold Noyes for articles by Newbold Noyes, © 1936 by The Evening Star Newspaper Company.

George Weidenfeld and Nicolson Limited for material from *Walter Monckton: The Life of the Viscount of Brenchley* by Frederick Winston Furneaux Smith, Second Earl of Birkenhead.

Printed and bound in Great Britain by
Butler & Tanner Ltd, Frome & London
for the publishers W. H. Allen & Co. Ltd,
44 Hill Street, London W1X 8LB
ISBN 0 491 01851 7

For
Pearlie Bernier
From the Fourth of July to forever
The kind of friend who enriches life

For
Bill Williams
From the Queen Mary, Birmingham,
Llandyssul and Newport, Wales
"Lord, keep my memory green . . ."

For
Al Weisman
From Yank, The Army Weekly,
The Stevenson Bandwagon, *and*
Chicago, Chicago, Chicago
His cause was people.
So sincere, so vital, and
when was there a kinder man?

Contents

Prologue

WHEN THE DUCHESS STOOD UP, she seemed so small, so frail. The fractured hip had taken away some of her easy grace. ("It's because it's only partly plastic; if it were all plastic, I could move more smoothly.") And yet, for a petite woman, there was this feeling of presence and size. If you analyzed it quickly, you always came back to her large, luminous, violet-blue eyes, piercing and intense. They were the kind of eyes that focused, drilled and rooted you. When she talked to you, it was only you she was interested in, and she made you know it. And you realized this was probably the simple way it all began, the way she so completely captured the heart of a king.

Quite apart from her eyes, she made a vivid picture: the trim figure; a simple, classic light violet dress; the beads and earrings both tasteful and dramatic. She looked as if she had "stepped out of a bandbox," not a hair out of place, the make-up muted. Her hair was high on her head, parted in the middle. "I'm putting my hair back to the Mrs. Simpson days," she said, smiling.

Her accent was neither Baltimore nor British, but something of a soft merge, pitched low, with the occasional suggestion of a slight lisp.

But the formidable thing about this woman, who was almost eighty, was that she looked alive and exciting, and almost twenty years younger.

She was waiting with her secretary, John Utter, and her other guests. Villa Roserie sat high on a hill, overlooking the ocean at Cap Ferrat. The grounds were large, all walled in, with an enormous swimming pool. The grass was lush and the silence complete.

Lunch was gay and laughing, the conversation easy, ranging from Watergate to the British sex scandals. The Duchess regarded the London scandals as far more interesting, and she said she found it fascinat-

9

ing how many British government people seemed to be popping in and out of bed. "But the British act as if they had invented sex." She had lived long enough among them, she said, to feel that they were the most moral people she knew. "They've always done it, but they never talk about it. Now, when they finally write about it, everybody seems so surprised."

A small edge of bitterness seemed to creep into her tone. "The British won't do anything unless there's money in it." As the talk turned to mutual friends there she added, almost sadly, "I didn't know I had any friends left in England."

She seemed to be so aware of everything else that was happening in the world. It was not simply a matter of having read the headlines; it was a matter of her understanding and her analysis. It was both pertinent and informed.

The food itself was simple but delicious; a fine wine, a small bird, a fresh salad, a whole fish ("Take the meat near the tail," she suggested. "It's the sweetest part"). Her wit was sharp. Somebody mentioned the cranberry health juice fad in the United States, and she asked, "Does it do for you what it does for the turkey?"

Two black pugs sat quietly nearby on a red satin chair and one barked softly for attention. The Duchess looked lovingly at them, remarking how comfortable they both looked, and how striking their black looked against the red upholstery. She explained that one of the pugs had belonged to the Duke, "and the other is mine, and completely possesses me. It's difficult to make the Duke's pug feel that I love him just as much as I do the other one. Sometimes they're both on my bed, fighting, and I have to have a whip handy to break them up. But then, it's nice to have two boys fighting for me, at my age."

One had to marvel at her. She was the perfect hostess. Her eyes were watchful of every guest, how they were served, whether they wanted or lacked anything. As a discussion lagged, her questions were fast and relevant. For a woman of any age, she seemed close to her prime.

At one point she said she had very few French friends, and she felt that the French found it difficult even to be friends with each other. Utter protested, reminding her of the various friends they did have. She said yes, but that he had more friends among them than she did, and that she really didn't know the French very well because she seldom ever met any of the French general public, or ever met many in the street. In that sense, she said, she felt isolated.

Her mention of isolation made her openly wistful. "Why don't we go somewhere tonight? I haven't been anywhere. How about Monte Carlo?" Then she added in a quiet aside, "I love poker. I think it's a marvelous game. And I like chemin de fer, but I don't gamble much. I always think what I could buy with the money I lose."

After the meal it was the Duchess who proposed, "Don't you want to come and talk?"

Utter and the guests went out to the pool, and she led the way into the drawing room.

Cap Ferrat looked quiet and misty below us, and she commented that it had not been as sunny as she had hoped. Then, suddenly, she turned and said, "You know, today is the first anniversary of his death."

The gaiety was gone from her voice now, and it sounded strained, almost flat.

"I didn't believe it when I looked at the calendar. A whole year. We had some friends who also died of throat cancer. I told him to stop smoking all those cigarettes. He started smoking all the time because he was always so nervous about making all those speeches when he was traveling around as Prince of Wales.

"He did cut down. He started smoking half-cigarettes in a holder. But I guess it was still too much; it all added up."

"I've never smoked," she said. "Maybe it was my grandmother's influence." She mentioned other influences. "You know, my friends all had more money than we did, but we did have at least one governor in our family and we did have a good background. And I was a happy child, I really was. My mother was always so gay, and what a great sense of humor she had. And my stepfather was very good to me."

Her face was almost shining now as she said it, the years all slipped away. Then her mouth tensed a little.

"The thing about Maryland is that they're tight, tight, tight. Maryland, my Maryland—they're the biggest snobs in the world. If you don't go to the Cotillion, you're nothing. And if you do, it's so boring. They never went anywhere outside of Maryland. They married each other and lived there and died there. They couldn't understand why I wanted to go anywhere else, but I did . . ."

She glowed when she talked about the Prince, how he knew more about the British Empire than anybody else, how he insisted on learning Spanish before going to South America, impressing the people there so much with his fluency that they took a lot of trade away from the United States and gave it to the British.

"He worked harder than any prince had ever done. He was the salesman of the British Empire. He told all this to me, and I listened, and I sympathized, and I understood; and I guess he needed that." She paused. "He might have been a great king; the people loved him."

Then, shifting unexpectedly, she murmured, "I never take any sleeping pills. Detective stories are my sleeping pills. Towards the end of the story, I always know how they come out."

At first, it seemed a non sequitur, but it fit.

She then described how she went to France and he went to Austria after the abdication, while her divorce was pending. "Everybody was watching us every minute, so that we shouldn't be together."

She was musing again. "We had many happy years together, even though a great many people thought we wouldn't. And you know what? We were different in a lot of ways. He was a country boy and I was a city girl. That's why we had two houses in Paris, one in town and then The Mill, which he loved. He loved gardening. He used to say to me, 'I always grow them and you always cut them.' That's why I want to sell The Mill now. It was his home more than mine, and I couldn't bear to be there any more. I couldn't stay at The Mill without him. Everything he did is still there."

As she said that, she was quiet a moment, digging deep into herself, the vividness of it causing a look of hurt to come into her eyes.

"He was so stubborn," she said. "When he made up his mind, that was it. I called him 'The Mule.' The thing is, he was so used to having everything he wanted all his life. I know he had a lot of girls before me, but he said I was the only one he wanted to marry."

She was quiet again after that, smiling at something secret inside. Then she said, "I told him it was too heavy a load for me to carry. I told him the British people were absolutely right about not wanting a divorced woman for a queen. I told him I didn't want to be queen. All that formality and responsibility. And I told him that if he abdicated, every woman in the world would hate me and everybody in Great Britain would feel he had deserted them. I told him that if he stayed on as king, it wouldn't be the end for us. I could still come and see him and he could still come and see me. We had terrible arguments about it. But he was a mule. He said he didn't want to be king without me, that if I left him, he would follow me wherever I went.

"What could I do? What *could* I do?"

12

PART I

1

THE HEADLINE in the Baltimore *Evening Sun* read:

MRS. SIMPSON HAS MORE
BRITISH BLOOD THAN KING[1]

That was true, but some of the other claims seemed more extravagant. One genealogist insisted that Wallis was technically a countess of
the defunct Holy Roman Empire, with her ancestry claiming six kings
of England, at least two Magna Charta barons, as well as French,
Scottish and Spanish royal houses along the way. Wallis' cousin, the
noted novelist Upton Sinclair, wrote that there was no question that
she was a relative of Pocahontas. He claimed that her maternal grandfather was a direct lineal descendant of Chief Powhatan, Pocahontas'
father.

No matter who the genealogist, however, there is no question that
her family tree had many distinguished branches, particularly in Maryland and Virginia. Governor Edwin Warfield of Maryland was one of
her father's ancestors and Governor Andrew Jackson Montague of
Virginia was one of her mother's. The Maryland Historical Society described the Warfields as "old, old Baltimore," and the Montagues are
similarly regarded as one of "the first families of Virginia."

William the Conqueror in 1086 ordered a general survey of the economic resources of England for taxation purposes. It described the
present and past holders of each piece of land, and it included several
references to Warfields. One of them was Pagan de Warfield, who
came from France with William the Conqueror,[2] fought for him in the
Battle of Hastings. William I rewarded him with a knight's fee, an
estate he called "Warfield's Walk," one of sixteen "Walks" that divided

15

Windsor Forest. Close by was Windsor Castle, which would figure so dramatically in the life of a king who abdicated his throne for a Warfield.

Into the family then came a mixture of Scottish, Welsh and even Dutch blood. Distinguished Maryland Society genealogist William R. Marye questions some heritage claims of kings and nobility. "If there are any," he said, "they would be very attenuated."[3] Marye, however, has definitively detailed Wallis' American heritage.

The original American Warfield came to Maryland from Berkshire, England, in 1662 and bought a large land tract near the Severn River for 8,000 pounds of tobacco. This Richard Warfield raised a family of six sons, who soon had estates all over the area known as Warfield's Forest, Warfield's Plains, Warfield's Right, Warfield's Range, Warfield's Hope and even Warfield's Folly. When Richard Warfield died, his bequests included such luxuries as silver spoons, leather-covered chairs and feather beds.

Virginia genealogists claim an equally distinguished history for the Montagues. And they do firmly claim a king. Sir Simon Montecute, who headed the House of Montague in the fourteenth century, married Aufrica, daughter of the King of the Isle of Man.[4] This isle in the Irish Sea, off the coast of Great Britain, is thirty-three miles long and twelve miles wide. When Aufrica's father died, Simon became King of the Isle, and his family reigned for more than fifty years.

The Montagues have long been pillars of British aristocracy, and the family's titular head is the Duke of Manchester. In *Romeo and Juliet*, Shakespeare noted that the Montagues were socially superior to the Capulets. This ancestral connection also makes Wallis a distant relation to the Earl of Sandwich.

Like the Warfields, the Montagues had original land grants from Charles II. First of the family to arrive here was eighteen-year-old Peter Montague of Bovency, Buckinghamshire, in 1621. He not only accompanied the new governor for the Colony of Virginia but married the Governor's daughter. He later represented his county in the colonial assembly, the House of Burgesses, and became a highly successful planter of tobacco, wheat and barley.[5]

A liberal sprinkling of both Warfields and Montagues served in the Revolutionary War. It was a Montague who saved George Washington's life by stepping in front of him to take the saber cut of a British soldier.

Both Warfields and Montagues were staunch Southern sympathizers in "the War Between the States" against "Mr. Lincoln's men." Unlike Virginia, Maryland did not secede from the Union. But Wallis' grandfather, Henry Mactier Warfield, "always bright, always cheery," [6] was one of the first Baltimoreans to demand secession. With the declaration of war, Warfield was arrested and sent to nearby Fort McHenry, along with his good friend Severn Teackle Wallis. Warfield later became the Democratic Reform Party candidate for mayor, the first president of the Baltimore Chamber of Commerce and a director of the Baltimore and Ohio Railroad and made his fortune in grain and flour export. Severn Teackle Wallis became a prominent lawyer and educator.

With the war's end, Baltimore soon sprang back to prosperity. Founded in 1729, this natural seaport had become a vital shipping center for tobacco and grain, and now it also became an important commercial center. With much of the South ravaged, a large number of prominent Virginia families moved to Baltimore. Among them were some Montagues from Richmond.

During those postwar years, the impact of Severn Teackle Wallis on Baltimore was so great that they put up a statue of him. His impact on his friend Henry Warfield was similarly strong, and Warfield named a son after him, Teackle Wallis.

Teackle Wallis Warfield was the only one of four sons who did not inherit his father's money-making ability. At the age of twenty-six, he was still a clerk while his brothers were all rich and famous. But he was not a family outcast, even if he was a black sheep. The Baltimore City Directory (1889–1896) lists him as living at 34 East Preston Street, the house of his mother and oldest brother. With his father's fortune and his family reputation, his social standing was set. He was a member of the exclusive Bachelor's Cotillion. The major excuse made for him was that he was sickly, tainted early with tuberculosis. He must have been a very appealing young man. The few portraits of him reveal compelling eyes, large and sensitive and penetrating, a long angular face, an impressive mustache. If his brothers were disappointed in him, his mother kept him close under her care.

It created a family crisis when T. Wallis (as he called himself) announced that he wanted to marry Alice Montague.

"Miss Alice" was absolutely lovely. The Baltimore paper referred to her as "one of the two beautiful Montague sisters." Her face had

17

sparkle, her laugh was rich, and there were always men clustering around her to hear it. In spite of her fiery temper and tart tongue she was the family favorite who could do no wrong. Cousin Lelia Barnett, wife of the commandant of the Marine Corps, said of her: "There was never anyone like Alice."[7]

The stream of suitors seemed to start when she was only thirteen, and she could have had the pick of almost anyone. Somehow she fell in love with this young man with the haunted face already marked with the stamp of death.

Why? There was no secret about his illness. Indeed, his oldest and most successful brother, Solomon Warfield, then the youngest postmaster in Baltimore, met the Montagues and stressed the seriousness of the disease. Because of it, T. Wallis could not expect to be wholly well again and both families were against the marriage.

Then why? T. Wallis was hardly handsome. A poetic face, yes. And there must have been something else, something special. Her family would say of her, many years and several husbands later, that "Miss Alice" always married the wrong man. On her own deathbed, she would tell her daughter Wallis how much alike the two of them were, ruled more by heart than head.

The heart won and the two lovers were quietly married at Saint Michael and All Angels Church in Baltimore on November 19, 1895, "in the presence of several friends."[8]

Exactly seven months later, on June 19, 1896, their child was born, at a summer resort in Blue Ridge Summit, Pennsylvania, just beyond the Maryland border. Their own doctor was out of town and so they called young Dr. Lewis Allen, then on the staff of the University of Maryland Hospital.

Newspaper society columns reported that Alice's mother-in-law, Mrs. Henry Warfield, was staying at the same Monterey Hotel at the same time,[9] and that Alice's sister Bessie and her husband, D. Buchanan Merryman, were registered at a nearby hotel.[10] Despite the prominence of both families, there was, however, no newspaper mention at all about the baby's birth. On July 5 there was an item: "Mr. Wallis Warfield, who has been very ill, is slightly improved."[11] And, on September 28: "Mr. and Mrs. Wallace [sic] Warfield have returned to Baltimore after spending the summer in the Blue Ridge Mountains"[12]—again, with no mention of the child.

They had hoped for a son and had prepared the name "Wallis."

When a daughter arrived, they kept the Wallis and preceded it by "Bessie," for Alice's sister, Mrs. D. Buchanan Merryman, and also for her cousin and godmother, Bessie Montague Brown.

A close cousin, Mrs. Elizabeth Gordon Biddle Gordon reported this conversation between "Miss Alice" and Dr. Allen:

"Doctor, is the baby all right? Has she all her fingers and all her toes?"

"She's perfect," answered Dr. Allen, adding, "In fact, she's fit for a King."[13]

T. Wallis, a wasted little man in a wheelchair,[14] had his baby photographed shortly before his death. In the last stages of tuberculosis, he could neither hold her nor kiss her, or even see her. He looked at her picture and said, "I'm afraid, Alice, she has the Warfield look. Let us hope that in spirit she'll be like you—a Montague."[15]

On November 16, 1896, the Baltimore *News* reported the death of T. Wallis Warfield, saying, "Mr. Warfield has been in failing health for about a year, and his death was not unexpected."

He was only twenty-seven.

2

TEACKLE WALLIS WARFIELD DIED four days before their first anniversary, leaving his widow with tender memories of much love, but no money. If Teackle's mother harbored any resentment against Alice, if she felt that the marriage had hastened his death, she still wanted her grandchild and so invited both of them to live with her and Solomon.

Alice's mother-in-law was then in her sixties and still always wore black for her husband, who had died years before. She had an aristocratic air, a thin face and tightly pulled hair parted in the middle. Her red brick house on fashionable East Preston Street, near Charles Street, had large, somberly furnished rooms and a well-stocked library. Her mother-in-law's bedroom and bath were on the first floor, Solomon's bedroom and bath on the second, and there were two bedrooms without bath for Alice and her daughter on the third floor. They were forced to use the bathroom two floors below.

Solomon became a vital part of their lives. He was a man of two faces. Then in his early thirties, he already had become one of Baltimore's men of distinction. Besides being the city's postmaster, he was organizing the Seaboard Air Line Railway and would become its president. He would also serve as president of the Continental Trust Company, consolidate the gas and electric companies of Baltimore, originate a plan to bring power to the city from the Susquehanna River and later be instrumental in connecting the east and west coasts of Florida by rail.

Like his father, he associated with the independent Democrats and ran unsuccessfully for mayor of Baltimore.

That was one face. The other was the author of a small, privately printed book that included some poetry,[1] the man largely responsible for bringing the Metropolitan Opera Company to the city and the diligent board member of the Museum of Art. He also kept a suite at the Plaza Hotel in New York and his intimates knew him as a man of many women. He had a collection of their photographs on his wall, all most warmly inscribed. And yet, he never married.

Bessie Wallis knew him as "Uncle Sol." To her, he was strict, cold, puritanical, perhaps trying to act as he thought a father might act, trying to counteract the permissiveness of her mother. His money supported them, put Wallis through school and even afterward sustained them.

The situation soon became awkward. Uncle Sol fell deeply in love with Alice, but it was not mutual. It would have solved all her problems, but he was not the man she wanted, with all his money. He was too somber and stiff for her. Therefore, when Bessie Wallis was five years old, she and her mother moved nearby to a quiet family hotel. Uncle Sol still made deposits to their bank account, but it was more quixotic, never a fixed sum on which they could budget.

Alice Warfield finally found a job making children's clothes for the Women's Exchange, and so Bessie Wallis still spent considerable time with her grandmother, whose imprint on the highly impressionable mind of the preschool tot was almost immeasurable. Grandmother Warfield had grown up in a Baltimore haunted by the ghost of slavery, when ladies used to spit when they passed a Northern soldier. "Never marry a Yankee," warned her grandmother, "and never marry a man who kisses your hand."[2]

Bessie Wallis might forget her grandmother's warning about letting men kiss her hand or marrying a Yankee, but she would never forget to brush her hair a hundred strokes each morning and a hundred strokes each night, and completely absorbed her grandmother's sense of perfection and punctiliousness.

Aunt Bessie was then a widow and she invited her sister Alice and Bessie Wallis to live with her. Alice was delighted. It gave Bessie Wallis more of a home, and it helped lessen her own loneliness. Aunt Bessie was a warm, lively woman, as witty and as pretty as her sister, and Bessie Wallis remembered her home as a place of fun and love.

When Bessie Wallis was six, it was time for school. She was then a skinny girl with big eyes, her hair in pigtails, tightly tied with a big black bow. Her teacher, Ada O'Donell, later described her as "an attractive, lively six-year-old who was full of fun and pep, and was well liked by all the children."[3] And, years later, she would introduce "Miss Ada" to her husband as the woman "who taught me all I know."[4] Miss Ada was the founder and teacher of a private school for some thirty neighborhood children, mostly of kindergarten age. Miss Ada also remembered, "Her mother worked hard, for she had little money of her own, but Wallis was always beautifully dressed, and appeared to have everything."[5]

Perhaps the indulgent mother gave the spoiled daughter too much. For her daughter's first party, Alice Warfield selected a white dress. Wallis stamped her small foot and said no. "I want the red one," she said, "so the boys will notice me."[6] But if Alice Warfield catered to her daughter on some things, she was stern on others. The breeding was good and so were the manners.

Bessie Wallis learned to curtsy to her elders, sit up straight during meals and speak when spoken to. And Bessie Wallis remembered the spankings, however occasional. Her mother believed her daughter should wear light clothes in winter to make her hardier and less susceptible to colds.

In those days, well-born women were not supposed to work, no matter how dire their financial straits. But Alice Warfield wanted greater independence. They moved to Preston Apartment House, still in the same neighborhood, and she started what was later referred to as "a boarding house." What she did was to invite other tenants in the building to be her dinner guests, and pay for it. An admiring friend said of her, "Broke and clever as she was, she probably could have driven herself to real success in the business world."[7]

This was an absurdly extravagant idea. Alice Warfield was never a businesswoman. She loved to cook and had a gift for it, but it was soon obvious that she was cooking more for pleasure than for profit.

A young medical student, Charles F. Bove, who later became a well-known surgeon in France, had rented a room from Mrs. Warfield when he was in his first year at Johns Hopkins. "I was particularly fascinated by the young girl who helped her mother serve the meals I took with the family," he said. "She was an exuberant child of twelve with . . . hair parted in braids, high cheekbones and a prominent nose that made one think of an Indian squaw. I teasingly called her Minnehaha and she responded with a wide grin."[8]

Alice Warfield was then slightly more than thirty years old, still a beautiful woman with a hectic social life, still living for laughter, and her laughter never stopped.

Bessiewallis (as people called her) was ten years old when she went to the well-known Arundell School in the heart of Baltimore. Arundell was highly disciplined, but Bessiewallis later insisted that she enjoyed every day.

There were other enjoyments. On nearby Cathedral Street, there was a marvelous shop called Sidenstrickers where you could buy five pieces of colored chalk for a penny, a box of decals for another cent. All those who still had a penny left could get something called Licorish Lash, or else a Bolster. A Bolster was an unwrapped piece of mixed peanut butter, chocolate and taffy candy. For other fun, there was roller skating at Mount Vernon Place, the historic center of the city, where the most luxurious homes overlooked four grassy squares with fountains. In bustling Baltimore, it was an island of dignity and graciousness.

At Arundell Bessiewallis found a heroine, Miss Charlotte Noland. Miss Charlotte, who a few years later founded the famous Foxcroft School, was then the athletics teacher. She was a woman of decisive speech, and she was a superb rider. Bessiewallis had been afraid of horses ever since one of her cousins had slapped the flank of her mount, which then bolted and threw her. Her general interest in athletics always had been minimal. Now, however, she tried to find some sport where she could excel and impress Miss Charlotte. She finally found it in basketball, which called for speed and maneuverability and aggressiveness, and she even became captain of the team.

Her mother decided to move again. She found a three-story brownstone at 212 East Biddle Street, on the outer fringe of the more fashionable area. Bessiewallis was shocked to discover why her mother had wanted to make the move. Alice wanted to marry again and she had picked her man.

Bessiewallis had met him and liked him. John Freeman Rasin had a pleasant personality with a loud, easy laugh and a gentle manner. Everybody called him "Young Free." His father, I. Freeman Rasin, had controlled state politics for more than thirty years, and Young Free had worked for him as his liaison with the ward workers.

He had been educated at Loyola College, clerked for the Board of Liquor License Commissioners and was then in the insurance business. Warfield family friends remembered him as a porcine-faced, heavy-set man, and "very ordinary." Again, for them, Alice had married the wrong man.

Socially, Young Free was an "out." Pedigree was the only social pivot in Baltimore. To be "in" you had to be born "in." Otherwise, you were always an "out."

For Bessiewallis, the news was a disaster. She wanted her mother for herself only. For years they had been alone together, shared all their innermost secrets. Now it would all change. She was then twelve years old. To persuade her to come to the wedding, she was told that she would be the first to cut the cake and would perhaps find "a ring, a silver thimble and a bright new dime." During the ceremony, "I slipped out," said Wallis, and began "probing" the cake. In the midst of this, the wedding party suddenly arrived and she heard the "roar of laughter."[9]

A wedding account described "the beautiful young daughter of the bride" who "wore a dainty gown of embroidered batiste laced with blue ribbons." The Baltimore *News* referred to her as "Miss Wallace Warfield." Even though they had misspelled her name, she was delighted that they had dropped the "Bessie." She hated the name of Bessie, she said, because it made her think of cows.

"My stepfather was very good to me," she said many years later. "He could not have been more kind, more loving."[10]

She had never really had a father before. Uncle Sol loved her, in his way, but he couldn't show it and she never felt it. Rasin was a man who showed and felt. His best present to her was her first dog, a French bulldog she called "Bully." It stirred in her a love for dogs that seemed to get stronger the longer she lived.

Alice (or "Alys," as she now spelled it) made a happy home for Rasin, filling it often with his friends. She joked that since he had not produced any children, she would call him "the seedless Rasin." They both decided that Wallis should go to summer camp for the first time when she was fourteen and that she should go to Burrlands. Wallis wanted, more than anything else, to go there because it was run by her idol, Miss Charlotte Noland, at her family home in Virginia. It was in the Piedmont section in a triangle between the Bull Run, the Cobbler and the Blue Ridge Mountains, not too far from where Wallis was born. The line the campers learned was "God smiled when He made those hills."

Older girls lived in tepees while the younger ones clustered in cottages. When they went anywhere, a quaint coach called "The Flying Yankee" accommodated all twenty of them. One place they went to for tennis and tea was an estate close by called "Glenora," owned by the Tabbs.

Seventeen-year-old Lloyd Tabb became Wallis' first "crush."

"Being full of romance and poetry at that age," Tabb remembered, "we would maneuver around and find a secluded spot in which to 'speak of love' and 'give the direct gaze.' " Tabb described Wallis as having "a touch of pathos and sweetness bordering on wistfulness." He admitted, however, that she was more sophisticated and advanced than other girls her age. He recalled, too, that the most sought-after spot for dates was "The Roost." It was an arrangement of seats in the branches of a large oak and one needed a stepladder to get up there. Tabb and Wallis were up there one night when they heard a rustling of leaves overhead. Tabb investigated and found a small group of Peeping Toms, some younger kids from camp. "I was very indignant," he said. "Wallis was highly amused. . . . Her ability to see the amusing side of things was very pronounced."[11]

The two of them read to each other everything from Kipling and Robert Service to *Monsieur Beaucaire* and the *Indian Love Lyrics* of Laurence Hope. Despite her eagerness and enthusiasm, he recalled how she would often "step out of the picture," withdrawing quietly into her own thoughts.

What impressed Tabb about her, as much as anything else, was her common sense and her simplicity. "No one who really knew Wallis well ever said anything against her," he added. She never acted "silly" around boys. "She was always very feminine but clever, and at times shrewd. . . . She was not impulsive; on the contrary, she seemed rather studied or thoughtful in determining on a course of action.

"We used to have close harmony parties on the porch, or down in the garden of our house," said Tabb. "Curiously enough, Wallis rarely joined in the singing [Tabb didn't know she was tone-deaf], though she obviously enjoyed the efforts of others, and was one of the best at thinking up new numbers. Having made suggestions, she would lean back on her slender arms. Her head would be cocked appreciatively, and by her earnest attention she made us feel that we were really a rather gifted group of youngsters."

There was one song, Tabb recollected, that Wallis did join in singing, and lustily. It was the old camp meeting hymn "Will There Be Any Stars in My Crown?"[12]

Tabb kept some of Wallis' letters for a long time, remembering that he had invited Wallis to visit Glenora another summer when she was visiting in Maine. She answered that she would be "thrilled to death" to come "if your mother really wants me." She then described where she was in Maine, "a peach of a place,"[13] and a party given for her that lasted until the end of the morning.

Burrlands also meant tying hair ribbons around pleated skirts for hobble-skirt races, blackberry picking, dips in the swimming hole, ferreting the marshes for frogs, killing a black snake in the cornfield and the annual variety show. They called this one "Dear Delightful Women." Four girls in evening gowns typified women who were "bad, bold, coy and cold." Wallis was one of them, but nobody remembers any more which one.

At Burrlands, too, Wallis had her first heartbreak. It wasn't a big break and it didn't last long, but she dreamed up an imaginary romance with thirty-five-year-old Philip Noland, Miss Charlotte's brother. It culminated when he took her on a ride alone in his two-wheeled cart. After she went home, she was distraught afterward when he never wrote to her. Her mother called it puppy love, but wisely added, "If you step on a puppy's tail, it hurts as much as if you step on a dog's."[14]

Wallis regarded these young years as the happy years. Freed of financial worries, her mother seemed completely content with her indulgent husband. Wallis also had a growing group of friends and "three good uncles." Each of them was highly successful, with large summer estates in the Timonium area outside Baltimore.

Uncle Emory was the religious uncle. He assembled everybody, family and servants, every morning for the ritual morning prayer. His place was "Pot Spring" and there Wallis learned how to play bridge and wear a corset. Describing the corsets to Aunt Bessie, she wrote, "Am crazy about them."[15]

Uncle Harry was the gentle uncle. Everybody called him "General" because he had been adjutant general of Maryland. Wallis remembered him as the kind man with the peaceful farm full of cows and meadows and lovely views.

And then there was Uncle Sol. His was Manor Glen, the family place originally given as a royal grant, and Wallis' grandmother spent her summers there. Uncle Sol had been bitterly hurt by her mother's remarriage. He was then so bitter that he even asked Wallis to come and live with him and her grandmother. He said she would have everything she wanted and would be the heir to his fortune. He made only one condition: Wallis must never again enter her mother's house.

Wallis flatly refused. Confiding all this to a friend,[16] she said, "Nobody can tell me not to see my mother."

Her friend said she was foolish, that she should have agreed and then still managed to see her mother on the sly, whenever she wanted to, and then one day she would be the richest woman in Baltimore.

"I've never forgotten that," the friend said, several generations later. "And I've always admired Wallis for doing it. She was only sixteen then and it took courage and principle and love to do what she did. It was to her great credit."[17]

The same friend, however, quarreled with Wallis' conception of another quality of her character at the time. Reminiscing about those early days, Wallis had said, "I was a serious little girl, I really was. You'd always find me with books under my arms. And very disciplined. I'd go to my room every day at five o'clock and do all my lessons. I had a marvelous twenty-four-hour memory, and it was best for tests. Not mathematics, I hated mathematics, but it was wonderful for history, and I liked history."[18]

This friend smiled at all that. "Wallis was a lot of fun, but hardly a serious student. Let's put it this way: she was as serious as I was, and I couldn't spell 'cat.' "[19]

Other of Wallis' friends of the time generally agree that she preferred boys to books.

"Wallis was in love with one of my father's choir boys whose name was Slater and whose father was a fireman in Brooklyn," said the former Anne Kinsolving, daughter of an Episcopal minister. "He had a beautiful voice, and Wallis was so mad about Slater that she used to come to evensong every Sunday afternoon at St. Paul's."[20]

Wallis at sixteen was now ready for a greater adventure; she was ready for Oldfields and fortunately for her, despite his ultimatum, Uncle Sol continued his sporadic support.

Oldfields is something special in Baltimore. Founded in 1867, it is one of the most distinguished boarding schools in the country, just for girls. Set on a high, gently sloping hill, surrounded by velvety lawns and old trees, it has several hundred acres of utter privacy, beyond Timonium, some fifteen miles from the city.

"Gentleness and Courtesy are expected of the Girls at all Times," read the sign over each room in the dormitory, and that was the tone of the place. Rising was early followed by prayers, classes, lunch, afternoon nature walks, dancing and music. The nights were divided into study hours, sewing, poetry readings and impromptu entertainment. Impromptu entertainment often included using dishpans for sliding down the icy hill and bed slats as skis.

Her friend Mary Kirk wrote home that Wallis was "simply wild" about the school and was "awfully enthusiastic" and the other girls "like her loads." She wrote how wonderful it was for the two of them to be together, "giggling as ever." But Mary was soon reporting that she was now afraid that Wallis didn't like it so much there and had said that she didn't think she would come back after Christmas. Mary correctly diagnosed it as a "little homesick spell."[21]

In truth, Oldfields in the winter was a special wonderland and Mary and Wallis loved to walk in the snow in the woods. They also made "the most beautiful snowman."

The school had a chicken pox epidemic, which included Wallis' roommate, and everyone was "scared to death" of getting it. Wallis didn't, but she did spend some time in the infirmary and came back "looking dreadful." She was soon bouncing busy again and involved "with everything that goes." Mary also reported that Wallis played "splendid" basketball[22] and made the team and was "excited to death" about going to an Army-Navy game with a friend and a school chaperone.

Later in the year the two girls decided to earn some money and they made a sign for the bulletin board:

WALLIS WARFIELD AND MARY KIRK MAKE BUREAU DRAWERS NEAT
IN THE OLD BUILDING DURING LENT FOR TWO CENTS APIECE—THE
CHEAPEST IN SCHOOL! WRITE FOR CATALOGUES.[23]

Since they were on the honor system, each girl responsible for reporting her misdeeds, and since talking after "lights out" was a misdeed, it made their midnight-feast tradition most difficult. One cottage of girls resolved it that year by meeting in the bathroom, promising not to speak a word. When they were all in there, they heard the key turn in the lock. Fortunately, the partition didn't quite go to the ceiling and they could climb out, but not before they had stuffed themselves and almost convulsed themselves with giggles.

The forty Oldfields girls wore middies, green serge bloomers, ribbed cotton stockings and green and white "sweat bands" on their brows.

It was one of the last years of long hair, before the bob, the last years of the kerosene lamp. One of the most popular sophisticated dancers of the time was Irene Castle, and one of the girls named her guinea pig after her.

Sunday was a day of order and silence while the girls learned the Collect, Epistle and Gospel for the day. Those who did not cry at the later hymn singing were regarded as "soulless." One of them remembered that choir rehearsals were once postponed for several weeks because a skunk had died under the rectory floor.

"Everything mattered so terribly, terribly much," said one of Wallis' schoolmates, Lucie Lee Kinsolving, "and we took ourselves so very seriously. We thought we were the most idealistic, romantic women of the country. We were in truth nauseatingly sentimental. We talked of nothing but boys, clothes and food."[24]

Oldfields had traditional rules, strict ones, and the strictest one of all concerned boys. Not only was it forbidden to see boys, but girls were not even supposed to write to them or receive letters from them.

One Friday morning in prayers, Miss Nan announced that she had discovered that some of the girls had been writing to boys.

"Well, it was awful and she almost cried," wrote one of the girls afterward.[25] Miss Nan then said she would see any girl who was guilty in her room after dinner. All afternoon and evening there were girls standing outside her office waiting to confess. Of all the girls in school, there were perhaps only a half-dozen who were not present. Everyone was scared and gloomy.

Wallis could not have been too scared. She had grown up with an equally strict grandmother and uncle and had learned how to handle them. Besides that, she had her own ideas about rules and boys.

"I used to take father's car and drive down a dirt road," said Carter Osburn, son of a Baltimore bank president. His father owned a Packard car, then one of the few in the city. "I wasn't allowed to have the car, but I took care of that. At a certain point in the road, I'd stop, and Wally could see the car from her dormitory window. The moment she spotted it, she'd slip out. I don't know yet how she managed it, but as far as I know, she never got caught. She not only got out, but she also got back in without being observed. She was very independent in spirit, adhering to the conventions only for what they were worth, and not for their own sake. Those dates were all the more exciting for being forbidden. I think for a while we were in love with each other."[26]

Carter Osburn was not very handsome, but he did have a car and he did have the courage to come. Another teenage suitor Wallis remembered was tall, dark and silent Arthur Stump. His car was only an old Ford, but he had easier access to it.

Much more handsome than either was Thomas Shryock, Jr., a highly pedigreed student at the nearby Country School for Boys. His father was a general and Thomas himself would later become a colonel in the National Guard. His memory of Wallis was warm and firm. "Wallis was one of the loveliest, sweetest and most charming girls I ever knew," he said. "I was madly in love with her in those days, and we saw a great deal of each other."[27]

To ensure variety, Wallis even sent a letter of invitation to her first boyfriend, Lloyd Tabb, telling him she was at Oldfields but expected to come into town for a few weekends. She would love to have him come down anytime convenient to him, she wrote. She added that she would not promise him "any excitment." On a previous weekend, though, she said, she had taken in two cafes.

How Wallis, intrepid as she was, managed to maintain such a highly charged social life in so strict a school as Oldfields seems almost understandable the more you know her. Her two closest friends were Mary Kirk and Ellen Yuille. Ellen came from Virginia, where her father was in the tobacco business with the Duke family. Tall and graceful, she came from a sheltered family and envied Wallis' naturalness and sophistication, her knowledge of boys and her sense of excitement. Mary came from a Baltimore family of famous silversmiths. A blue-eyed, freckle-faced girl with a lively smile and a trim figure, she was Wallis' closest confidante. Of them all, Wallis was the most aggressive, the most piqued by challenge, the most "fast." She was always ready for something new. If it was fun, she wanted to try it; if it was daring, she was ready to take the dare; if it was exciting, she wanted to be first.

"Wallis and Mary were both snappy, peppy girls, and we all liked them," remembered one of their former classmates, Mrs. Augustine Janeway. "But they were both boy-crazy."[28] Another classmate put it more specifically: "Everybody loved Mary and everybody liked Wallis. Mary was more open, Wallis was more cliquish. But Wallis was always jolly and fun and full of ideas, never rowdy or wild or cut-up. She had dignity, and we respected that."[29]

Another former classmate of Wallis, Mrs. Harold Kersten, remembered the time the two of them were the only students taking German. The teacher gave them two pages to memorize.

"I think this is ridiculous," Wallis told her friend. "You memorize one page and I'll memorize the other."[30]

"I guess I was naïve," said Mrs. Kersten, "but I asked Wallis how did we know that the teacher would call on us for the right page. Wallis simply told me, 'Don't worry, I'll handle it.' And she did. The teacher called on Wallis and asked her to recite the page I had memorized. Wallis distracted her, talking about something else, and then said, 'Shall I begin now?' She then started reciting the page *she* had memorized. She really was very clever. We were both the same age but she was much more sophisticated than I was."

Another of Wallis' characteristics that the students admired was her dependability. She kept her promises. If she said she would play basketball, she was there. She never disappointed anyone.

What made it most difficult at Oldfields was the watchful eye of Miss Nan (Anna Green McCulloch). Oldfields girls curtsied to her (the older girls kissed her), feared her and loved her. Her daily uniform was her long black dress, high-boned to her earlobes. She was the one to whom the girls confessed their sins under the honor system. Wallis once admitted to her that she had two jars of jam under her bed and an Edam cheese in her suitcase. Wallis also confessed to throwing a stone at the window of an abandoned mill and breaking it. It was during Lent and the punishment, which was to last through the holiday, was to listen to a teacher read aloud, every night after evening prayers, from a book on Gothic architecture. The dullness of it was unbearable. Wallis then got the bright idea that if she told the teacher how perfectly wonderful the book was, it would no longer be considered a punishment and the teacher would find another book. This, however, was one of Wallis' few ideas that did not work.

Then, in April 1913, Wallis got word that her stepfather had died. He had Bright's disease and her mother had taken him to Atlantic City for the sea air. One day, Alice Rasin found her husband dead in bed. They had been married less than five years. Wallis found her mother looking "so tiny and lost and pathetic that my heart broke."[31]

Miss Nan was memorably gentle with Wallis when she returned. Wallis remembers reading more books than she ever had. She played basketball again. The school had two teams: "Gentleness" and "Courtesy." Wallis played on the Gentleness team, but she did not play very gently. It was another way to get rid of too many emotions.

Ellen Yuille invited Wallis to spend the next summer at her family place in White Sulphur Springs. There was a handsome young man about twenty-one who lived nearby. His added attraction was that he came from a very wealthy, very social family, and he himself owned one of the only two cars in the immediate area. He and Wallis saw a lot of each other that summer.

One night Wallis told her friend that the young man had proposed marriage, and what should she do?

She was only seventeen. Her stepfather was dead. She and her mother were again dependent on the financial generosity of Uncle Sol. Perhaps the young man was the answer.

But at Oldfields, the girls had a dream and a program. The dream, as they put it in their song, was "... Hills for a heart to aspire to ..." And the program of the fourteen girls in Wallis' graduating class was: "Debut, travel, marriage."[32] She wasn't ready yet for marriage.

For the class of 1914 it was still a gentle time in a gentle world. In a friend's birthday book, Wallis wrote a quotation from *Much Ado About Nothing*: "I do much wonder that one man, seeing how much another man is a fool when he dedicates his behaviors to love, will, after he hath laughed at such shallow follies in others, become the argument of his own scorn by falling in love."[33]

For the end of school, there was the traditional May Day celebration. Young girls dance around the maypole, while the May Queen in a white dress with a crown of fresh flowers sits on her throne. Somebody

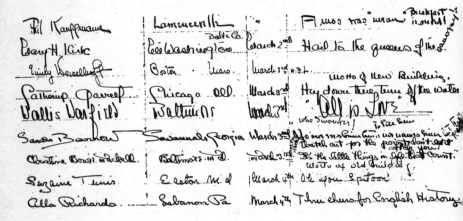

sings, "Come out, come out, my dearest dear . . . ," and each of the fourteen graduating girls brings a bouquet of wildflowers she has picked. "These sweet peas of delicate hue, we picked, dear Renée,* especially for you . . ." And Wallis brought "sweet arbutus, youngest child of spring . . ."[34]

There was a farewell dance and the girls and their guests signed their names and wrote their comments on life.

What Wallis wrote was short and simple:

"All is Love."[35]

---

* Renée duPont, later Mrs. John Donaldson.

3

THE WORLD OF EIGHTEEN-YEAR-OLD Wallis Warfield in 1914 was bounded by Baltimore and the Bachelor's Cotillion.

Outside of Baltimore it was peaceful early that summer. The United States was generally well fed and prosperous. President Woodrow Wilson was busy implementing his "New Freedom" program, pushing for a graduated income tax, an eight-hour working day and lower tariffs. The headlines on June 28 were concerned with the physical collapse of former President Theodore Roosevelt; a battle between two generals in Mexico; Jack Johnson winning a heavyweight championship fight; SUFFRAGETTES MARCH ON CAPITOL, with a prediction that they would get the vote by 1917; the latest gospel of "muscular Christianity," by evangelist Reverend W. A. "Billy" Sunday, a former baseball player; and a movie censorship decision by Mrs. Cyrus Niver of Philadelphia, who said that one yard of film is long enough for a kiss in a movie and that an embraced couple "should be torn from each other after 36 seconds."

The American public had other concerns:

HOT DEBATE OVER CORSET.[1]

Dr. Louise Eastman was quoted in the Des Moines, Iowa, *Register* as saying that as she became heavier she "found the 'straight front' prevented her from becoming bunchy." Dr. Flora Smith of Newark, Ohio, disagreed. She said she "could not see why women thought it necessary to improve on nature; neither she nor her mother had ever worn a corset."[2]

A more disturbing note to male Baltimoreans was the news that West Virginia had voted for Prohibition, the ninth state to go dry. Saloonkeepers warned patrons, "A camel can go nine days without a drink, but after July 1, you will have to beat the camel," and "Don't be alarmed if after July 1 you spit talcum powder."[3]

Horses were still going strong on Baltimore's cobblestone streets, and even an advertisement for the early automobile stressed that it would "pull like a team of horses." Biggest feature of the local movie houses was *The Perils of Pauline*. And the Baltimore *Sun*, discussing the debate on whether or not to permit baseball on Sunday, editorialized, "Sunday has become the gayest day of the week."

It was on that day, June 28, that a Bosnian Serb student, Gavrilo Princip—not much older than Wallis Warfield—fired two shots in the small city of Sarajevo and killed an archduke named Francis Ferdinand and his morganatic wife.

The murdered archduke was the heir to the Austrian throne and the assassin said he was avenging Austria's seizure of his country. The tiny tinder exploded into World War I, but it was then a matter of small moment in the United States. David Franklin Houston, a member of Wilson's Cabinet, wrote a memo:

> The weather was warm in July, and it was time for the annual holiday. What? Another little war in the Balkans? Serbia is in the Balkans, isn't it? A lot of fuss over an archduke. Called himself Francis Ferdinand. He probably didn't amount to much; he couldn't have with a name like that.[4]

Less than a year later, when the German submarine sank the Cunard liner *Lusitania*, carrying many Americans, the girls at Oldfields, singing hymns, "hysterically burst into the strains of 'Eternal Father, strong to save'..."[5]

That summer of 1914, Wallis visited her cousins, the Barnetts, at quiet, lovely Front Royal, Virginia. Mrs. George Barnett told her two shy daughters that she wished that they could be like Wallis, "who had such poise, manner and style and perfect taste in everything." But what the two girls marveled at even more was that she was "so popular with the boys."[6]

"She was a honey pot," said another cousin of hers, Basil Gordon. "She attracted men the way molasses attracts flies."[7]

Gordon was at Princeton, a mathematical genius who was most helpful to Wallis. She very much wanted to go to the Princeton prom and Cousin Basil was her only contact there. He was a very important contact, however, because he tutored several handsome, athletic but mathematically deficient seniors. He gave one of them a choice: either take his cousin Wallis to the prom or get another math tutor.[8] Wallis wore a deep sapphire-blue dress, cut very simply and strikingly, with American Beauty rose ribbons outlining the bodice. She was a belle at the ball.

She was a belle because her romantic mind had a practical focus. She knew herself very well. She knew her liabilities and how to overcome them with her assets. She was five feet four, but so slender as to seem taller. Her jaw was too square, her eyebows too bushy, but she had distinctive high cheekbones and a beautiful broad brow. Her hair was a rich medium shade of brown, and she kept it parted in the center, drawn off her face in soft waves, the back of it rolled into two coils, crossing each other. She wore no hair ornaments, and needed none. Her voice was low-pitched and she somehow made it dramatic and unmistakable. Her greatest single physical feature was her eyes, a changing violet-blue, but with a kind of dynamic, magnetic attraction.

"All her features are good," said one of her oldest friends, "yet, put together they do not make beauty. The effect is rather of a sparkling personality and good nature—more intriguing than beauty."[9]

Putting it more pointedly, a cousin remarked, "This charm was so enormous that it could and did captivate anyone, particularly the men, who came into contact with it. It was always a question how long the charm lingered after someone left Wallis' presence, but while they were there with her, there was no question about the intensity of the capture."[10]

She had absorbed her mother's gaiety, inherited her wit, learned her ready laugh. Mixed with all this were the good manners, started by her mother, deepened by her grandmother, intensified by Oldfields.

"Why, when we went to the theater, she would turn to the usher, smile and thank him for showing her the seat. It didn't make any difference who it was who did anything for her—a policeman, a newsboy, anyone—she was immediately grateful and courteous," remembered her old beau Tom Shryock.

"She had a great many admirers," added another dancing partner, Irvine Keyser. "She tended to be interested in boys. Girls were just people who happened to be around . . . and some of the young ladies were critical of her because she cut in on their preserves a bit."[11]

Keyser also recalled that Wallis was outspoken. "In those days, that was considered forward for a young lady."[12]

The outspokenness, however, made her more unique in a decorous society of shy, giggling girls. For men, it was an added attraction.

"For her time, she was very sophisticated," her constant escort Carter Osburn remembered. "You know there are stories about how she used to insist the young men in Baltimore take her out to places that were so expensive they could hardly afford to pay the bill afterwards. All I can say is I don't recall anything like that happening during the three years I went around with her."[13]

In those days you could sit in the "peanut gallery" of Ford's Theater and see a play or a visiting opera company for twenty-five cents. Parents still had bedtime rules and a strict chaperone system, but the young people had their own techniques. "We would say goodnight to our parents, and then later go out again—without our parents knowing it. All the girls knew how to do that," one of them said.[14]

By the summer's end, the air of gallivanting was gone and Wallis' serious concern had started. October was the time when the postman would or would not deliver an invitation to the Bachelor's Cotillion.

The Bachelor's Cotillion was the major social event for any would-be debutante.

Birth and connections were then almost everything in Baltimore. A favorite local story concerned Mrs. Rebecca Shippen, born a Nicholson and descended from the Lloyds of Wye House—some of the bluest blood in Maryland.

"Rebecca," queried a friend at tea, "did it ever occur to you that if Our Lord had come to Baltimore we wouldn't have met him, since his father was a carpenter?"

"But, my dear," replied Mrs. Shippen, "you forget. He was well connected on his mother's side."[15]

Baltimore is basically a city with a British background and British social customs. It was named after Lord Baltimore, and, even after the British went home, the Baltimoreans kept many of their social graces. Even in its beginnings, the city always had its class of rarefied aristocrats living in lordly mansions and going to fashionable balls. Local historians trace the Cotillion to a similar ball held in 1796, but it was not given the name "Bachelor's Cotillion" until 1870.

Somehow, gradually, the custom grew in Baltimore for a certain small, selected number of eighteen-year-old debutantes to "come out" at the Bachelor's Cotillion on the first Monday in December. So great did its prestige become that only the invited girls were regarded as debutantes.

The self-perpetuating board of governors invariably represent the oldest Baltimore families and they are seldom young, and rarely bachelors. Their decisions are absolute. In the year 1914, they selected only forty-seven debutantes.

Wallis was one of them. And why not? Her breeding was the best, her uncle one of the city's most important citizens, and her father had even been a member of the Bachelor's Cotillion.

She still had one main worry—her dress. Mr. Rasin had not left her widowed mother much money, and they could not afford Fuechsl's, where most of the debs traditionally went. In the end, Wallis and her mother designed a dress themselves.

Designing her own dress was more than a matter of mere economy for Wallis; it was a challenge to her driving desire to be different. Like every deb there, she wanted to be spectacular, outstanding, the absolute, striking center of attention. Personally planning her own dress would make the satisfaction all the sweeter. The final gown was made of white satin and chiffon, delicately trimmed with white beads. She felt queenly . . . and looked it.

Her escort for the evening was twenty-seven-year-old cousin Henry Warfield, Jr., arriving in Uncle Sol's Pierce Arrow with a huge bouquet of American Beauty roses. He gave her a quick, full look and said, "Kiddo, I can assure you that you will be the most enchanting, most ravishing, most exquisite creature at the Cotillion."[16]

It was all she needed. She laughed and was ready to go.

The mood at the Lyric Theater was almost magical. All the seats had been cleared and the outer frame of the floor looked like a continuous garland of flowers. A romantic reporter called it "a bower of beauty where light and color mingled to form an almost tropical atmosphere of warmth and fullness of life." The steps from the supper room to the dance floor were covered with satin pillows, a tradition that dated to the time just before the Civil War when there was no money available to decorate the Cotillion and so the Baltimore matrons ripped up their ball gowns and made them into cushions to give elegance to the scene.

The climax of the evening comes at eleven, when the orchestra stops and a whistle blows in the sudden silence to clear the floor. The senior governor then leads the couples through a simple marching figure called a "german." Somebody described it as similar to show horses' being put through their paces. Wallis' escort for this was her cousin Major General George Barnett in full dress uniform. Wallis wanted all the attention she could get.

Then the band played a one-step, a few foxtrots, but mostly waltzes, ending with a number called "Parfum d'Amour."

A social observer later tried to explain that there was some meaning to this snobbish elegance, that it really did launch these girls. They needed it because most of them weren't prepared for anything but marriage and most of them were not even prepared or ready for that. This ball gave them a lift, an increased self-confidence, almost a social strength.

But there was a letdown for Wallis. If this was the beginning, where was the end? Where was her Prince Charming? Where was her Jerome Bonaparte?

Baltimore's most romantic story concerned eighteen-year-old Betsy Patterson and nineteen-year-old Captain Jerome Bonaparte, youngest brother of Napoleon.

The dashing, debonair Captain Bonaparte stopped off in Baltimore en route to France, went to the races with a friend, saw Betsy, demanded an instant introduction, romanced her and overwhelmed her. William Patterson, one of the city's wealthiest men, discouraged the affair, sent his daughter away to forget. But the romantic Betsy swore she "would rather be Jerome's wife for an hour than the wife of another for eternity."

The willful Betsy finally had her way and they were married on Christmas Eve 1803.

The angry Napoleon Bonaparte refused to recognize the marriage, ordered the French consul to cut off his brother's allowance and insisted his brother return to France alone. His brother finally did.

Forbidden to go to France, Betsy went to England and gave birth to a son she named Jerome Napoleon Bonaparte. Pope Pius VII refused Napoleon's demand to dissolve the marriage, but the French courts did annul it. Jerome married again and became King of Westphalia, and Betsy and her son returned to Baltimore in 1834. At the family's request, the Maryland General Assembly annulled the marriage. But she never married again, never dropped the dream that her descendants would one day occupy the throne of France, and ultimately died in a rooming house on Cathedral Street at the age of ninety-four.

Every Baltimore girl knew the story by heart. Only a few knew one of her final phrases: "My ruling passions have been love, ambition, avarice. Love has fled, ambition has brought disappointment, but avarice remains."[17]

Wallis knew what money was, and wanted it. She and her mother had had too much financial insecurity, too much dependence. Wallis was also stirred by ambition. She wanted to be more than she was, and she wanted out.

Betsy Bonaparte had been most bitter about the fact that Napoleon had "hurled me back on what I hated most on earth, my Baltimore obscurity."[18]

But more than money, and more than ambition, Wallis Warfield now wanted love.

When she had inscribed in the Oldfields guest book "All is Love," she or somebody else wrote underneath, "and I wonder who it is?"

The dream love of many American girls at that time was the young Prince of Wales, then a boyish-looking twenty years old, a lieutenant in the Grenadier Guards in France. A newspaper report that December described him as "looking fit in spite of the enormous amount of work he manages to cram into the hours from daybreak until sometimes almost daybreak. One of his favorite habits is to vanish, to be discovered several hours later, interrogating wounded men in out-of-the-way corners."

Young American women avidly followed the doings of their romantic hero, and Wallis was no exception. She and Virginia Page kept a joint diary for a while, full of admiring entries about their hero. Wallis even inserted a picture of the Prince inside the diary pages. A romantic novel that fall called *His Royal Happiness*, by Mrs. Everard Cotes, was described as "a timely and startling international romance, relating the dramatic complications which arise when a Prince of England happens to fall in love with the daughter of the President of the United States."

Royal romance was the wishful daydream of any girl who had ever read *Cinderella*. One of Wallis' cousins remembered, shortly after the Cotillion, going to the hairdresser with Wallis and her mother. Her mother explained to the hairdresser that her daughter was going to a naval ball at nearby Annapolis and had to look her best.

"Ah," ventured the hairdresser, "you are setting her cap for a young naval officer."

Wallis' mother, ever quick with a comeback, answered, "No indeed, I'm setting her cap for a king."[19]

The 1914 social season for "the bevy of buds"[20] was as frenetic as any other. There were lunches, parties, balls, oyster roasts, football games, college hops, private dinners, the races. Most boring were the lunches. One of the debs that season, Banny Ner, who later became society editor of the Baltimore *Evening Sun,* remembered how dull they were because the same girls were seeing each other again and again, and "What do women, at the age of eighteen or so, have to talk about together?"[21]

Upton Sinclair, who shared that same social scene, listed the three topics of discussion, not very differently from Wallis' schoolmate Lucie Lee Kinsolving: marriage, clothes and good things to eat.

The most fun for the girls were the parties at the Baltimore Country Club, where the mood was more informal, the music merrier and all of it sometimes lasting until breakfast at dawn. Most parties were much more straitlaced, but there were rare scandals. One of them had taken place during an earlier social season, a costume party in the basement of Mrs. William Munnikhuysen's home on the highly respectable North Charles Street. The young people had transformed the place into "Hell" and dressed themselves as demons in scarlet tights. The champagne flowed very freely indeed. Afterward somebody wrote a limerick about it:

> There was a young lady named Nance
> Who attended the Munnikhuysen dance.
> She went down the cellar
> With a handsome young feller
> And now all her sisters are aunts.[22]

The obvious and prime purpose of the prolonged social season was husband hunting.

"What was thrilling to other debutantes," said Banny Ner, "was the fact that she [Wallis] had an early-afternoon beau. Imagine having a man at three in the afternoon to lighten the too-deadly-for-words atmosphere—an air thick with nothing but the vapid vaporings of women or (forgive me) girls of 18.

"Carter Osburn was always waiting to take Wallis home, to tea, or wherever she might want to go. He would jump and obey her every wish. He was wildly in love with her and, although no one really knew, the general inference was that Wallis rather liked Carter. To our girlish minds, it seemed it would be a 'go.' "[23]

Carter thought so too. "Between ourselves, we said we were engaged," he reminisced years later. "We thought we were serious and planned to marry."[24]

Maybe Carter was ready and willing, but Wallis was still searching elsewhere. Another friend, who became the Countess de Niezychowska, later recalled that Wallis "had more beaux than any other girl in town."[25] Mrs. Emily Sadler recalled that Wallis "was superlatively smart, without being beautiful, and she had poise and a knack for finding her way around that made most of us feel like clumsy children."[26]

Wallis wanted still one more big social splash—a ball of her own. Uncle Sol had had an impressive ball for her cousin Anita, and Wallis hoped hard for one of a similar size. It was true she had signed a statement with thirty-three other debs that they would refrain from any extravagantly elegant entertaining because of the war. But she fervently wished that Uncle Sol would not take that too seriously.

Uncle Sol, however, took the war most seriously. This was his other side, the sensitive man who liked music and poetry and pretty girls. He saw the war for the ugly horror it was. By 1915, it had indeed become a world war and the young men who had gone off singing "It's a Long Way to Tipperary" had soon smelled the stink of fear and death. Germany had marched through Belgium and burned ancient cities to the ground, and there were propaganda stories that they had cut off hands of Belgian babies. Each side made unfounded claims against the other of every kind of atrocity. Ambassador Myron T. Herrick notified President Wilson, "Situation in Europe is regarded here as the gravest in history."[27] Wilson, however, was determined to keep the United States out of war. But Americans were already taking sides. Baltimore women were busy making bandages for Belgium. It looked like a long war. A British newspaperman wrote:

Let us not put on paper caps and march through the streets waving penny flags, breathing beer and singing "Britons never shall be slaves." Let us not sing boastful songs! Honor may call us to fight, self-preservation may force us into the slaughterhouse; but let us wear on our sleeves the crepe of mourning for a civilization that had the promise of joy, and strike our enemy without a hiccup or a curse.[28]

That was Uncle Sol's mood, too. In this time of world trial, he was against the gaiety, the ostentation, the social display. He worked hard at a number of war-relief activities and notified the press that the report that he "will give a large ball for his debutante niece, Miss Wallis Warfield, is without foundation."[29]

Wallis was indignant, despairing, crushed. Baltimore was her world, pleasure was her principle, marriage was her future. War was too remote and unimaginable. Who wants to think of torn-up bodies when you're eighteen years old, dancing in a country club?

Cousin Lelia Barnett came through in the social crisis the following April. Since her husband was the Marine commandant, she had a dance in the ballroom of the Marine barracks in Washington with a sixty-piece Marine band. She furthermore corralled all the available unmarried Marine officers in the area. In addition, Wallis' many Baltimore friends made the necessary migration.

Then came tragedy. Grandmother Warfield died. It was the first important family death for Wallis. This was not the death of thousands of faceless soldiers; this was somebody warm and near and dear. One thing her grandmother had told her, something she would always remember: conscience was a "mirror" which only one person could see. She urged Wallis to look into that "mirror at least once a day."[30]

Looking into that mirror of conscience, Wallis would have seen a bright young woman—brighter than most—who didn't care that much about the world because she didn't know much about it. Her conscience was clear because she didn't know what she was violating. She wasn't yet willing to help others because she felt she still hadn't helped herself enough. She wanted first to shape herself into something stronger and more important. She didn't know what, exactly, only that she wanted more—more money, more power, more love, more fun.

It was all as vague and romantic and unreal as the picture of the Prince of Wales she had put into her diary.

4

To WALLIS, and teenage girls everywhere, the Prince of Wales was the Prince Charming of the world, all wrapped up with the glamour of royal mystery.*

* He was not only on tap as Prince of Wales but was answerable to all his other titles—everything from being Chancellor of the University of Cape Town to being a general in the Japanese army. He was Earl of Chester, Duke of Cornwall, Duke of Rothesay, Duke of Saxony (disused), Earl of Carrick, Baron of Renfrew, Lord of the Isles and Prince and Great Steward of Scotland, High Steward of Windsor, Knight of the Most Noble Order of the Garter, Privy Councillor, Knight of the Most Noble Order of the Thistle, Grand Master of the Most Distinguished Order of St. Michael and St. George, Knight Grand Commander of the Most Eminent Order of the Indian Empire, Knight Grand Commander of the Most Exalted Order of the Star of India, Knight of the Most Illustrious Order of St. Patrick, Grand Master of the Most Excellent Order of the British Empire, and Grand Cross of the Legion of Honor. In his closet hung the uniforms that enabled him to appear as head man of the Prince of Wales' Volunteers, the Prince of Wales' Own Scinde Horse, the Fourth Prince of Wales' Own Gurkha Rifles and the Third Prince of Wales' Canadian Dragoons. He was Vice Admiral of the Royal Navy, Lieutenant-General of the Army, Colonel of the Welsh Guards, Air Marshal of the Royal Air Force, Colonel-in-Chief of the Twelfth Lancers, Colonel of the Fifth Battalion Devonshire Regiment, Commandant of the Royal Canadian Mounted Police and Chief of the Boy Scouts in Wales; and he belonged to the Royal Scots Fusiliers, the Duke of Cornwall's Light Infantry, the Seaforth Highlanders, the Middlesex Regiment, the South Wales Borderers, the Wiltshire Yeomenry, the Eighth Punjabi Regiment, the Sixth Rajputana Rifles, the Twelfth Frontier Force Regiment, the Seventeenth Dogra Regiment, the West African Regiment, the Toronto Regiment, the Canadian Grenadier Guards, the Seaforth Highlanders of Canada, the First and Second South African Mounted Rifles, the Fifteenth Battalion London Regiment, the Ceylon Light Infantry and the Ceylon Planters' Rifle Corps. In the royal bureau drawers were the trinkets that go with a life of decoration and distinction: the Golden Fleece of Spain, the Elephant of Denmark, St. Olaf of Norway (with chain), the Italian Order of the Annunziata, the Russian Order

44

Could she have talked to him then, she would have been appalled by the lack of love in his life, and by his loneliness. The Prince had had nobody.

His father had recorded his son's birth in his diary on June 23, 1894: "White Lodge, Richmond Park. At 10.0 a sweet little boy was born and weighed 8 lb."[1] That was probably the maximum affection he ever showed for his son.

His mother, "very cold and stiff"[2] and unmaternal, "had no automatic or spontaneous understanding of a child's mind or ways." She felt she had done her duty by giving her husband an heir, but she agreed with Queen Victoria that "it is really *too dreadful* to have the first year of one's married life & happiness spoilt by *discomfort & misery* . . . I was furious at being in that position."[3]

Queen Victoria, however, was delighted with her first great-grandchild, "a very fine strong Boy, a pretty Child,"[4] pinched his cheeks, burst into tears and asked that he be named after her dead husband.

Christened Edward Albert Christian Andrew Patrick David, he was soon called David. His grandfather, the Prince of Wales, who later became Edward VII, commented, "He has large and vigorous lungs, the beggar."[5]

Six weeks after his birth, his mother left him for a month to vacation in Switzerland. For the rest of his boyhood, she and her husband saw their children at bedtime to kiss them goodnight. The Queen's official biographer regretfully noted that "between them, King George and Queen Mary managed to be rather unsuccessful and somewhat unsympathetic parents."[6]

Queen Mary's closest friend, the Countess of Airlie, put it more simply: ". . . she disliked the routine of child-bearing, and had no interest in her children as babies . . ."[7]

Writing to her husband on the subject, she noted, "Of course it is a great bore for me & requires a great deal of patience to bear it, but this is alas the penalty of being a woman."

The King, on the other hand, "frightened and subdued his children.

---

of St. George, the Military Order of Savoy, the Imperial Service Order, the Military Cross, the Siamese Order of the House Chalkri, the Rumanian Order of Michael the Braver, the Egyptian Order of Mahomed Ali, the collar of the Rumanian Order of Carol and the Chilian Order of Merit (first class). He held degrees from Oxford, Edinburgh, Toronto, Queen's University, Melbourne, Cambridge, Calcutta, Hong Kong, St. Andrew's and Cape Town.

When they were very young, he embarrassed them by chaffing questions, and as they grew up, he alienated them by continual criticisms, interspersed with fits of impatient anger." A close friend at court said that his manner toward them "alternated between an awkward jocularity of the kind which makes a sensitive child squirm from self-consciousness, and a severity bordering on harshness."[8]

His close friend, the seventeenth Earl of Derby, once complained to the King about the way he bullied his children, and he answered: "My father was frightened of his mother, I was frightened by my father, and I'm damned well going to see to it that my children are frightened of me."[9]

And so David was. The most dreaded words he could hear were that his father wanted to see him in the library. His father had injured his eardrum at sea and he more often shouted than spoke. Children were to be seen, not heard, and they occupied only "small, fixed niches" in his life. He was a stern-looking, bearded man, a father figure to his country but a fearful figure to his son.

"How came it that a man who was by temperament so utterly domestic, who was so considerate to his dependents and the members of his household, who was so unalarming to small children and humble people, should have inspired his sons with feelings of awe, amounting at times to nervous trepidation?"[10]

His nanny, Mrs. Lala, remembers the then Duke complaining, "Can't you stop that child crying?"[11] She also quoted his mother, saying: "Nurseries don't seem to be of much use any more. Nowadays children are all over the house."[12]

Coupled with this utter lack of parental love, David's first nurse was a neurotic who twisted his arm and made him cry just before he entered the room to see his mother and father so that they would quickly dismiss him. She also believed that the bouncing of a carriage was bad for babies and carried him in her arms for the first three months of his life. Three years later, without ever having a single day off, the nurse had a nervous breakdown.

It was therefore not unexpected that David would grow up to be a highly nervous child, a fidget, subject to easy tears. Furthermore, he was shy, hesitant, highly insecure. He was raised in a discipline of "don'ts." His happiest early memories were the late summer months when his father was away on "shoots," and he and his three brothers and sister were alone with his mother at Windsor Castle.

His mother had been the Princess Victoria Mary of Teck and her family called her "May." Her father was German and her mother was the Princess Mary Adelaide of Cambridge. A tall woman with shapely legs, Queen Mary never wore a shorter style dress because of her husband's conservative taste. She was the least assertive of women, seldom disagreed with her husband even though her mind was more original than his.

He was a simple man of principle, dedicated, selfless, highly religious. His belief in monarchy was almost devout. He once wrote that monarchy should be dignified, make government intelligible and interesting to the masses, strengthen government with religious tradition and be a moral factor for good. Above all, he had a sharp sense of duty and made all his sons memorize a Quaker precept he kept on his desk:

> I shall only pass through this world but once. Any good thing, therefore, that I can do or any kindness that I can show a human being, let me do it now. Let me not defer nor neglect it for I shall not pass this way again.[13]

The King was an excellent shot, loved to sail, enjoyed stamp collecting, organized his life with the punctuality of a railroad timetable. He disliked cocktails and women with bobbed hair or painted fingernails or gaudy hats. Yet, he was hardly spartan. He enjoyed all the royal comforts of fine food, expensive guns, jeweled cigarette cases, well-cut clothes. His concept of clothes was conservative and fixed, and anybody who disagreed was "a cad."

When it came time to marry, he never questioned Queen Victoria's suggestion that he wed the fiancée of his brother, the Duke of Clarence, who had just died.

What adult affection David got came from his grandparents the Prince of Wales and Princess Alexandra. He and his three brothers and sister stayed with them while their parents were away for many months on trips to India and elsewhere. The grandparents believed in fun and games and much affection, and the children had the run of the castle, and the strict nurses and tutors were kept out of bounds. They would concoct a drink made of salt and pepper and their grandma would delight them by pretending to gulp it down. She also insisted on bathing them whenever she felt like it while their grand-

47

father, a rotund, joyous man, roared with laughter at almost anything they did.

"Come in," David once shouted as somebody knocked on the door, "there's nobody here, nobody that matters, only Grandpa."[14]

Queen Victoria also reached out for her great-grandson whenever she could. At his christening, she had insisted that everything used in the ceremony be British made. David and the children called her "Gangan" and marveled at her turbaned Indian servants called "khidmatgars," who followed her everywhere. At his birth she was seventy-five years old, in the fifty-seventh year of her reign, wore black satin dresses and looked like a potato dumpling. Her British Empire covered a quarter of the earth's surface and almost a quarter of the earth's population. British sea power was supreme. In those days, a British schoolboy's definition of an "island" was "A piece of land entirely surrounded by the British Navy."

Queen Victoria's nine children and forty grandchildren ruled the courts of Europe. Her death in 1901 was the end of an era. David was then seven years old, in bed with the measles. With his grandfather as Edward VII, David got a glimpse of a more spirited social life at Sandringham. David remembered his grandfather as the only man who entered his nursery without trying to teach him something.

He had two men watching and teaching him now, Frederick Finch, who later became his valet, and Henry Hansell, his tutor. Hansell unsuccessfully urged David's father to send him to a preparatory school so that David could have the companionship and competition of other children his age, but the new Prince of Wales said that he had never gone to such a school, and neither would his son. "The Navy will teach David all he needs to know."[15] David often found Hansell standing on a hill, smoking his pipe and staring at the view. When David asked him what was so interesting in that dull view, Hansell answered, "For me, it is freedom."[16] Years later, David understood what he meant.

Monarchy had lost much of its meaning in the changing times. The Tudor despotism of the sixteenth century brought order to Britain after the baronial wars, gave the emergent middle class the stability it needed. Constitutional monarchy in the seventeenth and eighteenth centuries helped end the religious struggle in England, preserved the new industrial structure of society. British royalty in the nineteenth century survived mainly as a symbol and focus of national loyalty, the political power fully resting with the elected leaders of the people.

Monarchy gave the British people a color and splendor that their own lives too often lacked. Women saw in Queen Victoria "a compensating personality"; in Edward VII, "the fun-loving King they would like to be"; and in George V, "the father to us all."

Most of all, the life of monarchy was its mystery. "We must not let in daylight upon magic," wrote historian Walter Bagehot.

For a young boy to grow up in this heavy atmosphere of history, knowing that one day he too would be king—the pressure was unique and overwhelming. He got a bike on his seventh birthday. When he was reprimanded for riding it over the red geraniums, he answered: "What's the good of my being the Prince of Wales if I can't do as I like?"[17] He wasn't yet Prince of Wales, but he knew he would be.

He knew it when he and his brother Bertie sneaked out of bed, hurried to the bathroom, loaded up on wet sponges, crept around the gallery circling the ballroom and dropped them on the dancing guests. Another time they tied a rather smelly fish to a string and dangled it over secluded alcoves among startled visitors.

David knew it when he would tell his royal tutor in the royal manner, "Perhaps you are getting tired now and would like to rest."[18]

As a human being, Hansell was friendly; as a tutor he was remarkably uninspired. David found his classroom studies as constricting as the starched Eton collar he was forced to wear. He also found himself much more interested in nature walks than in cricket.

Even as a boy, David had that haunted look of wistful sadness. A courtier of the royal household remarked much later, "That look of melancholy . . . is something which I cannot trace to any ancestor of the House of Hanover."[19]

In a biography of his ancestor the Duke of Marlborough, Winston Churchill had written, "It is said that famous men are usually the product of unhappy childhood. The stern compression of circumstances, the twinges of adversity, the spur of slights and taunts in early years, are needed to evoke that ruthless fixity of purpose and tenacious mother-wit without which great actions are seldom accomplished."[20]

Of his own childhood the Prince had said, "As a kid, it was the very devil."[21]

He had no friends his age. His mother later set up an hour before dinner when her children collected in her boudoir. She had a cultivated mind and a soft voice and she would read to them, talk to them, teach them how to knit woolen comforters. It was more educational than emotional.

Many years later, a friend raised the question that since he was Queen Mary's first and favorite child, why had she not shown him more affection throughout the years?

His answer was curt: "Too German."* [22]

David entered the world of children when he was twelve and went to a naval training center at Osborne on the Isle of Wight. He was round-shouldered, undersized and skinny—so skinny that other boys soon dubbed him "The Sardine." They also decided he would look more interesting with red hair and poured red ink over his head. A hazing group also pushed his head under a raised window and slammed it down on his neck to remind him how a displeased British people had eliminated Charles I.

What made him most unhappy was that his tutor had not filled his mind full enough with the proper knowledge, and his studies were a monumental struggle. He stayed in the "dumbbell" class. So much did he dread bringing home his report that he once burst into tears in front of his father.

After two years he was transferred to the Royal Naval College at Dartmouth. The hazing increased. A cadet captain informed him that the time to prepare for bed—undress and into pajamas—would be cut from one minute to thirty seconds. It was a frantic period, about which he could never tell his parents.

It was about this time that David got a letter from his mother: "Do tell me whether you have time to clean yr. . . . teeth at night. I want to know . . ."[23]

The first two years at Osborne, he remembered feeling like "rather a lost dog."[24] At Dartmouth, though, he described it as "rather a de-

---

* George I, who could not even speak English, was brought over from the little German principality of Hanover to become Britain's king. Three other Georges followed, these being the son, great-grandson and great-great-grandson of the first. All married German wives and thus put queens of German blood on the throne. A brother of the fourth George, who also married a German spouse, became the parent of Queen Victoria, who likewise married a German, Prince Albert of Saxe-Coburg-Gotha. Thus Edward VII was of pure German descent. Edward changed the trend of German queens by marrying Alexandra, daughter of the King of Denmark; but his son George V went back to the German line for his queen. (Baltimore *Evening Sun*, December 4, 1936.)

cent time."[25] For him, this was high praise. Until then, he had had so little of the warmth of life, the companionship of people, the sense of doing a job.

Edward VII died in 1910, and nine kings, all related by blood, rode on horseback behind the funeral cortege. In the next twenty-five years that George V was on the throne, five emperors, eight kings and eighteen minor dynasties came to an end. It was Farouk, the then king of Egypt, who told Lord Boyd-Orr, "There will soon be only five kings left—The King of England, Diamonds, Hearts, Spades and Clubs."[26]

His father was now George V, and David was soon made the Prince of Wales. This also entitled him to the income of the Duchy of Cornwall, thousands of acres including valuable real estate in London. The Prince was pleased with his performance at his first official function as the Duke of Cornwall—returning a symbolic silver oar to the town. He was much more impressed at the coronation ceremony for his father, wearing a costume of silver cloth with a sword in a red velvet scabbard, kneeling at his father's feet at Westminster Abbey and swearing, "I, Edward, Prince of Wales, do become your liege man of life and limb, and of earthly worship; and faith and truth I will bear unto you, to live and die, against all manner of folks. So help me God."

Then he kissed his father and his father kissed him on both cheeks. "I was very nervous," he wrote in his diary.[27]

King George, in his diary of that day, recorded: "It was grand, yet simple & most dignified and went without a hitch. I nearly broke down when dear David came to do homage to me, as it reminded me so much when I did the same thing to beloved Papa, he did it so well."[28]

The ceremony to solemnize David as Prince of Wales took place at Carnarvon Castle, and David Lloyd George taught him some Welsh words: *"Mor o gan yw Cymru i gyd,"* which meant "All Wales is a sea of song." But David rebelled when he saw the costume he had to wear: white satin breeches with an ermine-edged mantle of purple velvet. He could only envision what his Navy classmates would say. His mother finally persuaded him, saying that his friends would understand that duty required him to do things that seemed "a little silly."[29]

His father then made him happy by permitting him to go on a delayed sea voyage for three months as a junior midshipman on the battleship *Hindustan*. He had barely learned how to swear properly before his father sent him to Paris to learn to handle himself in French society. He stayed with the Marquis de Breteuil, learned little French, but saw some of the bright side of Paris.

He was now eighteen years old, with the royal permission to smoke in public. He now headed for Oxford University, and he hated the idea.

What he loved, though, was the new freedom.

He was not regarded as a typical student. His suite of rooms at Magdalen College was redone to include the first private undergraduate bathroom, complete with tub. With him, in a nearby room, were his tutor, his equerry and his valet. Then, too, there were always the lurking photographers.

Oxford was a serious, studious place but the faculty consensus about the Prince was "Bookish, he will never be . . ."[30] He liked history and German, but he much preferred outdoor activity.

"You certainly have been doing a great deal," his father wrote him, "hunting two days, out with the beagles twice, golf and shooting one day, besides all your work, which seems a good deal for one week. . . ."[31]

Reassuring his father about other things, the Prince wrote, "I never smoke more than ten cigarettes a day."[32]

Once, on a visit home, his pool cue tore the green cloth on the table and his father forbade him to use the pool table again for a full year. Earlier, his father similarly had refused his request to use the golf course because he might "hack it up." But the King did slowly accept the Prince of Wales into his way of life, allowing him to come along on some of his "shoots." At one of them, the group killed some 4,000 pheasants, of which the King shot more than 1,000 and the Prince killed more than 300. At the end of the carnage, his father had a pang of conscience and said, "Perhaps we went a little too far today, David."[33] It was one of the first times the King talked to his son as one man to another.

He had his own checkbook, kept polo ponies, learned to play the banjo and the bagpipes, made the second-string football team. His diary entries at the time stressed that he was now a smooth dancer, and he added boastfully, ". . . I had no more than 8 hours sleep in the last 72 hours!!!"[34]

His fellow students at Magdalen treated him politely at first, then warmed up enough to nickname him "Pragger Wagger." He was still the Prince of Wales and somebody always scrambled to his feet when he entered a room, and he would have to say, "Oh, for God's sake sit down." But for those who tried to be too familiar, he could shout imperiously, "Call me 'Sir,' damn you!"[35]

He had no friends. There were those who adored him, swore by him, followed him, but always they were held apart by the magic and mystery of the monarchy. It was a wall that he never shattered as long as he lived. Because of it, he was always partly shy, partly sad, very introspective. Surely, one of the reasons for his later drinking was that it released him somewhat from all this, released his buried exuberance and flamboyance.

He did not do well at Oxford. He always said afterward that he learned more from people than from books. The college's final comment on him put it most politely: "[He will never be] . . . a British Solomon."[36]

During the Easter and summer vacations of 1913, the Prince made two trips to Germany. He enjoyed Germany much more than France because he picked up a greater fluency in the language, and besides, he had a great many relatives all over the country. He liked singing German songs and drinking German beer, and his younger cousins gave him a good taste of Berlin night life.

What surprised him was the number of people who wore uniforms "falling over each other with swords, spurs, helmets and what not."[37] What surprised him even more was his visit to his cousin Kaiser Wilhelm II. Instead of a desk chair, he sat on a wooden block shaped like a horse's body, on which was girthed a stirruped saddle.

He was now invited to more family functions and state affairs, and something new stirred in him, the beginning of a social conscience. He commented in his diary: "What rot & waste of time, money & energy all these state visits are!"[38]

One such ceremony was for Archduke Francis Ferdinand, heir apparent to the Austro-Hungarian Empire, and his wife. Only seven months later an assassin's bullets killed them at Sarajevo.

At Oxford he was proudest of the fact that he had joined the Officers Training Corps and earned his Lance Corporal stripes. He still looked incredibly boyish, slight, delicate at his full height of five feet six. When England went to war in 1914, he wanted to enter the Navy but they wouldn't have him because his presence on any ship might make it a prime target. He joined the Grenadier Guards instead, and felt like "a pygmy" in this unit of six-footers. When the unit went to France, the Prince was left behind "in a glass case." "A terrible blow to my pride, the worst in my life."[39]

The Prince began an intense personal campaign to get into action. He told the formidable Lord Kitchener, the Secretary of State for War, that he had four brothers to succeed him if he was killed. Kitchener answered that he wouldn't stop him if he were certain of that, "but I cannot take the chance . . . of the enemy taking you prisoner."[40]

The Prince afterward wrote his father: "I feel so ashamed to wear medals which I only have because of my position . . . Having never done any fighting, & having always been kept well out of danger!! . . ."[41]

He did, however, manage to get assigned to a headquarters in France, where he slipped away often by car or bicycle to talk to the wounded and visit the front. "A bad shelling will always produce the Prince of Wales," a regimental officer was quoted as saying.[42]

Touring the trenches one day, he returned to find his car had been destroyed by a direct hit and his driver killed. Another time, he had to crouch in a dugout for an hour, bracketed by shellfire. He saw the slaughter on the Somme, where 57,000 soldiers fell the first day.

An official photographer had been following him but the Prince had ordered him not to take any pictures. The man looked so dejected that the Prince walked over to him, picked up some of his equipment, remarked that it weighed "a ton." Then he asked how long the man had been following him with that load.

"About four miles, sir."

"Well, you certainly have earned a picture. You can have all the shots you want. Just tell me how to pose."[43]

Visiting a field hospital once, the Prince asked why one bed had been screened. The commandant hesitatingly informed him that the man was horribly wounded and was unfit for him to see. The Prince insisted. On the bed he saw a man so hopelessly shattered that he was almost unrecognizable as a human being. For a few moments, the Prince stood there, absolutely silent. Then he saluted the man and bent forward to kiss what could have been his forehead.

5

THE WORLD WAR was remote from Wallis but it would soon seem equally fearful and ugly to her. Shortly after her grandmother's death in the spring of 1916, a family conference decided that Wallis was too young to mourn too long. Arrangements were made for her to visit Lelia Barnett's youngest sister, Corinne Mustin, in Florida. Corinne's husband commanded the new Naval Air Station at Pensacola.

In her first letter home Wallis wrote that she had just met "the world's most fascinating aviator."[1]

Lt. (Junior Grade) Earl Winfield Spencer, Jr., was not only handsome but persuasive, dominating, virile—and he knew it. One of Wallis' friends called him "a beautiful-looking man . . . not the most talkative, but very flirtatious with the women."

In the U.S. Naval Academy yearbook, the limerick for him read:

> On the stage, as a maid with a curl,
> A perfect entrancer is Earl.
> With a voice like Caruso
> It's clearly no use
> To try to beat him with a girl.

It went on to call him "fiery and able," "brimming with happy spirits," a "merry devil," and "a good comrade—there could not be a better shipmate."[2]

He was twenty-seven, the twentieth naval pilot to win his wings. In those days a naval pilot had all the drama and glory of an astronaut fifty years later. For nineteen-year-old Wallis Warfield, whose boyfriends were mostly callow young men, "Win" Spencer came on like a charge of electricity.

Cousin Corinne had invited Spencer and two other young officers to lunch at her home the first day after Wallis' arrival. Corinne was one of the pretty, witty Montagues, a natural blonde with a loud laugh who had married a quiet man ten years older than she was. She knew exactly what Wallis wanted and needed.

An unattached fresh female face on a naval base becomes an automatic attraction causing all kinds of challenge and competition and so Spencer quickly staked his claim. He didn't have to try hard; Wallis was already caught.

Corinne, who called her cousin "Skinny," had no intention of running any chaperoned cocoon. Win was soon giving Wallis private lessons in golf, taking her on personal tours of the airport, spending long evenings at the country club telling her all about the fascinations of flying.

Wallis listened as if her life depended on it. She had a way of looking at a man's face, her eyes never leaving it. Her interest was avid and deep and flattering. Wallis could maintain a flow of chatter as easily as anyone, but she had an innate sense of timing with men, and she knew the place for silence.

She also knew when to be vivacious, to be "on."

"She oozes charm in the way an old-fashioned burner stove radiates heat," confided an old friend.[3]

Part of her charm, a great part, was her naturalness. She was what she was. She didn't try to put on any other face or any other accent. Nor did she pretend to any knowledge she didn't have. She also had the great gift of making men laugh, making them feel relaxed and "easy."

"I don't believe in saying anything mean about people," she reminisced many years later. "It's so much easier to say something nicer."[4]

Win had never met anybody quite like her. More beautiful women, yes, many of them. But never anyone so attentive and so bright and so much fun.

Now it was Win Spencer who was caught.

Corinne knew what was happening and let it happen. She had never seen Skinny so dazed before. Playing gin rummy with her, she realized that Wallis didn't even know the game was over.

For Wallis, the game had just begun.

If Win was ready, Wallis was ripe. It was her first sweeping love. She was transformed and daydreaming and eager. Scheduled to go home after a month, Wallis stretched it to two. Then, one night after a movie, sitting on the porch of the country club, Win asked her to marry him.

Win was handsome enough to have had his pick of any number of prettier women. Besides the other assets he had seen in Wallis, he had found deeper qualities in her than he had ever found in any other woman. Years later, in a reminiscence, he defined it as "strength of character," and said she had more of it than anybody he had ever known. It was a quality that Earl Winfield Spencer, Jr., needed more than anything else. Despite his dominating virility, he sensed that she was stronger than he was, and he wanted her for it.

Spencer came from a large suburban family in Chicago. His father was a member of the stock exchange there. Win had never before had any pressure put on him. Money was easy, women were easy, flying was easy. It now looked as if the United States would soon be in the war and Win wanted more than anything else to fight in it. He saw it as the high drama of life.

He now felt his first inner pressures. Before he fought, and maybe died, he wanted to belong to somebody. His mother had other sons, but Win wanted somebody to worry about him and him alone. He wanted somebody to truly care, somebody to listen to him, somebody with whom he could share everything.

Win had a core of weakness, and he knew it. He drank too much, and the drinking intensified all his pressures and all his needs.

Wallis had the strength and love he wanted and needed.

She told him then that she loved him, wanted to marry him. She had been bred tightly in social formality and there were rules: she first had to talk to her mother and Uncle Sol.

Alice Warfield Rasin looked at Wallis and saw her young self. Years later, when she was dying, she told Wallis how alike they both were: more heart than head. Now she had all the negative arguments. It had been such a short romance. Navy wives had to learn to live the strict life of conforming to so many regulations. Wallis was so restless, so impulsive, could she do it? Could she pinch pennies on the small Navy salary? We would soon be in the war, and Win would probably be part of it, possibly even die. She had been an early widow, and it was bitter and terrible—did Wallis want to be one, too?

Wallis listened to everything, shook her head. She was in love.

Uncle Sol had hoped Wallis would marry a Baltimorean of wealth

57

and distinction. He hedged his judgment until he met the man. Win arrived, won over everybody, especially the women. Wallis then went with him to Chicago and the Spencer family made it plain that they approved but that the young couple could not count on them for any financial support. Money, however, was not the main thing on their minds.

It is interesting that Wallis thought it necessary at this time, September 1916, to write a letter to Carter Osburn. Osburn had gone to Mexico with the U.S. Cavalry chasing after Pancho Villa. Osburn later remembered that he was sitting under a mesquite tree when the straggling courier returned with a single letter with the bombshell news from Wallis that she was marrying somebody else. "The temperature was about 116 degrees in the shade and we hadn't had any water for 24 hours," he remembered.[5] Wallis' letter did not improve the atmosphere. Years afterward, Wallis dismissed her relationship with Osburn as mostly a matter of car convenience. If this was seriously so, she would not have written that "Dear John" letter. For Carter Osburn, it had been a romance with many unspoken promises.

The Baltimore newspapers announced the engagement as something "of unusual interest to Society in Maryland, as well as in Virginia" and described Wallis as "one of the most popular girls in Society," noting: "Miss Warfield has been a belle ever since she made her debut two years ago."[6]

One of the calls to Wallis' mother, after the announcement, came from cousin Mrs. Elizabeth Gordon:

"Now that Wallis is marrying into the United States Navy," she said, "the next thing we will hear is that you are marrying an Admiral."

Alice Warfield Rasin laughed and answered, "A Paymaster would be more to my liking."[7]

Wallis had seldom been traditional, and neither was her wedding. She had, however, been confirmed at the Christ Protestant Episcopal Church, and she would be married there. The date was November 8. President Wilson had just been reelected on the slogan "He Kept Us Out of War," but most people knew that war was coming. It had touched Baltimore several months earlier when a German U-boat had surfaced in its port with a $10 million cargo of dyes and chemicals. The drama of an upcoming war and the uniformed groom heightened the wedding's excitement.

Wallis had her own views of a wedding and what should be worn. She designed gowns of orchid-colored faille and blue velvet for the bridesmaids. Ellen Yuille (then Mrs. William Sturgis) was matron of honor, and she remembered the large blue satin hat with orchid plumes that Wallis had her wear. For herself, Wallis, with the help of her mother and Maggie O'Connor, designed a gown of white panne velvet (velvet was *not* traditional) embroidered with pearls, and a tulle veil that had been in the family. In her hair she wore a coronet of orange blossoms, and she carried a bouquet of white orchids and lilies of the valley.

The evening ceremony with burning tapers made the aura more romantic but it was a nervous bride who found no emotional support in the stern face of Uncle Sol, who escorted her down the aisle. But Win was there, and the love in his face restored her.

6

Cousin Lelia Barnett told Wallis, many years later, that Wallis had married Spencer "out of curiosity."[1] She said it jokingly, but there was some truth in it. In every young woman there is surely the curiosity of what it means to live with a man. It is not simply a physical thing, but the curiosity of constant discovery.

Wallis got the first foreboding of troubles to come on their honeymoon in White Sulphur Springs, West Virginia. It was here at her friend Ellen Yuille Sturgis' summer house that another young man had once romanced her and asked her to marry him. Now she was staying at the staid, sumptuous Greenbriar Hotel. Soon after their arrival, just as they were unpacking, Wallis saw her handsome husband was unhappy. He had seen a notice in the room that no liquor would be served because the state was dry. She could see how important this was to him, but she was on her honeymoon. Win soon wiped the thought from her mind.

The officers' homes at Pensacola Naval Air Station were mostly similar bungalows with similar interiors and furniture. What made them special was the waterfront setting and the smell of the oleanders.

Wallis had long ago learned to sew. Now, she not only learned to cook and like it, she also learned to drink and like it.

"Wallis was a law unto herself," said a woman who knew her then. "She bossed everybody. And she was a great one for men. She really wanted other husbands to pay attention to her. Something else I remember was that she didn't seem to like children."

Others have echoed the same note about Wallis and children. If it was true, then why? She had grown up an only child with a mother who didn't often play the traditional maternal role. While Alice worked, or busied herself elsewhere, Wallis lived with her grandmother, who offered a mixture of sternness and kindliness rather than open affection. Since she had no younger brothers or sisters, she was deprived of an opportunity to understand young children. Nor did she have many children her own age to play with. Finding herself so much with adult company made her more self-sufficient and mature, and distorted her view of normal childhood. The idea of having children may have clashed with her ideas of independence.

Then there was the money. She and her mother had to scratch for it. They were forced to rely on the generosity of others. Wallis did not want ever again to be so dependent. Even if she could have children, she probably didn't want them until she could well afford them.

There was, however, the question of whether she *could* have children. After her mother died, an attendant nurse revealed that the mother had said that Wallis could never have any children.

For anyone, there is the obvious psychological phenomenon of not liking what you can't have.

At Pensacola Wallis found Navy life was confining, lonely, fearful. The sound of fear was the crash gong. It meant a plane had gone down. Once the gong sounded, and it was Win. He had been forced down in the bay but he was rescued unhurt. Wallis grew to hate planes and developed a fear of flying that lasted all her life.

The only talk of war now was: When? The expectancy intensified the frenzied fun of their Saturday nights in town. Then they all let loose. After a certain amount of drinking, Win wandered onto the dance floor to do impersonations. Saturday night made it all seem like a merry-go-round.

The merry-go-round seemed over on April 6, 1917, when the United States entered the war. Win eagerly expected a combat assignment, and now, suddenly, Wallis began to realize what war might mean. It was no longer a faceless soldier dying in a dreary trench; it was her husband; it was the crash gong.

Win, however, had been a first-class senior air instructor and the Navy decided to put him in command of Squantum Naval Air Base near Boston. He was angry, frustrated; Wallis was delighted.

What saved Wallis from loneliness was her curiosity, her restlessness. Win's work was so consuming that he seldom came home before nine at night, so exhausted that he went straight to bed. Home then was a hotel apartment in the Back Bay section of Boston.

Reginald Thomas, who was stationed at Squantum, remembered Wallis driving her husband to work every morning and returning to take him home at night. She had a small automobile, with which she did her own shopping, and she was a familiar figure at the beach, sunning herself.

What can you do in Boston when you're a stranger, and alone? She had had her fill of the chatter and the bridge with other Navy wives. She saw the city as a treasure trove of history and she wandered everywhere, visiting the museums and antique shops. It was not the life she had imagined on Biddle Street or at Oldfields or Christ Church. It was a quiet introspective life, but there was a great sense of freedom in it. She shaped her time as she shaped herself. Her mother once told her never to be afraid of loneliness. She said that loneliness had its purpose, that it taught us to think.

Thinking about herself then, Wallis had little to regret. She loved her husband and he loved her. The war made everything uncertain, but it only made them get more meaning and pleasure out of whatever time they did have together. The transfers were uprooting, but there was something always exciting about going someplace new.

Win did so well at Boston that the Navy reassigned him to command a naval air station near San Diego. Befitting her new status, Wallis found a high-ceiling bungalow with a large living room and a generous patio.

She was now in a new element, a new life style. The "brass" came through in a steady stream, and there were always dinners and parties. She enjoyed being the wife of the commanding officer of an important post; she liked being the hostess, keeping the conversation alive, the mood enjoyable.

"Actually, she seldom said anything brilliant," commented a woman who knew her well, "but she supplied large amounts of the candor that seems to be wit at the moment, especially if one has had three or four highballs, and the chatter is both loud and fast. Wallis caused uproarious laughter when she said things most other people would leave unsaid, and instead of saying them, screamed them—and kept screaming them not only at midnight, but at one, then two, and even at three A.M., with as much gusto as when the party started. By four A.M. she usually had a jolly idea about everybody going out and stealing the milkman's wagon for a joyride."

Wallis thrived. She liked parties and she liked people and life was suddenly rich and beautiful. She broadened her social reach, moving into the more prestigious circle at nearby Coronado. Her friends were now the daughters of admirals, the owners of polo ponies, and she even had herself photographed with Charlie Chaplin.

One of the unexpected social events at the Hotel del Coronado was a ball for the young, handsome Prince of Wales, who arrived in April 1920, aboard the HMS *Renown*. "We attended the ball," Win remembered, "and the Prince was pointed out to us early in the evening; but neither Wallis nor I commented except to murmur our surprise."[2]

This was the way of life Wallis always had wanted: the easy grace, the perfect taste, the unpressured pace, the high style, a whole corps of exciting friends ready to explore anything fresh and different.

If Wallis blossomed, Win seemed to disintegrate. The war was over and he had never had the combat he so badly wanted. To make it worse, he had lost a brother in the war. His drinking increased. Wallis always enjoyed being flirtatious, and freely admitted it. Win saw these flirtations as something more serious. Always a jealous man, he became more violent. Wallis had a temper of her own and they had frequent yelling matches, and sometimes he would hit her and she would throw things.

Win even had changed physically. The lean, handsome body had grown fat and gross. He was no longer the man she had married or the dream she had dreamed. As for Win, he had married Wallis for an inner strength that she didn't even know she had. Now that their marriage had gone sour, she had found this strength in her bitterness and no longer wanted to share it.

Win was twice reassigned elsewhere on a temporary basis, but Wallis did not join him. Her mother came to visit and stayed a while. But they could no longer confide in each other as they once had. Wallis had become a more private person. She could involve herself in all kinds of things, but she found it hard to give of herself.

It was the same with friends. It wasn't really friendship she gave; it was a kind of camaraderie: a relaxed air of goodwill, a sense of cheer, a friendly feeling—but not friendship. She gave no deep confidences, no close secrets. The failure of her marriage was her own failure, and not for disclosure. The heartache of her husband was part of the core of her inner self.

Wallis had a large circle of acquaintances, and a few felt they were her friends, but there were no intimates.

What had happened with her mother was hard to understand. These two were so much alike. Perhaps if Wallis' marriage had been happier, the air between them would have been easier. Her mother had warned her, and the warnings had come true. Alice was ready with sympathy and Wallis wanted none of it.

She did not feel quite free with her Coronado crowd. She was, after all, a married woman without a husband, living alone in her own house. It took an edge off the pleasure. The future seemed more uncertain, more lonely.

Then in the summer of 1920 came some good news. Win had received a permanent assignment to help set up the new Bureau of Aeronautics in Washington, D.C. The job seemed important, with a potential, and Win was genuinely excited about it. It looked like a fresh beginning.

It was, for a while.

The nation's capital had a new atmosphere in 1920. The Republicans nominated Warren G. Harding, and the American people would elect him to bring the country "back to normalcy." The war had left the world "in crutches, with its arm in a sling." And shell-shocked too. The United States had gone deep in debt; inflation had shrunk the dollar almost in half.

These were all things the American people wanted to wipe out of their minds, particularly the young people. Wallis was then twenty-four years old and she felt herself one of them. The new creed of the young at the start of the 1920s said that the purpose of life is to express yourself, realize your full individuality; that there is nothing unclean about the body, that it is a shrine to be adorned for the ritual of love; that it's stupid to pile up treasures to enjoy only in old age when we can no longer enjoy it fully, that we should seize each moment as it comes and use it intensely; that Puritanism is the great enemy, that every convention preventing the full enjoyment of the moment should be shattered and abolished; that women should be the economic and moral equals of men; that we should remove our individual repressions and be happy.

Edna St. Vincent Millay wrote a stanza which became the battle cry of the generation:

> *My candle burns at both ends;*
> *It will not last the night;*
> *But ah, my foes, and oh, my friends—*
> *It gives a lovely light!*[3]

The phrase "Flaming Youth" soon gained wide circulation. A historian described this attitude by saying, "They believed in a greater degree of sex freedom than had been permitted by the strict American code; and as for discussion of sex, not only did they believe it should be free, but some of them appeared to believe it should be continuous." The concept was perhaps best summed up in the sentence "I have a right to do anything that doesn't harm anyone else."

This was the world Wallis Warfield Spencer was living in; these were the times and this was the mood. To understand this is to understand better why she could make her monumental decision.

She had decided that her marriage was too degrading. They lived in an apartment-hotel with thin walls and it shamed her to know that their violent arguments had become public property, that her husband's drunkenness could no longer be confined to her inner being, that she was married to a man who could also be physically brutal. She no longer wanted to live with him.

Divorce was unthinkable, said her mother. Love could turn to loathing, but marriage was a sacred vow. Separation yes, but divorce never. A divorced woman was a disgraced woman, a lost woman. And it was a family shame that would not be erased.

Wallis steeled herself to confront Uncle Sol. To her, he represented an image rather than an emotion. He was her family elder, the source of her income, her father's brother but never really a substitute father.

The emotion was there. He was not a dry man. He had lived and loved, and done it well. Why should he only show her his puritanical face? His friends knew him as a delightful companion and yet, to his niece, his favorite niece, he could never communicate any feeling, any love. He showed her only a soul as stiff as cardboard. He listened to her explanation and her pleading and his answer was flat and final. No divorce. She must try again.

So much was Wallis' awe of this man, and so much was her financial future dependent on him, that she did try again. Win tried, too. But the importance of his job had bogged down in bureaucracy and paperwork and he could only find refuge in more drink. More drink, which meant more jealousy, more violence.

Win wanted more than she could give, and she could give nothing.

Her mother had moved to Washington in 1921 to try to make a new life of her own. She had gone to work as a hostess in the Chevy

Chase Country Club. One day Wallis appeared, with a request: Could she move in?

In answer to a query, several generations afterward, Wallis said, "The physical side of love is a vital ingredient, but many men and women have learned to their sorrow that physical attraction alone cannot sustain a marriage."[4]

7

Perhaps it was the deep disapproval of Uncle Sol, perhaps it was inertia or lack of funds, perhaps it was the lingering fear of the final step of cutting herself absolutely loose—but Wallis did not at that time seek a divorce. Instead, she acted as if the deed was done.

Washington in 1921 was in transition, the Democrats out and the Republicans in. It gave a certain spice to the cocktail talk, everybody wondering what the new President Harding would do. He was such a handsome man with a sincere face and a magnificent figure. He seemed like a warm-hearted regular fellow who liked poker and golf and an occasional drink.

"The truth about it is that he was altogether too urbane, too good-natured, too generous-hearted, and too fond of having a good time for his own good. . . . The simple fact is that my dear old friend just did not like to work," confided the U.S. Senator from Indiana James E. Watson. It was the kind of comment that got around quickly. It marked the man as it marked the expectations of his administration.

Win was again transferred, early in 1922—this time in command of a gunboat in the Far East. Wallis started to spread herself socially, first through her cousins, then through friends. What gave Washington society its special color and variety, its code and distinction, came from the fact that it was the nation's capital. The big social word was "precedence." Government officials and foreign embassies all obeyed the protocol of rank. It firmly dictated the order of who sat next to whom, and every Washington hostess learned to regard this as holy. So complicated did this sometimes become that some hostesses almost met the fate of the centipede in the old verse—the one who paused unexpectedly to contemplate which foot properly came before which foot and found itself unable to walk at all.

This rigid rule of social precedence put the wife of a Navy lieutenant on a very low level indeed, but Wallis was still delighted to be part of the scene.

Wallis found herself listening and learning politics just as she had had to learn cooking. "I like to know what other people think," she said long years later, "but I would never express a political opinion."[1]

If she held back on that, she held back on little else. This was the day of the hip flask, the "IT" girl, the rising time of the flapper, the night club, the air of novelty and anything goes. Wallis felt that she was twenty-six and old enough to do anything she wanted to do.

She moved into the Georgetown house of Dorothy McNamee, the daughter of an admiral, whose naval husband was also in the Far East. Mutual friends noted that it spoke well of Wallis that Dorothy McNamee wanted her to share a home. She was a quiet, shy, sensitive woman who was much respected as a talented artist. She and Wallis had the same qualities of humor and self-respect and natural honesty and directness.

Wallis, however, was looking for something more, and she soon found him.

She got a call from an old Baltimore friend and one of her bridesmaids. She had been invited by a blond, good-looking diplomat from the Dutch Embassy to a small dinner in Washington that coming week and was asked to bring a girlfriend. Would Wallis want to go?

Wallis was delighted. Foreign embassies had a special attraction for young Washington women, and vice versa. Foreign diplomats, particularly the young ones, caused a quicker female flutter with their flattering attention, their ardor, their insistence.

Present at the dinner was Washington's most eligible bachelor. At thirty-five, Don Felipe A. Espil, the first secretary of the Argentine Embassy, was described by one of Wallis' friends as "delectable," "that beautiful hunk of man." A slim, dark six-footer, he spoke with a strong South American accent "which made him even more attractive."[2] Society editors called him "dashing," and he was always impeccably dressed.

What gave Espil his special distinction in Washington was that he was a Renaissance kind of man with a broad range of abilities and interests. Ever since he had come to the United States in 1916 as a practicing attorney, he had had a love affair with the country and learned all about it. He could talk knowledgeably and excitedly about anything from big league baseball to the latest trends in music to esoteric economics. He was an excellent golfer, a superb bridge player, a wonderful horseman and a connoisseur of wine, women and song. He described himself as "a diplomat by accident,"[3] but few diplomats worked harder in Washington, or knew more. He rose early, read voraciously—at least seven newspapers and the Congressional Record. Everybody knew him as a bon vivant, and he was, but he was usually the first to leave a party, to ready himself for the morning's work.

When Espil gave a party, everybody wanted to come because they knew everything would be the best, the guests as sparkling as the wine. He somehow managed to keep up a frenetic social life and yet attend all the important Congressional committee hearings. What impressed everybody most about Espil, however, more than his magnetism and his good looks and his intelligence, was his warmth and sincerity. Needless to say, ambitious mothers had their eligible daughters all lined up and waiting.

Espil impressed Wallis as he did everybody else. Wallis managed to catch and hold his attention that night. If she ever effervesced, she did then. And, before the evening was over, Wallis invited everyone at the dinner to come to an eggnog party at her place that week. She now knew what she wanted.

Later that night, Wallis escorted her friend to the Union Station to put her on the train to Baltimore. The two went into the ladies' room to "freshen up" and Wallis seemed to be looking into the mirror for a long time as if she were cataloguing her liabilities. "With faces like ours," she said aloud, "how are we going to get anywhere?"[4]

It seemed hopeless. Besides any inadequacies she saw in her face, her figure was more boyish than buxom, with more angles than curves, and her legs were slightly thin. Espil was a man's man who had everything, including the most beautiful women in Washington. Why would he ever want her?

But that night at dinner, Espil saw something in her that stirred him. He came to her eggnog party, then invited her to lunch with him at the Hotel Hamilton. The lunch was a weekly get-together of a swinging set of sixty young diplomats who called themselves "The Soixante Gourmets."

Wallis was lucky that afternoon. She knew one of the members, Wilmott Lewis, who was going with her cousin Ethel. Lewis publicly announced all the virtues of the Montague women, and urged every member to marry one. Then when Wallis made some witty remark, Lewis said, "Oh, the Montaguity of it all!"[5]

Espil took Wallis back to those lunches again and again, and then to dinner and to parties, and the word was soon out that the two were a duet and should be invited together. In the "precedence" social world of Washington, Wallis found herself suddenly lifted several rungs higher into a new stratum.

Back in Baltimore, her friends thought Wallis was "a woman of the world," but in Washington she soon saw how far she was from true sophistication. To keep up with Espil, she had to keep up with the news, keep up with the world, keep her bright mind honed to the quick. Wallis had much to learn and Espil had much to teach. As she later put it, "He acted as both teacher and model in the art of living . . . in many respects the most fascinating man I have ever met, with principles of steel and a spirit that bubbled like champagne."[6]

Espil stirred her, excited her, overwhelmed her.

"Wallis was mad about him," said her friend.[7]

Espil gave Wallis a final polish of high style. He pulled out of her a maximum of her potential, enriching all the many assets she already had. He made her see so much of the cocktail party trivia for what it was and opened up her mind to an excitement of new ideas. He did all this not simply because he liked her and enjoyed being with her, but because he had learned to love her.

He saw in her a woman whose energy and spirit matched his. They shared the same zest for life. Beauty alone no longer intrigued him. He had had his fill of the blank beauties. Of course there were the lovely ones who also had sharp minds, but here was a woman who could make him laugh, who said what she thought, who never seemed to pretend. Such a direct honesty was refreshing and captivating.

Wallis possibly had another attraction for Espil—she was still safely married. Friends who knew them both at the time insist that Wallis was much more in love with him than he with her. They also claim that Wallis was plainly jealous. While Espil escorted her everywhere and often, he occasionally went with other women. This was the first time Wallis had ever showed any jealousy; she had never had to before —she was never that deeply interested in any one man. This new, painful reaction was a measure of the depth of her feelings. Wallis' single great ambition in life was to marry Espil.

"She would have gone to Argentina or anywhere else, if he wanted to take her. He was a Catholic, but I think she would have converted, if he asked her. She would have done anything. I've never seen a woman so much in love," said a friend who knew her then.[8]

Wallis' ambition was to have Espil permanently, but Espil's ambition did not include marriage with Wallis Warfield Spencer. He was nine years older than she and he had a clear concept of his future. He wanted to be the Argentine ambassador to the United States, and so he would be. To best fit that post, he needed money, and he had none. Of course, neither did Wallis. Beyond that, it would hardly help his career to marry a Protestant who was also a divorcée, whose husband was still alive. Argentina was a strongly Catholic country and such a choice might kill his diplomatic hopes. What he wanted and needed was a wealthy wife who had as many of the other desired attributes as possible. This was not Wallis. She was wonderful to be with, marvelous to love, but not the woman he wanted to wed.

She made it easy for him by being increasingly jealous and possessive. Her friends had always said of Wallis that she had a practical mind, that she was basically a realist, that she kept her heart and mind compartmentalized and seldom lost her cool.

This was not true of her in 1923. Perhaps she felt she would never find another man like Espil, and she could not and would not lose him. Perhaps she felt that she was twenty-seven, and this might be her last chance at such full love. She always before had been able to shape her fate, reach her goal, get her man. Such failure was new to her. So was this inability to control herself. Control had always been a point of personal pride. But this was a love richer than she had ever known. She had loved Win Spencer in a romantic physical way, whereas with Espil it was a love without boundary, a wild and mature love with a man who could teach her everything because he knew everything. And she didn't want to lose him; she didn't want to lose him! The more jealous she became, the more time he spent with other women; the more possessive she tried to be, the less he saw her.

Then, one day, he made it plain it was all over.

Never had she been so crushed, so empty, so forlorn. It was the summer of 1923. It seemed like the end of her world. Then came an escape, a surprise invitation from Corinne Mustin, the cousin she had visited in Pensacola. Corinne's husband had died and she wanted a change of scene. She was going to Paris. Would Wallis join her?

Wallis jumped at the chance. She had no money so she petitioned

Uncle Sol. Again, at first he was the puritan, the public official, the straitlaced citizen, cold and severe. Two young women alone in Paris was immoral and unheard-of. Before she left, however, he thrust a small wad of bills in her hand to cover expenses.

Several women close to Wallis through the years have freely admitted her many special qualities, and have openly envied them. "But she has no warmth," they add, "she has no heart."[9]

These were women who did not know her in Washington. Those who did knew that she was then warm and loving and alive. Espil not only had made her mind tingle but had made her soul sing.

Other critics have called Wallis a cold, unawakened woman. The truth was that she was a warm woman who had been frozen. She had been hurt as badly and deeply as any woman could be hurt, denied the strongest love of her life. The coldness had come from that, a newly insulated wall around her heart. Espil had brought her passion to a peak and then thrown her into a chasm. Nobody would ever do that to her again if she could help it. The hardness had come then.

"She would kill me, if she ever knew I told you," confided one of her close friends, "but I think she expected Espil to join her in Paris. He never came."[10]

The men in Paris were young, good-looking, pleasant. She enjoyed being with them. They passed the time. They filled an emptiness. Espil had filled more than mere emptiness; he had filled her deep and real need. He had made her conscious of what she had been missing her whole life. And there was no doubt that his intellectual awakening of her intensified her love for him and her understanding of others. All other men now seemed callow and incomplete compared to him.

From then on, there was only so much of herself that Wallis would give. Friendly, yes. Cordially correct, certainly. Confiding, only partly, and seldom. Warmly intimate, almost never. Friends could talk to her, but never deeply reach her.

She stayed on alone in Paris, even after Corinne had gone home. There seemed nothing better to do, nowhere else to go. Friends suspected that she drank more than she used to. She felt rootless and lonely. Suddenly, into that loneliness came a stream of letters from her husband in China. He was also rootless and lonely. He still loved her very much, he said. He wanted her back. Couldn't they try again? The Navy would send her to him in China.

She wondered: Was it worth trying? He had been the first romance in her life and there was once love. Time seemed to have dimmed some of the ugliness between them. She herself had gone through her own fire of suffering. She saw things now in a new perspective, a new dimension. Her pain had brought more maturity with it. And now, of course, she had a new need.

To a friend she said, "Well, it's the only way I'll get to the Orient, so I guess I'd better go."[11]

And her friend commented afterward: "Wallis was always a very sensible woman. She always said she would never let tomorrow get in the way of today."[12]

Wallis wrote to Win that she was returning to Washington, and would consider what he had written, and make her decision later. Was it possible that the "sensible" Wallis delayed her decision because she had the lingering hope that Espil might still want her?

8

WASHINGTON, D.C., was more a merry-go-round than ever when Wallis returned in the summer of 1924. President Harding had died in office, replaced by his Vice-President, Calvin Coolidge. One newsman's reaction was "Calvin Coolidge—President! My God!"

Investigations into White House involvement in the Teapot Dome scandal had produced sensational revelations, deeply implicating a former attorney general and secretary of the interior. They had disposed of valuable oil lands to oil companies without competitive bidding and fattened their pockets in the process. President Harding was proved innocent but others would go to jail and one committed suicide.

Washington corruption seemed symptomatic of the age. The Ku Klux Klan offered a new program of hate. Everybody winked at Prohibition, and people transformed raw alcohol into gin by adding water and juniper drops. Washington cocktail parties started at five in the afternoon and often lasted until three or four the next morning. Magazines began printing articles about companionate marriage, and nymphomaniacs became the heroines of literature.

More women bobbed their hair, wore dresses up to their knees. "Silent Cal" Coolidge seemed out of tune with the times, a small man with a sheepish grin who looked "like the farmer looks on Sunday." He preached economy in government, promised not to rock the boat or interfere with business, let everybody live and let live. In an age of cynicism and corruption, he promised a time of quiet. Another prophet from France, Dr. Emile Coué, tried to improve America with the slogan "Every day, in every way, I am getting better and better."

Wallis tried to believe the Coué philosophy. She wanted to. But

Espil, again, had said no. He had found another woman he wanted more. Wallis no longer wanted to linger. Washington seemed a city with more lion hunters than lions, more people having parties to advance themselves rather than to enjoy themselves. The whole mixed-up scene made China triply attractive and she wrote Win that she was coming.

The voyage to China took more than six weeks and Wallis had all the time she wanted to look into the mirror of her conscience. She was emotionally down, and she needed a brass ring to grab, an exhilarating lift. She now wanted this marriage with Win to work; she wanted it desperately.

Win met her at Hong Kong, with the news that he had stopped drinking the day he had learned she was coming.

Their first days together were all she could have wanted. Win was at his best, and so was she. More than anything else now, she wanted this to have a happy ending, she wanted to belong, she wanted to be part of somebody.

And then one night Win came home very late and very drunk.

She was tougher now. She had more walls within herself. She wanted more, but always expected less. Her tears were mostly interior now, but sometimes, even now, she found herself almost breaking. "If I saw her cry, I would die," said one of her closest friends. "I've never seen her cry; I've never seen her even come close to it. She always has been in complete control of herself."[1] Not always, but the witnesses were few.

Win tried again when Wallis had a serious kidney infection. He seldom left her side. His devotion was obvious and touching. After an interval, though, things got worse again. Win started drinking before breakfast. Then he started humiliating her, insisting that she accompany him to certain sing-song houses to meet his former girlfriends.

Wallis suddenly had her fill. Their final farewell was more sad than bitter. He agreed to continue her separation allotments and she headed for Shanghai, where somebody had said she might get an easy divorce in an American court.

Shanghai was then one of the most sophisticated, most cosmopolitan cities in the world. Anything could happen there, and usually did. Wallis moved into the Palace Hotel on the Bund, a haven for other Navy wives. She soon had friends. Her neighbor was a minister's daughter who carefully explained that all respectable women should drink gin because it looked so much like water. Wallis also soon had an escort, an Englishman named "Robbie" who introduced her quickly into the pleasure-seeking swirl of moonlight dinners, swinging night clubs and parties. Wallis loved the exotic food, the cheap living and the excitement of this different world. She also discovered that a divorce there was more complicated than she had thought. Still, she liked being in limbo.

Part of the attraction in Shanghai was the atmosphere of spontaneity and it did not seem outlandish to her to accept an invitation from another Navy wife to go shopping in Peking, almost a thousand miles away. The other woman dropped out when she was warned not to go because Chinese bandits often stopped the trains.

Wallis, however, was piqued, curious, willful as always and determined to go. The long journey started on a broken-down coastal steamer, continued on an antique train.

"And the bandits did stop the train," she reminisced later. "But they were very polite bandits, and they let us go on. It was really very exciting."[2]

Peking was a world beyond Wallis' imagination.

"It was one of the best, most exciting times of my life," she said almost fifty years later, her eyes glittering as if it were all yesterday. "Can you imagine a place where there are ten men for every woman!" She repeated it as if the fact still seemed unbelievable. "Ten men for every woman!"[3]

This was the city Kublai Khan rebuilt centuries before, a city then called Cambaluc.

"You must know that the city of Cambaluc hath such a multitude of houses, and such a vast population inside the walls and outside, that it seems quite past all possibility," wrote Marco Polo. He told of the twelve gates, which were closed each night, and "the streets are so straight and so wide, that you can see right along them from end to end and from one gate to another." These were the roads on which the elephants and camels came, bringing with them the luxuries of the world. "As a sample, I tell you, no day in the year passes that there do not enter the city 1000 cartloads of silk alone . . ."[4]

The great Khan so conceived the city that it had within it the Tartar City in the north, a square with walls almost fifteen miles in length, and the Chinese City in the south with walls almost as long. Within the Tartar City was another square called the Imperial City, its red-plastered walls more than six miles long, and within that

76

still another square, the Forbidden City, its violet-colored walls more than two miles long.

Peking was a city of squares within squares, walls within walls. The walls kept out the world, and the bandits. They were not only physical, they were psychological, exactly the kind of walls Wallis wanted. The world outside had gone sour for her. Where could she ever find a land so apart and so magical as this? The dynasties of emperors were part of history and the Republic was still in swaddling clothes, but Peking was its own private place and the giant wooden gates shut tight every night.

Wallis moved into the Grand Hotel de Pekin, but not for long. Her cousins the Barnetts had told her of a close friend at the U.S. Legation, and there was also Gerry Green, a warm friend she had met in Paris. Then she discovered Katherine Moore Bigelow, whom she had known as a young widow in Coronado, California. Katherine now had a handsome husband and a beautiful house and they insisted she stay with them.

The husband was Herman Rogers, whom Wallis described as "unusually attractive." Besides that, he was rich, charming, intellectual, athletic. A Yale graduate, World War I artillery major, champion polo player, student of history with a special interest in China, Rogers had all the money he needed to wander anywhere in the world, and he did.

The Rogerses lived in the Tartar City near the Hatamen Gate in a beautifully decorated house built around a large courtyard.

Nothing could have suited Wallis better. When she called it one of the best, most exciting times of her life, she meant it. "We were young, we were gay," she tried to explain.[5]

The knowledge that she was at the end of her young years, almost thirty, surely gave the pace of pleasure more intensity, an extended gaiety. With so many available men, her only daily question was: Which one? She herself told of the "dashing British military officer"[6] and the "gallant" Italian naval officer[7] who wrote such lovely poems for her.

She wanted both the men and the poetry.

The Rogerses made their home her home. They even provided her with her own servant, an *amah*, and her own rickshaw boy with her own rubber-tired rickshaw.

The pleasure cycle never stopped. Somebody always was giving a dinner party and there were so many favorite restaurants—one had the prize eunuch cook formerly with the Dowager Empress of China. Dancing started at eleven, seldom stopped until three in the morning.

Peking's social life in those days has seldom been duplicated. Money bought much and the dollar bill seemed to stretch forever.

Of the 2,000 foreign residents, about a fifth of them belonged to the "red, white and blue ghetto." Foreign diplomats especially enjoyed giving parties on a lavish scale. A favorite place was the racetrack just outside the city walls. The different clubs tried to outdo each other with Chinese delicacies: bamboo shoots with shredded ham and sea slugs, à la Szechuan; white fungus cooked in wine; fried fish lips; roast turtle; fried bears' paws; ducks' tongues; pudding of the seven heavenly flavors.

Herman Rogers caught some of their high jinks on movie film: the women wearing knee-length dresses and boudoir caps or bandages on their foreheads, and the men in tight trousers and high collars, all of them acting slightly silly for the camera. One sequence caught Wallis kissing Rogers, laughing hilariously into the camera, then kissing him again. Other scenes, at the races, showed some intimate glimpses of the English colony, "with Wallis as ever the life and soul of the gatherings." Cecil Beaton, who saw the film, also commented, "She seemed much less individual then, her hair thicker, her head bigger, her body fatter."[8]

Wallis loved to go shopping. Chinese shopkeepers soon called her "a woman of face," which meant that her taste was superb. She kept her rickshaw boy busy taking her to Silk Street, Pewter Lane and Jade Street. She became particularly enamored of and expert with jade. She learned to judge the color, cut and quality of it, and shopkeepers sent her special trays of jade to inspect, even on Sundays. A Peking specialty was the jade tree, a foot high with berries of carnelian or quartz or topaz or amethyst, leaves of jade and blossoms of crystal, pink or clear or mauve or smoky.

Her monthly allotment from Win hardly financed her shopping and Wallis needed outside sources to supplement. She did have a small income from a trust fund her grandmother had left her, but she found a fresh way to augment her income by using her control and her coolness. She played poker often, and won fairly consistently. Her host, Herman Rogers, had backed her at first, until he saw how good she was.

Wallis stayed with the Rogerses more than a year. They became her most intimate friends. Herman Rogers was more than that. He taught her most of what she knew about China, took her on long walks on top of the city walls, talked to her about his book on mythology, stirred her mind as Espil had done, even persuaded her to learn Chinese.

"I really tried to learn the language," she confessed long afterward, "but I was just no good at it; I'm tone deaf and Chinese has different tones on different levels and they all have different meanings."[9]

Nor did Wallis ever get to know the Chinese people. Chinese intellectuals kept clear of the foreign crowd. She saw the people of the streets: old men with thin beards and happy faces, because age was highly respected; a young girl with a jade flower in her hair; an old woman in black silk trousers and a short blue jacket; men wearing thick padded robes with fur collars and triangular fur hats; the barber twanging his tuning fork; the screaming seller of "sugared horse blossoms"—made to resemble a horse's tail, a sweet of sugar, oil and flour. She knew their faces, their bells and noises, but she never ever knew any of them. She knew only one Peking native well, her rickshaw boy. He was in an accident one day, and was killed.

"I went to his funeral," she said years later, "and I was the only one there who cried. I asked Herman Rogers why the Chinese people didn't cry and I'll never forget what he said. He told me it was because they considered death a desired end."[10]

Weekends were perhaps the most fascinating time for Wallis. Peking sat on a gold and sepia plain in the shadow of blue Western Hills. Only fifteen miles from the city the slopes of these hills were covered with temples. Herman Rogers had rented one of them. The giant Buddha there was losing its gilt, but everywhere there were tiny tinkling bells, sounding with the slightest breeze.

Their temple even had an enormous Oriental bed platform along the back wall and two adjoining rooms with cots where they divided the men and women.

Wallis, Herman and Katherine traveled part of the distance by car. Servants sent in advance would be waiting at an appointed place with donkeys, while another group of servants was already preparing dinner at the temple. It was a Chinese safari, with all the comforts.

In the peace of that place, Wallis had much to think about. Herman Rogers was an ideal man, most considerate and attentive and affectionate. He was the kind of man she could fall in love with easily, but he belonged to somebody else, a close friend. Her own life was still too disrupted for her to disrupt other lives.

She had been there more than a year, an unbelievable year, and the pleasure of it would remain prime in her memory as long as she lived. Without that year, she might have been a torn, disturbed woman, marked with a sign of failure. Instead she now felt a surging self-confidence, a renewed strength of purpose, an eagerness to search for new beginnings.

It was time now to tie up the loose ends of her life. It was time to get her divorce. It was time to go home.

9

THE MARVEL of any woman is that the men in her life speak well of her long after she has left them. This seems particularly true of Wallis Warfield. It stands as a test of quality. Her break with Spencer had been clean and final. It was a long, lonely voyage home, the ship going from Japan to Seattle. On her arrival she was seriously ill and had an operation. Heading east afterward, the train stopped in Chicago and Wallis had an unexpected visitor and companion to New York: Win Spencer. He had heard about her operation, knew she was still weak, felt he should be with her for the last lap of her trip. He had been home on leave.

It was a parting gesture, a tender, sensitive ending to a sweet-sour marriage.

New York City was not a place in which she wanted to linger. She and Win had spent the final few days of their honeymoon there. Her dear friend Ellen Yuille tried to persuade her to stay awhile. She was getting married to Wolcott Blair and wanted Wallis to be at her wedding. Wallis couldn't face the trauma of a wedding now. Besides, she already had made arrangements for her divorce and she wanted to get things started. Ellen understood. There was no time for confession then, however much Wallis needed it.

Wallis had learned that the cheapest, simplest divorce would be in Virginia, where she had spent so many summers when she was young. Her cousins the Barnetts had a magnificent Southern mansion with spacious rooms set high on a hill near the picturesque town of Front Royal. Lelia Barnett recommended a brilliant young lawyer and friend of the family, Aubrey Weaver. The highly successful Weaver had made his local reputation by saving a man on a self-defense charge after he had supposedly shot somebody in the back during a poker game. The jury presumably had not been prejudiced by the fact that the victim was a baseball umpire.

Weaver suggested that Wallis lodge at the Warren Green Hotel in nearby Warrenton, opposite the Fauquier County Courthouse. The courthouse, which Wallis faced every morning, was an undistinguished mid-nineteenth-century cream-painted brick building with a four-column portico on a narrow front above a high flight of steps.

Warrenton sat in the foothills of the Blue Ridge Mountains, not far from where Wallis was born. It served as county seat for a prosperous, fertile farm country, but it was also a meeting place for the old and new Virginia, particularly during the hunt season. Farmers in overalls and the "horsey" set in breeches mixed on the crowded little business street. The few steep streets were liberally shaded by old trees, and, after the horsey people left, the town again became a sleepy, pleasant place of fewer than 1,500 people.

Virginia law required that Wallis reside here for a full year.

The Warren Green Hotel once had been a tavern, then a private school, finally an inn. The one saving grace of this rambling red-brick, three-story building was its double veranda. Otherwise it was a small, typical, commercial hotel that catered primarily to traveling salesmen and a few permanently retired older people, who had all the choice rooms with private bathrooms.

The traveling salesmen were rough and ready with the latest joke, the backslapping, the loud laugh, the flirting and the kindness, here today, gone tomorrow. Wallis got to know a great many of them in the course of the year. Her more permanent escort was somebody she had known since they were children in Baltimore, Hugh A. Spilman. Still a bachelor, Spilman was then a banker in Warrenton, handsome, blond and curly-headed. He made sure Wallis met the most interesting people in the area, attended the best parties. These were not only Virginia people but weekend people from Washington, only several hours away. Wallis soon got the Washington news that Espil was romancing his future wife, Courtney Letts, a lovely, wealthy daughter of a United States senator. Perhaps Wallis remembered the cliché: If you carry a torch long enough, it gets burned out.

She rediscovered another old romance when she called Lloyd Tabb, who lived nearby. He had been her first beau. After Burrlands, Tabb had visited her in Baltimore, when he had returned there for the winter back in 1911, saw her as often as three times a week, and celebrated New Year's Eve with her. Now, fifteen years later, he found her equally attractive, but the fire was gone.

What greatly impressed Tabb, though, was a quality of sympathy and consideration he now found in her. The parent of a dear friend was ill. Despite her time of trial, Wallis telephoned and asked if she could come and visit. She then canceled her previous engagement and drove twenty miles to spend the afternoon with him.

Peking friends remembered Wallis as "the woman who didn't give a damn." Warrenton citizens remembered her as the woman who seemed "very much alive" and had all the beaux she wanted.

She tried to give her room at the Warren Green Hotel a feeling of home and yesterday. Out of her steamer trunks came the Chinese screens and lacquer boxes and brocades and her collection of "lucky elephants"—tiny ones carved out of jade and ivory and turquoise and amber and a dozen other stones. She even adopted a dog called Sandy. From her hotel window, she could see the daily street scenes on the two main streets. In the distance was the beautiful country of Virginia she had known so well.

The large country homes were crowded during the hunt season, when the women wore formal gowns and the men their pink hunt coats. The Warrenton Gold Cup Race for gentlemen jockeys was an outstanding local event, guests coming from everywhere.

When the hunt was over and Warrenton's quiet became too oppressive, Wallis went to New York City for a visit. She stayed with her oldest friend and closest confidante, Mary Kirk Raffray. Mary had married a Frenchman and they lived on Washington Square. It seemed hard to remember that, not too long ago, at Oldfields, they were just two giggly girls who constantly broke the rules by chattering and whispering long after lights out.

Mary was a very gay, very pretty girl, with a short, pouter-pigeon figure. "She loved to laugh and she and Wallis got along wonderfully well together," said a mutual friend.[1]

There was probably nobody else with whom Wallis could be more frank and intimate. And nobody else would be more sympathetic and understanding. If ever Wallis needed this kind of friendship, she needed it then.

Mary had two other guests for dinner that first night: Mr. and Mrs. Ernest Simpson.

Ernest Aldrich Simpson was a deceptive man with a complex personality. A tall, well-built man with blue eyes, light brown hair and a mustache, Simpson was described by a friend of Wallis as "a very, very nice man, but nothing truly exceptional, and really, I suppose, quite ordinary. But everybody likes him."[2]

This description was misleading, because beneath the quiet likable façade there were several other Simpsons. There was Simpson the intellectual Harvard graduate, a sensitive human being, a tireless traveler. He had a particular interest in Dickens, owned several original manuscripts, knew all about him. His large library included a remarkable collection of A. A. Milne. He stunned Wallis once by talking Latin with a friend. He was also fluent in French, expert in wine and history and the arts. There was Simpson the businessman, and few men knew more about shipping, or worked harder. His father owned a British shipping firm and Ernest handled the American office. There was Simpson the hobbyist. He not only was an authority on antiques, but could read the markings on old silver the way the average person reads the newspapers. There was Simpson the wit. A dry wit, and reserved, but funny. There was Simpson the Anglophile. His father was British, his mother American, and he had migrated between them when they separated. But he enlisted in the Coldstream Guards during World War I, plainly preferring the British attitudes, clothes and manners, and became a British subject, "more English than the English."

Simpson had a wife and daughter, but Mary told Wallis that Ernest and his wife were no longer happy together. Mrs. Simpson was a slight, silvery-haired woman whose great-grandfather had been chief justice of Massachusetts. Interviewed years later, Mrs. Simpson said she had liked Wallis, who was "much more clever than I am."[3]

It wasn't simply Wallis' cleverness that attracted Ernest Simpson, it was the same thing that attracted all men: her spirit and her gift of laughter.

Wallis saw Ernest Simpson several times after that dinner, once as a guest at the Simpson home, and then several times when he was invited alone to play bridge at Mary's house.

She admired Mary, who had created a position for herself, operating a boutique. Wallis saw her own immediate future as a darkening problem. She was too restless to manage a shop or sell in a store. She did feel she had some talent in fashion design and decided to enter a competition. The prize was a job on a fashion magazine. It was an essay contest; Wallis wrote one on spring hats. The editors said no.

Then came the job offer. One of her old friends, Elizabeth Key Lloyd, had become Mrs. Morgan Schiller. Morgan Schiller was an important manufacturer of tubular steel and construction elevators in Pittsburgh. When Wallis discussed her need for a job, he looked at her and thought, Why not? It was obvious that Wallis knew nothing about steel, business, mathematics or engineering, but Schiller decided that Wallis "could hypnotize anyone into buying anything in the world."

She went to Pittsburgh, immersed herself in steel, finally learned that it wouldn't work out because she just couldn't seem to add up an order. She still extended her stay in Pittsburgh for several weeks because her friend Elizabeth had arranged a whole series of parties and invitations for her to meet the most eligible bachelors in town. Her inability to sell had not detracted from her other talents.

Wanting to get some kind of glimpse into the future, Wallis spent ten dollars to find out from an astrologer that she would have two more marriages and would become a celebrity after she was forty.

It seemed most unlikely. Beyond her divorce, her future looked murky and highly unpalatable. As her mother had put it, a divorced woman was a lost woman.

Wallis saw her mother often. Alice had refused to let herself disappear into the woodwork of a Baltimore apartment. As the hostess of the Chevy Chase Country Club, she was able to keep her personality alive and her contacts warm. At the age of fifty-six, she had found herself another husband, Charles Gordon Allen. She had finally married the right man. And when they photographed her sitting on her husband's knee, she inscribed the picture, "Alice on her last lap."[4]

Wallis always saw her Aunt Bessie in Washington, too. They had a warm rapport. Aunt Bessie, unlike her sister, had never remarried. This did not narrow her mind or squeeze her soul. She knew all the jokes, hung "naughty" pictures in her bathroom and always said exactly what she thought. That summer of 1927 Aunt Bessie decided to go to Europe, and invited Wallis along. Wallis again jumped at the opportunity. At different stages of their tour of the Mediterranean, assorted young men attached themselves, including a Philadelphia lawyer and a young Irishman. Aunt Bessie was the perfect chaperone because she had long ago decided that Wallis was old enough to know what she was doing.

Wallis was old enough to decide that she preferred Paris to Warrenton, and so she stayed on after Aunt Bessie left. Reading the Paris *Herald* one day, Wallis was startled by the news that her Uncle Sol had died. It disturbed her that nobody had tried to contact her, and she sailed immediately for home.

Upon Uncle Sol's death, all the trains of the Seaboard Air Line Railroad stopped running for five minutes. His honorary pallbearers included Nicholas Murray Butler, the president of Columbia University. And his will itemized a fortune of almost $5 million.

Wallis was Uncle Sol's favorite niece. Everybody in Baltimore fully expected her to inherit the bulk of his fortune. There is little question that he originally planned just that. Wallis' final decision for a divorce, against Uncle Sol's strong warning, had cost her dearly. Two months before his death he revised his will. Most of his money now went to establish a memorial to his mother, a home for aged and indigent gentlewomen. The will provided that a room in the home should be set aside for his niece, if she should ever want it.

"If my niece, Bessiewallis Spencer, wife of Winfield Spencer, shall survive me, I give to the Continental Trust Company the sum of $15,000 in trust, to collect and receive the income arising therefrom, and to pay over the income to my niece in quarterly installments, so long as she shall live and not remarry."[5]

The puritanical businessman had predominated in the end over the sensitive lover of life.

Wallis had no qualms in joining some of her other relatives in contesting the will.

Wallis now received another warning, this one from her bright young lawyer, Aubrey Weaver, in Warrenton. If she wanted a divorce, she'd better get back quickly to the Warren Green Hotel and maintain her resident requirement. Wallis hurried back.

Weaver's daughter, Mrs. Helen Livingston, remembered her father telling her that he had asked the local judge, "Just let me have this one, Judge, and I won't bother you any more for a long time."[6]

Weaver kept the divorce questioning as simple as he could. Desertion was the charge. Wallis testified: "We lived together until the early part of 1920; at that time my husband went to Florida. There was some estrangement between us but in the early part of 1921 we adjusted our differences and resumed our marital relationship and we lived together until June 1922."

At that time, she said, he moved to the Army and Navy Club.

Asked if she had tried to bring about a reconciliation, she said she had written to him several times. She said he had written her this letter:

I have come to the definite conclusion that I can never live with you again. During the past two years, since I have been away from you, I have been happier than ever before.

The letter ended with: "Please be kind enough not to annoy me with any more letters. Yours, Win."

The letter was carefully couched to include all the necessary legal requirements but it did seem that he forgot himself at the end, signing it, "Yours, Win."[7]

The pro forma letter fooled nobody, but the judge gave Weaver his case and gave Wallis her divorce.

"It was just a matter of incompatibility," Weaver philosophized afterward. He added that Spencer had come to the courthouse just before the divorce was granted, "and we all sat around and talked very cordially. Wallis and he shook hands and parted friends."[8]

The date was December 10, 1927.

Wallis was then thirty-one years old. She didn't want to stay with her newly married mother. She had imposed too much on her friend Mary. She didn't want to share her miseries or her memories with any other relatives or friends. She wanted nobody's pity.

She decided to stay on at the Warren Green Hotel. She had run out of options.

10

WALLIS LIKED NEITHER the horse nor the hunt, but she liked the people who did. She spent more time with her cousins the Barnetts at Front Royal, less than an hour away.

The Barnett parties were in the grand style, befitting the spacious Southern mansion, the enormous rooms, the long covered porch and the beautiful grounds. Their parties had scintillated with the presence of the most interesting people. Mrs. Barnett's daughters noted how many men always seemed to group around Wallis.

"She must have had thirty different proposals while she was here," said her favorite Warrenton escort, Hugh Spilman. "I know I proposed to her regularly once a day."[1]

Wallis felt she was marking time in Warrenton, and she was. A letter arrived from her old friends Katherine and Herman Rogers, who had moved from China to the French Riviera, inviting her to stay with them. They lived in a villa called Lou Viei near Cannes, and Wallis quickly accepted.

Ernest Simpson had moved to London, after divorcing his wife, and became head of the British offices of Simpson & Simpson. He and Wallis had seen much of each other when he was still in New York. He had courted her with flowers and theater and persistent attention. He had outlined his future, and asked her to share it.

Remarriage was the easiest and most obvious option after her divorce from Spencer. She was tired of running, tired of searching, tired of swinging. She had had the travel, the freedom, the fevered love that failed. She was also tired of the gnawing fear of lack of money.

Simpson offered security. He was not wealthy, but he was financially comfortable, with an assured fortune in his future. As he was the oldest son, the shipping firm inevitably would be his. He also offered stability. He was perhaps a little vague about some things, but he was sensible and practical, with a distinguished manner and conservative taste. Stability was the one quality her life always had lacked.

Even his looks radiated dependability—his shoulders squarely set, his complexion a clear pink and white. It was so flattering to have a man want you more than you wanted him.

Simpson wanted Wallis because he felt she could give him more than he could give her. He had all the solid virtues and he wanted a wife to lighten his life. Wallis wanted Ernest Simpson, not only for the security and stability but because she honestly felt she loved him. At least she thought so. It was a love more quiet than overwhelming, but she felt it was there. She accepted his proposal, then moved into a small London flat.

They were married on July 28, 1928. Simpson called the civil ceremony in the city Registry "a cold little job."[2]

The honeymoon was happier. Simpson planned a motor trip through France and Spain in his new yellow Lagonda. For a staid man, it looked like a bright beginning.

Back in London they took a year's rental of Lady Chesham's house at 12 Upper Berkeley Street, near Marble Arch in London. It was small but pleasingly furnished, with pine-paneled walls, gleaming old silver and bright chintz. Wallis unpacked the treasures of her travels, including her collection of "lucky elephants." She soon needed all the lucky elephants she could find.

Ernest made sure Wallis had all the help she needed: a butler, maid, cook and chauffeur. Wallis, however, still preferred to do her own shopping. She was a good buyer and was never cheated. She knew what was fresh, she knew the sizes, quantities and cuts of meat, and she always knew what she wanted. She had a fixed budget, however generous, and considered it a challenge to keep within it, and did.

Her married life soon fell into a pleasant pattern. Housekeeping in the morning, an occasional lunch with a friend, perhaps shopping or visiting in the afternoon, a social evening of dinner and bridge. On weekends, Ernest took her all over the London he loved, pointing out the historic markers on houses where the great men of England had worked and lived, the character of the side streets where tiny parks seemed to appear out of nowhere, the inherent beauty of the buildings themselves. Wallis' awe of her husband increased, and, years later, she said of him, with pride, that he was "an intellectual."

Wallis described that time as "a blissful existence." Gone was her restlessness. Replacing it was a security more solid than she had ever known.

But there was loneliness too. She knew almost nobody in London. Most of their friends were her husband's, and most of them British. Wallis' American openness seemed to startle and freeze some of them.

Aunt Bessie came to visit, and so did Cousin Lelia Barnett, who was to be presented at court. Wallis helped to pick the feathers and her train. Wallis' mother couldn't come because she was too ill, and so Wallis and Ernest went to see her in Washington. She hadn't wanted Wallis to come because her daughter had always seen her smiling, and she couldn't smile now. She was thin, bedridden, emaciated and partly blind. "Oh, Wallis . . . have you come to see me die?"[3]

The prognosis on her mother's condition was serious, but nobody could say how long she would last. Wallis reluctantly decided to return to England with her husband.

Stanley Baldwin was still prime minister in 1928. He had come to power two years earlier, with the slogan "We cannot beat the Labour Party by abuse; we must do it by offering the country something better." Like much of the world, England started sliding down the drain of depression and Baldwin's "government of mediocrities" seemed to offer "nothing better," and so they too were turned out of office the following year. George V had a serious lung infection that weakened his heart that winter, and the Prince of Wales hurriedly arrived in London. Wallis was on her way to pick up her husband when she saw a black car race into the street at St. James's Palace, and the sentries stiffened. She caught a "glimpse" of "a delicate, boyish face, serious and absorbed."[4]

Ernest extended his weekend tours to the English countryside, all carefully planned and detailed. Wallis found it enchanting at first, exploring all the ancient castles and cathedrals, but then she found it a bit wearing, and finally slightly boring. She realized that her husband was more interested in places while she was more interested in people. She also discovered that her husband preferred the utter silence of a discreet hotel lounge while she liked the noise and laughter of a pub.

Wallis got the news in October 1929 that her mother was dying. By the time she arrived at her bedside, Alice was in a coma. Three days later, she was dead.

The two were so much alike—the wit, the heart, the gaiety. Both were more concerned with today than tomorrow, both preferred men to women, both knew how to milk life. They had led their separate lives, but Wallis knew that nobody understood her better than her mother did, nobody worried about her more, nobody loved her more.

Returning to London, Wallis concentrated on looking for a home of their own and finally found it in an apartment building at 5 Bryanston Court. Ernest knew more about antiques than she did, and the two of them scoured the city to find the pieces they needed. Wallis picked comfortable sofas and chairs, made sure her husband had a whole wall for his bookshelves. Dignified without being pretentious, the apartment suited them exactly.

Dominating the dining room was a mirror-top table, large enough to seat fourteen guests. Somerset Maugham's wife, Syrie, suggested a dozen high-back dining chairs upholstered in white leather and tall crystal vases filled with flame-colored flowers. The living room was pale chartreuse, with cream and beige furnishings.

Wallis finally had her own home and new friends too, with whom she felt comfortable. Most of them were part of the large American colony in London. Benjamin Thaw was first secretary of the United States Embassy, and Wallis had known his brother in California. Thaw's wife, Consuelo, was the oldest of the famous Morgan sisters. Her younger sisters were twins, Thelma and Gloria. Gloria had married Reginald Vanderbilt, and was living in the United States. Thelma, however, was the Viscountess Furness, internationally known as the woman who had currently captured the heart of the Prince of Wales.

The three Morgan sisters were particularly proud of saying that they were descendants of the grandees of Spain. Actually, their father, Harry Morgan, had been the American consul at Lucerne, Switzerland, and their grandfather, General Judson Kilpatrick, had served as American minister in Santiago, Chile. Their grandfather had married a local beauty, Louisa Valdivieso, and Thelma and Gloria especially had inherited her dark Chilean coloring. Both slim and elegant, Thelma and Gloria often wore the same gown in contrasting colors: Thelma might wear a white dress and black gloves when Gloria wore an identical gown in black with white gloves. Thelma had married young, and unsuccessfully. Her second husband, Lord Marmaduke Furness, whom she called "Duke," was a millionaire shipping magnate with a notorious reputation with women. Friends called their relationship "a marriage of convenience." It was particularly convenient for the Prince of Wales.

Lady Furness remembered being at home at 21 Grosvenor Square, in either late 1930 or early 1931, when her sister Consuelo called to ask if she could bring a friend for cocktails. "Mrs. Simpson is fun," her sister said. "You will like her."[5]

"Wallis Simpson was 'fun,' and I did like her," Lady Furness commented afterward. "At that time she did not have the chic she has since cultivated. She was not beautiful; in fact, she was not even pretty. But she had a distinct charm, and a sharp sense of humor. Her dark hair was parted in the middle. Her eyes, alert and eloquent, were her best feature. She was not as thin then as in later years—not that she could be called fat, even then; she was merely less angular. Her hands were large; they did not move gracefully, and I thought she used them too much when she attempted to emphasize a point."[6]

Lady Furness' memory was that the Prince of Wales arrived, prepared for a quiet evening with her alone and unhappy at the prospect of a party. "No, darling, just a few friends," Lady Furness told him. "You know most of them." She then told him about Wallis Simpson, saying, "She seems to be fun."[7] And then she introduced them.

Wallis had a different memory of her first meeting with the Prince of Wales. She firmly fixed the date as November 1930. Her friend Connie Thaw had called asking if she and Ernest could substitute for the Thaws as chaperones that weekend at her sister Thelma's party at Melton Mowbray. Oh yes, by the way, the Prince of Wales would be there.

The usually cool Wallis felt flustered. She didn't even know how to curtsy. Ernest, however, was delighted and honored. English society was more a matter of concentric circles than of layers. One seldom skipped from one to the other, and almost nobody ever moved into the hub, the royal family. The Prince of Wales would one day be His Sovereign Majesty.

Wallis took curtsy lessons from a friend on the train—put left leg well behind the right one and descend slowly. What made it funnier was that her instructor was a man.

Wallis and Ernest arrived in the late afternoon in a thick fog,

Wallis feeling feverish and wishing she were in bed. As Thelma introduced them to the Prince of Wales, Wallis saw the "sad look" around his eyes, the "golden hair," the "turned-up nose," the "utter naturalness."[8]

The Prince of Wales had still another version of that meeting. He remembered it a year later, also at Mowbray. He remembered the thick fog, and the fact that Wallis had a cold. With that remarkable memory of his, he also recalled their first conversation, after the introduction. He had commented that she must miss American central heating.

"A mocking look came into her eyes. 'I am sorry, Sir,' she said, 'but you have disappointed me.'

" 'In what way?'

" 'Every American woman who comes to your country is always asked the same question. I'd hoped for something more original from the Prince of Wales.' "[9]

The Prince smiled, moved away to his other guests, but the echoes of that passage lingered.

Thelma, Lady Furness, afterward insisted that there had never been any conversation about central heating and, if so, Wallis' answer would have been "not only bad taste but bad manners."[10] Nor was there any electric tension, any instant spark between them. "This is utter nonsense," Lady Furness said. "Wallis and I became great friends; actually I came to regard her as one of my best friends in England, and the Prince and I would often include Wallis and her husband in our parties."[11]

"Wallis Simpson was as nervous and as impressed as any woman would have been on first meeting the Prince of Wales."[12]

11

On the day the Prince of Wales was born, a Radical member of Parliament, James Keir Hardie, told the House of Commons: "The assumption is that the newly born child will be called upon some day to reign over this great Empire. In due course, he will be sent on a tour around the world, and probably rumors of morganatic marriage will follow. And the end of it will be that the country will be called upon to pay the bill."[1]

It was a prophecy eerily accurate.

At the end of World War I, the bachelor Prince was twenty-five. His father told him that he could mingle with other people but he could not be like them. "You must always remember your position and who you are."[2]

And the question he then asked was, Who *am* I?

The Prince now knew the boundary of his courage and the rising tide of his recklessness. He loved steeplechasing, won a fair share of races and took no more falls than anybody else—but his got world-wide publicity. Will Rogers asked him, "How are you falling, Prince?" His answer came quickly, "All over the place!"

Both the Prime Minister and his parents asked him to stop steeplechasing, and he did.

Automobiles were new and he bought a Daimler and enjoyed driving it as fast as he could until, again, his father wrote: "I must beg of you not to drive fast and to be most careful when you are driving, it makes Mama and me most anxious. . . ."[3]

He enjoyed playing polo, got a bad crack in the eye and a fast note from father. "I hope you are not overdoing it in the way of exercise."[4]

But, best of all, years later, he learned to fly his own plane, and thrilled to the freedom of it—until he again got the paternal word.

The paternal word was the reminder that the motto of the Prince of Wales was *Ich Dien* ("I Serve"). His was the job of doing all the things the King had no time or inclination to do. It meant making speeches, planting trees, launching ships, laying cornerstones and showing his face everywhere. The Prince called the job "princing."

He had been bred for it and now the mold fit.

The war brought to the surface his great reserve of energy and restlessness and curiosity.

Lady Airlie remembered the Prince visiting her at Ashley Gardens in March 1919. He had known her all his life and he could confide in her more easily than in his own mother.

"He sat for over an hour on a stool in front of the fire smoking one cigarette after another and talking his heart out."

"I don't want to marry for a long time," he said. "But at twenty-five I can't live under the same roof as my parents. I must be free to lead my own life."[5]

On the advice of Lloyd George, the King decided that his restless son start a series of tours of the British Empire to strengthen relations with the peoples of the Commonwealth.

The more he traveled, the more popular he became. The world saw his conscientious sincerity, his naturalness, his shy smile, his sense of fun and his youth and handsomeness. The greatest single impression people had about the Prince was that he really seemed to care. When he shook hands, he looked at every face; when he asked questions, he truly seemed to listen. And his vitality was incredible:

"He can dance till four, board a train or plane immediately afterwards, arrive somewhere before breakfast, review the troops (in the proper uniform), shake two thousand hands, make a speech, play two rounds of golf, attend an official luncheon, drive through the streets, unveil something, shake another thousand hands, make another speech, review more troops (in another uniform), put in an hour's squash, climb into fancy dress, and dance till four. This is no exaggeration."[6]

When in Canada he shook so many hands that his right hand swelled and turned painfully black; he simply retired it to a sling and started shaking with his left. Somebody in the crowd would say, "Put it right there, Ed,"[7] and another would yell, "I touched him!"

Before touring he had been warned: "And never miss an opportunity to relieve yourself. Never miss a chance to sit down and rest your feet."[8]

"My father always wore a top hat and he was surprised that I didn't follow his tradition. He didn't have to go around the big industrial plants that I did."[9]

Nor had King George ever toured as many slums as his son did. For one such slum tour, they brought up a Rolls Royce and the Prince refused. "I'm sorry, I'm not going to ride in that."[10] Some officials couldn't understand that. In many ways, the Prince found himself colliding with the Establishment in an attempt to revivify it.

The watchful father-king always let his son know when he disagreed, and he disagreed often.

"My father doesn't *like* me," the Prince once confided to a friend. Then he added, even more sadly, "Not at all sure I particularly like *him*."[11]

When a member of Parliament referred to royalty as "a gang of lazy, idle parasites, living on wealth created by other people," the Prince was reported to have said, "Parasites, maybe, but idle—never!"[12]

In his six years of touring the world as the Number One Salesman of the British Empire, the Prince had gone to forty-five countries and colonies, covering over 150,000 miles. He had planted enough memorial trees to fill a forest, laid enough cornerstones to build a city. "I could have qualified as a self-contained encyclopedia on railroad gauges, national anthems, statistics, local customs and dishes, and the political affiliations of a hundred mayors. I knew the gold output of the Rand, the storage capacity of the grain elevators at Winnipeg, and the wool export of Australia; and I even have held my own on the subject of the chilled-beef trade of the Argentine."[13]

In all this, he disobeyed the advice of his father's Keeper of the Privy Purse, Sir Frederick Ponsonby,* who warned him not to run the risk of making himself too accessible to people. Echoing Bagehot, Ponsonby had said, "The monarchy must always retain an element of mystery."[14]

The King and Prince disagreed on this as they did on many things. Congratulating his second son, the Duke of York, on his marriage in 1923, King George wrote: "You have always been so sensible & easy to work with & you have always been ready to listen to any advice & agree with my opinions about people & things that I feel we have always got on very well together. Very different to dear David."[15]

It was the same Duke of York who later noted how difficult it was

---

* Ponsonby had served as the principal private secretary to Queen Victoria, and George V had said of him, "He taught me to be a king."

Her mother   Her father

Bessie Wallis Warfield
With grandmother Warfield

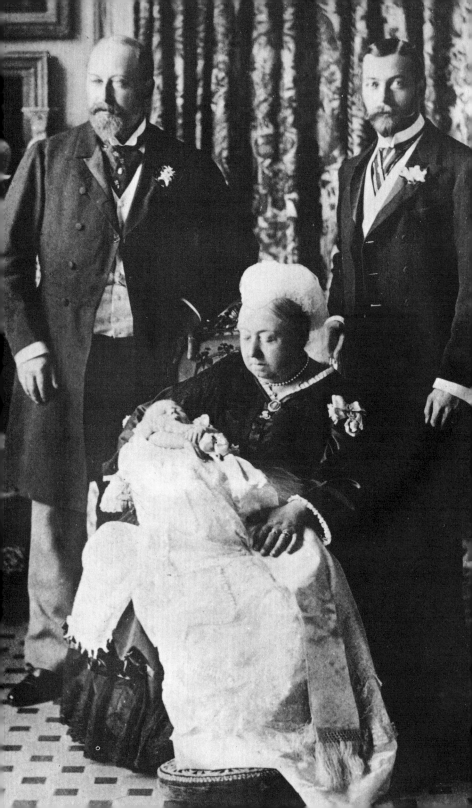

The young Bessie Wallis and her home at 212 East Biddle, Baltimore

pposite] Three kings and a queen: Edward VII [left], George V [right], and ictoria holding Edward VIII; [below] The royal residence at Windsor

Wallis the schoolgirl; scenes at
Oldfields

Edward the soldier and [opposite]
Edward, Prince of Wales

The Prince—a
young man in a
hurry

*Wallis—a belle of
Baltimore*

Wallis marries Lt. Earl Winfield Spencer of the Naval Air Corps . . . but marriage changes them both.

The Prince—salesman of the British Empire

Wallis meets a most fascinating man,
Felipe Espil.

The Prince meets Lady Furness.

Then the Prince falls in love . . .

Wallis was then married to Ernest Simpson. Simpson found sympathy in Mary Kirk Raffray, Wallis' best friend, who later became the third Mrs. Simpson.

Wallis ponders her problems at her flat in Bryanston Court.

The Prince and Wallis:
The courtship continues.

The King is dead! ...

... Long live the King!

Prime Minister Stanley Baldwin gives Edward VIII his choice: the throne or the woman he loves.

With Walter Monckton

The Archbishop of Canterbury

With Winston Churchill

Her time of trial

With Aunt Bessie

The King's retreat:
Fort Belvedere

They still had each other.

At Cannes: Herman
Rogers, Katherine
Rogers, Wallis,
Lord Brownlow

The wait for her divorce from Simpson.

And then the wedding at the Château de Candé, where they celebrated with champagne.

Left to right: Aunt Bessie, Reverend Jardine, the Duchess and the Duke, Mrs. Fern Bedaux and Randolph Churchill; partly visible in background, "Fruity" Metcalfe

At Candé: the grand salon, where the civil ceremony took place; [above] the bedroom

Before the war: with Hitler in Germany

*During the war: with the
Red Cross in France*

*Dancing at a
USO club
in New York*

SOLDIERS DIED AT PRAYER HERE

During the battle of Britain, they served in the Bahamas.

Jimmy Donahue became an intimate friend.

Elsa Maxwell became an
occasional critic.

Refuting rumors of a rift

He had his golf . . .

The only home they owned: The Mill, outside of Paris.

She had her fashions . . .

Their dogs were their family.

He had been a myth.

Their love had been a legend.

British royalty finally received them at a memorial for Queen Mary.

And then, one day, the myth was dead . . .

. . . but the legend lived on.

to have serious talks with their father because their father treated his four sons as if they were all the same, and they were all totally different in character.

"It was very difficult for David," his brother continued. "My father was so inclined to go for him. I always thought that it was a pity that he found fault with him over unimportant things—like what he wore. This only put David's back up. But it was a pity that he did the things which he knew would annoy my father. The result was that they did not discuss the important things quietly. I think that is why David did not tell him before he died that he meant to marry."[16]

One of their points of conflict concerned marriage. An entry in the King's diary read: "Now they are all married, except David."

On his American tour, one of the headlines read:

HERE HE IS, GIRLS—THE MOST ELIGIBLE BACHELOR
YET UNCAUGHT[17]

A woman reporter sent to interview him about his love life returned to the office and told her startled editor that she had spent several hours dining and dancing with him, then burst into tears, saying, "It was all too sacred; I could never write about it."[18]

Just before he left, another woman reporter asked him if he would ever consider marrying an American girl.

His answer was yes.

He made it plain that he didn't want a loveless marriage, a politically planned marriage. World War I had closed much of the royal marriage market and the Prime Minister had advised the King in 1920 that the country would not tolerate an alliance with a foreigner for the Prince of Wales. There were still some eligible princesses in Greece, Holland and Denmark, but the government now openly preferred that the Prince marry within the English or Scottish nobility.

The Prince, however, had come home with the American girl very much on his mind. He kept whistling "A Pretty Girl Is Like a Melody," to his father's distaste. (He also taught Lady Airlie the words to "Yes, We Have No Bananas," and she in turn taught it to Queen Mary, both of them singing it at the top of their voices.)

He did not tell his father about some other lyrics sung to the tune of "Three Blind Mice":

Here's our Prince!
See how he smiles!
Did you ever see such a smile in your life!
Lucky the princess he takes to wife!
Amongst all the girls there's a deadly strife
For our Prince!

The Prince felt all the signs and hints of unspoken parental pressure to push him into marriage. Gene Tunney, the cultured heavyweight boxing champion of the world, came to see him, and the Prince said, "So you are retiring because you are getting married. I sometimes think that I shall have to retire because I'm not."[19]

One of the bawdy tunes of the day aimed at the Prince's dissipation:

England's Virgin Queen was Bess,
I'll be virgin King, I guess,
And the greatest sport in Merrie England.[20]

He rationalized it by saying that he worked hard and played hard. He was up early, then to the Bath Club for a game of squash, back by nine, a hot bath, shave, breakfast and ready to work by ten. In the evening, though, he liked to go to the theater, preferably a revue or a musical comedy—he adored Ethel Merman and dated Beatrice Lillie. In the late evening, often to the early hours, he liked dining and dancing at such private night clubs as the Kit Kat, which had thirty peers among its members, and the Night Light, which had four princesses and two dukes on its board. The one he liked best was the Embassy Club on Old Bond Street, run by an Italian restauranteur of much discretion.

The Prince simply wasn't ready for marriage. There was never any shortage of available women for him, anywhere in the world. But he always had kept himself carefully self-contained. Women were casual encounters, some lasting only slightly longer than others. To one of them he gave a jeweled vanity case inscribed: "To Pinna, forever, forever, FOREVER."[21] The truth was that he felt he could not give himself forever to anybody; he could not "give" at all. It took time to find a "forever" girl with whom he fell fully in love.

It is a strange coincidence that Ernest Simpson's sister, Maud Kerr-Smiley, claimed to have given the ball toward the end of the war where the Prince of Wales met his first true love. Her maiden name was Winifred Birkin, and she was then the wife of the Right Honorable Dudley Ward, Liberal member of Parliament, a man twenty years her senior.

"Frieda," as her friends called her, was not the kind of woman a playboy Prince was supposed to want as a playmate. For one thing, she was not very much interested in the cocktail set; she preferred thinking people and was strongly interested in politics. "She was one of the brightest women I have ever known," said a friend of the Prince. "She was very witty, very sure of herself, and nobody awed her, not even he."[22]

That might have been an initial attraction, the lack of awe. Perhaps, too, the Prince was psychologically sick of being known as a playboy, perhaps she represented an intellectual challenge, a new public profile, a refreshing change as well as a defense. More probably, she represented a compelling need. He desperately wanted somebody to regard him as a human being.

Frieda was not only bright, she was pretty, very pretty. Lady Cynthia Asquith called her "a pretty little fluff." She was petite, shorter than he was, and he liked that. She had a neat figure and a charming face. Hers was the art of the storyteller with a great reliance on exaggeration. Frieda had an amusing way of detailing what happened to her during the day, magnifying little incidents into really good stories. Everybody enjoyed her gossip, and she poked fun at herself as much as at others. Her most distracting liability was a birdlike, mincing, almost squeaky voice.

The Prince went wherever Frieda invited him. His taste in music was popular, with a passion for jazz, but she was a great lover of more serious music. A newspaper report described them sitting together at a concert, with Mrs. Dudley Ward explaining to the Prince how artistically the Mendelssohn music had been blended with the Tennyson scenario.

A friend revealed long afterward that Frieda kept a cottage at Le Touquet in France where the Prince could go for quiet and comfort. She also gave him a dog as a souvenir of her affection. On his sporadic trips he cabled her often, telling how both he and the dog missed her.

The two were reported golfing together all over England, and often dancing till dawn. Throughout all this, the Prince maintained his friendship for the Right Honorable Dudley Ward and they occasionally attended prize fights together.

The relationship lasted more than ten years.

"I know he was in love with her because he told me so," said Lord Brownlow, one of his closest confidants.* "He was always writing to her and she seldom wrote to him. He was always traveling so much, you see. Of course she was very much married, but I know he proposed to her, and she said 'No.' She was English and she knew the royal rules about divorce, she knew the King would never approve of his son's marriage to a divorcée.

"He once told me that he was on a train en route to Calcutta, after a long week in Delhi, and he was in the dining room, and he suddenly started thinking about her, and he was so lonely for her that he started sobbing, and just couldn't stop. He absolutely adored her."[23]

It tells much of the loneliness of the man. He must have known, as well as Frieda, that marriage was impossible. One of her early attractions for him might well have been the fact that she was married, and therefore "safe." But this constant traveling, with almost no human contact, always on the move, never staying long enough anywhere to get to really know somebody—it only magnified the importance of the one woman who did treat him as a human being.

Frieda, however, had become deeply interested in somebody else, a handsome bachelor named Michael Herbert. She was interested enough in Herbert to divorce her husband in 1930. And Herbert was interested enough in Frieda to leave her £80,000 ($400,000) when he died three years later.

The Prince, meanwhile, had found another "true love," Thelma Furness. She was the exact counterpoint to Frieda Ward; she had the beauty without the brains.

He met her at a weekend party in the country, and asked her to dance.

"My knees would not stop shaking," remembered Lady Furness. "I was thankful for my long dress."[24]

"She was very beautiful," admitted Elsa Schiaparelli, "but she was heavy to talk to. She was gay and friendly and chattering, always chattering. But she had no sense of wit or repartee. She was what the French call 'frou'—vague."[25]

---

* Lord Brownlow's title dates from 1776, and his possessions extend over 26,000 acres in England. He is Lord Lieutenant of Lincolnshire, where he has his seat at Belton House, Grantham. His son and heir was a godson of the King and named Edward.

Lord Marmaduke Furness was Thelma's second husband, but her name also had been associated with several prominent actors. She was a Roman Catholic but then she and the Prince never talked about religion, or marriage.

"I remember we were at a party together," said a woman friend of the Prince. "Thelma had come running in and grabbed my hand and took me upstairs to the powder room, breathlessly saying that she had something to tell me. It seems she had been away at some country home that weekend, and met the Prince, and it happened that they were both on the same train coming back to London. Well, imagine her surprise when the Prince's equerry knocks on the door of her train compartment and asks if she would please join the Prince in his compartment because it was such a long trip, and he was bored."[26]

Later, describing the course of their romance, Thelma told of the coincidence of meeting in Kenya, both of them on separate safaris. She joined his, which had portable bathtubs as well as wine coolers. "This was our Eden and we were alone in it. . . . His arms about me were the only reality; his words of love my only bridge to life. Borne along on the mounting tide of his ardour, I felt myself being inexorably swept from the accustomed moorings of caution . . . Each night, I felt more completely possessed by our love, carried even more swiftly into uncharted seas of feeling, content to let the Prince chart the course, heedless of where the voyage would end."[27]

She afterward detailed some of the Prince's other attractions:

"I found in him what at that time I most wanted and needed. Not only was he fascinating to me in terms of his own personality, but he was the perfect companion for my emotional hurt. He was the antithesis to Duke [Lord Furness]; he was an antidote to Duke. Duke was rugged, blustering, carelessly self-indulgent; the Prince was shy, gracious, meticulously considerate."[28]

And, he was also the Prince of Wales.

If the Prince was an antidote to Duke, Thelma was an antidote to Frieda.

"We talked a great deal, but mostly about trivialities," Thelma confessed. "The Prince was not a man for abstract ideas or ponderous thoughts; nor was he interested to any extent in the theater, books or art. Our talk was mostly about people we knew, or had known, and about places we knew and liked. And this was enough."[29]

It was certainly enough for the Prince of Wales at that time.

133

Thelma offered him warmth and love. He could relax with her. They shared a great many people and places and common interests. She even helped him practice his Spanish before he went on a South American tour. She was not as stimulating as Frieda intellectually, but Thelma had other compensations.

She was his escape hatch. The royal world had hemmed him in on too many sides. He had loved the challenge and danger of steeple-chasing, the fun of flying his own plane, and his parents had made him abandon both. He had a small set of friends interested in night clubs and poker and private parties and he found an increasing solace in whiskey.

None of these friends was an intimate.

"You couldn't be intimate with him," said one of them. "My God, how could you be intimate with him when the Royal Family isn't even intimate with each other?"[30]

The love that the Prince of Wales gave Thelma Furness was almost superficial. He still felt himself a cold, remote human being. He had loved Frieda Ward, but she had never fully fulfilled him. Thelma Furness filled a need, but it was not his deepest need.

And then he met Wallis Simpson.

134

12

"I CAN REMEMBER the Jubilee of Queen Victoria," Winston Churchill told the voters in Peckham, the south of London, in 1931. "Nine kings rode with our Queen that day and princes and potentates from the ends of the earth came to honor her. In those days England was the world's ironmaster, the world's shipbuilder, the world's banker, the workshop of mankind. You voters have it in your power to bring those days back again."[1]

Nobody had that power any more. Great Britain at the beginning of the 1930s was "optimistic, phlegmatic and self-confident," but it had just emerged from a paralyzing general strike and was then in the midst of a more paralyzing economic depression. The establishment still preferred its closed self-contained circle of hereditary amateurs against self-made professionals, the "old-boy" agreements stultifying the dynamic.

British industry was a hundred years behind the times in equipment and production methods. The Prince of Wales reminded people at the British Industries Fair that their salesmanship and marketing methods were out of date and that the happy Victorian days of automatic British sales were gone forever. The British people had ushered in their second Labour government, Ramsay MacDonald replacing Baldwin as prime minister. MacDonald was a man of colossal vanity who told an American friend, "Oh, I'm so weary—I'd love to retire from politics now but who would there be to carry on my work?"[2]

Reconstruction, Restoration and Recovery were still unfulfilled slogans. The international order of the Versailles peace treaty after World War I was visibly crumbling. The fascism of Hitler and Mussolini was on the rise. France and Italy were no longer friends. Japa-

135

nese troops invaded Manchuria. And yet, speaking for the British government, Lord Robert Cecil told the League of Nations Assembly: ". . . There has scarcely been a period in the world's history when war seems less likely than it does at present."[3]

The American stock market crash in 1929 drastically hurt the purchase of British goods and the use of British ships. British unemployment rose far above 2 million. Prime Minister MacDonald quickly avoided the blame. *"We* are not on trial; it is the system under which we live . . . It has broken down everywhere, as it was bound to break down."[4]

J. B. Priestley wrote of two Englands, the traditional England of Shakespeare and history books and fox hunting and West End clubs, and the bleaker England of harsh industrial towns, grimy rows of houses and the noise of factory workers before dawn. London saw its first pathetic "hunger marchers."

Visiting a soup kitchen in an English provincial town some years before, the Prince of Wales saw the poverty of men wearing coats without shirts under them. Choosing houses at random, he held the hand of a hungry woman in childbirth, listened to a miner tell him he had not worked for five years. A New York *Tribune* reporter found him pacing up and down, pressing his hands together, saying, "What can I do? What can be done?"[5]

In an earlier speech, he had asked "that every man and every woman may enjoy the just proceeds of their labor, and that every child born into the country may have a sporting chance."

Press publicity of his trips and his reactions caused enough political comment so that his father called him in for criticism. On controversial questions, royalty, like children, must be seen and not heard. George V did not tell his son that when the miners went on strike and Lord Durham said they were "a damned lot of revolutionaries," His Majesty exploded and said, "Try living on their wages before you judge them!"[6]

These were some of the watershed years of British prewar history, but they were only newspaper headlines to Wallis and Ernest Simpson. They were subjects one discussed during the afternoon cocktail hour, but only obliquely, without too much heat. If their knowledge was not deep, whose was? Even Winston Churchill, in those days, wrote kind words about Hitler and Mussolini.

Wallis and Ernest were more apt to discuss the art of gracious living, the standards of public taste, the lack of a flowering of art, architecture, music or poetry for more than a generation. It is also most likely that they discussed D. H. Lawrence's most recent book, *Lady Chatterley's Lover*.

Lawrence had kept up a crusade against conformity, against the "social attitudes that put the human spirit in chains." "Man is one, body and soul; and his parts are not at war with one another," he wrote. Sexual love was humanly good and humanly necessary, he said, but there must be a total meeting of mind, spirit and body in the physical act.

How much of this there was in the love and marriage of Wallis and Ernest Simpson is a matter of serious question. He adored her; there was no question of that. He tried hard to enrich her mind with English history, with travel: his business took him to many countries, and she often went with him. They enjoyed the theater, seldom missing a new play. He stirred her mind and her imagination. She had pride in his intellect, boasted about it. She saw him as a man of size and dimension and her respect for him was deep. There were certainly more quiet evenings than she would have liked, too much book reading at the contemplative fireside. Yet he was not so stodgy that he didn't enjoy parties and dancing. He was a handsome man and he had a quiet charm that was most effective with women, and she took pleasure in that, too.

She discovered qualities in him she had never known. On a tour of Holland with Aunt Bessie, they were awakened at midnight with the cry of "Fire," the people pouring out of their rooms in various stages of undress. Ernest ordered her to take Aunt Bessie to the lobby and he would soon follow them. She then saw him carefully packing his suitcase and yelled at him to forget their clothes while there was still time.

She was increasingly worried when he failed to appear. The firemen would not let her go back to look for him. The smoke was heavier now. Suddenly there was Ernest at the head of the stairway, immaculately dressed, complete with bowler hat, suitcase and umbrella.[7]

He had that kind of propriety, that kind of courage.

She knew that, and she loved him for it. But it was a comfortable love, and the passion was banked.

Ernest wanted nothing more than he had. She had brightened his life considerably, as he had hoped she would. He shone reflectively in the fact that she was an excellent hostess, knew how to put people at their ease, could talk brightly about anything. He was pleased with her expansion of their social life, her adjustment to his private world. He loved watching her wit in action and hearing her laugh. She had warmed his home and his heart, and he was grateful. One day the shipping firm would be his and he could give her more of everything she wanted: he knew her taste for the best in clothes, jewels, antiques. He wanted more than anything to please her. It was a good marriage; it might have lasted their lifetimes.

Looking around her apartment at Bryanston Court, at her porcelain fishes and lacquer boxes and screens and lucky elephants, she may have been wistful of her more romantic memories in Peking, but then she must have contrasted that lost rootlessness with her sure sense of security.

This was Wallis as Mary Kirk Raffray found her at the end of May 1931. It was Mary's first trip to London, and Wallis took her immediately to lunch with Connie Thaw, entrancing Mary with the news that the Prince of Wales came there often to meet Connie's sister Thelma Furness.

She and Wallis were long past the giggling stage, but they talked that first night until the early hours. Wallis surprised Mary by telling her that she and Ernest mostly saw Americans because she found the British dull and uninteresting.

Mary liked everything about the Bryanston Court apartment except Wallis' bed in pink plush. She loved the hot bar for towels in the bathroom but found the separation of bath and toilet inconvenient. She liked the formality of having several wines at lunch and dinner, and being announced to the hostess when she arrived anywhere. Ernest impressed her by always wearing "white tie" full dress whenever they dined out. She thought the naïve patriotism of the British both childish and stirring.

Wallis filled their next weeks with lunches at the Ritz, chic dinners and a continuous round of parties. At one party given by two Argentines at their embassy, she found herself talking to the son-in-law of former Prime Minister Stanley Baldwin.

Ernest took a day off to show Mary Westminster Abbey and she found it so fascinating she forgot to search for her ancestor. Ernest also took her and Wallis poking around the shops on the small side streets near Shepherd's Market, and then to Kensington to see a traditional military tournament with the cloak and dagger fencing of the eighteenth century.

They also saw the trooping of the colors from the private windows of the Admiralty—and, alongside an admiral. Mary marveled at the slow march of the men and the Scottish pipes and the shining silver armor and the red plumes on the helmets. She got a "swell look" at the King and the Prince of Wales riding past them, and wondered if she would ever meet the Prince. Wallis said the chances were slim because they had no parties booked where he was supposed to appear, but she would see what she could do. She did well, and Mary did meet him at a party and made "a splendid curtsy."[8]

Mary carefully observed a typical Wallis dinner: cocktails with sausages (not on skewers), caviar with vodka, soup, fish, white wine, champagne and then brandy, all of it ending about three o'clock in the morning, everybody exhausted, "but Wallis' parties have so much pep that no one ever wants to leave."[9]

Wallis was sorry when Mary finally had to return home. They had talked so much that it made her gay again.

After Mary's visit Wallis was cheered when several friends suggested that she be presented at court.

"Very well, I'll do it," Wallis reportedly said, "if it doesn't cost anything."[10]

There were problems. One had to be presented by someone who already had been at court, and a British citizen. A more major hurdle was the Lord Chamberlain's Office, which screened out undesirables from the long list of applicants. Most undesirable was the divorcée. No account was taken of who was at fault in the divorce. Their Majesties held this inflexible rule not only because they regarded their marriage vows as sacred but because "they knew extremely well the feeling of the British masses on the subject."

Divorcée Wallis Warfield Simpson was nevertheless accepted at court. The whisper was that Thelma Furness, then already a warm friend of Wallis, had asked the Prince of Wales to use the necessary leverage.

Thelma loaned Wallis the same feathers and train she had worn at her own court presentation. The gown came from Consuelo, Thelma's sister. "She could not wear my dress," said Thelma, "because she is not my size; I am taller."[11] Wallis bought a band of aquamarines to hold the plumes in place and then impulsively bought an aquamarine cross four inches long and wore it suspended from a cord around her throat.

Court presentation offered the kind of dramatic spectacle that quickened her pulse.

It was a scene from another age, the gentlemen-at-arms in their white-plumed hats, crimson and gold uniforms; the King and Queen on their thrones, sitting under the great durbar canopy which they brought back from India; the scarlet and gold State Room of Buckingham Palace banked high on all sides with hydrangeas and roses, and a concealed orchestra playing popular music. Assembled was an audience of diplomats and wives from every corner of the Empire, "the dominion over palm and pine."

Presentees and sponsors moved in a line toward the throne, their names pronounced aloud as they swept to the floor in deep curtsies to the King and Queen, then moved along into the adjoining room for tea. Another presentee that day was Adlai Stevenson's sister, Mrs. Ernest L. "Buffie" Ives.

As the royal family left, Wallis overheard the Prince of Wales tell his uncle how ghastly the women looked under that light. At Thelma's party afterward, the Prince complimented Wallis on her dress and she reminded him of his "ghastly" remark.[12] He smiled and said he didn't realize his voice had "carried so far."[13]

An exciting postscript for Wallis was the Prince's offer to take them home in his car. It was a small beginning of the growing informal feeling between them, his acceptance of them. He politely refused their offer to come up for a drink, but asked to be invited again. It would be almost a year before he got that drink.

It was a good year for the Simpsons: a trip to Scotland, Wallis' troublesome tonsils removed, a holiday in southern France, a greatly increased social life.

Wallis discovered one of the gravitational pulls of London society was the tendency of American wives of British men to stick together. This had begun a generation before in the time of Lady Randolph Churchill, Winston Churchill's American mother, the former Jennie Jerome of Brooklyn, New York, who had made one of the first great international marriages and served as a buffer for other American brides. Bryanston Court was only a few blocks from Lady Randolph's home.

One of the most celebrated American brides of Wallis' times was Lady Sackville, once better known on the American stage as Meredith

Bigelow. She lived at one of the magnificent historic houses of England called Knole. Wallis found it intriguing to dance to lively American music from a gramophone record under the spectacular Queen Anne chandelier.

Thelma and Wallis saw a lot of each other that year. They both liked to talk, but Wallis was more ready to listen. It was therefore no great surprise when the Prince of Wales invited the Simpsons for a weekend at Fort Belvedere.

"The Fort" was the Prince's private place. Only twenty-five miles from London, close to the edge of Windsor Forest, it looked like an ancient castle. It is built of warm, cream-colored stone that softens any forbidding look into a kind of serenity. A green lawn slopes gently toward a semicircular stone battlement, where more than thirty ancient Belgian cannon point toward London.

"The house is an enchanting folly," wrote Lady Diana Cooper, "and only needs fifty red soldiers stood between the battlements to make it into a Walt Disney colored symphony toy . . . The Fort centers round the swimming pool, which has an elaborate equipment . . . long chairs, swabs, mattresses and dumbwaiters bearing smoking and drinking accessories in abundance. It is some little way from the house, so showers cause a dreadful lot of carrying in and bringing out again for the next fitful sunray . . . The comfort could not be greater, nor the desire on his part for his guests to be happy, free and unembarrassed. Surely a new atmosphere for Courts? . . . The Prince reminds me of myself at Bognor—over-restless, fetching unnecessary little things, jumping up for the potatoes or soda-water. . . ."[14]

The Prince himself greeted Wallis and Ernest and showed them to their room. She may not have known then that the nearby Windsor Forest was where her Warfield ancestors once had lived.

When Wallis and Ernest came down for cocktails they found the Prince, bent over a large flat screen, doing needlepoint. Shyly, he explained that he had learned it from his mother. After dinner they played phonograph records and danced. Before midnight, the Prince was ready for bed, and that was the signal for other guests. The rest of the weekend was pleasant, uneventful. Ernest was most impressed with the Prince, even when the Prince drafted him to help cut laurel. Wallis went away realizing that her conception of the Prince of Wales was idealized and romantic. In reality he was a slightly built man in a turtleneck sweater who liked to putter in his garden.

There was more travel for the Simpsons in 1932, and Wallis' Baedeker education continued, this time in Tunis, France and Austria. She also had a flare-up of her stomach ulcer.

"I always kept the day-to-day tensions of living bottled up in me."[15]

Not only did she bottle her daily tensions, but she was always on watch for the disapproving eyebrows of her husband's British family and friends. She lived in a world where one seldom showed anger or drank too much or laughed too loudly. She lived with the feeling that she was always on exhibition. Deeper within herself were her secret compartments—the men and loves of her life, the frustrations and dreams.

That fall there were other weekends at The Fort. One day at the hairdresser's Wallis found an old friend from Baltimore under an adjoining metal hood. She lifted up her own hood and said in an excited voice, "Guess what? I'm in the Prince of Wales set!"[16]

She said it as if something wonderful had happened, and for her it had. For her, it meant that she had made it. On the social merry-go-round she had grabbed the long-awaited brass ring. She would no longer have to watch her husband's friends; they would have to watch her.

That spring of 1933, Wallis returned to the United States for a two-month visit with Aunt Bessie and friends. After the stiff etiquette of London, it was relaxing to hear somebody say, "Hi Wally, whatcha been doin'?"

There is little likelihood that she saw Don Felipe A. Espil, although she surely learned what happened to him. He had gone to The Hague as minister from Argentina in 1928, then minister to Denmark in 1930, and finally, in 1931, he became ambassador to the United States. His ambition achieved, he then married the woman he wanted, the beautiful and wealthy Courtney Letts of Chicago, named on the list as one of the ten best-dressed women in the country. Before accepting Espil she had had two previous husbands; and she was not a Catholic. By then, however, Espil no longer had to worry about a marriage that might hurt his career.

Wallis also spent some time in Baltimore seeing the races at Pimlico, visiting old friends. The news was out about her court presentation and the Prince of Wales set, and her reception was much warmer than it might otherwise have been. What they said of her, admiringly, behind her back, was that Wallis may have been slightly tacky as a young girl, but my, she has developed an extraordinary style, and she does walk so well.

The wealthy Baltimoreans she knew had changed some of the landscaping for their homes, but their furniture inside seemed unchanged, except for being recovered. Traditional Baltimoreans simply didn't want things changed.

Wallis enjoyed change. She was delighted when her friendship with Thelma and the Prince seemed to flower on a fresh basis. The Prince (and Thelma) surprised Wallis on her thirty-seventh birthday with a party at a Jermyn Street restaurant. The Prince even gave her a present—an orchid plant that he promised would bloom again in a year. And so it did.

Ernest Simpson and the Prince also enjoyed each other. Each was a serious student of history, and they had long talks, going into dates and detail. "They would talk about a lot of things that would bore me," Wallis said afterward, "and I often wondered when they would shut up."[17] The Prince was actually supposed to have been Simpson's sponsor when he became an English Mason.

Thelma Furness had some news for the Prince and Wallis in January 1934. She was going to the United States for a six-week visit with her twin sister, Gloria. "Three or four days before I was to sail, I had lunch with Wallis at the Ritz," remembered Thelma. "I told her of my plans, and in my exuberance I offered myself for all the usual yeoman services. Was there anything I could do for her in America? Were there any messages I could deliver? Did she want me to bring anything back for her? She thanked me, and said suddenly, 'Oh, Thelma, the little man is going to be so lonely.'"

"Well, dear," Thelma answered, "you look after him for me while I'm away. See that he does not get into any mischief."

"It was later evident," said Thelma ruefully, "that Wallis took my advice all too literally."[18]

Discussing her life with an interviewer, years later, Lady Furness was asked if she would live her life the same way all over again, if she could.

"I would do it all again," she said. "The only thing I would NOT do again is introduce Wallis Simpson to the Prince of Wales."[19]

It made all the gossip columns in the United States when the Prince called Thelma while she was visiting a Hollywood movie set. Thelma also got long and frequent cables from the Prince, all carefully coded "to conceal their intimate nature."[20]

One of the jokes circulating the country at the time was "If the Lord saved Daniel from the Lions' den, who will save David [the Prince] from the fiery Furness?"[21]

Shortly before sailing for England, Thelma Furness met Aly Khan. Thelma was almost thirty and Aly was only twenty-three. Aly's father, the rotund Aga Khan, was regarded by the Moslem Ismailis as the divine descendant of the Prophet. This not only made Aly one of the wealthiest men in the world, but an international celebrity. He was a dark, handsome, soft-spoken young man who loved to race cars and chase women. He believed in the inherent and inalienable superiority of the male, and he worried about nothing since he had nothing to worry about. Women loved his attentiveness, his gaiety, his impetuousness and his readiness to do anything, anywhere, anytime. He frankly regarded himself as the best horseman, the best dancer, the most attractive man on the international scene.

Of course he knew that Thelma belonged to the Prince of Wales. This made her all the more intriguing that night at dinner. For the next few days, his attention was so intensive that it made headlines back in Britain. One cocktail quip was that Thelma now had both the White Prince and the Black Prince.

Thelma boarded ship exhausted, overwhelmed but happy. She found her cabin crowded with roses, each bouquet with an endearment from Aly. One of them said: "You left too soon." As the ship was on its way, the phone rang.

"Hello, darling. This is Aly. Will you have lunch with me today?"

She was flattered by the ship-to-shore phone call, and gaily answered, "Where will it be, Aly? Palm Beach or New York?"

Aly laughed. "Right here. I'm on board."[22]

Their togetherness aboard ship only increased the size of the headlines.

Wallis, meanwhile, was not idle in London. She and Ernest invited the Prince to a small dinner party at Bryanston Court. She prepared a meal of her Baltimore specialties, and he was delighted with it.

But what he liked at Bryanston Court more than the food was the utter informality. He had thought he had found a haven in The Fort, but even there he was not free. There was always the necessary protocol, the watchful servants, the knowledge that the world could always find him there. At Bryanston Court, with Wallis, he enjoyed the remarkable feeling of being in a comfortable, completely relaxed home.

Soon afterward the Simpsons were again weekending at The Fort. Wallis found herself alone with the Prince one evening, and he was talking as he had never talked before. He explained the problems of being a Prince of Wales, the frustrations and the satisfactions. He outlined his own private hopes of what monarchy could be and could contribute to the world and the times.

"He told all this to me and I listened and I sympathized, and I understood; and I guess he needed that."[23]

He told her about his social service plans for the unemployed, and she was delighted that she had read in the papers about the Council of Social Service, and wanted to know more about it. She also wanted him to describe his typical working day. As he talked, she sensed the loneliness of the man.

"But I am boring you," he suddenly said to her.

She begged him to continue, and he looked at her searchingly, then slowly said, "Wallis, you are the only woman who has ever been interested in my job."[24]

It was a fateful moment.

13

THE PRINCE gave a dinner at The Fort soon afterward for Wallis and her close friends Ellen and Wolcott Blair. Blair had given the big ball for the Prince on his first visit to Chicago. Ernest Simpson was out of town on business.

The surprise came when Wallis and the Blairs were leaving. Instead of saying good-by, the Prince climbed into their car with them. When they asked where they could take him, he simply said, "I'm going with you to London." Before Ellen Blair could ask another question, Wallis kicked her to keep quiet. The Blairs then drove Wallis to her home, and the Prince got out with her.

The next morning Wallis called Ellen and said, "Do you know what time he left? One-thirty in the morning!"[1]

After that, the Prince could not seem to keep away. He had found a home where he could unwind more thoroughly than he could unwind anywhere else. He had found a woman who filled his most basic need.

"He once stayed so late that I had to tell him we were having our dinner, but if he were willing to stay, we could stretch it to three. And he was willing," she remembered years later, still smiling at the memory. "I told our cook, Mrs. Rolph—she was a big woman—and she got so excited that she went and got her fancy apron for 'my Prince,' as she called him."[2]

At first Ernest Simpson was flattered, then amused by the Prince's frequent and often unexpected arrivals, but then his enjoyment diminished. He loved his wife and he liked his privacy and wasn't interested in sharing either—even with the Prince of Wales.

"It reached a point when Ernest said to me, 'Is the little man coming to dinner again tonight? When are we going to have dinner by ourselves?' I told Ernest that I didn't know, and I asked him whether I should tell the Prince not to come. Then he was quiet and he said, 'No, not if it gives him so much pleasure.' "[3]

Thelma Furness returned to England in March 1934 and found a changed picture. It is difficult to know what she expected. Did she think the Prince was so firmly hers that the highly publicized Aly Khan affair would accentuate his feelings instead of cooling them? Or, more likely, had she been so overwhelmed by Aly Khan that she didn't care, and felt she could cope with the Prince when she returned? If so, she did not know her man. The Prince was never one to brook competition. Whatever the game was, he always wanted to win.

Thelma claimed that she and the Prince had dinner at her apartment the first night after her arrival. The Prince, more stiff than usual, had said to her: "I hear Aly Khan has been very attentive to you."[4]

Thelma said she then went to Wallis for advice. "It is quite evident I chose the wrong friend," she said ruefully, afterward. She insisted that Wallis then said to her, "Darling, you know the little man loves you very much. The little man was just lost without you." Wallis' maid then interrupted to say that the Prince of Wales was on the phone—for Wallis. Through the open door, she heard Wallis say, "Thelma is here," and expected Wallis to call her to the phone.[5] Wallis returned, saying nothing about the call.

Wallis remembered it differently. She remembered Thelma at her apartment, asking her point blank whether or not the Prince was "keen" on her. Wallis answered that she felt the Prince liked her, but definitely was not in love with her.

They were all together that weekend at The Fort.

"I noticed that the Prince and Wallis seemed to have little private jokes," said Thelma. "Once he picked up a piece of salad with his fingers; Wallis playfully slapped his hand. I, so overprotective of heaven knows what, caught her eye and shook my head at her."[6] The Prince never liked to be touched, no matter how familiar the friend.

"Wallis looked straight at me. And then and there, I knew 'the reason' was Wallis—Wallis, of all people! . . . That one cold, defiant glance that told me the entire story. I knew then that she had looked after him exceedingly well."[7]

Somebody else at The Fort that night described it still differently: It was a small dinner party, and Thelma was not there. There was a banging on the door, so loud, sounding as if somebody was trying to break in. It was Thelma. She stormed in, and she and the Prince and

Wallis all went into the library. The only voice anybody heard coming from the room was Thelma's. She then stormed out as she had stormed in. The Prince returned to the dinner party, coldly polite, and Wallis, similarly cool.

The next day Lady Thelma Furness and Aly Khan were in a fast car headed for Spain. One of the popular songs of the time was "I Danced With the Man Who Danced With the Girl Who Danced With the Prince of Wales." Aly Khan, feeling he had won the race and the chase, could be much more direct than that.

These were the days when the Prince seemed to be an inevitable part of the Simpson household. These were the days, too, when Ernest Simpson seemed to be abroad on business an increasing amount of the time.

What Wallis had started as "a flirt" had flowered into something that would soon shake an empire. Forecasting a devastating love affair for the Prince of Wales, Count Louis Hamon, in the September 1933 issue of the *National Astrological Journal,* had written: "If he does, I predict that the Prince will give up everything, even the chance of being crowned, rather than lose the object of his affection."

The Prince of Wales was caught, obsessed and desperately in love with Wallis Simpson.

Why?

The Prince himself testified that his initial attraction to Wallis came from her sincere interest in his work. It probably did. And there is no need to question that Wallis' interest was sincere. She was doing what came naturally to her—she made the man who was talking to her feel that he was the most important, the most interesting man in the world.

One must necessarily add that Wallis unquestionably had done a little more homework on the Prince's likes and dislikes, and his special areas of concern, so that she could talk more knowledgeably about them with him. It is similarly certain that his royal aura made him even more fascinating to her. It never, however, changed her "naturalness" and "forthrightness," two attributes that particularly impressed the Prince. She enchanted him when she vigorously defended her point of view at a party, something he seldom saw in the women of his set. Analyzing herself, and her own attraction to the Prince, Wallis thought that it may well have been her independence of spirit and directness that "astonished, amazed and amused him."

The fat and friendly Lord Castlerosse, who knew the Prince well, said of him that he had "an inferiority complex. Mrs. Simpson has built up her man . . ." Castlerosse's view was that Wallis had said to the Prince, "My boy, you're not the fool you think you are. You're a grand fellow!" As a result, said Castlerosse, the Prince "threw out his chest."

"The attraction between them is NOT sex," insisted Castlerosse.[8]

A much closer friend of the Prince, a man who knew him in his earliest youth, disagreed: "Her hold over him must have been sex," he said. "She must have given him something in bed that no other woman ever did. She must have made him feel more vital, more masculine, more satisfying."[9]

Discussing Wallis' lack of bodily beauty, one of her Oldfields friends said, "But she had a lot of what we called SA [Sex Appeal]."[10] Bernarr MacFadden, publisher of *Liberty*, trying to pinpoint the secret of why the Prince was caught, wrote that "the intricate technique of enticing masculinity can hardly be learned without experience . . . such feminine charms cannot be acquired solely in the beauty parlors." And to win a prince, he said, "What woman would not stoop to conquer."[11]

Wallis, of course, had been married twice before. She had known many men. In her year in China she had learned much about their concepts of life and love. She knew what it was to be fulfilled.

The Prince had never known true fulfillment. He had been in love with Frieda Ward, but it was not fully reciprocal. He may have loved Thelma Furness, but it was only physical. After their affair had ended, years after, Thelma told several friends that the Prince of Wales was a most unsatisfactory sexual partner. His primary problem, she said, was premature ejaculation.

Partly explaining this, a friend who had known him well and had gone swimming with him often said that the naked Prince was most unprepossessing as a man. "To put it bluntly," he said, "he had the smallest pecker I have ever seen. Can you imagine what this did to him? Here are all these beautiful women all over the world, all ready and willing to go to bed with the Prince Charming of the world, all of them expecting the most eventful romantic night of their lives. And the ones who made it with him, can you imagine their disappointment? And can you imagine how he felt?"[12]

It might explain why he delayed getting married. It might explain why his affairs were mostly with the more experienced married women. It might explain his shyness, his massive sense of insecurity. It also might explain some of the unfounded widespread rumors of homosexuality: his boyish look, his needlepoint, dressing as a woman at a ship's costume party, his voice becoming high-pitched when he became angry.

A brash American, who got to know the Prince well, once jokingly remarked to him that his bedroom must be very crowded. The puzzled Prince did not understand and the American explained that there were so many people who said so many specific things about what happened in the Prince's bedroom that there had to be a nightly audience. The Prince was not amused.

What happened in their bedroom can only be a guessing game, and an improper one. These were not two people who would ever discuss such things with anyone. And if they wouldn't, who could?

For the Prince of Wales, there were other things almost as important as sex. Wallis was one of the few people in the world who made him laugh, laugh out loud. Friends said they could see him at the dinner table, leaning forward, just waiting for her to make some remark so that he could roar with laughter. He had lived a life of protocol and propriety. Laughing out loud was almost as bad as drinking too much. With her, it was wonderful, a rare release for him.

Something else Wallis did was to mother him. He had never really known his mother when he was a boy except for the afternoon bow and the goodnight kiss. Wallis had a delightful way of bossing him, without being coy about it. *"Don't* eat that, Sir," she'd say, smiling, taking a caviar canape out of his hand. "Have this instead."[13] And she would give him some cream cheese on toast.

She made sure he was dressed warmly enough when it was cold, persuaded him to cut down his smoking and actually took a drink away from him when she felt he had had too much. He loved it. Nobody ever had cared that much for him before.

"At first none of us thought anything about it—another girlfriend," said one of his closest confidants. "But then he started to flaunt her, brazenly showing her off in public everywhere, making her very important socially. And there was something else: the previous two always called him 'Sir' in public. For all the years I've known him, I would still never dream of calling him anything but 'Sir.' This one called him 'David.' "[14]

It happened gradually. She was most careful at first. She was, after all, still Mrs. Ernest Simpson.

Simpson naturally knew what was going on. As much as they had a common interest in business, government, tradition and history, the Prince of Wales was not making nightly calls to see him. The growing number of daily phone calls from His Royal Highness were not for him either. And one would have had to be blind not to see the shining eyes of the Prince follow Wallis wherever she went.

What could he do? He was a quiet, gentle, sensitive man and he knew Wallis was past the stage of confrontation. He knew that Wallis saw herself in a romantic setting beyond her imagination, the flattering adoration of her Prince Charming. The royal glamour was irresistible. He also knew Wallis' heedlessness, her tendency to push problems away, to deal with consequences only when they had to be faced.

Confronting Wallis then would have brought on this crisis of consequence, and he didn't want to lose her or hurt her. Nor could he confront His Royal Highness. That seemed unthinkable.

His only option was to wait and hope. Something might happen to break it up, and then her dream would be over and Wallis would be his again.

Ernest found increasing excuses to leave the Prince and Wallis alone. "He looked like a tailor's dummy in a window and often acted that way," said a friend of Wallis' about Simpson.[15] He did sometimes look like one in his Savile Row suits, but he never really acted like one. His withdrawal from their lives was the only option he felt he had. His real emotions seldom surfaced. He and Wallis had long silences when they were alone together. What could they say? Only once did he show his indignation. She remembered him slamming the door once when she refused to go on a trip with him because she was going away with the Prince.

The Prince's favorite brother, George, married Princess Marina of Greece in November 1934. Wallis didn't want to go to the wedding, but the Prince insisted. Prince Christopher, the uncle of the bride, remembered the Prince excitedly saying to him, "Christo, I want you to meet Mrs. Simpson."

"Who is she?" he asked.

"An American . . . she's wonderful."

Prince Chistopher noticed how heedlessly the Prince of Wales pushed past other people at the party toward her. Christopher later remembered Wallis as "a pleasing but not beautiful woman who never stopped talking."[16]

The Prince also introduced Wallis to his father and mother, the only time Wallis ever would meet the King and Queen. Queen Mary later remembered that her son had introduced Wallis, saying, "I want to introduce a great friend of mine," and she had shaken hands with her without thinking much about it.[17]

"If I had only guessed then I might perhaps have been able to do something," the Queen said.[18]

Aunt Bessie had come to visit again, and to chaperone. Wallis wanted her to join them at Biarritz. As a chaperone, Aunt Bessie was ideal. She understood the new morality of the times, and sympathized with it. She was so guarded with all Wallis' confidences that she never gave a single interview about her niece, although she actually lived to be a hundred. Were it not for her niece, the world of Aunt Bessie would have been bounded by a few streets in Washington. Wallis opened up Aunt Bessie's horizons, and she loved "little Wally" for it. Whenever Wallis wanted her, Aunt Bessie came.

The Baltimore *News-Post* picked up a press association story, featuring it as a local-girl-makes-good item, misspelling Wallis' name as "Wallace" and describing her as a descendant of Governor Warfield of Maryland. "Wales danced with her until 3:30 in the morning," the story said.[19] A follow-up story five days later, which did spell her name right, added that "the friendly attention which the Prince of Wales has been paying American-born Mrs. Ernest A. Simpson, formerly Wallis Warfield of Baltimore, at Biarritz, is giving international society something to romanticize about."[20]

The Prince had rented a beautiful, almost inaccessible villa at Biarritz called Mer de Monte. He also reserved a secluded table at the Bar Basque, where he and Wallis had their daily aperitif, and the Biarritz swimming pool had a special entrance built for their more private use.

Lady Furness was reported to have passed through Biarritz at the time. The French Countess de Villeneuve was the one who saw her in a draped hat and quipped, "Has Lady Furness decided to take the veil, now that she no longer sees the Prince?"[21]

The yacht they used for the cruise itself belonged to Lord Moyne, a Conservative Party leader. On it they toured the Spanish coast, the Prince and Wallis often taking picnic lunches in quiet inlets, dining unnoticed in small bistros, strolling along empty beaches on Majorca. Wallis thinks those were the days when they actually fell in love.

The Prince had known it long before, but maybe Wallis referred to her own feelings. Until then, perhaps, she felt herself swept along, scene by scene, as part of a romantic mood, an interval that would somehow end. Being alone with him so much, in those settings, she now saw the seriousness of the man and his need for her.

Some have said of Wallis Simpson that she had a tough, male aggressiveness and that even her body had nothing softly feminine about it, nothing curvy, only sharp, hard angles. She also could be decisive and determined. The Prince, like Win Spencer, came to her for her strength.

Two New York dancers, Jane Dickson and Lora Lane, were performing at a night club in Cannes when the Prince invited them to join his party at his table. The Prince told them, "I'm not dancing." Wallis then explained, "Too much exercise isn't good for him." The Prince then poured champagne for them and further explained, "I'm not drinking." And Wallis added, "We're not drinking much any more."

Wallis made a move to leave shortly after midnight, but the Prince said, "Let's stay till one."

"All right," she said, "until one, but no later."

Exactly on the hour, they rose and left.[22]

A newsman at Cannes reported: "The Prince of Wales is evidently enjoying his sojourn in Cannes, for today he decided to remain three days longer. He sent to Marseilles the airplane that had come to take him to Paris."[23]

Another reporter earlier had described the unbelievable spectacle of the Prince of Wales—one of the most restless men in the world—patiently waiting two hours at a hairdresser's while Wallis had her hair done. Still another reporter described how well they danced the rumba together.

None of these articles appeared in any British newspapers, which maintained, as always, a discreet silence on royal romance.* And

---

* Sometimes a discreet silence was broken. There had been a previous press reference to another royal romance—but most oblique. A sporting paper in the nineties headlined a news column: "Nothing between the Prince of Wales and Lily Langtry." The next week, in the same space, was the remark, "Not even a sheet."

nobody in Cannes knew that the Prince had given Wallis a tiny velvet case containing a diamond and emerald charm for her bracelet. Her body may have been angular, her manner sometimes aggressive, but Wallis Simpson loved all the female luxuries of jewels, clothes, perfume.

Neither of them wanted their trip to end. Herman and Katherine Rogers joined them on a quick trip to Italy. They stayed for a week at a small villa on a tiny island on Lake Maggiore. The Prince then felt forced to leave because he had to join his parents for the launching of the *Queen Mary*.

Wallis went to Le Havre with Aunt Bessie, who was heading home again. Aunt Bessie understood and approved of many things, but she would not have thought the gift of jewels proper. Wallis was still a married woman. Before she got on the ship, the plain-speaking Aunt Bessie warned her that she was moving into dangerous waters. Wallis refused to listen. "I know what I'm doing," she said.[24]

She didn't know. She only knew how romantic and unreal everything was, and how she loved it. She and the Prince hated cats and loved dogs; he gave her a cairn terrier puppy called Slipper. He asked her to share the Royal Enclosure during Ascot Week. In February 1935, she went with him on a skiing trip in Austria, waltzed with him in Vienna, then impulsively traveled with him to Budapest to listen to gypsy violins. One of the many reporters and photographers following them everywhere remembered how much more quiet the Prince was now—the last time in Budapest he had kept busy shooting the street lights. They made no attempt at secrecy. Except for Great Britain, the world now knew all about Mrs. Wallis Simpson.

The British public did not know, but the society leaders did. Wallis soon received an invitation from Lady Maud Cunard, who liked to call herself "Emerald." A petite, animated American, married to the leading British shipping magnate, Emerald corralled the most important and interesting people in England for her parties.

Emerald loved to mix them and stir them up and gleefully watch the fun. A friend jokingly described her as "looking like a third-dynasty mummy painted pink by amateurs." But she might well have been painted red, warning of danger, because nobody knew what she might say next. Her knowledge of politics was vast and her knowledge of politicians was intimate. Wallis said she felt like a schoolgirl when she listened to Emerald. She did warn Wallis of one thing: never express any political views because people would automatically assume she was voicing the Prince's opinions. Wallis never forgot that.

It was well to warn her. At one of Emerald Cunard's parties, Wallis found herself sitting next to Joachim von Ribbentrop, special envoy of Adolf Hitler. She met Ribbentrop again at a supper party that same week at the home of the German ambassador to Great Britain, Dr. Leopold von Hoesch, who was a good friend of the Prince and had been ambassador since 1932. The Prince enjoyed these parties because it gave him a chance to speak his fluent German. He often liked to explain that his mother and grandfather were German and that made him three-fourths German.

Wallis Simpson impressed Ribbentrop. He sent roses to her and a memo to Hitler. His memo commented that both the Prince of Wales and Mrs. Wallis Simpson seemed most friendly to the German cause.

The Prince seemed to give some proof of this. In June 1935 he addressed a convention of the British Legion and urged them to visit Germany to shake hands with the men they had once fought. The speech caused a world stir. In a memo to the U.S. State Department, Ambassador William E. Dodd wrote, "It is difficult to conceive of any announcement better calculated to appeal to the prevalent German conception than the announcement by the Prince of Wales ... Hardly had the news been published in Berlin than statements in support were elicited from Göring, Hess and Ribbentrop. All the press, on June 12th, seized up the statement of the Prince of Wales with the greatest avidity."[25]

George V was not pleased.* He told his son again never to discuss politically sensitive subjects before alerting the government.

King George did not then discuss something that displeased him even more. He had been getting detailed reports about the latest affair of his son. He expressed his concern to the Archbishop of Canterbury, Cosmo Lang. The Archbiship tried to mollify him, suggesting that the Prince had had previous friendships. But King George, stiff and stolid as he was, had a sensitive perception about his most stubborn

---

* He was not displeased with the Prince's pacifist feelings, however, which echoed his own: "H.M. [George V] fired up and broke out vehemently, 'And I *will* not have another war. I *will* not. The last war was none of my doing, & if there is another one & we are threatened with being brought into it, I will go to Trafalgar Square and wave a red flag myself sooner than allow this country to be brought in. . . .' " (Frances Stevenson, *Lloyd George*, p. 309.)

son. He worried aloud to the Archbishop that this affair was more serious than the others.

The King and Queen celebrated the Silver Jubilee of their reign that summer at a state ball at Buckingham Palace. It escaped nobody there that the Prince of Wales invited Wallis.

As the Prince and Wallis danced past the King, she thought she felt the King's eyes searching her, filled with "an icy menace."[26]

She may well have been right.

Several months later, the King told Blanche Lennox, wife of Lord Algernon Gordon-Lennox, "I pray to God that my eldest son will never marry and have children, and that nothing will come between Bertie and Lilibet and the Throne."[27]

His meaning was plain. His was a vision of the future. As a father, he had had no relationship with his son David, but as King, he knew him well. From all the reports he had read and heard, from what he himself had seen at the state ball, he knew that this was a love that was stronger than his son. He knew that the British people would not countenance a divorcée as queen, that such an issue would tear apart the country. His whole life had been dedicated to the British monarchy and he hated anything and anybody who would hurt it. He surely hated Mrs. Simpson and he may well have hated his son that night.

Wallis and the Prince were oblivious to hate. Nor were their minds marching too far into the future. They had too much to content them. Those who had not yet heard of Wallis Simpson in the British social circles soon did. She now found herself an integral part of the Prince's life in almost everything. Her phone was always ringing with his queries on party invitations, menus, furniture rearrangement and even flowers.

Wallis once called Constance Spry to give her precise instructions on the flowers for a party. Constance Spry, who previously had had a free hand in arranging the Prince's flowers, promptly called the comptroller at St. James's Palace: "Look, have you by any chance got a new housekeeper called Mrs. Simpson?" There was a long pause before the comptroller answered: "Mrs. Spry, any orders that come from Mrs. Simpson should be instantly complied with."[28]

The Prince gave Wallis a free hand in redecorating The Fort, and Wallis brought in her new friend Lady Mendl, the former Elsie de Wolfe. One of the fashion leaders of the world, Lady Mendl aided

Wallis' further education on the subject. "In those days, Wallis didn't dress well at all," a friend recalled. "I remember she once came in wearing a big floppy hat and it looked terrible on her. Lady Mendl not only taught Wallis what kind of clothes to wear, but where to buy them."[29]

What Wallis had that was her own was a sense of taste. It was excellent. Style was something else, something she was willing to learn. She had a visual memory and she learned style not only from Lady Mendl but from looking sharply at what the best-dressed women wore at parties and dinners. Her new social status had opened every door. After much search and discussion, Wallis went to Schiaparelli, one of the best fashion designers in the world. "Scap," as her friends called her, and Wallis quickly liked each other, and Scap soon made most of her dresses. "Her taste was good and quiet," the designer recalled, "and she always paid her bills, then and afterwards."

Wallis always loved jewels, particularly rubies, sapphires, aquamarines, emeralds and diamonds. The men in her life were conscious of this and were most generous. None was more so than the Prince of Wales. It was one of the things that most impressed Sir Samuel Hoare when he met Wallis, and he remembered "not only her sparkling talk, but also her sparkling jewels." However, he concluded, "Very American with little or no knowledge of English life."[30]

Wallis admitted that his judgment was just.

As much as they were together, and as often as they spoke on the phone, Wallis still had her own life to live and the Prince still kept to a crowded schedule of royal duties. The duties were mostly ceremonial: presentations to make, people to greet, meetings to attend, quick trips around the country. Wallis still had her home to maintain and a husband to worry about. The strain between them had increased; the silences were longer. Some of the comments about Ernest Simpson had turned into cruel, ugly jokes. One of the least of them was that Simpson was going to write a play called *The Unimportance of Being Ernest*, in which the hero cries out, "My only regret is that I have but one wife to lay down for my King."[31]

Talking about his personal dilemma with a close friend,[32] Simpson confided that he felt as if he was living in an armed truce, "as if I was meddling in English history."

Ernest seldom went to The Fort for weekends any more. Everybody who did, however, automatically regarded Wallis as the hostess. The butler brought menus for inspection and maids minded their dust. Wallis was now the mistress of two homes.

Her social circle kept spreading with her notoriety. One of the guests at The Fort was Lady Diana Cooper, actress and author and close friend of the former Mrs. Frieda Ward. Mrs. Ward had divorced her husband in 1931. Lady Cooper described her visit in a note to a friend in July 1935:

"This stationery is disappointingly humble—not so the conditions. I am in a pink bedroom, pink-sheeted, pink Venetian-blinded, pink-soaped, white-telephoned and pink-and-white maided.

"The food at dinner staggers and gluts. *Par contre* there is little or nothing for lunch, and that foraged for by oneself American-style . . . We arrived after midnight (perhaps as chaperones). Jabber and beer and bed was the order. I did not leave the 'cabin's seclusion' until 1 o'clock, having been told that no one did. H.R.H. was dressed in plus-twenties and vivid azure socks. Wallis admirably correct and chic. Me bang wrong! Golf in the afternoon, only the Prince and Duff playing, Wallis and me tooling around. It poured and we took shelter in a hut and laughed merrily enough with other shelterers . . . A splendid tea arrived at 6:30 with Anthony Eden and Esmond Harmsworth. Dinner was at 10. Emerald arrived at 8:30 for cocktails, which she doesn't drink although the Prince prepares the potions with his own poor hands and does all the glass-filling.

". . . The Prince changed into a Donald tartan dress-kilt with an immense white leather purse in front, and played the pipes around the table after dinner, having first fetched his bonnet. We 'reeled' to bed at 2 A.M. The host drinks least. . . ."[33]

Ernest Simpson still remained his wife's proper and legal escort at the increasing number of parties where the Prince of Wales was always present. Harold Nicolson, a distinguished writer, scholar, diplomat and statesman, recorded in his diary his impressions of them at a number of places. One of the best bright minds in government, Nicolson was a sophisticated, handsome man of grace and wit, who had served the Foreign Office in a variety of posts from Istanbul to Berlin and had been elected to Parliament in 1935.

At a dinner at Lady Sibyl Colefax's in December that year, he described a conversation with the Prince in which Wallis was an interested listener. "He talks a great deal about America and diplomacy. He resents the fact that we do not send our best men there. He knows an astonishing amount about it all. 'What can I do?' he says. 'They will only say, "Here's that bloody Prince of Wales butting in." ' One finds him modest and a good mixer."[34]

Nicolson was with them again the next month at the premier of a new Noel Coward play, *Tonight at 8:30*. He gave his first view of Wallis, who was there without her husband.

"Mrs. Simpson is bejeweled, eyebrow-plucked, virtuous and wise. I was impressed by the fact that she forbade the Prince to smoke during the *entr'acte* in the theater itself. Our supper party at the Savoy Grill afterwards goes right through, but I find the Prince gazing at my tie and collar in a mood of critical abstraction—the eye of Windsor blue surrounded by jaundice. Nobody pays any attention to him, and what is odd is that the waiters do not fuss unduly. The Prince is extremely talkative and charming. I have a sense that he prefers our sort of society either to the aristocrats or to the professed highbrows or politicians. Sibyl imagines that she [Wallis] is getting him into touch with Young England. I have an uneasy feeling that Mrs. Simpson, in spite of her good intentions, is getting him out of touch with the type of person with whom he ought to associate.

"Go home pondering on all these things and a trifle sad. Why am I sad? . . . Because I think Mrs. Simpson is a nice woman who has flaunted suddenly into this absurd position. Because I think the P. of W. is in a mess. And because I do not feel at ease in such company."[35]

Such was Wallis' charm that she soon made Nicolson feel perfectly at ease with her. Both of them were at another Colefax lunch in April, along with Winston Churchill and J. I. Garvin, editor of the *Observer*. Garvin held forth on the need to make Italy an ally and Churchill disagreed but added, "We must retain that command of the Mediterranean which Marlborough, my illustrious ancestor, first established."[36] Wallis and Nicolson both listened intently. She learned more at such luncheons than she did from books.

At another party, Wallis again found herself in conversation with Winston Churchill. Since his break with the Conservative Party leadership, he had become an almost-forgotten man in politics. He had known the Prince since he was a child. It was also Churchill, as home secretary, who went to Carnarvon Castle and read the proclamation creating him Prince of Wales.

Churchill might have thought how fascinating it was that his American mother, Jennie Jerome, a girl from Brooklyn, had once been in love with a Prince of Wales who became Edward VII. And here was Wallis Simpson, a girl from Baltimore, who was in love with another Prince of Wales, the grandson of the man who had loved Jennie.

The change in the Prince himself was obvious. Churchill was not the only one to note the improvement in his drinking and smoking habits. And the new joy in him.

Then George V was suddenly ill again, and this time it was critical. It was shortly after midnight, January 20, 1936, when Wallis got a call from the Prince telling her that his father had died.

During one of the accession ceremonies the following week, the Prince had invited Wallis to watch the pomp and circumstance from an unused palace apartment at St. James's. Suddenly, Wallis looked up to see His Majesty next to her, watching. As the Guards band played "God Save the King," Wallis felt tears in her eyes, and turned to him, and said, softly, that now she realized how different his life would be.

He pressed her arm gently, and said, "But nothing can ever change my feelings toward you."[37]

PART II

14

".. . WE, THEREFORE, the Lords Spiritual and Temporal of this Realm
. . . do now thereby with One Voice and Consent of Tongue and
Heart, publish and proclaim, That the High and Mighty Prince
Edward Albert Christian George Andrew Patrick David, is now, by
the Death of our late Sovereign of Happy Memory, become our law-
ful and rightful Liege, Lord Edward the Eighth, by the Grace of God,
of Great Britain, Ireland, and the British Dominions Beyond the Seas,
King, Defender of the Faith, Emperor of India . . ."

It was an awesome idea that he reigned over 486 million subjects
scattered all over the world, an empire on which "the sun never sets."
Nobody, however, knew better than Edward VIII that monarchy was
rapidly becoming a mirage.

"As a boy I saw Kaiser Wilhelm II, my father's first cousin, at a
shooting party at Sandringham," he said, "an occasion also memorable
to me for my first ride in a horseless carriage. I remember the visit of
Czar Nicholas II with his family to Cowes only eight years before
this unfortunate Emperor, another of my father's first cousins, was
murdered by the Bolsheviks. The dashing Alfonso XIII of Spain, who
married one of my father's first cousins, often came to Britain to shoot
or play polo. My parents, as Prince and Princess of Wales, had in fact
ridden in Alfonso's wedding procession in Madrid in 1906 when an
anarchist's bomb burst under the King's coach, killing many people
but sparing him and his British bride. And the plump and jovial King
Carlos of Portugal, who in 1908 met an untimely end from an assassin's bullet, was also during my childhood a guest at Sandringham.
While I was an undergraduate at Oxford I was called to Windsor
Castle by my father when he entertained the elegant Archduke Franz
Ferdinand, heir-apparent of the Austro-Hungarian Empire."[1]

Gone was the doctrine of divine right; gone was the belief in the ringing remark of James I in 1609: "Kings are justly called gods, because they exercise a manner of resemblance to Divine power on earth . . . They have the power to exalt low things and abase high things and to make of their subjects like men at chess."

Edward VII reputedly once introduced his son Prince George as "the last King of England." And when George V died, his last words were: "How is the Empire?"[2]

George V's funeral came on a raw, wintry day. His Majesty arrived without a coat. Knowing his susceptibility to colds, Wallis urged him to wear one.

"But I haven't a fur coat here," he said.

"Well, your brothers have," she had answered.[3] His Majesty then reluctantly put on his father's coat, and he and his three brothers marched behind the draped gun carriage that carried the coffin. Secured to the coffin was the imperial crown, taken from the Tower of London, but the jolting of the carriage caused the Maltese cross on top of the crown to jar loose and fall to the ground. This spectacular cross, a square diamond with eight more substantial diamonds and 192 smaller ones, was duly retrieved. His Majesty resisted the impulse to pick it up himself, but was overheard to mutter, "Christ, what will happen next?"[4]

It became the muttered theme of the year, the omen of things to come.

When he had been Prince of Wales, novelist D. H. Lawrence had written a poem about him, calling him the "alien, diffident boy, with nerves tired out, whose motto is, *Ich Dien*—I serve!" Now it was "Three cheers for the King—hip, hip, hurray! hip, hip, hurray! hip, hip, hurray!"

Prime Minister Stanley Baldwin told Parliament of the new king, "He has the secret of youth in the prime of age." And *The Times* of London editorialized approvingly his "unerring eye for the distinction between dignity and solemnity . . . Men not books are his library . . ." It also noted solicitously that he lacked "the help and counsel of a consort."

They were both soon to sing a different song.

In his first broadcast as king, he told the British people, "I am better known to you as Prince of Wales—as a man who, during the war and since, has had the opportunity of getting to know the people of nearly every country in the world, under all conditions and circumstances. And, although I now speak to you as King, I am still that same man who has had that experience and whose constant effort it will be to continue to promote the well-being of his fellow men . . ."[5]

His was a crowded calendar those first few months as king, and Wallis saw him more irregularly, although he was still unfailingly calling her. Beyond the steady procession of ceremonies and inspections and visits and appointments, the King had the daily job of "doing his boxes." These were the special locked red boxes full of Foreign Office dispatches and telegrams and Colonial Office reports, all kinds of statements he had to read and understand and approve and sign, all manner of honors and appointments he had to grant. One of the boxes brought the secret minutes of Cabinet meetings to update him on all that was happening. The King also automatically became admiral of the fleet as well as field marshal and marshal of the Royal Air Force, each of which required specific duties. In addition, he had to supervise his own vast household, with all its staff and administrative detail, as well as the management of his two royal estates at Sandringham and Balmoral.

With all this, he wanted to be the first modern king of the twentieth century. His father had never even flown in a plane. He wanted to be a king who was not only concerned about his people, but understood them. Queen Victoria had been surprised to discover there were such things as railroad tickets. He knew it scandalized some citizens that he carried his own umbrella or wore a bowler hat or didn't go to church regularly every Sunday. Still, he wanted his people to accept him as he was.

The final coronation ceremony was scheduled for May 1937, more than a year away. Before that there were several accession ceremonies. At the first when he appeared beside Wallis at a courtyard window in St. James's Palace, he had been caught by photographers, raising the question "Who *is* that woman?"

Wallis was still unknown to the general British public early in 1936. At "The King's Maundy" before Easter, when the King wore his full regalia at Westminster Abbey to distribute the traditional silver pieces to the poor, he stared so directly and often at Wallis in the reserved section of visitors that she flushed and looked down, and several present took note.

With the King at the Abbey was the Archbishop of Canterbury, the Most Reverend Cosmo Gordon Lang, primate of all England, next in "precedence" to the royal family, preceding even the prime minister. Great Britain was unique in that it had a national church, an "island religion," of which the King was the defender of the faith.

In trying to clear the somewhat strained air between them, the Archbishop had told him, "I want you to know that whenever the King questioned your conduct I tried in your interest to present it in its most favorable light."[6]

His Majesty quietly resented that his conduct or character should be questioned. Again, it was an omen.

Edward VIII had become king at a time of heightening turmoil. Nazi Germany was rearming at a frenetic rate, intensifying its dictatorship and making threatening gestures to reoccupy the Rhineland. Italy had invaded Ethiopia, ignoring League of Nations sanctions. "England," wrote John Gunther, "is the most dangerous country in the world because it is the only one capable of going to war on behalf of another country."[7] Prime Minister Baldwin's British government, however, was keeping its oars in.* The British people preferred disarmament and wanted to remain politically cut off from the Continent. So pointed was this feeling that when a heavy storm stalled all channel traffic to France, a newspaper headline poster read: CONTINENT ISOLATED.[8]

Still, in 1936, Edward VIII was less concerned with any looming war than he was with his personal future. He had scheduled his first formal dinner at York House and told Wallis he wanted her there because, "Sooner or later, my Prime Minister must meet my future wife."[9]

This was the first time he had ever mentioned marriage to her. In his own mind, it had been something definite and decided for months. He wanted her with him always. He no longer could consider sharing her with anybody, as he once had shared Frieda Ward and Thelma Furness. He wanted her to live with him, not with Simpson. He now felt he needed her with him more than ever. Wallis, too, felt his need. But she could not have believed marriage was a possibility. There were too many hurdles. He belonged to his heritage. And yet,

---

* In justifying his foreign policy, Baldwin told a friend, "I want it to be said of me that I never sent a single Englishman to die on a foreign battlefield."
"But Prime Minister," the friend countered, "don't you see that you are piling up troubles for the future that will kill a million Englishmen in the next war?"
"Ah, that," said Mr. Baldwin calmly, "is a problem for my successor." (Isabel Leighton, *The Aspirin Age*, pp. 188–189.)

here he was, saying what he was saying, and here she was, believing it.

She could have said a flat "No" then, as Frieda Ward had said "No." That was the moment, that was the time. If she had, then he would have had to face it, accept it, adjust to it. Instead, she said that he mustn't talk that way, that the idea was impossible, that "they" would never let him marry her. Hers was the answer of a woman who wanted to keep on dreaming. The King smiled confidently at her and added, "I will manage it somehow . . ."[10]

It was a dinner that caused controversy. Prime Minister Stanley Baldwin and his wife were the guests of honor. Also present were Mr. and Mrs. Charles Lindbergh, just back from Germany; Alfred Duff Cooper and his wife, Lady Diana; Lady Cunard; Commander Lord Louis Mountbatten and Lady Mountbatten; and several other guests, including Mr. and Mrs. Ernest Simpson. All the names appeared in the *Court Circular,* a record published daily of the doings of the royal family.

Many members of British society saw the *Court Circular* announcement as a public declaration by the King of his feelings for Wallis Simpson. The American-born Lady Astor, the first woman to sit in the House of Commons, was particularly aghast.

"Nancy Astor is terribly indignant at the King for having invited to his first official dinner Lady Cunard and Mr. and Mrs. Simpson," Harold Nicolson recorded in his diary. "She says that the effect in Canada and America will be deplorable . . . and she deplores the fact that any but the best Virginian families should be received at Court. I stick up for both Emerald Cunard and Mrs. Simpson, but I refrain from saying that, after all, every American is more or less as vulgar as any other American. Nancy Astor herself, by her vain and self-conscious behavior in the House, cannot claim to be a model of propriety. In any case, she is determined to tell the King that although Mrs. Simpson may appear at Court, she must not appear in the Court Circular. I suggest to her that any such intimation would be regarded by H.M. as a gross impertinence. She says that when the dignity of the United States and the British Empire is involved, it is her duty to make such sacrifices."[11]

The Baldwins had a similar feeling, but a different view. Both were sharply aware of Mrs. Simpson, and Mrs. Baldwin particularly resented the forced meeting. Baldwin's biographer summed up her feeling: "Mrs. Simpson has stolen the fairy prince."[12]

The idea that Wallis was the King's mistress was a special affront to the puritanical Mrs. Baldwin. Discussing how disagreeable sex was to them, a friend of Mrs. Baldwin asked how could she bear to have four children.

"I shut my eyes and thought of England," she said.[13]

Her husband had a milder view of Wallis' appearance. It was the first and only time he met her and he said only that she "intrigued" him.

Baldwin was surely more concerned when he read the *Court Circular* for the next formal dinner at York House. The distinguished guest list included the Duke and Duchess of York; the new First Lord of the Admiralty, Samuel Hoare; the King's new private secretary, Major Alexander Hardinge; the Winston Churchills; the new Viceroy of India; Lady Diana Cooper; and Mrs. Wallis Simpson. Only Lady Diana Cooper and Mrs. Simpson had been present at the previous dinner. Most carefully noted was the fact that Mr. Simpson was *not* present. If the earlier *Court Circular* had been the King's announcement about Mrs. Simpson, this was now his clarion call. As the King later put it to Prime Minister Baldwin, "The lady is my friend and I do not wish to let her in by the back door, but quite openly."

Wallis was now so socially important that she had only to crook her finger and almost anyone in British society would come to her. They came because they knew the King would be there.

The couple appeared socially more often and more openly now. At one dinner party in June at Lady Colefax's, they found themselves again with Harold Nicolson, as well as Artur Rubinstein, Lord and Lady Brownlow, Lady Diana Cooper, Noel Coward, and the Churchills among others. The King told Nicolson that the Lindbergh dinner had gone well. Mrs. Lindbergh had been shy at first, he said, "but with my very well-known charm I put her at ease and liked her very much." Rubinstein played Chopin until after midnight, and was about to play more when the King said, "We enjoyed that very much, Mr. Rubinstein." The King started to say good-by to people when Noel Coward began singing "Mad Dogs and Englishmen," and "No, Mrs. Worthington," and the King promptly resumed his seat.[14]

Wallis and the King plainly preferred Noel Coward to Artur Rubinstein. And this was their kind of party, where people even sat on the floor. His parents could never have imagined it.

One of Wallis' earlier social coups had been to bring together at her dining table two arch-rivals, Lady Emerald Cunard and Lady Sibyl Colefax.

"I dine with Mrs. Simpson to meet the King," a guest that evening later reported in his diary. "Black tie; black waistcoat. A taxi to Bryanston Court; an apartment dwelling; a lift; butler and maid at the door; drawing room; many orchids and white arums. The guests consist of Lady Oxford, Lady Cunard, Lady Colefax, Kenneth Lindsay, the Counsellor of the U.S. Embassy at Buenos Aires plus wife, and Alexander Woollcott. Mr. Ernest Simpson enters bringing in the King. It is evident that Lady Cunard is incensed by the presence of Lady Colefax, and that Lady Colefax is furious that Lady Cunard should also have been asked. Lady Oxford appears astonished to find either of them at what was to have been a quite intimate party. The King passes brightly from group to group.

". . . Then dinner. I sit between an indignant Emerald and the wife of the U.S. Counsellor at B.A. Opposite is Woollcott, and both ends of the table go gaily enough but for continued fury on Emerald's part. The King talks to Mrs. S. and Lady O. all the time. Emerald cannot bear it, and begins shouting 'Your Majesty' aloud. That doesn't go at all. Sibyl then starts telling a funny story which goes even less well. Then the women go and we sit on for hours talking to our Sovereign over the port. I must say, he is very alert and delightful . . . at last at 1 A.M. the King retires.

"Something snobbish in me is rather saddened by all this. Mrs. Simpson is a perfectly harmless type of American, but the whole setting is slightly second rate."[15]

Ernest Simpson now thought so too. The King had become increasingly open in disclosing his feelings for Wallis, and Simpson was tired of waiting for the situation to right itself, tired of waiting for his wife's dream to disappear, tired of expecting her to come back to him. He had played the role of the proper gentleman, but he was angry, perhaps more angry at himself than anyone else.

Finally he confronted Wallis.

"She told him that he could trust her to look after herself; she enjoyed the attention she received and saw no harm in it."[16]

He could hardly have believed this. Still, he had expressed himself on the subject for the first time.

Mary Kirk Raffray visited the Simpsons for part of that summer. She had come because Wallis needed to talk to someone, and Mary was almost her only intimate friend. Mary was then having her own marital problems and needed Wallis, too. At first Mary listened with sensitive understanding, but the longer she stayed and the more she listened, the more her sympathies veered toward Ernest. Mary had known Ernest since 1924; she had been the one who had introduced them. It was easy for Ernest to turn to Mary, to confide in her, and this was a time when Mary wanted to be needed. She was much like Wallis in personality, but had more open warmth, and was "less calculating"—perhaps because she had not been hurt as much.

Still, when she returned to the United States, she continued the charade, telling the waiting reporters that the relationship between the King and Mrs. Simpson was "perfectly innocent." Wallis' cousin Mrs. Anne Suydam, who also had seen her recently, loyally echoed this, saying, "Ernest is the only man Wally ever loved. Her whole heart and soul are his, and when they are together they are the picture of adoration. Simpson is proud of his wife, trusts her and has no suspicion. They understand each other, and that's what counts . . . at least that was the case when I last saw them together."[17]

A newspaper article, supposedly quoting a royal source, said: "Mr. Simpson regards the friendship of his wife and the King as purely platonic." The article added that the relationship "has been so distorted by mystery and ill-founded rumor that it has placed these three persons in an invidious position." It further noted, "In well-informed circles, Mr. Simpson's name has been mentioned among others who are likely to be honored on the Coronation List."[18]

Indeed, the King had offered Simpson a title. It was in a kingly tradition. Roger Palmer became the Earl of Castlemaine in the seventeenth century because he quietly approved the fact that his wife had brightened the life of Charles II. Simpson, though, saw the offer for what it was, and refused it.

At home in Bryanston Court the situation worsened. The atmosphere became increasingly tense. What could Wallis tell him: that she was full of guilt and self-recrimination but that the fantasy was too great, that her love for him, the quiet love that it was, could not compete with the royal romance, that the main feeling she had for him now was pity, and pity wasn't enough? What could she *tell* him? In the end, she told him nothing.

Then one evening, when she wasn't home, the King came to see Ernest Simpson. He was obviously distraught, pulling at his tie, pacing the floor and finally he blurted out what he had come to say:

"I *must* have her!"

"I was so dumbfounded," Simpson confided to a friend[19] afterward, "that I simply sat down. Then I suddenly realized that I had sat down in the presence of my King!"[20]

Shortly afterward, Simpson and the King had lunch at the Guards Club. With them was their mutual friend Bernard Rickatson-Hatt, who later reported their conversation.

"Simpson told the King that Wallis would have to choose between them, and what did the King mean to do about it? Did he intend to marry her? The King rose from his chair and said, 'Do you really think that I would be crowned without Wallis by my side?' "[21]

Wallis, of course, already had made her choice. Ernest Simpson moved to the Guards Club.

The most biting comment on the soon-rumored divorce came from Ernest Simpson's first wife. Interviewed in New York she said, "I doubt very much the reports that Mr. Simpson and his wife are contemplating a divorce. I see no reason why either of them should wish it. The present Mrs. Simpson has enough of 'what it takes' to steal a man. Mr. Simpson walked out on me while I was ill in a hospital in Paris."[22]

The King was now exultant. He arranged with his legal adviser to select a proper divorce solicitor for Wallis. His name was Theodore Goddard. Since the London court calendar was heavily booked, Goddard recommended divorce action in nearby Ipswich.

To consummate his fresh happiness, the King planned a summer cruise along the Dalmatian coast. He had initially planned to settle in a villa on the French Riviera, but the government had vetoed this because of the war in Spain and the political uncertainty in France. They further vetoed his embarkation from Venice because it might seem to lend an air of British approval to the Italian conquest of Ethiopia. The King, however, would not compromise on the yacht he wanted. Instead of the aged royal yacht, he wanted the biggest, the best and the most luxurious. This was the *Nahlin,* a floating villa.

The guest list was a cozy one: The Perry Brownlows, the Duff Coopers, the Mountbattens, Lord Dudley and Wallis' dear friends from Peking and the Riviera, Katherine and Herman Rogers. The Rogerses, more than any other friends, had shared the ebb and flow of Wallis' fortunes. Had there been no King and no Mrs. Rogers, Herman might have shared even more.

The King traveled to the rendezvous port in Yugoslavia incognito using the title "Duke of Lancaster." Wallis' luggage, however, had letters eight inches high announcing: MRS. ERNEST A. SIMPSON. Nor could the cruise be considered secret when the yacht had an escort of two British destroyers, HMS *Grafton* and *Glowworm*.

The yacht cruised along the Dalmatian coast. It is one of the most enchanting water journeys, the hilly coast rising into mountains, the towns quaint and uncrowded, the very still, very blue Mediterranean filled with picturesque red-sail fishing boats, the cherry orchards seeming to come down almost to the sea and the absolutely isolated sandy beaches, perfect for picnics.

The two of them would go rowing together to some quiet cove, walk unnoticed in a remote village. Wallis even managed to go to a shop to buy the King some swim trunks. At one of the larger towns, a random photographer caught them hand-in-hand.

The idyllic privacy, however, didn't last long.

As soon as word got out, everyone wanted a glimpse of the famous couple. Lady Diana Cooper told of "the impossibility of landing because of the yelling, jostling crowd that does not leave the King space to breathe. If he walks to the sights (the churches and old streets) they follow shouting 'Cheerio!' and surround him so that he can see nothing." She talked of the crowd "cheering their lungs out with looks of ecstasy on their faces."

"The King walks a little ahead talking to the Consul or Mayor, and we follow, adoring it. He waves his hand half-saluting. He is utterly himself and unselfconscious. That I think is the reason why he does some things (that he likes) superlatively well. He does not *act*. In the middle of the procession he stopped for a good two minutes to tie his shoe. There was a knot and it took time. We were all left staring at his behind. You or I would have risen above the lace, wouldn't we, until the procession was over? But it did not occur to him to wait, and so the people said: 'Isn't he human! Isn't he natural! He stopped to do up his shoe like any of us!' "[23]

She described the King as wearing "spick-and-span little shorts, straw sandals . . . no hat (the child's hair gleaming) . . . and two crucifixes on a chain around his neck . . ."[24]

People seemed to stare at Wallis as much as they stared at him. They cheered, gave her flowers, wanted to touch her. "*Zivila ljubav*," they shouted, and Wallis found out what it meant—"Long live love . . ."

Whenever they were walking together and a photographer popped up, Wallis was discreet enough to drop two paces back so that the King would be in the picture's foreground. She explained that the King didn't mind photographers, but that he didn't like to be surprised by them. Before the cruise, all pictures of the King showed him sad and worried—the story was that he had not smiled since his father's death. The pictures now flooding back to England revealed him really happy for the first time. A London weekly magazine broke the news blackout on the King's vacation with a front-page picture of him and Wallis, with the caption "The Duke of Lancaster and a Guest."[25] American magazines shipped to England with articles on the subject had the stories physically snipped out before their circulation.

It seemed fitting that this "most beautiful yacht in the world" had an American Indian chief, in full headdress, on its prow. The Adriatic fjord they leisurely entered was the Bocche di Cattaro, the wall of the mountain so high that it darkened the light, making the beautiful country look almost sinister. The town was tiny and poor, no shops or hotels or bars, a few pathetic Japanese lanterns with single candles at the quay. The King was anxious to move on but a ceremony had been scheduled and so the group reluctantly waited aboard ship.

Suddenly, every mountain peak seemed to be set afire, every house and every mountain path along the steep shoreline lit with flaming torches, thousands of peasants holding the torches, singing folk songs, all along the fifteen miles of the gorge. The guns from the nearby forts boomed and echoed through the ravines. In response, the King's bagpiper walked around and around the deck playing "The Skye Boat Song," while the King shouted explanations of the bagpipes to the crowd.

As the yacht eased out slowly past this magnificent serenade, His Majesty whispered to Wallis that these people were doing all this for her because they "believe a King is in love with you."[26]

She told him it was madness, that he must show more discretion or that the whole world would know their secret.

Discretion, he said, was not a quality he particularly admired.

Greece was brown rocky earth, ships that looked as they had in Homer's time, mountains that climbed right into the clouds. King George of Greece came on board at Corfu.

"We fixed our King up in white flannels and blazer and yachting cap," said Lady Diana Cooper, telling of the hurried preparations to get ready for the Greek king's six unexpected guests. "Wallis left us to arrange it all. They came and stayed two hours and we behaved badly and were cliquish, catching each other's eyes and yawning and looking miserable. The King played up best."[27]

The two kings were cousins, and the King of Greece confided that he didn't have a single friend he could trust, and his life was very sad. "I hope you have better luck," he said.[28]

The sea was green now, the olives immense, the air smelled so fragrant. Wallis, the King and the Duff Coopers landed at a broken quay, climbed an endless flight of steps flanked by symmetrical cypresses that led to a charming statue of Empress Elizabeth with a superb view and to a huge, hideous house. Sitting alongside the King of Greece later at dinner at his own magnificent villa, Wallis acted as naturally as if she had grown up amid royalty. "Wallis was doing splendidly, the wisecracks following in quick succession, the King clearly very admiring and amused."

Even in the informality aboard ship, there was some protocol. "At meals he [the King] gets served last, with the result that there is never anything left for him. The fool stewards don't realize it and go on passing the sauces and extras to his meatless plate, so that every day he has to say at least once: 'Yes, but I do want something to eat.' "[29]

Their trip to Turkey was a Foreign Office request, as Britain had just concluded a commercial trade agreement there.* Turkish dictator Mustafa Kemal Atatürk treated Wallis as if she already were a queen, seating her alongside the King in the parade and next to him at dinner. His Majesty wanted it that way, and Wallis loved it.

For the first time she believed everything was possible. The King's closest friends deferred to her. Other kings and leaders respected her. She could not only cope with them, and easily, but she enjoyed them as human beings, and they enjoyed her. If she married her king, she now felt she could play her part as his queen.

His being there alongside her, always, his face shining with love, made it all seem more and more possible.

* "Edward VIII was the first sovereign of a great power to visit Turkey since Kaiser Wilhelm II, and the effect on the still relatively young Republic was profound. It is no exaggeration to say that the self-confidence that the King's gesture gave to the pro-British party in Turkey influenced the country's conduct in the war immensely to our benefit . . . 'Edvard,' as he is often remembered, is the most popular Englishman in Turkey to this day." (Christopher Sykes, *The Observer*, London, September 23, 1958.)

The cruise was over but the King was reluctant to let it all end. Atatürk made available his private train and His Majesty and Wallis went to Budapest and Vienna. For them, it was a romantic return. At the Hussar Restaurant on the Kärntnerstrasse in Vienna, the King and Wallis could summon a certain waiter and tell him, "Just like the last time," and the waiter knew just what menu to repeat. At the Rotter Club in Vienna, the King sang his songs in German, just as he had done before, and Wallis hummed along. Their presence at the Emke night club in Budapest received much publicity but it was too late to help the club. "Not even the King and his soul-mate could save our most famous night club,"[30] the local paper commented the next day, when it was shut down because of back taxes.

Press observers reported how contented the King looked, how much he smiled and laughed, how little he drank, how late he and Wallis danced every night. Dancing the gypsy czardas one evening, Wallis was reported wearing a dinner jacket made of spun glass, a single glittering diamond in her hair. Another report mentioned a $750,000 emerald and diamond necklace.

Wallis personally arranged for the King's appointment with a famous Viennese otologist, Dr. Heinrich Neumann. The King had persistent pain in the ear and Neumann was a world authority. He had caused considerable controversy earlier because he had refused to operate on Adolf Hitler, saying, "As a Jew, I cannot risk it, because if I am unsuccessful, he would say that I failed on purpose."[31]

When the King came for his appointment, the porter stopped him at the door and asked who he was. "My name is Edward. Please lead me to Professor Neumann."[32] The professor successfully diagnosed the ear problem as something more painful than serious. Later, when the Nazis were threatening Vienna, the King arranged for Neumann to come to Britain.

Reporters were now swarming all around the King and Wallis, and they made little effort to conceal themselves. One reporter interviewed a bartender at the Hotel Bristol, where they had stayed. "Mrs. Simpson now talks with a British accent," said the bartender. "Last year when she was here with him, when he was Prince of Wales, she talked like an American who was just beginning to pick up some of the British way of speech."[33]

Wallis had picked up much more than a British way of speech on this trip. If the King had been in love with her before, he was obsessed now. She had bewitched him as few men had ever been be-witched. Or, as *Le Journal* put it, "She's his oxygen. He cannot breathe without her."[34]

He left her only after she promised to join him soon at Balmoral Castle, where he wanted her to meet still more of the royal family.

Wallis first went to Paris for a few days. The cruise had been too unreal. As relaxing as it had been for the Mountbattens and the Duff Coopers and the Brownlows, who had done it so many times before, it was nevertheless a nervous strain for her. She felt their eyes always on her, their ears always open.

She could never know what they were thinking, but she could always guess. And guessing hurt. She was on stage center, always on, and there was no intermission. Now she needed one.

She stayed at the Hotel Meurice with Mrs. Gilbert Miller and Mrs. Erskine "Foxy" Gwynne. The three spent an afternoon drinking martinis, chattering about everything and everybody, when the phone started ringing. The calls came in quick succession, each from abroad, each for a different woman. The call for Wallis came last. It was from the King and he was lonely for her, he said. It was Sunday and he was bored and he didn't know what to do with himself.

"Why don't you go to church?" suggested Wallis. It was one of the few times he did so while he was king.

The calls completed, the three women had another round of mar-tinis and Foxy Gwynne felt buoyed up enough to ask Wallis a ques-tion:

"What are you going to do with His Nibs?"

The martinis had mellowed her, but not that much. These were her friends, but the stakes were too large.

"I'm not going to do anything," she replied. "I'm married to Ernest and I'm hoping to stay married as long as he wants me."[35]

Her next stop was London.

15

WALLIS LINGERED LONG ENOUGH in London to discuss with her solicitor more details of her divorce, which was scheduled for October 27, some six weeks away. She also took time to move out of her apartment at Bryanston Court. It must have been a wrench; she was not simply closing down an apartment and opening up a new life, she was also storing a whole part of herself away into another of the many secret compartments of her being. Guilt feelings, sadness, question marks.

There had been an exchange of notes with Mary Kirk Raffray about Mary and Ernest Simpson. Mary not only sided with Ernest but had fallen in love with him. A sharp exchange of letters ended their long friendship. With Mary gone, Wallis found herself very much alone.

She still had Katherine and Herman Rogers. When the King had invited her to Balmoral, she had asked that they come too. She had the courage to face a roomful of social lions, but she wanted some support when she faced a castle full of royal lions.

Balmoral Castle was something outside of Wallis' experience. It was the site of the annual royal family get-together, an autumn ritual begun by Queen Victoria. She had loved this cold, drafty, granite castle, 600 miles from London, on the moors of Scotland. Her prince consort, Albert, had built it in the valley, on the right side of the Dee River, surrounded by the thickly wooded firs and larches, looking so much like the German landscapes he loved. It was his gift to her and she eventually—after his death—spent almost half of every year here. Just as she always wore black and always turned down his bed, as if he were alive, so did she treat his castle as if it were a shrine. Edward VII liked it little. It was too grim for him, too dark. The only gay things were the masses of Michaelmas daisies outside the ground-floor windows. George V preferred Sandringham, but came here anyway for the autumn holiday. King George's friend J. H. Thomas, secretary of state for the colonies, who had once been a locomotive engineer, told the King frankly that he thought Balmoral was "a bloody dull house."[1] Edward VIII found it too formal for his taste, but he liked the exhilarating air while stalking deer and shooting grouse.

For the autumn get-together, not only did the family collect but so did the prime minister, archbishops and cabinet ministers and admirals and dukes and duchesses. King Edward had invited the Dukes and Duchesses of Marlborough, Buccleuch and Sutherland, and the Earl and Countess of Roseberry, but he omitted the political and religious figures. Instead, he invited Wallis and the Rogerses. Not only did he invite them, but he broke another tradition by driving his own car to the Aberdeen railway station to meet them, jauntily wearing his kilt and his tam o'shanter.

This caused much more furor than he had anticipated. Several months before, he had excused himself from an invitation to attend the cornerstone ceremony for a new royal infirmary at Aberdeen. His given excuse was that he was still in mourning for his father, and he asked the Duke and Duchess of York to represent him. The day of the infirmary ceremony was the same day that the King gaily drove down to meet Wallis at the Aberdeen station. Scottish reaction was bitter. Chalked on one wall was an ugly reference: "Down with the American whore!" Playwright Sir James Barrie told Geoffrey Dawson, editor of *The Times*, to expect at any moment a Scottish minister to denounce the sins of the court.

The King's brother, the Duke of York, and his duchess, who lived six miles away, were equally unhappy about the incident. The Duchess, a commoner herself but of noble British blood, said, "Everyone knows more than we do; we know nothing. Nothing!"[2]

Queen Mary did not come to Balmoral. Her excuse was that she was busy moving out of Buckingham Palace to Marlborough House. The King had lunched with her on his first day home. They had talked about everything but the one thing that was uppermost in both their minds. Her mail had been heavy with letters from British citizens overseas, urging her to stop the gossip about the King. Queen Mary showed Lady Airlie a clipping from the Baltimore *News-Post* saying that Mrs. Simpson would marry the King as soon as her divorce was made final. Lady Airlie said she couldn't believe it and then remembered something His Majesty had said to her sister when he was Prince of Wales. "It's no use, Lady Salisbury. Bruce and I are two old bachelors. Neither of us will ever marry any woman unless we really love her."[3]

The older aristocracy had never liked the King, even when he was Prince of Wales, mainly because he had never really liked them. They were too pompous for him; they weren't "fun." This did not mean that he had the kind of democratic instinct that would wipe out class prejudices, not at all. In one sense, he was still a snob. He preferred people of his own set and class and background. He defended the Guards Division's snobbishness as "tradition, discipline, perfection and sacrifice."[4] He disliked the people at court, the old-line dukes and duchesses, not because of their class, but because too many of them were stuffy and boring. Some of the cold, drafty feeling Wallis experienced at Balmoral emanated from some of the other guests.

One morning Herman Rogers took movies of the King demonstrating an Austrian game involving a bow and arrow. Lord Louis Mountbatten and the Duke of Kent both fared badly, which made everyone laugh.

"As they sat on the terrace, waiting for lunch, the ladies looked untidy and relaxed," noted Cecil Beaton, who had seen the film. "The Duchess of Sutherland looked enormous in a dowdy hat, Mollie Buccleuch was made to look very squat and square in tartans. Neither Mary Marlborough nor begoggled Edwina Mountbatten were flattered by the camera; only the Duchess of Kent looked romantic, with her hair untidily blowing, and tied with a baby-bow of ribbon. Every few feet of film, the King appeared with Wallis. She looked very different from the others, neat and tawny in smart clothes and a black felt hat."[5]

The dukes and duchesses and the King's brothers and their wives were not unaware that Balmoral's royal bedroom, formerly occupied by King George and Queen Mary, was now the bedroom of Wallis Simpson. They resented her not only for what she was—an outsider, an interloper—but for what she was doing to their king. She was not one of them, and she never would be, no matter what the King did, or tried to do. They would be polite, but never cordial; they might even defer, but they would never accept.

Wallis afterward insisted she had enjoyed her stay at Balmoral. It seems hardly likely. Her easy quips and soft laughter might melt a

Greek king or a Turkish dictator, but the true British aristocracy can only be melted by time, generations of time.

If Balmoral made Wallis pause, it was not for long. On the chessboard, she still owned the King. He now became her landlord, too. She moved into a four-story house on 16 Cumberland Terrace, facing Regents Park. She sublet it, but the original lease belonged to the crown.

And the King was a unique landlord. He sent her long-stemmed roses every day, gave her a royal Buick driven by his own chauffeur, phoned her several times a day and was her nightly guest.

London bobbies kept the curious away, saying, "This is Crown property, move along, move along . . . ordinary people don't live here y'know . . ."[6]

The King breakfasted with his mother on his return to London, and again, neither mentioned Wallis Simpson. Queen Mary afterward confided to Lady Airlie: "Your sons are about the age of mine, Mabell, and you have had to bring them up without a father. Tell me, have they ever disappointed you?"[7]

Lady Airlie answered that all children sometimes disappoint their parents, but that one had to remember that they had their own lives to live.

"Yes, we can apply that to individuals, but not to a Sovereign," Queen Mary observed. "He is not responsible to himself alone." She was then silent for a moment, and continued, "I have not liked to talk with David about this affair with Mrs. Simpson . . . in the first place because I don't want to give the impression of interfering in his private life, and also because he is the most obstinate of all my sons. To oppose him over doing anything is only to make him more determined to do it. At present, he is utterly infatuated, but my great hope is that violent infatuations usually wear off."[8]

There was another pause and she added, "He gives Mrs. Simpson the most beautiful jewels." Lady Airlie then saw bright spots of crimson on Queen Mary's cheeks as she quietly added, "I am so afraid that he may ask me to receive her."[9]

Except for the top levels of British society, Wallis' name was still unknown in Great Britain. In the United States, though, the headlines were bigger than ever:

THE YANKEE AT KING EDWARD'S COURT[10]
THE MOST ENVIED WOMAN IN THE BRITISH EMPIRE[11]

She told photographer-artist Cecil Beaton, "I don't want you to call me by that name of Mrs. Simpson, which the American press has made me loathe."[12]

Cecil Beaton's manner and style had made him a fixture in court and society circles and he had entree everywhere. He was, in fact, a distant relation to Ernest Simpson. Beaton had met Wallis five years before at the Three Arts Club Ball. He remembered her then as "somewhat brawny and rawboned in her sapphire-blue velvet. Her voice had a high nasal twang." He had renewed the acquaintance more recently and found her "bright and witty, improved in looks and chic . . . I liked her immensely." It was mutual, and Wallis was most pleased to pose for him.

London *Observer* fashion editor Alison Settle often helped Beaton set up background for his portraits. One day Beaton called her to borrow marble busts of the young Queen Victoria and her prince consort. At Beaton's studio, Alison Settle couldn't recognize the woman waiting for her portrait. "Now let me think, where have I seen her?" she wondered. "I know she has her nails done next to me at Elizabeth Arden." But she did notice that the woman's make-up was all wrong for a sepia photograph. "I'm awfully afraid you'll have to have your face washed and redone. The make-up girl will be here in a minute or two." She next looked around the setting and saw two more royal busts, including one of Queen Alexandra. "My, we have gone royal today, haven't we?" she said, loud enough to be heard. Back at her office, she suddenly realized whom she had seen. "Good heavens, that was Mrs. Wallis Simpson!"[13]

Beaton made his own faux pas when he suggested pinning scrolls of ermine in the background. "Don't do anything connected with the Coronation with me. I want none of that now," she sharply told him. Her look at him was equally sharp when he asked her to lower her chin "as though bowing."

Beaton's camera saw Wallis as "soignée and fresh as a young girl. Her skin was as bright and smooth as the inside of a shell, her hair so sleek, she might have been Chinese."[14] But the memory that stayed even longer with Beaton was the sad, suffering look in her eyes.

He brought proofs of the photographs to her house at Cumberland Terrace, along with his sketching tools. She seemed brighter then, spoke amusingly in staccato sentences "punctuated by explosive bursts of laughter that lit up her face with great gaiety and made her eyebrows look attractively surprised."[15]

Wallis found she could talk to Beaton. He was a man of sophistication, flip and irreverent and funny. Nothing fazed him or awed him. His portraits were kind, but they were not façades; they had depth.

"And what absolute nonsense all this was about marriage," Wallis told him. "How could English people be so silly. There is no question of marriage," she continued. Beaton told her he had bet against any marriage, and added, "But maybe you'll ruin me."

"No, I expect I'll be very poor and you'll clean up."[16]

Could she really have believed that then? The King had been so strong and certain on the subject. Was it her Balmoral visit that brought her doubts back? Or was this all simply part of the continued smokescreen?

At that moment the butler announced His Majesty, and the King entered in high spirits, quickly examined Beaton's set of prints, picked his favorites and added, "I want the lot."

Beaton remembered they then had a broad discussion of the news ranging from South Wales unemployment to the Spanish Civil War. Britain had decided to follow France's example and stay aloof. The Germans and Italians already were supplying men and arms to General Franco and the Soviet Union was doing the same for the government forces. The King impressed Beaton with his memory for names and statistics and his sense of humor. He quipped that Atatürk of Turkey must have taken the title from the American expression "Attaboy."[17]

Wallis afterward brought out snapshots of the *Nahlin* trip. It might have been any family living room, where everybody comments on vacation pictures. There was no trace of stiffness or pomp. It was as if the King were in his own home. And it was one of the major reasons the King so much wanted Wallis. She created that feeling of naturalness whenever she was with him.

Wallis showed a picture of herself and the King, both in shorts, and commented, "That's sweet, isn't it?"[18] Then she reminisced about the crowd in the Yugoslav town of Korčula, where the people all came down to the dock to meet them. "Do you remember it?" she asked the King. "It was swell."[19]

Beaton sketched the King, but something his sketch didn't catch was the mood of the man afterward—talking very fast, eating green grapes stuffed with cream cheese, restlessly darting around the room ringing bells, untying parcels and looking very very happy.

16

"I KNOW I am not good enough to be your Queen," Elizabeth Wood-ville told the dissolute Edward IV in 1464, "but I am too good to be your mistress."[1]

"Elizabeth perceived that the impression which she had made on Edward IV was so deep as to give her hopes of obtaining the highest elevation. She obstinately refused to gratify his passion, and all the endearments, caresses, and importunities . . . proved fruitless against her rigid and inflexible virtue. His passion, irritated by opposition and increased by his veneration for such honorable sentiments, carried him, at last, beyond all bounds of reason, and he offered to share his throne as well as his heart with the woman."[2]

Wallis had no such parallel with Edward VIII. She already had given the King her passion and her heart and that was part of what had caught him.

"It is a great mistake to assume that he was merely in love with her in the ordinary physical sense of the term," noted Walter Monckton, whose friendship with the King dated back to their days at Oxford. "There was an intellectual companionship, and there is no doubt that his lonely nature found in her a spiritual comradeship . . . She insisted that he be at his best and do his best at all times, and he regarded her as his inspiration . . . To him, she was the perfect woman."[3]

The King had his own firm standards of right and wrong, however unconventional they often were. As Monckton put it, "One often felt that the God in whom he believed was a God who dealt him the trumps all the time and put no inhibitions on his main desires."[4]

His main desire was marriage. He felt he and Wallis were made for each other and there was no other honest way of meeting the situation. The difference between Wallis and Elizabeth Woodville is that Wallis, at one time, would have happily settled for being the King's mistress.

Bernard Rickatson-Hatt, editor-in-chief of Reuters, Wallis and Ernest's old friend, said he thought "her intention was to have her cake and eat it. She was flattered by the advances of the Prince of Wales and the King and enjoyed his generous gifts to her to the full. She thought that she could have them and at the same time keep her home with Simpson."[5]

Rickatson-Hatt added that Wallis often made Simpson extremely unhappy, and then overwhelmed him with kindness and affection to make it up to him. He further described her as a woman who "likes the good things of the earth and is fundamentally selfish . . . capable of hardness."[6] He further felt that if the King had not been obstinate and jealous, the affair would have run its course without breaking up the Simpson marriage.

Indeed, it might have happened just that way. But the King had introduced a new note for Wallis: ambition. He was the king and the emperor. He always had had what he wanted, and he wanted her. He did not want her as the mistress of Buckingham Palace; he wanted her as his wife; he wanted her as his queen and empress. And he promised her he could make it happen, that he knew what he was doing, that he could "fix things." He was so persistent and so convincing that she finally allowed herself to believe him. She believed him because she had an amazing ignorance of British law and custom and the powers of the king, and also because she wanted to believe him. She wanted to believe that the girl from Baltimore could actually see her fairy tale come true, could truly become the queen of Great Britain and the empress of India.

It was then, and only then, that she had agreed to divorce Simpson.

Discussing Mrs. Simpson with Nicolson, Ramsay MacDonald, the former prime minister, contended that nobody would mind about her if she were a widow, that she alone was the person who could remedy the situation "but there is always the possibility that her head (which as a head is not exceptional) may be turned."[7]

"Sibyl [Lady Colefax] says that at any rate up till last July there was no indiscretion at all," Nicolson recorded on October 6, 1936, "and that Wallis seemed really to understand the responsibility of her position. But since the *Nahlin* things have gone more recklessly.

There is the new house in Regents Park. There is that Balmoral episode. Rob [Robin Maugham] thinks that the thing is really serious and will shake the foundations of monarchy. I feel sad about it since I like Wallis Simpson. The King resents the suggestion that Wallis is not as good as anyone else or that he must confine his friends to those whose names look well on the Court Circular. Nor will he be so disloyal as to cut out Mrs. Simpson from the Circular when she comes to stay. But there is seething criticism which may develop into actual discontent."[8]

Wallis and the King regarded their marriage and their future as their magnificent secret, which they would share with nobody. Both were naturally suspicious. They had both been hurt and toughened. If Wallis was "capable of hardness," so was the King. Both felt that they now could have the kingship and each other, but they must tell nothing to anybody.

And whom could Wallis consult? Mary Kirk Raffray had gone home, after declaring her love for Ernest Simpson and ending their friendship. Aunt Bessie had not yet arrived. Wallis had no other intimates except the Rogerses, who were in Cannes. She therefore willingly accepted the King as the sole source of advice and information. Making it a mystery only heightened the excitement of the drama and the romance.

The charade was even maintained before Walter Monckton. When Wallis agreed to a divorce, the King brought her to Monckton for advice. A man of medium height with thinning hair and thick glasses, Monckton had been attorney general to the Duchy of Cornwall when the King was Prince of Wales. A brilliant barrister, he had also advised the Nizam of Hyderabad. The King had often said how much he admired Monckton's mind and respected his judgment.

He also knew how intensely loyal Monckton was and had confided to him as to few others. In his first days as king, he had told Monckton that he could not bear to feel that he would be cooped up in Buckingham Palace, that the British people must take him as he was—a man different from his father and determined to be himself. He said that his public life belonged to the people, and he would be available when wanted, but his private life was his own, and he wanted to live it the way he had always lived it.

And yet, even to Monckton, he said nothing at that time about his intention to marry. The King said only how much he resented the fact that Mrs. Simpson's friendship with him brought her so much publicity and might interfere with her prospects of securing her freedom. Wallis, later, and privately, told Monckton that she wanted to be free of her present marriage, "that she was getting older, but might well meet with someone with whom she might happily marry. She said to me in the little lane behind the exits at Harcourt Buildings that it was ridiculous to imagine that she had any idea of marrying the King."[9]

Monckton agreed that it was ridiculous. He agreed even though he had heard, months before, that Ernest Simpson had told Sir Maurice Jenks that the King had informed him that he was in love with his wife and wanted to marry her. Monckton refused to believe that the King had actually said this, and suspected an attempt at blackmail.

But Monckton underestimated the intensity of the King's love. He believed that "when the stark choice faced them between their love and his obligation as King-Emperor, they would in the end each make a sacrifice, devastating though it would be."[10]

This was the King's hour. He saw this as his lonely battle. He had both courage and obstinacy, but no man ever needed advice more than he did then. Three hundred years before, Edward Clarendon had written of King Charles: "His single misfortune was (which indeed was productive of many greater) that he never made a noble and worthy friendship with a man so neere his aequall, that he would frankely advize him, for his honour and true interest, against the current, or rather the torrent of his impetuous passyons."[11]

Many of the King's friends indeed cared less for his welfare than for their own amusement. Even the few who adored him, and willingly served him loyally, still called him "Sir," even in their most relaxed moments; they were not his "aequalls."

The King did have available to him the best advisers in Britain. Winston Churchill "with his hundred horsepower brain"[12] was only one of them, but the King still did not speak. It was Monckton, not the King, who finally went to Churchill for advice. As the divorce proceedings came closer and the publicity worsened abroad, Monckton was concerned as to its impact on the King.

He watched Churchill pace up and down his rooms at Morpeth Mansions, pondering the question.

"I can hear him now," Monckton recalled. " 'Life is a tease. Joy is the shadow of sorrow, sorrow the shadow of joy.' He told me how he refused to sit at a table with people who criticized the King. But he was plainly anxious about what I told him. He was all against divorce proceedings in which he saw no advantage; the presence of Mr. Simpson was a safeguard. Moreover, he was anxious that I should make plain to the King how important it was that his friendship should not be flaunted in the eyes of the public."[13]

This was precisely the kind of advice the King did not want; this was certainly one of the main reasons he sought no counsel. He did not want to hear what he knew they would tell him.

When Monckton reported Churchill's advice, the King simply said that he didn't see why Mrs. Simpson should stay tied to an unhappy marriage simply because she was his friend. He dismissed the suggestion that he keep their friendship quiet by saying he was not ashamed of it and was not going to hide it or deceive people.

The King did ask for help from two of Britain's most prominent press lords, Beaverbrook and Rothermere, but on a much more pointed matter.

With Wallis' divorce imminent, the King was much concerned about publicity. His concern was for her. Lord Beaverbrook, who owned the *Daily Express* and *Evening Standard,* already had informed Wallis' solicitor, Theodore Goddard, that he planned to publish a story about it. Beaverbrook was an old friend of Goddard, who tried to persuade him to kill the story, but Beaverbrook refused. Then, on October 13, Beaverbrook was invited to "name your own time"[14] for a meeting with the King. It is most interesting to note that Beaverbrook's engagement book lists the name of Mr. Ernest Simpson the day before he saw the King.

William Maxwell Aitken Beaverbrook was a Canadian who made his fortune amalgamating cement mills. He joined the British Cabinet in 1918 as minister of information in charge of propaganda. A short man with a bullet-shape head and dynamic energy, Beaverbrook barely knew the King. Nor did he share Churchill's romantic feeling for the monarchy. He had, however, memorized a passage by Edmund Burke: "The world is governed by go-betweens. Those go-betweens influence the persons with whom they carry on intercourse by stating their own sense to each of them as to the sense of the other; and thus they reciprocally master both sides."[15]

The King asked Beaverbrook to be a go-between to get the cooperation of the British press to give minimal attention to Wallis' divorce.

He told Beaverbrook that he felt it was his duty to protect Mrs.

Simpson because she was ill and distressed by the notoriety caused by her association with the King. He gave no hint of any idea of marriage. Goddard had told Beaverbrook that His Majesty had no such intention. "And I believed it," said Beaverbrook. He not only believed it, but he so assured the other British publishers.

Lord Ponsonby, once a page to Queen Victoria, had said of royalty, "Let us in decency leave the private lives of these servants of the people alone. We expect too much from them. Cannot we in return respect their privacy?"

Beaverbrook arranged "a gentlemen's agreement" among British publishers in regard to the divorce. The New York *Daily News* afterward commented that the trouble with British newspaper publishers "is that most of them think of themselves as statesmen first and publishers second."

The King had calculated the divorce date most carefully. After a decree *nisi* was granted, English law required a wait of six months before the divorce was made final. The delay was originally provided in case a child should be born to the divorced wife. This meant that Wallis would be free on April 27, 1937. The coronation ceremony was announced for May 12. This gave the King adequate time to marry Wallis before the coronation. He even had decided on his eventual argument to the Prime Minister: "No marriage, no coronation."

His argument could not have been more ill chosen.

Wallis left London early in October to go to Felixstowe, near Ipswich. Goddard said it was necessary to establish residence in the area several weeks before the divorce petition. Felixstowe was a remote village on the east coast of England where the river Gipping flows into the sea. October was off-season and the resort was absolutely dead.

Wallis arrived in the King's Buick driven by the King's chauffeur, accompanied by a cook, a maid and two friends, Kitty and George Hunter. No one in town knew who they were, and nobody cared. Even with her tiny house packed with people, this was still one of the most lonely times in Wallis' life.

She walked the long, empty beach and thought how far she had come from 212 East Biddle Street. Always characterized as the kind of person to whom you would go if you were in trouble, to whom could she go? She was a woman alone. She still had no realization of the overwhelming nature of the events to come. She still felt confident that her king could cope with anything.

She did not have to wonder about the true depth of his love for her. She knew that. But what about her own love for him? The King was not Don Felipe A. Espil. He was not the tall, strong, brilliant, overpowering man's man who swept her off her feet. The King was handsome in a boyish way with his warm smile and open charm. He had his own stubborn kind of strength. He was a marvelous dancer. They both liked the same kinds of things: people rather than books, popular music more than opera, lively friends instead of pompous ones, bistros instead of banquet halls.

He was sincere, affectionate, anxious to laugh, even more anxious to please her. More than all this, he was a king and an emperor and the most eligible bachelor in the world.

Beyond everything, though, he needed her; he needed her far more than Espil ever did.

"She loves him, though I feel she is not *in* love with him," summed up a perceptive friend.[16]

Her love was not a passionate love, not an overwhelming love, but she was surely swept along by the high drama of their romance, the continuing excitement of it.

Was it enough? Wasn't it more than anyone else ever had?

Whatever the answer was, it was too late to turn back.

"When I was a little boy in Worcestershire, reading history books," Prime Minister Stanley Baldwin once told a friend, "I never thought I should have to interfere between a King and his mistress."[17]

Baldwin was as British as roast beef and John Bull. A short, stocky man with a blunt face, baggy tweeds and the inevitable pipe in his mouth, he was then in his seventieth year, ready for retirement. His critics called him colorless, made much of the fact that he often seemed to prefer his pigs to people and that his political slogan was "When in doubt, don't." He was slow of speech, strongly conservative and liked to refer to himself as a "plain man."

A former *Times* editor, Wickham Steed, raised the question: "Is Stanley Baldwin the luckiest of incompetent politicians or the subtlest of competent statesmen?"[18] And Harold J. Laski provided his answer: "Mr. Baldwin has the Englishman's genius for appearing an amateur in a game in which, in fact, he is a superb professional."[19]

Neither strikingly clever nor intellectual, Baldwin went to Harrow and Cambridge and admitted, "I did nothing at the university. I attribute such faculties as I have to the fact that I did not overstrain them in youth."[20] His "old school tie" loyalty to Harrow, however, was almost as deep as his religious principles.

"When the call came to me to form a government," he wrote, "one of my first thoughts was that it should be a government of which Harrow should not be ashamed . . . I will, with God's help, do nothing in the course of an arduous and difficult career which shall cause any Harrovian to say of me that I have failed to do my best to live up to the highest ideals of the School."[21]

His father was chairman of the Great Western Railway, head of Baldwins, Ltd., one of the giant iron and steel works, and also served as a member of Parliament. Stanley Baldwin quietly succeeded his father in all three areas. His first speech in Parliament opposed the eight-hour working day. He had run his business on a paternalistic basis, a just and kindly employer acting as head of a family, and he felt government ought to be run the same way.

Baldwin was a political unknown when Andrew Bonar Law chose him as his parliamentary private secretary and later as chancellor of the exchequer. Bonar Law was reported to have said of Baldwin then that he was too honest to intrigue against him and not clever enough to get into trouble.

When Bonar Law retired in 1923 because of illness, King George had to pick a successor between two Tory leaders, Baldwin and Marquis Curzon of Kedleston. When he chose Baldwin, Curzon complained, "Not even a public figure. A man of no experience—of the utmost insignificance."[22] After his selection, Baldwin told the press, "I don't need your congratulations, but your prayers."[23]

"Every morning, we kneel together before God," Baldwin's wife said, "and commend our day to him, praying that some good work may be done in it for us. It is not for ourselves that we are working, but for the country and for God's sake. How else could we live?"[24]

His secretary said of him that he was more of a preacher than a statesman, that he felt things deeply and his conscience was more active than his intellect. He himself confessed to a "somewhat flabby nature" that preferred "agreement to disagreement." His first premiership lasted less than a year and he was replaced by the first Labour government of Ramsay MacDonald. Baldwin returned in 1924 with a tremendous majority, struggled through the general strike of 1926, ran for reelection in 1929 on the slogan of "Safety First" and lost. In 1935, he again became prime minister, with the slogan "I think you can trust me."

But in 1936 Baldwin was in trouble. His foreign secretary, Sir Samuel Hoare, had caused an international uproar by making a deal with Premier Pierre Laval in Paris permitting Italy to keep what it had conquered in Ethiopia. A cohort described him as wearing the air of a man crushed by some appalling disaster. His days in office were supposedly numbered. Germany further complicated the international scene by marching into the Rhineland. Baldwin had known how Hitler's enormous rearmament program compared to England's pitiful pace but kept his "lips sealed."

"Supposing I had gone to the country and said that Germany was rearming, and that we must rearm, does anybody think that this pacific democracy would have rallied to that cry at that moment? I cannot think of anything that would have made the loss of the election, from my point of view, more certain."[25]

Asked if he had talked to any of the European leaders, Baldwin was equally blunt, and said no, he hadn't, because he didn't like them.

Baldwin maintained his outward, pipe-smoking calm, but his secretary wrote, "Within him storms a chaos,"[26] and, "Every burden becomes a nightmare."[27] Friends observed his facial tic become chronic, and he greatly increased his habit of snapping and cracking his fingers. Fearing a nervous breakdown, his doctors had insisted he take a rest of several months.

Before he left, Baldwin was aware of the growing concern about the King and Mrs. Simpson. Word had come to him, as it had to Walter Monckton, from Sir Maurice Jenks that the King had told Ernest Simpson he wanted to marry his wife. Baldwin also had received repeated urgings from the King's principal private secretary, Major Alexander Hardinge, that he should and must speak with the King on this matter. Hardinge, along with everybody else, was outside the King's orbit of full confidence. Because of his position, however, Hardinge, more than anyone else, knew exactly what was going on.

Aside from his natural reluctance to intervene in the private life of his sovereign, the Prime Minister felt that no constitutional issue could arise as long as Mrs. Simpson remained married to her husband. With the divorce hearings set, the issue became more immediate.

Fully recovered and rested, the Prime Minister was weekending at Cumberland Lodge, the home of Lord FitzAlan, with a small group including Alexander Hardinge. They were all key establishment people concerned with the future of the crown. Hardinge had been assistant private secretary to George V since 1920. His father had been viceroy of India, ambassador to France and Russia, and permanent undersecretary of state. His great-grandfather had fought in the Battle of Waterloo and received Napoleon's sword from the Duke of Wellington. The Hardinge family motto was "For King and Country." Even though he was the King's private secretary, Hardinge saw his greater duty to the monarchy rather than the monarch.

Hardinge was a simple, unpretentious man of middle height with a drawn face and a full mustache. His heritage put him in the social circle just below that of the royal family. His service with King George had made him into an important social conduit. Indeed, it was this familiarity with the court circle that earned him his job as principal secretary to the King. The King would have preferred Sir Godfrey Thomas, who had been his private secretary and friend for seventeen years, but Thomas felt himself inadequate and recommended Hardinge. The King had not known Hardinge well, but he was reputed to be a man of honor, without political guile, punctilious and efficient. He was supposedly not the kind of man who would spring surprises.

It was Hardinge, though, who finally impressed the Prime Minister that he must try to persuade the King to stop the Simpson divorce. Baldwin agreed. Only a year before, he had said in a speech: "If in any cataclysm the Crown vanished, the Empire would vanish with it. It is a link which once broken can never be repaired, and so long as the tradition to which we have been accustomed, the tradition which guides those who sit on our august throne, so long as that tradition lasts, it will be blest to our country and no power on earth can break it."[28]

The King was having his own country weekend, a shooting party at Sandringham, when Hardinge telephoned him. They set the meeting for Tuesday morning at Fort Belvedere. The Prime Minister was plainly nervous, and almost apologetically asked for a whiskey and soda. He offered to pour one for the King, who answered, severely, that he never took a drink before seven in the evening. Then the air relaxed slightly as they both began puffing their pipes.

"You remember, Sir, when we came up from Folkestone together, you said I might speak freely to you about everything? Does that hold good when there is a woman in the case?"[29]

The King said yes, it did.

The Prime Minister said he was talking also as a friend, then detailed the growing rumors at home and abroad and its potential damage to the monarchy. Finally, he asked, "Must this case really go on?"[30]

The King simply said, as he had before, that it would be wrong to try to influence Mrs. Simpson just because she happens to be a friend of the King.

Why did he feel he had to lie? Why couldn't he have said then that he loved Mrs. Simpson and wanted to marry her? What kind of game was he playing? One conclusion was that the King hoped to avoid a confrontation before the divorce became final. He could then marry the woman he loved and present His Majesty's government with a fait accompli.

Baldwin went away that morning feeling that "the ice had been broken," and complimented the King on the beauty of his garden.

The worried King called his friend Walter Monckton, told him about the Baldwin talk, then said, "Listen, Walter, one doesn't know how things are going to turn out. I am beginning to wonder whether I really am the kind of King they want. Am I not a bit too independent? As you know, my make-up is very different from that of my father. I believe they would prefer someone like him. Well, there is my brother Bertie."[31]

Speaking of the succession even before Edward became king, Baldwin reportedly remarked cryptically, "The Yorks will do it very well." Baldwin also told Labour Party leader Clement Attlee that he had grave doubts whether the new king "would stay the course."[32]

Unlike the American Constitution, the British Constitution is not a written document. What governs the United Kingdom is an accepted body of principles, some of them written, but others based entirely on tradition. Most traditional of all is the very existence of the British Cabinet. Parliament therefore has the flexibility to meet the changing conditions of the Empire. Constitutionalism in England is what *is* done. In *The Forsyte Saga* Galsworthy wrote, "You always have to give England time. She realizes things slowly."

The British Constitution did not prevent the king from marrying anyone he wanted unless she was a Roman Catholic. To marry a Catholic, he had to surrender the throne to the next Protestant heir in line. Until they were twenty-five years old, members of the royal family could not marry without the king's permission.

As king, though, Edward VIII could marry whom he wished no matter what her nationality, race or position in society. Nor was there anything prohibiting marriage to a divorced woman. Nor was it illegal for any clergyman to perform such a ceremony.

Four years before, the Archbishop of Canterbury expressed his "desire" that the Anglican Church should not solemnize any marriage involving a divorcée whose husband or wife was still alive. Since the king of England was also the Defender of the Faith, this did raise a problem. But a more major factor was the Statute of Westminster, passed in 1931, which decreed that the Imperial Parliament ceased to be sovereign over the Dominions. The only symbolic link was the crown. On any royal marriage, the Dominions would have to be considered.

These were all things the King knew, thought about and worried about. But he later told Monckton that he had made up his mind about marrying Wallis in 1934 and his decision was as hard-set as concrete.

Reaction from the Dominions already had started to filter in. Prime Minister Mackenzie King of Canada spent the night of October 26 with Baldwin telling him that Canada would be hostile to the King's marriage to Mrs. Simpson. An article in a Canadian newspaper quoted a lawyer as saying, "If the United States wants a Queen, why not crown Mrs. Simpson in Washington?"[33]

Dominion newspapers referred to the American press treatment of the Simpson affair as "mud stirred up by hooligans."[34] Columnist Walter Winchell considered the matter in a different light: ". . . Readers are more interested in people who are 'living' than in those who are 'dying' . . . People in love are alive . . . People who aren't are dead . . ."[35]

One American newspaper headline announced:

FIVE-TO-THREE HE DOESN'T MARRY HER![36]

The story compared the British social scene to a glass of ale: aristocracy was the froth on top, workers were the sediment, and the middle class was the strong body of the drink that made it a good drink, and the middle classes didn't want Wallis as queen.

Among the steady stream of critical letters from overseas Britons to *The Times*—none of which was ever printed—editor Geoffrey Dawson read one that caught his attention. Signing himself "Britannicus," the reader wrote a nine-page letter detailing "a perfect avalanche of muck and slime"[37] in the American press, which, he said, transformed the American view of Great Britain "from a sober and dignified realm into a dizzy Balkan musical comedy . . ."[38] Among other items, he listed stories that Queen Mary was being evicted from Buckingham Palace to make room for Mrs. Simpson, that Wallis should be enlisted to collect the British war debt to the United States, that the King had bawled out the Prime Minister for complaining about his intended marriage.

"I cannot refrain from saying that nothing would please me more than to hear that Edward VIII had abdicated his rights in favour of the heir presumptive," the letter concluded. "In my view, it would be well to have such a change take place while it is still a matter of individuals, and before the disquiet has progressed to the point of calling in question the institution of monarchy itself."[39]

As editor of *The Times*, Geoffrey Dawson at sixty-two was one of the dozen most important people in Great Britain. *The Times* was The Thunderer, the voice of the establishment. There were those who said Dawson, a flush-faced man with thinning hair, lacked the editorial courage to match his editorial independence, that he liked to steer silently rather than lead, that he preferred being the pilot fish rather than the shark. Other critics saw him as a snob who only sought out important company. They admitted he was a man of uncompromising honesty, except with himself. His friends saw him as a brilliant writer, discreet, hard-working, conservative, a man of strong religious principles who believed utterly in Lord Milner's concept of England and the Empire as a great moral force.

Dawson saw the Britannicus letter as further evidence that the Simpson affair was diminishing that moral force and promptly took a copy of it to Buckingham Palace to show his friend Alec Hardinge, the King's secretary.

Dawson and Hardinge shared the Milner concept of Empire. Dawson had been part of the "Milner Kindergarten" in South Africa and Hardinge was Milner's stepson-in-law.

Lord Beaverbrook later said of Dawson that he was the main villain in the plot against the King "by methods many would condemn" and that "he pursued his quest with a vigor that seemed more like venom."[40]

Hardinge told Dawson that he already had brought in "big guns" to bear on the King, and mentioned the meeting with Baldwin. That evening Dawson dropped in on the Prime Minister at 10 Downing Street with another copy of the Brittanicus letter. Baldwin told Dawson that the letter would strengthen his hand in dealing with the King, but he felt he could make no further move until the King gave some intention of marriage. Dawson, too, felt it prudent to hold his fire.

The invisible man at that meeting was the Archbishop of Canterbury, Cosmo Gordon Lang. At Magdalen College at Oxford, when he had been dean of Divinity, the undergraduates called him "Cosmo." They remembered his beautiful voice, strong personality and superfluous and inappropriate sermons. Dr. C. C. J. Webb in the Senior Common Room also recalled that "he certainly appeared to get on best with the socially prominent undergraduates."[41]

As archbishop, he kept his own diary on what he called "The King's Matter." In it, he discussed the charm and the promise that "were not always wisely directed." He later said of the King, "It was clear that he knows little and, I fear, cares little about the Church and its affairs."

What concerned the Archbishop most was the coronation service in May, when he also had planned to open his campaign of "A Recall to Religion." If he had to administer the sacrament of Holy Communion to a man married, or about to be married, to a person who had twice divorced her husband, such a surrender would not only make a mockery of the campaign but would shake the foundations of the church's influence and teaching.

". . . the thought of my having to consecrate *him* as King weighed on me as a heavy burden," he wrote in his diary. "Indeed I considered whether I could bring myself to do so. But I had a *sense* that circumstances might change. . . ."[42]

The change was coming. It began on October 27, at Ipswich.

17

Don't talk of your alien Minister
Nor his Church without meaning or faith!
The foundation stones of its temple
Are the bollocks of Henry VIII[1]

HENRY VIII was infatuated with Anne Boleyn and married her in 1533, in defiance of Clement VII. Before that, he had made the church subservient to the crown, created his own archbishop of Canterbury and ordered his marriage to Catherine made invalid because of her sympathy to Spain, the unlikelihood that she would have more children and the illegality of the original papal dispensation to permit their marriage. Pope Clement promptly excommunicated Henry VIII, and Henry broke with Rome, stopped all payments to the Pope and had himself made supreme head of the Church of England.

The Church of England, then, was born out of Henry VIII's wish for divorce, but for a considerable time thereafter no church was more strict in its prohibition against divorce. The essence of that prohibition was that marriage can only be dissolved by the natural death of one of the parties and is indissoluble while both live.

It later took an individual act of Parliament to permit divorce, and then it was made available only to the powerful and rich. Everyone else was faced with the cliché answer: as you have made your bed, so you must lie in it. It took many years to accept the American attitude that marriage was more of a social habit than a sacrament. Adultery became the only accepted excuse for divorce and the Matrimonial Causes Act of 1923 established complete equality between the sexes in any grounds for divorce. It also cut the cost of divorce and extended its jurisdiction to the Court of Assizes.

Some 80 percent of divorces were undefended. It was considered gentlemanly for the man to assume the blame of adultery, even if he was not guilty. There was the accepted farce of using an unknown professional woman at a resort hotel, with the evidence of the chambermaid arriving in the morning with tea to find them in bed together. The difference, however, between British and American divorces was that the divorce decree took more time in Britain.

So blatantly false was the charade needed to achieve divorce that even the Church of England, at its convocation in 1936, asked for some amendment to the law, "provided that any proposed amendment does not tend to make marriage a temporary alliance or to undermine the foundations of family life." A. P. Herbert, author of a satire on divorce, "Holy Matrimony," felt so strongly about the need for divorce reform that he got elected to Parliament and proposed a law to ease divorce and eliminate the humbug of collusion. The Simpson divorce put the whole question in a national spotlight.

Few places seemed more unworthy of world headlines than the quiet farming town of Ipswich. It had little of tourist interest: Cardinal Wolsey was born here, the son of a butcher; Charles Dickens used the local White Horse Hotel for a scene in his *Pickwick Papers* about a lady in yellow curl-papers; the great British actor David Garrick made his debut here on a site then occupied by the Salvation Army. Ipswich was also, historically, the scene of a Viking raid. Otherwise, the big attraction was a small art museum and a weekly market day.

More important for Wallis Simpson, Ipswich was the county seat of Suffolk, with a Circuit Court of Assizes where judges assembled four times a year to deal with county cases.

"It was all badly handled," said Lord Brownlow. "The timing was wrong, the place was wrong, everything was wrong. The town was crawling with Secret Service and Security people. All those newspapermen and photographers crowding into the small village only exaggerated the event. The fact that Wallis had a very prominent Solicitor to handle her divorce, a Solicitor known to be tied in with the King made the situation even worse."[2]

The international press arrived in Ipswich in great strength. The few British reporters were mainly there as observers. In 1926 Parliament had passed an act restricting published reports of divorce proceedings. The establishment argument was that this prevented injury to public morals since there were often intimate details of sexual perversion, including a surprising number of ingenious variations of sadism and masochism. Some observers hinted that the establishment was really protecting its own, since there was a disproportionate number of broken marriages among the aristocracy and since it was the sexual perversions of the aristocracy that caused the greatest newspaper scandal.

This ruling, however, would not have normally prevented the British press from exploiting the Wallis Simpson story in a dozen different ways, had not the King made Beaverbrook extract their promise to treat the story lightly.

Wallis had not slept much the night before. On her mind, surely, was an oversize mixture of concern and ambition, doubt and hope.

She knew she had the best possible legal advisers, solicitor Theodore Goddard and his rotund associate Walter Frampton. To act as her barrister in court, she had Norman Birkett, K.C., a bespectacled lean man with a hawk nose who was considered one of the most distinguished and expensive legal counsels in Britain. Birkett, who was knighted soon after the trial, went with Monckton to lunch with the King at Fort Belvedere several days before the divorce hearing. "Norman was deeply impressed with the King's straightness and kindness and devotion to Mrs. Simpson and was captivated by his charm."

Birkett and Goddard assured Wallis Simpson that all the loose legal ends had been carefully buttoned up and that the hearing would be quick and quiet. Barrister Birkett had so arranged his leading questions that Wallis mainly had to answer, "Yes" or "No."

All the logistics had been carefully planned: The strict security outside the courtroom, so strict that even a former mayor of Ipswich found difficulty gaining entry; the rearrangement of public seats in the courtroom so that all seats facing the witness box were left vacant; the issuance of only thirty tickets to the press, their seats so placed that they could only see the back of the witness.

More than two dozen photographers parked themselves on nearby roofs waiting for Wallis' arrival. The particularly enterprising photographers who got too close to the courthouse had their cameras smashed by the police. Security men also discovered a newsreel crew renting an apartment with windows facing the courtyard, and they sent them packing too.

Goddard and Frampton called for Wallis in their own car, so that she would avoid attracting attention in the royal Buick. The plan was for her friends and staff to take her car with her luggage directly to London while she drove home with Goddard after the hearing. Everything was precisely timed. As soon as their closed car raced into the courtyard police slammed shut the seven-foot-high gates. Wallis pulled her large hat low over her eyes.

It was the first case scheduled that afternoon, listed on the court calendar as "Simpson, W. vs. Simpson, E.A."

She sat waiting in the so-called "barrister's well" near her solicitor's table. A man sat on either side of her, and seven policemen, four of them in plain clothes, stood facing the spectators during the entire hearing. Indoor cameras were banned.

Wallis wore a navy blue woolen suit, a blue and white polka dot scarf, a single ring on her left hand. She remembered being so tense that she hardly knew what was going on. One reporter described her composure as "queenly."[3] Another mentioned her "spasms of coughing."[4]

The presiding judge, His Lordship Justice Sir John Hawke, a short, elderly, heavily jeweled man with a ruddy face, wearing a snowy, close-fitting wig and a crimson ermine-trimmed robe, made his traditional arrival, heralded by guardsmen in scarlet tunics and black busbies blowing silver trumpets. An enterprising reporter discovered that Hawke had been legal adviser to the Duchy of Cornwall, which was still responsible to the King. Hawke seemed a stern, solemn man with his broad-rimmed eyeglasses on the tip of his nose.

Wallis was called to the witness box. A bailiff handed her the New Testament, on which she swore to tell the truth, the whole truth and nothing but the truth. Most observers agreed that her voice was clear and firm.

"Frequently her tongue moved rapidly in nervous movements from cheek to cheek," wrote one reporter. "She looked, to one seeing her for the first time, like a middle-aged woman of the upper classes. She had a wen on the right side of her chin. She told a most ordinary story."[5]

She answered questions as to where she lived and when she had married, and whether or not there were any children.

Then Birkett asked:

"Did you live happily with the respondent until the autumn of 1934?"

"Yes."

"What was the change?"

"He was indifferent and often went away for weekends alone."

"Did you complain about this?"

"Yes, I did."

"Did he continue to do what you complain of—going away alone and staying away weekends?"

"Yes."

"On Christmas Day, 1934, did you find a note lying on your dressing table?"

"Yes."

The note was passed on to the judge, the barrister suggesting that it was in a woman's handwriting.

Justice Hawke read it, then said: "It may be in a woman's handwriting, but it's not very legible." He was then given a typewritten transcript of the letter. "This is evidence against nobody," he said, after reading it. "I do not understand it."

Birkett, however, continued his questioning of Mrs. Simpson.

"Did the finding of the note cause you considerable distress?"

"It did."

"Did you complain to your husband at that time?"

"No, I thought I better not, in the hope conditions would improve."

"Did they improve?"

"I'm afraid they did not."

She then testified that she had received another letter, addressed to her but intended for her husband,* and that afterward she had sought counsel and hired detectives. Birkett then submitted a letter she had afterward written to her husband.

Dear Ernest:

I have just learned that while you have been away, instead of being on business, as you have led me to believe, that you have been staying at the Hotel Bray with a lady. I am sure you realize this is conduct which I cannot possibly overlook and must insist you do not continue to live here with me. This only confirms the suspicions I have had for a long time. I am therefore instructing my solicitors to take proceedings for divorce.[6]

---

* The letter was a warm, loving note from Mary Kirk Raffray, thanking Ernest Simpson for some roses.

Then came the usual witnesses, the maid and the floor waiter from the Hotel de Paris, in Bray-on-Thames in Maidenhead. They had seen Mr. Simpson and another woman, had brought morning tea to them in their double bed. No, the other woman was not Mrs. Simpson. The night that Simpson supposedly was in bed with this other woman was July 21, his eighth wedding anniversary.

Justice Hawke seemed dissatisfied, started raising a question, and Birkett broke in, "I assume that what your Lordship has in mind . . ."[7] The justice testily demanded how Birkett could possibly know what was in his mind.

At that point, no one could predict what the judge would do.

The judge's question concerned the name of the other woman. It had not been mentioned in the trial, only in the original petition. Her name was Buttercup Kennedy.

Wallis felt that the judge was definitely hostile. He hardly looked at her throughout the whole trial and seemed to resent being involved in the case.

Almost reluctantly, Justice Hawke decided, "Well, I suppose I must come to the conclusion there was adultery in this case." Then he added, "Very well, decree *nisi*."[8]

"With costs, my Lord?"

"Yes, I suppose so."[9]

It was all over. It had lasted nineteen minutes.

Almost instantly, Wallis was whisked out of the courtroom through a side door, and the door firmly shut in the face of the reporters. Before they could open it she was already on her way to London.

18

KING WILL WED WALLY

THAT WAS the New York *Journal* headline the day after Wallis' divorce, followed by an unsigned story reportedly written by publisher William Randolph Hearst, after an interview with the King. Without hedging, the story simply said that Edward VIII planned to marry Wallis as soon as her divorce became final in April. The article argued that royal marriages were outmoded; that the King's brother, the Duke of York, was happily married to a commoner, "a lady of the people."[1] It added that the most important thing for the peace and welfare of the world was an intimate understanding and relationship between England and the United States and that the King's marriage with "this very gifted lady"[2] might help bring about that beneficial cooperation.

"Primarily, however," the article concluded, "the King's transcendent reason for marrying Mrs. Simpson is that he ardently loves her, and does not see why a King should be denied the privilege of marrying the lady he loves."

The American press had given the Simpson divorce an enormous play. There was considerable speculation that the court case had been royally rigged to please the King. A Briton remarked caustically, "The courts of law are open to all—like the Ritz Hotel."[3] George Buchanan, an MP from Glasgow, put it more sharply: "The whole law courts were set at defiance for this one man. A divorce case was heard when every one of you knows it was a breaking of the law. The law is desecrated. The courts are thrust aside."[4] His point was that the court had blandly accepted a patent fraud as acceptable evidence.

Even though faked adultery was a standard ploy all over the world, it angered many righteous Britons that their king would indirectly make use of it.

"Princes might rather expect to be lamented than to be envied, for being in a station that exposeth them," wrote Charles Halifax in the seventeenth century, "if they do not do more to answer Men's Expectations than Human Nature will allow."[5] Or, as a more modern Briton put it, "A Prince may have his fun, and Lord love him for it, but once he becomes King, he better behave himself properly."

Shortly after the turn of the century, *The Times* of London editorialized that the king "is the most visible embodiment of the Monarchial principle; and any personal default of his gives a shock to the principle which is mischievous and even dangerous."[6]

The king was not a human being; he was a myth, "the most universally popular personality in the world." The great difficulty in being a myth is that most people tell you what they think you want to hear.

This king saw himself first as a human being, and a modern one. "You are out of date," he once told Sir Samuel Hoare, "you know nothing of the modern world." Hoare later mused, "If I thought too much of the past, he seemed to me to think too little of it."[7]

On that day of Wallis' divorce, the King properly and punctiliously saw all his appointments, but the human being readily admitted that deep in his mind, he was at Ipswich with Wallis.

One of his appointments was with Prime Minister Mackenzie King of Canada. "It had been hoped," said Geoffrey Dawson in his diary, "that the P.M. of Canada might have said something on this occasion about the growing anxiety in his own country. He was in a strong position to give such a warning; but it was quite clear from his conversation with me that he had done nothing of the kind—had indeed, if anything, made matters worse by discoursing on the King's popularity in the Dominions."[8]

The King got the news of the divorce shortly after lunch and called Wallis soon after she arrived home at Cumberland Terrace. They had their reunion at her home that night, the two dining alone. He had been lonely and restless without her. For him, it had been almost unbearable.

"I saw him when she'd gone away for a fortnight. He was miserable, haggard, dejected, not knowing what to do," Winston Churchill said.

"Then I saw him when she'd been back for a day or two, and he was a different man—gay, debonair, self-confident. Make no mistake, he can't live without her. . . ."[9] The affair was reaching the point where Wallis could no longer think of living without him, either. His way of life had now become hers. A royal wish was a command. They would make an unexpected arrival late at night at the Embassy Club —when there were no tables—and a table would suddenly appear. He would notice her eying a sable coat and suddenly she would have one. He knew how she loved emeralds, and one night there was a surprise emerald necklace. He made it seem as if he held a magic wand and everything she wanted could be conjured with a flick.

The first weekend after her divorce, reporters knew she was at Fort Belvedere because it was announced that the King had called his mother from there to inquire about her cold. Queen Mary had asked Lady Airlie, "Has there been a great deal of gossip, Mabell—I mean, here in London?"[10] Lady Airlie said there was and then asked the Queen if the rumor was true that she had received Mrs. Simpson.

Queen Mary said that it was not true, that "she had promised the late King never to receive her."[11]

Queen Mary had a royal side that was steel, but she still gave a mother's sigh when she said, "He's very much in love with her. Poor boy!"[12]

With Wallis back, the King decided to tell her about the Baldwin visit. The news frightened her but he was blandly reassuring. Wasn't he the king with the magic wand?

Hostesses now flooded Wallis with invitations. Her friends, the Gilbert Millers, of New York and Paris, threw a party for her. Gilbert Miller, a prominent theatrical producer, had felt it was not proper to invite both Wallis and the King until she was divorced. The Millers had a magnificent house in London and that night there were a large number of uninvited guests who had heard about the guests of honor. As the party kept getting larger, Mrs. Miller finally told them all: "You might as well go home; the King is not coming."[13] And they went.

The King much preferred small groups of intimate companions. One of his oldest American friends arrived for a visit, "Doc" (Milton W.) Holden. They had met in Paris during World War I when Doc was in the Lafayette Escadrille. Doc could see how much Wallis had changed the King. As a young man he had been introspective, partly shy. With Wallis, he was buoyant.

"When she first met me, and knew what an old friend I was, she set out to charm me, and she got me hook, line and sinker," said the lean, wiry Doc. "She could charm anyone. She was a brilliant talker. And very natural. Which is probably what first won him."[14]

Aunt Bessie arrived, too, in early November 1936. She was full of funny stories of her ocean crossing, when she kept overhearing people talking about the King and Wallis, and had to keep a straight face. Wallis confided in Aunt Bessie as she could in no one else, and Aunt Bessie reported on the American press, said that some paper had tried to denigrate her early background. One American article related that Wallis had queried a Warfield uncle asking him to document their heritage and genealogy—because the press was treating her as if she was a plumber's daughter. The article claimed that the Warfield uncle had cabled back: STOP ACTING LIKE THE PLUMBER'S DAUGHTER.[15]

The King, meanwhile, continued acting like the King. He addressed Parliament, asserting his "Declaration Insuring the Maintenance of the Protestant Faith by the Crown."

"I, Edward VIII, do solemnly and sincerely in the presence of God, profess, testify and declare that I am a faithful Protestant. . . ."

It was supposed to have been a day of pageantry, a colorful procession through London. But it was pouring rain and the King sped to Parliament in a closed car. The House of Lords was filled with colorful robes, all emitting a faint odor of mothballs. He was tense when he started speaking but then his voice became strong and vigorous.

Among his other daily duties the King had to receive all new ambassadors. Hitler's new envoy from Germany was Herr Joachim von Ribbentrop. Ribbentrop's predecessor was the King's friend Hoesch.

One of the many ugly whispers against Wallis was that she was being used by the Germans to influence the King in their favor. Much was made of her meetings with Ribbentrop at the Cunard and Hoesch parties, months earlier, but there was no need for Wallis to influence the King with regard to the Germans; he already was prejudiced in their favor.

According to Fritz Hesse, press attaché at the German Embassy at the time, Hoesch claimed that he had been "on terms of intimate friendship"[16] with the King for many years, and that he had made a direct appeal for the King's support when the Nazis marched into the Rhineland.*

Hesse said he listened in on another phone when the King called Hoesch:

"Hullo, is that Leo? David speaking. Do you know who's speaking?"

"Of course I do," said Hoesch.

"I sent for the Prime Minister and gave him a piece of my mind. I told the old so-and-so that I would abdicate if he made war. There was a frightful scene. But you needn't worry. There won't be a war."[17]

The account seems most improbable. War was the furthest thing from Baldwin's mind. Nor would he brook such royal interference in foreign affairs.† The King's pro-German feeling, however, was an open secret. He similarly favored Mussolini. When the Italians conquered Ethiopia and Emperor Haile Selassie fled to London, Anthony Eden suggested that the King should receive him. The King refused because he felt the Italians and Mussolini would not like it if he did.

Ribbentrop was a suave former champagne salesman, who reported to Hitler that Mrs. Simpson, like the King, was favorable to the Germans. Wallis Simpson insists that she was not, although she certainly made no attempt to bait him like her good friend Lady Emerald Cunard did at one of her parties. "Tell me, dear Ambassador," Emerald said sweetly, "what does Herr Hitler truly think about *God*?" And, later, "We all want to know, dearest Excellency, why does Herr Hitler dislike the *Jews*?"[18]

Wallis would never have permitted herself such pointedness on a political question. It was Lady Cunard who had warned Wallis of this.

There were few important dinner parties in London that month where Wallis' name was not mentioned.

Harold Nicolson recorded in his diary a dinner at Lady Sibyl Colefax's. "The party consists of the Winston Churchills, Duff Coopers,

---

* When German troops marched into the demilitarized Rhineland on March 7, 1936, an open breach of the Locarno Treaty that might have meant Allied military countermeasures, "Hitler waited nervously for the first reactions . . . sighed with relief: 'At last! The King of England will not intervene. He is keeping his promise.' " (Albert Speer, *Inside the Third Reich*, p. 72.)

† Philip II of Spain reproached an ambassador of his at Rome for having been too punctilious in his negotiations and having stood up too strongly for a mere "convention." The ambassador replied, "Your Majesty himself is only a convention." (*The New York Times*, undated editorial.)

Somerset Maugham, the Mountbattens, Philip Sassoon, Artur Rubinstein, Desmond MacCarthy and others. I sit between an American woman and the Duchess of Rutland. I discuss with the latter the great Simpson question. Mrs. Simpson has now obtained her divorce, and there are very serious rumours that the King will make her Duchess of Edinburgh and marry. The point is whether he is so infatuated as to insist on her becoming Queen or whether the marriage will be purely morganatic. The Duchess of Rutland is very sensible about the whole thing, and does not believe that he would do anything so foolish. Nonetheless I gather from other people that there is considerable danger."[19]

Geoffrey Dawson committed to his notes the fact that one could not go anywhere without hearing such Simpson talk and referred to the subject as "His Majesty's obsession." Even at a meeting of the Literary Society, he said, literature was abandoned and some speculated on the possibility of a representation to the King on the Simpson subject by senior officers of the Brigade of Guards, who were "the only people for whose opinion he had any respect."[20] Baldwin, too, received increasing pressure to talk again to the King, but he was still reluctant to make any further move, hoping "the young man would see sense."

The young man could see nothing but Wallis. She alone had gauged him correctly, and knew that there was no limit to his love, that he would give up everything and follow her anywhere. She was still, however, moving as if she were a character in a play, saying lines she had to say, constricted by a plot over which she had no control. Nor did she seem to have any overall understanding about the significance of the play itself.

No matter how close the friends, she denied to everybody that she and the King had the slightest intention of marrying. The idea was absolutely ridiculous, she said. Kitty Hunter later burst into tears in front of Walter Monckton, saying that Wallis had fooled her to the last by always declaring that she would never marry the King.

Wallis not only fooled Kitty Hunter; she fooled everybody. The tragedy was that she fooled herself. She simply did not understand the parliamentary hazards; she truly believed it would all work out well.

Cecil Beaton asked her where she planned to go for the coronation. "A flat again?"

"A flat is much easier to run," she answered. "This house is so far away. I'd like Claridge's, but there is the disadvantage of public exits."[21]

During this time the King already had resolved on his argument to force British government acceptance of Wallis as his queen: "No marriage, no coronation." But he had still not confided his marriage intentions to anybody. Wallis could act her part with aplomb, because she was hiding a romantic secret, not a passion. The King, however, was transparent.

A few royal friends muttered hopefully that this too would pass away. "You know how fickle our David is." Mention was made of King Manuel of Portugal, who lavished his love and several million dollars' worth of presents on an exotic French dancer named Gaby Deslys in 1908. A revolution pushed him off his throne, and when he lost his throne he lost his dancer.

History was searched for any kind of comparable case. William I of Hohenzollern did give up the beautiful Polish Princess Elise Radziwill in 1826 when it was decided that his rank was higher than hers. Napoleon forsook Josephine for another emperor's daughter, and his brother Jerome Bonaparte left his Baltimore bride to marry a German princess. Justinian waited for the Empress to die before he married a bear feeder's daughter, Theodora, who helped him rule the Eastern Empire in the fifth century. Louis XIV wed the brilliant Madame de Maintenon, but kept the marriage secret and couldn't even attend her funeral. Four of Henry VIII's six wives were commoners. Mary of Scotland married a commoner and so did the Black Prince, son of Edward III. Henry II wed Eleanor of Aquitaine, the divorced wife of the French king Louis VII. The wife of James II was a commoner. And George IV married the twice-widowed Mrs. Maria Anne Fitzherbert, a Roman Catholic, before he became king. However, in 1795 he denied the marriage and made a political union with Princess Caroline of Brunswick, even though he turned against her just a year later and went back to Mrs. Fitzherbert.

If Wallis believed her cousin's claim that she was descended from Pocahontas, she could have claimed that this Indian princess had married a commoner, John Rolfe, in 1614.

All this made interesting cocktail conversation, but none of it applied to the King and Wallis.

They were playing their own game, making their own rules. Wallis at that time had every expectation of becoming queen, and the King had every hope of making it happen. Both were naïve, romantic and politically immature. The King, particularly, had never acquired the gift of patience, the willingness to accept criticism, and he seemed to have an abject lack of ability to understand his present political position. He counted too much on his popularity with the British people, the masses of whom were still totally ignorant that there even was a Mrs. Simpson. Had he permitted the press to open up the subject earlier, had he confided to his people and built up his case with them, he might have had their support and their strength. His prime reason for keeping the subject publicly closed was to protect Wallis from massive publicity. This decision was a defeating one.

On the King's calendar was an inspection of the Home Fleet. "No one could deny his surpassing talent for inspiring enthusiasm and managing great crowds," noted Sir Samuel Hoare, then first lord of the Admiralty. "He seemed to know personally every officer and seaman in the Fleet . . . In my long experience of mass meetings I never saw one so completely dominated by a single personality . . . Elbowing his way through the crowd, he walked to the end of the hall and started community singing to the accompaniment of a seaman's mouth organ. When he came back to the platform, he made an impromptu speech that brought the house down. Then a seaman in the crowd proposed three cheers for him, and there followed an unforgettable scene of the wildest and most spontaneous enthusiasm."[22]

With "For He's a Jolly Good Fellow" still ringing in his ears from that mass of men, how could he not feel that he was popular enough to get anything he wanted? Inwardly, he later admitted, he had been tired and worried during the inspection, but "outwardly, he showed no sign of weariness . . . his bright and vivacious conversation never lagged."[23]

Interviewed by an American newspaper, a member of Parliament, James Maxton, expressed the opinion that the naval review was "designed to overcome the vehement objections to a possible marriage," and that the King, "finding himself in difficulties with the aristocracy is on a campaign to consolidate his personal popularity . . ."[24]

The trip, of course, had been arranged long before, but there was little question that the King was strongly aware of his impact and its meaning.

The King came home tired and drained, ready for a hot bath. Waiting for him were the usual red dispatch boxes, one of them marked: URGENT AND CONFIDENTIAL. He opened it to find a letter from his principal private secretary, Alec Hardinge.

Geoffrey Dawson noted in his diary on November 13 a visit to Buckingham Palace to see Hardinge that day, "and he showed me, since I happened to be there, the draft of a letter to his Royal master which he had felt impelled to write after a sleepless night. It was his first and only intervention—an admirable letter, respectful, courageous and definite . . ."[25] Two days earlier, Dawson had talked to the Archbishop of Canterbury, who told him he had decided against any active intervention in the Simpson affair, feeling it would do more harm than good.

Hardinge had kept the King aware of the incoming flood of protesting mail from overseas British subjects, as well as a resolution from British former servicemen that the thought of Mrs. Simpson stepping into Queen Mary's shoes did not commend itself to them. Hardinge and Prime Minister Baldwin had had dinner on November 12, the Prime Minister wanting to know if there was any change in the King's relationship with Mrs. Simpson. Hardinge said he saw no change. Baldwin then said that he planned a meeting with senior ministers to discuss the matter the following morning. That morning Hardinge wrote his letter to the King.

"The King's Private Secretary is a solitary figure, and ploughs a lonely furrow," Hardinge later noted, explaining why he had allowed Dawson to see the letter. "At this moment of anxiety and distress I desperately needed an outside opinion as to the general wisdom and propriety of my letter, as well as its accuracy; and, it seemed to me, no one could help me more over this than a man with the discretion, experience and integrity of Geoffrey Dawson, who was at the same time 'very much in the know.' . . ."[26]

It was a fateful moment. That letter would set in motion a succession of inevitable events. Geoffrey Dawson had it within his power to alter it all. He did not.

"What can be said of a Private Secretary who discussed his master's affairs with the editor of an opposition newspaper and even disclosed the contents of a letter of severe criticism that he meant to send to his employer? Bad. Worse still when the master is a King, and the servant a public official."[27]

Hardinge's letter read:

Sir,

With my humble duty.

As your Majesty's Private Secretary, I feel it my duty to bring to your notice the following facts which have come to my knowledge, and which I *know* to be accurate:

(1) The silence of the British Press on the subject of Your Majesty's friendship with Mrs. Simpson is *not* going to be maintained. It is probably only a matter of days before the outburst begins. Judging by the letters from British subjects living in foreign countries where the Press has been outspoken, the effect will be calamitous.

(2) The Prime Minister and senior members of the Government are meeting today to discuss what action should be taken to deal with the serious situation which is developing. As Your Majesty no doubt knows, the resignation of the Government—an eventuality which by no means can be excluded—would result in Your Majesty having to find someone else capable of forming a government which would receive the support of the present House of Commons. I have reason to know that, in view of the feeling prevalent among members of the House of Commons of all parties, this is hardly within the bounds of possibility. The only alternative remaining is a dissolution and a General Election, in which Your Majesty's personal affairs would be the chief issue—and I cannot help feeling that even those who would sympathize with Your Majesty as an individual would deeply resent the damage which would inevitably be done to the Crown, the cornerstone on which the Empire rests.

If Your Majesty will permit me to say so, there is only one step which holds out any prospect of avoiding this dangerous situation, and that is for Mrs. Simpson to go abroad *without further delay,* and I would *beg* Your Majesty to give this proposal your earnest consideration before the position has become irretrievable. Owing to the changing attitude of the Press, the matter has become one of great urgency.

I have the honour, etc. etc.

Alexander Hardinge

P.S.—I am by way of going after dinner to-night to High Wycombe to shoot there to-morrow, but the Post Office will have my telephone number, and I am of course entirely at Your Majesty's disposal if there is anything at all that you want.[28]

Before sealing the letter, Hardinge went to 10 Downing Street to show it to the Prime Minister to find out if he "would have any objection to my passing on to the King this information which he had given me in strictest confidence the night before."[29] Hardinge had hoped the Prime Minister, after reading his letter, might postpone the ministerial meeting until he heard the King's reaction. Baldwin was not available, and Hardinge left a copy of his letter with a staff member.

The King saw that letter as the crisis of his kingship. He was both shocked and angry. He felt he had been betrayed. Soaking in his tub, thinking about it, rereading the letter, he decided that the letter had been motivated and directed by Baldwin, that its prime purpose was to threaten him with the government's resignation unless he gave up Wallis.

"They had struck at the very roots of my pride," the King remembered afterward. "Only the most faint-hearted would have remained unaroused by such a challenge."[30]

The letter not only struck the roots of his pride, but his very being. He could not, would not, ever give up Wallis.

"With the King's straightness and directness there went a remarkable determination and courage and confidence in his own opinions and decisions,"[31] Walter Monckton noted. "Once his mind was made up one felt that he was like the deaf adder 'that stoppeth her ears and refuseth to hear the voice of the charmer.' The trouble was that on this matter his mind was made up by himself long before he knew it, and this is the explanation of what must have seemed to many a strange and obtuse obstinacy."[32]

Wallis and Aunt Bessie were weekend guests at The Fort, and the King had decided he did not yet want to share this new worry with Wallis. He first wanted to discuss it with a friend he could trust, Walter Monckton.

It was two days before he could manage to break away from Wallis to meet Monckton.

Monckton read the letter, agreed on the need for prompt action. The King then asked Monckton to be his liaison with the Prime Minister. They sat in the Empire Room at Buckingham Palace, which the King used as his sitting room, and for the first time he told Monckton that he planned to marry Wallis Simpson. He added that he had often wished to tell him before, but had refrained because he felt it would embarrass Monckton to know. Earlier, Monckton would have found the fact incredulous; now he was no longer shocked. In recent weeks he had seen and felt the intensity of the King's love for Wallis, a fact that he had much underestimated.

The King wanted to fire Hardinge but Monckton persuaded him not to, because it would openly indicate a breach over Mrs. Simpson. Monckton counseled patience.

Returning to The Fort from tea with the Duke and Duchess of Kent, Wallis sensed that something important had happened. The King told her about meeting Monckton, showed her a copy of Hardinge's letter and left the room.

Wallis read it unbelievingly. Fairyland came crashing down and the fearful reality flowed in. The King had lost his magic wand. She had never genealogically qualified as Cinderella, but the glass slipper had fit, and now, suddenly, it had shattered.

Deep within her she had always worried that it was too good to be true, too impossible to last. On that *Nahlin* cruise, the kings had treated her like a future queen and she almost felt like one. At parties, she saw how people deferred to her, listened to her respectfully. The jewels were real, the fur coats were real and the King's love was the most real. Only the world was unreal, and the future.

The King returned and Wallis told him that there was only one thing to do: she must leave the country immediately.

The King said she would do no such thing, that he would never give her up.

She tried to convince him of the hopelessness of their position, that it would mean tragedy for him and catastrophe for her. The King, however, answered that he was going to send for Baldwin and confront him at the palace the next day. ". . . if the country won't approve of our marrying, I am ready to go."[33]

The self-controlled Wallis finally broke down. "David, it is madness to think, let alone talk, of such a thing."[34]

But, as Wallis said of him: "When he made up his mind, he was like a mule. I suppose that's because he was so used to getting everything he wanted."[35]

19

THAT WINTER OF 1936 showed, more than ever, the mark of American influence in England. Bing Crosby records were big hits, and singers all over Britain picked up his crooning style: the swaying and tapping and heavy breathing, the body as close as possible to the microphone. Equally popular were the American musical films like *The Goldiggers* and the swing bands of Louis Armstrong, Benny Goodman and Duke Ellington. "Monopoly" had replaced mah-jongg. The Scots were not particularly happy with the new swinging hit based on "Loch Lomond," sung by Ella Fitzgerald. Imported American humor included the "Knock-Knock, Who's There?" jokes and "She was only a plumber's daughter, but . . ."

There were so many cars and so many road deaths (7,000 a year) that motorists were finally required to take driving tests before they could be licensed. The new fad was "keeping fit," and *The Times* of London that November promoted "a great national effort to improve the physique of the nation"—picking the King as an example of the "fit" man.

The Irish Sweepstakes had become big business, and so had the football pools. Darts, a fixture of working class pubs, now became as upper class as bridge. There were more and more luxury movie houses being built. *The Count of Monte Cristo* was most popular of the Sunday radio serials. The cartoon image of England was David Low's bald, fat Colonel Blimp, with his walrus mustache and his cliché remarks on world issues in the *Evening Standard*. Jitterbugging had not yet arrived, but it soon would. The mood and tempo of England were now on a faster beat than the foxtrot.

There is no question that Edward VIII was in tune with this new mood. He was always ready to go somewhere else, try something new. Seated, he wanted to be up; up, he wanted to move. He would walk swiftly around a room, humming to himself, something popular or a Scottish folk tune. He was a "fit" man, with unlimited energy, clear eyes, healthy complexion. He loved flying and skiing and golf. And he saw Prime Minister Baldwin and his government as a collected group of fuddy-duddies who belonged to a different England of a different age. He now saw them as his enemies. "To use a good American expression," he told Wallis, "they are about to give me the works."[1]

Monckton had counseled delay, but the King wanted confrontation. Monckton implied that the King's decision might well have been pushed by Wallis Simpson. In his diary, he wrote, "I wanted him once more to wait and be patient, but he discussed the matter with Mrs. Simpson after leaving me and decided to send for Mr. Baldwin and tell him of his intention to marry."[2]

Her own description of her meeting with the King when he showed her the Hardinge letter revealed her as emotional and distraught. This is a probable picture. But Wallis long ago had been toughened and she had a fighting instinct. She also had a lot of common sense. It is quite conceivable that she saw the King's stubbornness as a major asset in any meeting with the Prime Minister.

November 16. The setting was somber; not The Fort but Buckingham Palace.

The King and Baldwin met that Monday evening, surrounded by history. The King made his point quickly. "I intend to marry Mrs. Simpson as soon as she is free to marry." He added that if he could marry her as king, it would make him a better king. If, however, the government opposed the marriage "then I was prepared to go."[3]

Baldwin had been puffing peacefully on his pipe, and the King's statement startled him.

"Sir," he said, "that is most grievous news, and it is impossible for me to make any comment on it today."[4]

The King watched Baldwin leave in his small black car, which looked to him like a "black beetle."[5]

The King's next meeting, two hours later, was more emotional, more difficult. Dressed in his white tie and tails, he appeared at Marlborough House to have dinner with his mother and sister Mary. There was the usual royal small talk about painting the outside of Buckingham Palace before the coronation and the record work of his mother's favorite charity, and then, after dinner, the King told them what was in his heart. At first, they seem sympathetic. Then, when he stressed his willingness to give up the throne, he could see the shock on their faces, the disbelief. The Dowager Queen Mary saw the monarchy as something sacred and the vital word in her life still was "Duty."

The King asked his mother to meet Wallis but she would not "unbend." Despite her distress, her control was complete and she made only a restrained effort to dissuade her son. He was still the King.

Years later, she would write him:

"You will remember how miserable I was when you informed me of your intended marriage and abdication, and how I implored you not to do so, for our sakes, and for the sake of the country. You did not seem to be able to take in any point of view but your own . . . I do not think you have ever realized the shock which the attitude you took up caused your family and the whole Nation. It seemed inconceivable to those who had made sacrifices during the war that you, as their King, refused a lesser sacrifice . . ."[6]

The Dowager Queen was driving alone with Lady Airlie and they saw a newspaper placard: DOES THE KING KNOW?[7]

"I suppose that means what people are saying about him?" Queen Mary burst out. "He won't believe it. It's no use telling him. The whole thing is too dreadful."[8]

Prime Minister Baldwin came to call on the Queen Mother the next morning, and she greeted him briskly by saying, "Well, Mr. Baldwin, this is a pretty kettle of fish!"[9]

Baldwin had maintained his reputation of not moving until he had to, but when he had to, he moved quickly. He called in Clement Attlee, leader of the opposition Labour Party, and asked for his party's judgment on the issue. Attlee said his people had no objection to an American becoming queen, but he added, "I was certain that they would not approve of Mrs. Simpson for that position."[10]

Baldwin knew that there was nothing in the British Constitution that prevented the King from marrying Wallis Simpson and making her his queen. He also knew that once the King was crowned, there was no legal power to force him to abdicate. His only threat was the resignation of his government, which would force the King to try to form another. Getting Attlee's backing meant that the King's job of forming another government would be almost impossible.

Wallis had never felt more isolated. The King told her little of his meeting with Baldwin and almost nothing of his dinner with his mother. It was almost as if he wanted to spare her anything but good news, and the news seemed all   bad. Wallis still felt then that his power as king was much greater than it was. He insisted to her that he would work things out in his own way, and she had to believe him. She also wanted to believe him. But she had no real knowledge of what was going on, or the growing size of the issues. It was like being alone on an empty street, feeling the first shaking of an earthquake and not knowing what would fall first.

"Had a long talk with Sibyl [Colefax]," Harold Nicolson recorded in his diary. "She had been spending last Sunday down at Fort Belvedere with nobody else there beyond a new naval equerry and Mrs. Simpson. She had a heart-to-heart talk with the latter and found her really miserable. All sorts of people had come to her reminding her of her duty and begging her to leave the country. 'They do not understand,' she said, 'that if I did so, the King would come after me regardless of anything. They would then get their scandal in a far worse form than they are getting it now.' Sibyl then asked her whether the King had ever suggested marriage. She seemed surprised, and said, 'Of course not.' Sibyl then suggested that it would be a good thing if certain Cabinet Members were told of this, and were in a position to deny the story of an impending marriage. Mrs. Simpson readily agreed to this and authorized Sibyl to see Neville Chamberlain. Unfortunately Neville is ill in bed with gout; but Sibyl was able to send him a message through Mrs. Chamberlain and derived the distinct impression that Baldwin had been told by the King that he was determined to marry Mrs. Simpson after the Coronation. Sibyl agrees with me that Mrs. Simpson is perfectly straightforward and well-intentioned, and that it is quite possible for the King to have spoken to Baldwin before raising the matter with Wallis herself . . ."[11]

There is no better evidence than this of Wallis Simpson's political naïveté. She knew that the King had told Baldwin about their proposed marriage. Could she actually believe that Baldwin would *not* confide this information to his Cabinet ministers, particularly to his potential successor, Neville Chamberlain? This was not even a point of politics; it was basic common sense. Was she so distraught that she had lost hers? Being cut off from all information, being pressed by well-meaning friends, did this contribute to her air of near panic?

218

It was one thing for her not to tell Lady Sibyl Colefax that the King wanted to marry her; it was quite another thing to agree to let Lady Colefax tell this to Cabinet ministers.

The King had his own distressing concerns; he had to break the news to his three brothers, individually. His brother Bertie took it the worst. Bertie, the Duke of York, would succeed him as king were he to abdicate. Bertie, so shy, with his serious stammer, could not even say what he felt.

None of this could interfere with the King's calendar of duties. Thirty hours after he saw Baldwin, he was on his way to South Wales for a two-day inspection trip of the impoverished mining towns.

It had been a generation since the nervous young man had been crowned Prince of Wales at nearby Carnarvon Castle. There was no pageantry now in the hillsides of black slag and the dingy houses of Pontypridd and Cwmbran and Blaenavon in the Rhondda and Monmouth valleys of Wales.

Rhondda was once a coal-mining hub and now the towering chimneys were smokeless, the machinery rusty, the people bleak and despairing. The two twelve-mile-long valleys, separated by a thousand-foot ridge, were dotted with tiny grimy towns full of ill-paved streets and ugly hovels. These were the "tragic valleys" because foreign tariffs had caused oil to replace coal. A young man said he had never had a job. The frowning King said, "Terrible . . . terrible . . ."[12]

Dowlais, "the blackest spot in Wales," once had a mighty iron and steel works that used to employ 9,000. "Eight years ago," said a government official, "its furnaces lit up the entire countryside. Now . . . every family is on relief."[13]

The King said, "Something must be done!"

The welcoming signs in the windows were pathetic.

HELP US, OUR NOBLE KING! and THIS IS A POOR TOWN, LOYAL.[14] And there were clusters of wildflowers decorating the doors and faded British flags fluttering on broomsticks.

A group of Welsh unemployed handed the King a letter:

"This is a stricken valley," it read. "Slighted by the dead hand of poverty . . . Our women grow prematurely old . . . Our children are stunted. . . . Will an impoverished people be able joyfully to celebrate Your Majesty's Coronation?"[15]

After hours of this, the King called P. Malcolm Stewart to a conference in Mountain Ash. Stewart was a dapper, square-jawed former commissioner for South Wales whom the people called "Prime Minister of Straightforwardness," making a play upon his initials. Stewart had resigned two weeks earlier because the government had flatly rejected his plan to revive Welsh prosperity, building plants to extract oil from coal, giving tax incentives to new industries.

The King's Welsh tour hit a political nerve. The "Something must be done!" phrase made the headlines all over Great Britain. The British public was stirred by the idea that they had a new kind of king on the throne. Twenty-four hours later, Chancellor of the Exchequer Neville Chamberlain ordered a new study of Stewart's proposal and promised, ". . . We will carry out any of them which may seem useful . . ."[16] Privately, Chamberlain was incensed at this popular picture of a sensitive king and an insensitive government. Reporting in the *Daily Herald*, Hannen Swaffer described a dinner that night with the King "banging his fist on the table with insistence," saying that something would be done.

Baldwin feared political consequences, and he was right. Labour MPs in the House of Commons called for quick legislation to attract industry to South Wales. The King had become labor's champion against the forces of wealth and power. Newspapers used the phrase "Populist King." Respected papers such as the *News Chronicle* wrote, "The King is above and outside politics. What he has done is in the sole interest of truth and public services . . . The man in the street feels that Whitehall stands condemned . . ."

The King's stand was not a new social consciousness. During the depression he had talked to a man at Tyneside who had been out of work for five years. "What response could I make to that tragic disclosure? That the Monarchy was not responsible for his plight? That the Government was doing all it could? That he only had to be patient? What possible solace could that have given to a man who has been on the dole for five years?"

The King's tour and his statements did not endear him to the government leadership now pondering the Simpson affair. The *Daily Telegraph* warned that grave damage would result if the King's visit was represented as "a rebuke to ministerial authority." The inference was that the King had stepped out of his royal bounds. Chamberlain's anger was typical. Conservative Party leaders who had felt a certain sympathy for the King and Mrs. Simpson now hardened against him. They wanted a decorative king, a unifying king, not a troublemaker. A royal lion with teeth was potentially dangerous.

Wallis then had a visitor, Esmond Harmsworth, the chairman of the Newspapers Proprietors Association, the man who had helped Beaverbrook and Monckton arrange the "gentlemen's agreement" to silence the press. His father was Lord Rothermere, publisher of the *Daily Mail*, one of the few papers to champion the King.

Harmsworth was the first to broach the possibility of a morganatic marriage. This is a form of marriage historically used in Europe between a male member of a royal house and a woman who is a commoner. The wife does not take the husband's rank, and their children do not succeed to his titles. Since the British Constitution did not recognize such a marriage, it would require special legislation.

Wallis liked the idea and promised to discuss it with His Majesty.

Some time later Anne Fremantle wrote that she remembered her cousin Harry, who was lord lieutenant of Monmouthshire in Wales, complaining that the King, instead of spending the night with him as protocol dictated, "insisted on sleeping in his train with Mrs. Simpson . . ."[17]

The train trip to Wales takes only three hours and Wallis might have come for a quick visit and returned to London the next morning. She might well have wanted to tell the King about Harmsworth's new idea, but the King did not like the idea, mainly because it demeaned Wallis. The last such morganatic marriage in the royal family had been ninety years earlier. But he told Wallis, "I'll try anything in the spot I'm in now."[18] He then authorized Monckton to check on the legal precedents and possibilities, and he authorized Harmsworth to suggest the idea to Baldwin. Harmsworth reported that Baldwin was willing to consider the idea, but seemed unenthusiastic.

The night the King returned from Wales, Wallis already had left for dinner, not expecting him so soon. The King then invited Aunt Bessie to dine with him. Aunt Bessie felt then, as she told him later, that she hoped he would not abdicate, that she knew Wallis could make him happy, but he should consider carefully before choosing his personal happiness before the wishes of his country.

The more Wallis thought of morganatic marriage, the more she liked it. She knew that royalty was forced to walk a constitutional tightrope, strictly limited in their movement and action, and that they had a world audience that never stopped watching. If the British Empire was a myth preserved by an emotion, then its king must maintain this balance. Royalty were born and trained to be ropewalkers; they knew how instinctively. Wallis had tried, but she didn't like it.

The focus was too sharp and the strain was too much. She liked the position and the prestige, but she hated the formality and stiffness. She was a natural woman who liked her freedom. As queen, she would be poured into a plaster form. As a morganatic wife of a king, she would be the most socially powerful woman in the British Empire. More than that, she knew, better than anybody, the King's dependence on her judgment and her will. As his wife, she would be more than a queen and she would give him enough of her force to make him a better king.

Morganatic marriage had been a German idea. German royal families made a particular point of equality by birth, *Ebenbürtigkeit*. Only by such equality, they thought, could there be a complete and perfect marriage. Royal "house laws" on a morganatic marriage specified that no other marriage could take place during the lifetime of the contracting parties.

Technically, there were no British precedents. The closest case in the royal family was in 1847 when the Duke of Cambridge married an actress, Louisa Fairbrother, who already had borne him two sons. This was not morganatic because his father, George III, had refused to grant him permission to marry and therefore, according to the Royal Marriage Act of 1772, he was not legally married at all.

All Wallis knew of morganatic marriage was that it was something that had happened to the Hapsburgs. The Hapsburg slogan: "Let others wage war; thou, happy Austria, marry." The British, however, associated morganatic marriages with rulers such as Carol II of Rumania, who dissolved his morganatic marriage to marry a Greek princess and then left her to elope with Madame Lupescu. The King felt the whole concept was "strange and almost inhuman,"[19] but at Wallis' insistence he was willing to consider it as a possibility.

Walter Monckton had advised the King that "even in the unlikely event of the Cabinet approving a morganatic marriage, special legislation would be required, and the prospect of such a bill's ever passing Parliament was dubious."[20] Beyond that, the approval of the cabinets of the eleven Dominions was required.

The politically naïve King felt his great power was in the Dominions, because of his personal popularity. The decision, however, was not a decision of the people. It was a decision of the cabinets, and the King was much more popular with coalminers than political leaders, whom he had made little attempt to befriend.

He consulted Sir Samuel Hoare, first lord of the Admiralty, and

Hoare was sympathetic but convinced that Great Britain and the Dominions would never accept Mrs. Simpson as queen because of her divorces, that the Baldwin Cabinet was a stone wall of opposition. That same day the King visited Alfred Duff Cooper, minister of war. Cooper, who had gone with him on the *Nahlin* cruise, also urged patience, suggesting he go through the coronation, let the issues settle, then marry whom he pleased.

The King ignored Hoare's warning, rejected Duff Cooper's advice and then put his head on the chopping block. He asked Prime Minister Baldwin to come to see him.

Get Your $10,000 Post Insurance Policy—See Page 32

Sports Edition ★★★★★★★ COMPLETE FINANCIAL	**New York Post**	Sports Edition ★★★★★★★ COMPLETE FINANCIAL

THREE 3 CENTS   FRIDAY, DECEMBER 4, 1936   THREE 3 CENTS

CAN'T BE KING AND MARRY, EDWARD TOLD—WALLIS FLEES

THEIR EYES GAZE INTO THE FUTURE

BALDWIN ISSUES ULTIMATUM IN COMMONS SPEECH

Premier Says Morganatic Wedding Is Impossible—Goes to See King —Resignation Possible

LONDON, Dec. 4 (UP)—Members of the royal family, bitterly opposed to King Edward's apparent determination to fight for the right to marry Wallis Simpson, were reported today to be ready to desert England. Should the King undertake to make his romance the subject of an election, it was said, Queen Mary threatened to retire into grief-stricken seclusion for the rest of her life.

The Duke and Duchess of York, heirs to the throne, were said to be ready to leave the country. Other brothers of the King were represented as taking a similar attitude.

BRITISH SHIP HELD —REBELS ACCUSED

WPA PROJECT HEAD RESIGNS

MRS. SIMPSON FLEES TO FRANCE

Bronx Lyons Roars Back At Britain's

Lon... Also Hears Spanish Fas- ...ook Russian Stea ...

Protests Layoff Policy as Workers End Stay-In

Pauses at Rouen, Then Motors to an Unknown Destination

Borough President James J. Lyons of The Bronx today introduced a measure at a meeting of the Board

LONDON, Dec. 4 (AP)—Prime Minister Stanley Baldwin told the House of Commons today that the Government will not give its consent to King Edward to marry Wallis Warfield Simpson and have the throne.

Baldwin already had talked to the Labour Party leader, Clement Attlee, who assured him that, "despite the sympathy felt for King Edward and the affection his visits to the depressed areas had created, the party—with the exception of a few of the intelligentsia who can be trusted to take the wrong view on any subject—were in agreement with the views I expressed." His views: They would object to a morganatic marriage. Baldwin next sought out the Liberal Party leader, Archibald Sinclair. Sinclair agreed completely with Attlee and Baldwin.

Baldwin now could operate from strength. He had isolated the

King. The King could still marry whom he wanted, but the Baldwin government would then resign and neither Attlee nor Sinclair would agree to form another government.

Discussing the morganatic idea with his secretary, Tom Jones, Baldwin said, "Is this the sort of thing I've stood for in public life? If I have to go out, as go I must, then I'd be quite ready to go out on this."[21] He knew, of course, even as he said it, that he had the full support of his Cabinet and the opposition leaders, that he could easily carry the issue in the House of Commons; he knew he would not have to go out at all. Backed by this knowledge, Baldwin came to Buckingham Palace to meet the King.

It was November 26. The King asked Baldwin what he thought of morganatic marriage. Picking his words carefully, Baldwin answered that he had not yet "considered it." However, he said, if the King wanted his "horseback opinion," he firmly felt that Parliament would never pass such a bill.

The King asked if he was certain of this.

"Sir, would you like me to examine the proposition formally?"[22]

It was a crucial question. Until that moment, the King was his own man. The Prime Minister could discuss and advise, but not enforce. The King's agreement for a formal examination of the subject had a deeper meaning. It meant that he could not seek "advice" elsewhere, that he was respectfully bound to accept the "advice" of the government as its formal will and decision. And, as the Prime Minister explained, a formal examination of the question meant consultation with the Dominion cabinets as well as the British Cabinet.

"Yes, please do so," insisted the King.[23]

Although he did not know it, that phrase signaled the end of his royal future.

The next day Beaverbrook called on the King. He had gone to the United States and the King had asked him to return immediately.

Beaverbrook's friendship with Edward had never been marked, nor was he imbued with any special fervor for monarchy. "I asked Beaverbrook," wrote Randolph Churchill, "why, if he was so far from being a monarchist and one who scarcely knew the King, he had put himself to so much trouble on his behalf. He replied laconically: 'To bugger Baldwin.' "[24]

The hate there was deep. It had begun as a fight between them in the Conservative Party with Beaverbrook backing Empire preference

224

against Baldwin's belief in free trade. It then grew into a struggle for party control. Baldwin's predecessor Bonar Law had made Beaverbrook privy to inside information, and Baldwin ended this practice. Speaking of Beaverbrook and Rothermere, Baldwin called them press barons not worth bothering about. "They are both men I would not have in my house,"[25] he said. In a speech on behalf of Duff Cooper, Baldwin lashed out at both men.

"What are their methods? Their methods are direct falsehoods, misrepresentation, half-truths . . . What the proprietorship of these papers is aiming at is power, and power without responsibility—the prerogative of the harlot throughout the ages."[26]

The last dramatic phrase came from Baldwin's first cousin, Rudyard Kipling. It was a phrase Beaverbrook and Rothermere never forgot, or forgave.

Beaverbrook urged the King to withdraw his request for permission to make a morganatic marriage. He wanted the King to keep his throne at all costs, marry the woman he loved and let Baldwin resign. He believed that it would be possible then to form a King's Party, drawing strength from Tories, Socialists and Liberals, and that both major parties would hesitate to let this upheaval happen, "that the King had only to persevere in order to prevail."

Beaverbrook also proposed that the King let him and Rothermere and other friendly publishers begin their press campaign to bring the King's case to the people.

The King hesitated.

"His anxiety was intense, but he was anxious about the wrong things," Beaverbrook noted. "All his energies should have been devoted to the main issue, which was the struggle to remain on the Throne and to marry in due time. If he had carried out a well organized campaign, he would have attained his end and finished Baldwin politically forever. But he was preoccupied with other things, principally with protecting Mrs. Simpson from hostile publicity, or indeed from publicity of any kind, at whatever cost or sacrifice."[27]

Beaverbrook had met Wallis once. He saw her as a simple woman, plainly dressed, "and I was not attracted to her style of hair-dressing."[28]

"Her smile was kindly and pleasing, and her conversation was interspersed with protestations of ignorance of politics and with declarations of simplicity of character and outlook, with a claim of inexperience in worldly affairs."[29]

Beaverbrook, however, was careful to observe that she did engage in political conversation at one time in the evening "and then she showed a liberal outlook, well maintained in discussion, and based on a conception which was sound."[30]

He was also interested in the fact that there were six women at the dinner, and five of them greeted Wallis Simpson with a kiss. "She received it with appropriate dignity, but in no case did she return it."[31]

The King had kept much of his political maneuverings away from Wallis, but that evening they discussed the morganatic marriage at length.

"When the King telephoned me late at night," said Beaverbrook, "and told me Mrs. Simpson preferred morganatic marriage to becoming Queen, I knew my urgings were in vain. The morganatic marriage was what Mrs. Simpson wanted, and what Mrs. Simpson wanted was what the King wanted."[32]

Beaverbrook was absolutely right. Wallis could not and would not seriously advise him on alternate parliamentary ploys because she understood none of it. But she did fully grasp the significance of being a freer, more flexible power behind the throne without the disadvantage of sitting on it, in full and constant view of the world. On this she could take her stand, and the King was happy to oblige her. The mere fact that he was still maneuvering for alternative solutions indicated clearly that he was in no hurry to abandon the kingship. And neither was she.

She now knew that she was a notorious lady. Cumberland Terrace had become a tourist attraction and she hated to go out. Then came the threatening letters, ugly ones. Finally the King himself received word of a threat to blow up her house and called her quickly to suggest that she and Aunt Bessie move to The Fort for a while, and not tell anyone where they were going. He came around himself to get them.

Before this, Wallis had maintained a pretense of normalcy. She so convinced everybody that there was not the remote possibility of marriage that Harold Nicolson recorded in his diary, "I believe quite sincerely that the King has proposed to Mr. Baldwin and has not proposed to Wallis. I feel unhappy about the whole thing. I got such a sensible letter from her today."[33]

It was such a game, such a romantic game!

Friends of theirs at the time insist they "never acted like people who wanted to overthrow the Church of England. They acted like a couple in love who wanted to get married, and were plainly horrified by the momentous events this simple desire had set in motion."[34]

"They seemed to think you could leave the throne of England the way you get up out of a chair and you couldn't help loving them for it, they were honestly so damn naïve."[35]

Not everybody loved them for it, and least of all the Duchess of York. If the King abdicated, her husband would succeed to the throne. She was concerned about her husband's health, his physical ability to cope with the crown.

The King and Wallis arrived unexpectedly at Windsor Castle for tea one day and the governess for the two children, Elizabeth and Margaret, observed her with interest. "She was a smart, attractive woman, already middle-aged, but with that intimate friendliness American women have. She appeared to be entirely at her ease; if anything, rather too much so. She had a distinctly proprietary way of speaking to the King. I remember she drew him to the window and suggested how certain trees might be moved, and a part of the hill taken away to improve the view."[36]

"Crawfie, who is she?" asked Elizabeth.

Governess Marion Crawford later heard the Duchess of York say sadly, "We must take what is coming to us, and make the best of it."[37]

Making the best of it was a great strain on the King and Wallis, too. The King shielded her as much as he could from the bad news, but she knew him so well now that she could tell simply by looking at him, no matter how hard he tried to conceal it. A friend noted:

"I saw the King and Wallis during that time, and I never saw two people so *tired*. He was tired from his long battle to make Wallis Queen, which he was absolutely determined to do, and she was tired from trying to please him and please everybody else too. They both acted like zombies when other people were around, and the only time they showed a spark of the old liveliness was when they were alone together. I know, because I looked out of a window once and happened to see them alone. I give you my word, they looked like *kids*."[38]

A Dr. Arthur Frank Payne diagnosed for a New York newspaper that all indications revealed to him that the King was on the verge of a nervous breakdown and that his love for Wallis Simpson proved to be the exact psychological medicine that saved him.

There was no disagreement that Wallis was the King's balance wheel. So often they felt that they were two alone against the world. Wallis described the change at The Fort. From an enchanted castle, it had become a beleaguered one. Jock McGovern, Labour MP, brought before the House of Commons the question of whether it was wise for the government to spend money on coronation plans "in view of the gambling going on at Lloyd's over whether this Coronation ever would take place." The King, meanwhile, kept up with his duties and appointments. He even vetoed the buttons and color and cut of some of the Coronation Guards' uniforms.

The British Cabinet met in special session on Friday, November 27, to hear Baldwin's full story of the affair for the first time. He told them that he felt the morganatic marriage was both undesirable and impracticable and that the government must choose: accept the King's wife as queen or accept his abdication. The King opened his red box the next day to read the minutes of the secret meeting, but found them blank on the question.

Filling him in on what had happened, Beaverbrook emphasized that the King had put his head on the execution block. "All that Baldwin has to do now is to swing the axe."[39]

Beaverbrook wholly believed that the plot against the King was primarily directed by Baldwin, Geoffrey Dawson and the Archbishop of Canterbury. The King believed it, too. But the three men were such kindred spirits that no plot was necessary. None of them wanted Wallis Simpson as queen or as a morganatic wife of their king. They believed such a marriage would severely damage the unity of the British Empire. The Archbishop, moreover, saw it as a serious blow to the church. If the King wanted Wallis, they did not want the King.

The Archbishop, who had kept in the background, now emerged. He met often with Baldwin, Dawson and Hardinge. Hardinge had never resigned, never discussed his letter with the King, but had continued to work on the King's daily business. When the King asked Monckton to visit he always had him come by a circuitous route of stairways and elevators so that he would not pass by Hardinge's office. But Hardinge always seemed to know when he was there and invited him to come and drink and talk. The two men were old friends from Harrow. Monckton and Baldwin were also old friends, both on the board of governors at Harrow. The old school tie kept the conversations cozy, but they changed no results. Monckton had made it clear that everything was tending toward abdication.

228

So there was no need for a political plot. The King not only had boxed himself in, but had provided the box. The Archbishop had had a sense that circumstances might change, and they were changing.

The King's political friends became fewer as the issue became sharper.

"That man has done more harm to his country than any man in history,"[40] former prime minister and Labour leader Ramsay MacDonald told a friend. While Labour leaders liked the King's open sympathy for the workers, they worried that he might open the royal populist pattern for future kings. They foresaw a similar time when a more conservative monarch might continue the precedent and act against Labour.

Ramsay MacDonald's more specific concern was the effect of the affair on American, Canadian and British prestige. Nor did he feel that the British people were with the King on this issue. "The upper classes mind her being an American more than they mind her being divorced. The lower classes do not mind her being an American but they loathe the idea that she has had two husbands already."[41]

Wallis did have a handful of friends canvassing the establishment on her behalf. Lady Oxford, the former Margot Asquith, spent some time with Geoffrey Dawson and was "full of Mrs. S's good sense and good influence on H.M. and seemed to think even now that their relations need never provoke public comment."[42]

The comment, however, was coming, and soon.

"The *Times* had kept silence now for something like three months in the face of a great deal of pressure and ridicule from both sides of the Atlantic," Dawson wrote in his diary. "I had always felt very strongly that we must be the first to speak. The rest of the Press has quite openly been looking to us for a lead . . ."[43]

The press explosion was already primed.

His Majesty, meanwhile, kept telling Wallis that there was still hope, that nothing was final, that he hadn't stopped trying.

His equerry, Colonel Piers Legh, noted his nervousness, the way he constantly changed the carnation in his buttonhole. "He just kept putting in one, ripping it out ten minutes later, and putting a fresh one in. It nearly drove me crazy, but of course he obviously didn't know he was doing it."[44]

Wallis still found herself besieged by British friends begging her to give up the King. Walter Monckton wrote in his diary, "The easy view is that she should have made him give her up. But I never knew any man whom it would have been harder to get rid of."[45]

Privately, Monckton told a friend that the King would have committed suicide rather than give up Wallis Simpson.

20

VICTORIA REGINA WAS PLAYING in New York with Helen Hayes in the part of Queen Victoria. In an opening scene, the Queen said, "British Kings have married commoners in the past, and they better do it again."

The audience burst into wild applause.

At the same time, at the Empire Theatre in Leicester Square in London, there was the American movie *Libelled Lady*. At the end of the film, one of the actresses said, "What do you mean? I have been divorced from Simpson for three years!" There wasn't even a murmur from the audience at the coincidence of the name "Simpson" and "divorce."[1] The British public was still unaware of the whole affair. The blackout of the press was still complete.

American magazines still had all references to the Simpson affair torn out before they were circulated in Britain. *Esquire* magazine published a short story with a character named Mrs. Simpson, and that, too, was torn out.

People all over the United States were interviewed for their opinions. A Mrs. Rita Carle in Washington, D.C., said: "I think it would be perfectly wonderful to have her Queen exactly 200 years after 1776. After all, she comes from the aristocracy of Baltimore."[2] Frances Burn, a dancer at the Earle Theatre, also in Washington, said: "From her pictures, she's attractive, but not beautiful. She must have 'something.' It must be terrific. I wish I knew what it was."[3] And Beatrice Abbott added: "Whenever a door is closed behind the two, the reading public snickers. For all we know, they may be playing tiddle-de-winks."[4]

Mariana Sands, the daughter of Admiral Fulham, told reporters,

"I haven't had a great many women friends. As an Admiral's daughter, brought up in naval bases and with the Navy, I have known men much better than women. But if I had to be cast away on a desert island for a year with only a woman for company, of all the women I have ever known, I would choose Wallis Simpson because of her vitality, her gaiety, her real understanding of companionship and conversation."[5]

The Maryland legislature proposed a resolution granting permission to the King of England to marry the "distinguished lady from Maryland."

A forceful American newspaperman, Jack Beall of the New York *Herald Tribune*, managed to get one of the few interviews with Wallis Simpson. She told him, "I think it is terrible the way the papers in America have been treating me."[6]

Beall asked her whether she thought the matter was going to interfere with the coronation. "No, I don't think it will." Then she added quickly, "No, I can't say anything about that, really."[7]

Beall then remarked, "Did you know, Mrs. Simpson, that they have organized in America a 'Simpson for Queen' movement?"

Wallis Simpson burst into laughter and all she could say was "Oh no!" and "Not really?"[8]

Wallis was so concerned about the American press that she invited Newbold Noyes, then an associate editor of the Washington *Star,* to come and report her side of the story. Noyes had married her cousin Lelia Barnett, and she had known him since she was eighteen.

Noyes tried to reassure her that at least 70 percent of American newspaper articles were favorable to her. She was hard to convince because of the many threats and hate letters she had received. "It isn't that I'm afraid of threats like that but I'm sorry that people feel that way. If they knew the truth, I'm sure they'd feel differently."[9]

"The Wallis Simpson I recalled was carefree and laughing, some jest always on her lips," wrote Noyes. "The Wallis Simpson I found was still as gay, still as witty, but now she smiles more often than she laughs and the occasional faraway look in her eyes hints of cares that never show on the surface."[10]

She was then wearing a brocaded gown, black and sleeveless and close-fitting, with a high, square-cut neck, a dazzling bracelet of diamonds and rubies, the rubies in her ears in an old-fashioned setting. Fastened at her waist were two orchids. She wore no rings.

"The poise of her head upon a slender and well-modeled neck, typical of her whole bone structure, is lovely and proud," Noyes wrote. "She has what the French call 'fine points'—slim ankles and wrists. Her hands are strong and capable, with not very long fingers. Her feet are quite tiny. Her figure is trim, but in no sense boyish. She moves like an eager thoroughbred."[11]

Noyes listed five predominating characteristics of her personality: companionability, loyalty, simplicity, vitality and naturalness. In addition, he included the capacity of being a good listener as well as a good talker, the ability to laugh at the right places, "and her laughter is genuine."[12]

Madame Schiaparelli put it more simply: "She's always go-go."[13]

"Some say she is a saint," commented Lord Ponsonby on Wallis, whom he had never met. "Others say she is an adventuress. Neither is true, I'm sure. But there is no doubt that she has caused the most remarkable situation to arise in the British Monarchy."[14]

The noted author H. G. Wells wrote for the American press, "I never have yet heard one single word or suggestion that she was anything but a perfectly honorable, highly intelligent, and charmingly mannered woman. Why shouldn't the King marry her and make her his Queen? . . . Mrs. Simpson is far better fitted to be the King's wife than any possible bride that might be forced upon him to replace her."

And about the King, Wells felt, " 'Authorities' do not like him. People in privileged positions shiver slightly at the report of him. He flies about in airplanes, arrives unexpectedly, and looks at things, instead of traveling in a special train . . . He betrays the possession of a highly modernized mind by his every act, he is unceremonious, he is unconventional, and he asks the most disconcerting questions about social conditions. . . . They know quite clearly within themselves that, if he cannot be humiliated and discredited into political impotence by forcing him to renounce, in most glaring publicity, his desire to marry this excellent consort, they would be happier without him."[15]

It all was very true. The circle immediately around the royal hub was most anxious to get rid of this king. Lady Nancy Astor, who had known the King from his "princing" days, felt she could talk to him frankly about this. An American from Virginia who had become more British than the British, and even a member of Parliament, Lady Astor later admitted, "I went to see him myself and begged him not to do as

233

he was doing." When the begging didn't succeed, she "spoke hotly and loudly."[16]

Lady Astor represented a unique segment of opinion. The visitor books at her Cliveden estate cut across class and politics. Here came the prime ministers, the important editors, the budding politicians, the socialists and the fascists. *Times* editor Geoffrey Dawson was a frequent visitor. Yet, out of this melange came a predominant impression that a great part of the Cliveden set, Geoffrey Dawson among them, felt that Hitler's demands were "reasonable" and should be appeased. Baldwin and Neville Chamberlain seemed to share this view.

Harold Nicolson called Lady Astor "a kindly but inordinately foolish woman" with "a subversive influence." "The harm which these silly, selfish hostesses do is really immense. They convey to foreign envoys the impression that policy is decided in their own drawing rooms ... they create an atmosphere of authority and responsibility and grandeur, whereas the whole thing is a mere flatulence of the spirit."[17]

It was sometimes more than that. Nicolson himself recorded in his diary a clandestine meeting of Herr von Ribbentrop and some Cabinet ministers, from which "the German Ambassador did acquire the idea that there existed an influential minority in England prepared, if only the British Empire were left undisturbed, to accord Nazi Germany a free hand against Russia, and the resultant mastery of Europe."[18]

This Cliveden set was the same group that "the small, pretty, red-haired" Ellen Wilkinson, Labour member of Parliament, accused of using Mrs. Simpson's "influence over King Edward for their own purposes."[19]

It made small sense, however, that this same group of pro-German political figures in the establishment would therefore try to force the abdication of a pro-German king.

Of all people, no political leader wanted war with Germany less than Stanley Baldwin. His secretary, Tom Jones, had gone to see Hitler to arrange a Hitler-Baldwin meeting. The meeting never took place because Baldwin did not want to fly and "did not much like the sea."

The King's views toward Germany were much closer to Baldwin's than they were to Churchill's.

The weekend of November 28, the King and Wallis went to The Fort, though never again would it be a retreat of peace or quiet. Couriers came and went, and the King found it increasingly necessary to excuse himself from Wallis for still another meeting in another room. The outside world was no longer outside. The King no longer tried to hide the gravity of the situation but he still tried to save Wallis the details. He would only tell her that "nothing is yet final."[20]

This only accentuated her anguish. She always had a worry-prone imagination, and now she had everything available to feed it. The worst of it was her feeling of uselessness. The snowball had become an avalanche and she felt too small to fight the whole British Empire. The King was too agitated to give her a short course on the British Constitution and Monckton had been told to keep his secrets from her.

Aunt Bessie tried to mollify Wallis, keep her on an even keel. She dredged up all the funny stories, the memories of the young years. She tried to inject her common sense into this seemingly senseless situation. Most of all, she offered tea and sympathy, and love. She became mother and sister and friend. Wallis needed all of them.

On Saturday, Geoffrey Dawson received a note from Monckton and Hardinge, urging that he maintain press silence on the subject. Dawson had put several needles in print, but they were as thin as they were sharp, obvious only to those who were "in" on the happenings. On the appointment of a governor general of the Union of South Africa, Dawson editorialized on the importance of keeping the crown and its representatives remote from "glaring public scandal." And in his survey on parliamentary affairs of the week, he had a sentence inserted about the House of Commons "proving itself a Council of State which is able to demonstrate its solid strength in any crisis which may arise, whether foreign or domestic."

Dawson visited the Archbishop of Canterbury on Sunday afternoon "and found him very anxious, as he was bound to be."[21] The white-haired, thin-lipped Archbishop was fully aware of the King's final crisis. On Monday afternoon, November 30, Dawson checked with Baldwin. "The Dominion replies were coming in, and were all confirming S.B.'s views that 'morganatic' legislation was impossible anywhere in the Empire."[22]

Monckton later noted that "The King never set high hopes on securing legislation on the morganatic marriage,"[23] but remarks from the King indicated that he had, indeed, set the highest hopes on it.

Monckton earlier had felt impelled to present to the King his collected observations based on a broad range of discussion with leaders on all sides.

"People do understand the strength of the tie which holds you two together, and they appreciate what an appalling sacrifice is asked of both of you if you are to carry on alone. But they think that even so, you cannot throw up the job without letting the whole side down irretrievably in the eyes of the whole world."[24]

Even as he wrote this, Monckton knew that Edward VIII was long past such appeal.

The King came to Wallis, more visibly crushed than ever. His options were fewer. The doors were all closing. He knew the people loved him, if he could only somehow let them know exactly how he felt.

Wallis listened, wondering, and an idea suddenly stirred within her. She knew how hostile the American press was to President Franklin D. Roosevelt, and how he reached beyond them by going on the radio with his "fireside chats." The King was absolutely marvelous on radio. She had heard him. His voice had a moving quality. Why not? Why shouldn't he do it? The people would respond, she knew they would. He could talk to them from his heart, as he had talked to her. Wasn't it worth trying?

The King listened to her entranced. Of course. That was it. The people *would* listen, and they would understand. It wasn't a political problem; it was a human problem. Of course, he would have to get parliamentary permission to make the speech, but how could they deny it to him?

He was fervid in his excitement, kissed her appreciatively and hurried off to his study.

Much has been made of the theory that His Majesty really didn't want to be king, that he used the Simpson affair as an excuse to get out. He had said elsewhere that a king could only advise, encourage and mourn.

Bored as he often was with it, though, he had been born and bred to it. It was not easy to let go. The letters "R.I." after his signature meant *Rex Imperator*—"King Emperor." Where can you go after you've been on top of the mountain? What would he do with the rest of his life?

There was also this: he knew how much Wallis wanted him to stay on as king; he knew how romantic it all was to her; he knew how she gloried in the glamour of her position.

If they were together, the *Rex Imperator* could be exciting, and maybe even important. With her strength and her encouragement and

236

her energy and her love, he could give the kingship a dimension it had not had in centuries. Perhaps he *could* be a populist king?

Without her, it would have no meaning.

So, for his heritage, for her, for his vision, he clung tenaciously to the crown. He did this in his own instinctive, often immature way, without taking the best advice even of those who wished to support him.

"I told my brothers, my mother and even my Prime Minister not to come near me because I didn't want them involved in this. It was my decision. I made it, and that's the way it should have been."[25]

The elderly but still potent Lloyd George, who would have been one of his staunchest supporters, had gone to the West Indies long before the Simpson storm broke. He did send back a message: "A nation has a right to choose its Queen, but the King also has a right to choose his own life; if Baldwin is against them, I am against Baldwin."[26]

Winston Churchill, whose earlier support might have been most valuable, had been briefed by Beaverbrook, but kept to the sidelines. And the King still refused Beaverbrook's persistent plea to let him launch a campaign to the people, to arouse a public rally to the King.

Then the dam broke. Or, as a wit put it: "Then came a blow with a Blunt instrument."

Blunt was the name of the Bishop of Bradford in Yorkshire, a personal friend of the Queen Mother. Dr. A. M. F. Blunt was scheduled to speak to his diocesan conference on the coming coronation. He had been to London, a conference called by the Archbishop of Canterbury, and the Archbishop had confided his fears about the contemplated morganatic marriage. Blunt also had met with Baldwin, who seemed similarly worried about growing press support for a morganatic marriage. In his speech, Bishop Blunt sternly said that the King should be commended to God's grace, which he would need abundantly to do his duty faithfully. "We hope that he is aware of his need. Some of us wish he gave more positive signs of his awareness."

When an explosion is primed, the smallest spark can set it off. Bishop Blunt afterward said he only meant to chide the King for not being a devout churchgoer. The Yorkshire *Post*, however, saw in the speech a resentment against the Simpson affair, and editorialized on it in full. Had the editor of the Yorkshire *Post*, Arthur Mann, not circulated a copy of his article to the London morning newspapers, the King might have had a few days more grace.

That was Wednesday, December 2, and the self-controlled British press exploded. Dawson felt the hour was too late to give the story its proper treatment the next day, and so contacted the other London editors to make sure that they, too, were waiting. Besides printing the Blunt speech. *The Times* of London restricted itself to publishing a prophetic leading article on the wonderful reception that the Duke and Duchess of York received in Edinburgh. It was more than a coincidence. It discussed "the special affection for the Prince in whose posterity another race of Scottish descent may someday be called to the Imperial Throne."

Wallis and the King expected their whole world to end the next day.

Shortly before the storm broke in the British press on the Simpson affair, there was an interesting aside. Watchful reporters discovered Ernest Aldrich Simpson at Southampton waiting at the dock to meet Mary Kirk Raffray, who had gone home to complete arrangements for her divorce from Jacques Raffray. Simpson and Mary traveled to London in the same railway compartment, then separated on the platform of Waterloo Station, ran out by separate doors, jumped into the same taxi and curled up together on the floor to hide from reporters. When the newsmen found them and begged them to sit up and show themselves, they did so, screaming with laughter.

Mary Kirk alone had managed to pull Ernest Simpson out of his deep depression, out of his growing stolidity. One of the reasons he had married Wallis was to get some of that spirit, and it was one of the reasons he would marry Mary Kirk as soon as they were both free.

Despite any understanding Simpson may have had with Mary Kirk, he still felt it necessary to do a most unusual thing. Simpson, the naturalized subject, loved Great Britain. It wasn't the Coldstream Guards he had joined in the war or his bowler hat and umbrella, it was his acquired reverence for monarchy and the Empire. It was now ingrained in him, a highly emotional thing. No matter how much he had been embittered personally by what had happened, he saw it done by the King as a man, not by the King as a monarch. Within himself, he could blame neither Wallis nor the King. He was sensitive enough to understand the inevitability of the affair. Besides, now he had Mary Kirk.

The idea, though, that the King might abdicate seemed monstrous to him. He thought he could stop it. The divorce would not become final until April and all he had to do was refuse to cooperate.

Through intermediaries he made his offer to Monckton, then to Baldwin, and finally to Wallis. All of them felt that only the King could decide, and so Simpson went to see him.

The King was touched, deeply. The loyalty and honesty of the man was manifest. He was putting king and country above self. Yet this was the last kind of sacrifice he wanted. What Simpson didn't understand, what nobody seemed to understand, was that Wallis meant more to him than being king.

December 2 had been a busy day for the King. Beaverbrook had called that afternoon to confirm the end of the "gentlemen's agreement" to control the press silence. He felt the initial press reaction would favor Baldwin, but the sympathy could be reversed and a strong case made for the King's marriage. Even then, though, the King was still reluctant to do anything that would increase publicity.

Beaverbrook did not tell the King that he was trying another tack, a direct approach to Wallis. The night before, at Stornoway House, he had had dinner with a small group of the King's friends. Among them were Monckton, Esmond Harmsworth, the King's solicitor George Allen, and Lord Brownlow. "They all decided I had the best entree to Wallis," recalled Brownlow afterward, "and that I should see her and try to get her to leave him."[27]

Wallis was staying at The Fort, and the King would be at Buckingham Palace all day because he had a late appointment with Baldwin. The timing, then, was perfect.

"I did see her," said Brownlow, "and I told her how we all felt and why it was important for her to make the break. But I wasn't sure of the impact."[28]

Although she maintained her composure, the impact was considerable. There had been a pile-up of pressure on Wallis from more and more people—not only her friends, but friends of the King. At first she had thought that the King could do no wrong, and it was an impression he had encouraged; but now, increasingly, she sensed how wrong it all was. She could see the King's increased nervousness. He smoked constantly and always seemed to have a handkerchief out, wiping away perspiration, even when the perspiration wasn't there. The way he held the handkerchief against his head was "as if to ease some hidden pressure or pain."[29]

And then the threatening letters had become more fearful:
"Beware, the fate of all Kings' mistresses will soon be yours!"[30]
And another, postmarked from Mayfair, on expensive stationery:
"Had you been living 200 years ago, means would have been found
to rid the country of you, but no one seems to possess the courage
required to order you back to the U.S.A. where marriage is a mockery,
so it has fallen to my lot as a patriot to kill you. This is a solemn warning that I shall do so."[31]

Still, it wasn't all that clear cut. How could she leave him now when
he needed her most? Who would listen to him, argue with him, pat
his head, hold his hand? Still, leaving might simplify everything, clear
the air, calm the whole situation. For Wallis, the afternoon was turmoil.

It was torment, too, for other people.

Prime Minister Baldwin asked Geoffrey Dawson to see him late
that afternoon. His appointment with the King was at six. "He seemed
indeed to be nearly at the end of his tether and sat with his head in
his hands on the table, probably just glad to have someone with him
till the time that his interview came," Dawson later wrote.[32]

The King's last caller, before Baldwin, was a polar explorer, Lincoln
Ellsworth, who had expressed interest in buying the King's ranch in
Canada.* Ellsworth had just returned from a flight across the Antarctic
and told the King how vast and empty it was. His Majesty musingly
remarked how delightful it must be to think of a whole continent
without a prime minister or archbishop, or even a king.

Part of the reason for the Prime Minister's concern was that the
situation was still fraught with uncertainty. He had all the political
strength on his side, but this king was both impulsive and emotional
and no one could predict absolutely how he might move—rally a King's
Party, fight for public support, or even renege on the morganatic marriage and bide his time. Someone had quoted Baldwin as saying, "Love
is for grocers, not kings."

Baldwin would later tell Parliament, "His Majesty is not a boy. He

---

* The Canadian ranch comprised 1,600 acres of deeded land and 2,400 more
of pasturage leased from the Dominion government. Ranch superintendent
Dr. W. L. Carlyle, a former professor of agriculture, imported twenty-seven
shorthorns from four farms in Cornwall and Devon and sixty-five Shropshire
sheep, eleven wild Dartmoor ponies and three racing mares. (*The New York
Times*, December 3, 1936.)

looked so young that we all thought of him as our Prince, but he is a mature man with a wide and great experience of life and the world."[33]

The King did not feel that way. He later admitted that he felt his world was disintegrating.

During the Baldwin meeting, he was overheard to say: "No, and again No, and No again!"[34]

But most of the meeting had gone quietly. Baldwin told him that the returns from the Dominions were still incomplete, but it was now clear that they would not approve of a morganatic marriage.

"His Majesty said he was not surprised at the answer to him," Baldwin later told Parliament. "He took my answer without question and never referred to it again."[35]

The Prime Minister again summed up the King's three options: give up the marriage, marry against his minister's advice or abdicate.

"Believe me, Sir, it is my sincere hope, and the hope of the Cabinet —that you will remain our King."[36]

"Whether on the Throne or not, Mr. Baldwin," the King answered, "I shall marry; and, however painful the prospect, I shall, if necessary, abdicate in order to do so."[37]

The King returned to The Fort that night to find Wallis with Aunt Bessie and their cousin Newbold Noyes. Wallis curtsied to him, as she always did in the presence of others, just as she called him "Sir."

"You must be very tired, Sir," she said.[38]

The King apologized for being late, bowed slightly to Wallis, assured her he was not tired, but explained, "It has been an unusually busy day."[39]

He had changed clothes at the palace and came wearing his Highland kilt.

"Would you like a cocktail, Sir?" asked Wallis.

"No, thank you," said the King. "I don't think I feel like one."[40]

Wallis prepared an old-fashioned, Southern style, for herself and Noyes—bitters on a lump of sugar, a couple of large pieces of ice and a jigger of bourbon.

The talk was inconsequential. The King kept the conversation smooth and easy with no lulls or tenseness visible. They mostly discussed grouse shooting and jigsaw puzzles. He and Wallis had been working on a jigsaw map of France. The map was half-completed and the King absentmindedly picked up an odd-shaped piece and fitted it in.

"I wish I had watched more closely," Noyes noted afterward. "That piece might well have had a dot on it labeled Cannes."[41]

The red-coated butler announced, "His Majesty's dinner is served."[42]

The menu was typical: clear turtle soup, a lobster mousse with a light piquant sauce, roast pheasant with soufflé potatoes and a mixed green salad, frozen fresh pineapple and a toasted cheese savory; a bright Bordeaux wine during dinner and a liqueur with coffee. On the table were lighted tapers, the china and table service with the King's crest. The dinner table itself was square mahogany, glowing with a soft patina. At the table, whenever Wallis wanted to tell the King something she did not want the servants to overhear, Noyes noticed that she spoke in German "and the King replied in the same language."[43]

Talk generally concerned world politics and the affairs in England and the United States. The King referred always to the "United States of America." Wallis took an active part in the conversation and Aunt Bessie mostly listened.

"Knowing the broad-mindedness and chivalry of your country," the King told Noyes, "what I cannot understand is the attitude of your press toward an American woman who is my friend."[44]

Noyes repeated what he had told Wallis, that the American press overwhelmingly favored Wallis. The conversation turned to the marriage.

"If you marry, Sir," Noyes said to the King, "the woman you so honor will be one of three things. Correct me if I am wrong."[45]

The King asked him to name the three things.

"Your morganatic wife, the Queen of England, or shall we say, Mrs. Windsor, wife of the abdicated King of England."

"Nearly 67 percent correct, but no more," said the King. "There is no such possibility as morganatic marriage for an English king."[46]

It surely startled Wallis to hear that then from him, for the first time, knowing that he had just met with Baldwin.

"It would seem apparent then, Sir," Noyes continued, "that there are but three possible outcomes to this situation. Wallis becomes Queen. She becomes Mrs. Windsor, subsequent to your abdication. Or you renounce any intention of marrying her."

"Again, only 67 percent correct, Mr. Noyes," said the King. "You should confine your possibilities to the first two—the only two that exist."[47]

Noyes kept probing for their future plans and Wallis, somewhat embarrassed at his persistence, laughingly dismissed the subject, by saying: "If this keeps up, he will make you propose to me in front of him, Sir."[48]

Noyes noted afterward: "I have watched the eyes of King Edward VIII as they followed Wallis Simpson. I have watched the play of expression upon her face as she looked at and talked about the man she loves. And if I ever saw two people wholly, deeply, almost unbelievably lost in each other, I saw them then."[49]

"I understand that in your country there are certain marriages where the bridegroom has to be—shall we say, cajoled," said the King. "You didn't by any chance bring a shotgun with you, did you?"[50]

His Majesty then asked Wallis if she would like to take a walk. It was not walking weather: the fog had come in, damp and gloomy, but they set off down the flagstone path, and he told her what a bad day it had been, what Baldwin had said, what the newspapers would probably say in the morning.

He had no choice, he said; he could not and would not give her up—he had to abdicate.

They were both silent in their misery, each feeling sorry for the other.

She told him again that he must, at all costs, at all sacrifices, keep the throne.

Then she told him that she had decided to leave the country, that she should have done it long before.[51]

This time he did not try to stop her. He almost sounded relieved that she had made up her mind on this. He knew what was coming, and he wanted her as far away as possible from the hurt of it.

That evening the King still had calls to make. In his anguish and concern, and in his political immaturity, he still felt he could somehow control the impact of the press.

The King saw *The Times* as The Thunderer, the voice of his enemy Geoffrey Dawson, and he expected it to make a dramatic attack on Wallis.

"In the late evening, as I was struggling with the paper," Geoffrey Dawson noted in his diary, the Prime Minister called him, not once but twice, before midnight, ". . . the only time I think I ever heard his own voice on the telephone—to say that His Majesty was worrying him to find out, and if necessary stop, what was going to appear in

The Times. He understood that there was to be an attack on Mrs. Simpson and 'instructed' the Prime Minister to forbid it. In vain S.B. [Stanley Baldwin] had explained that the Press in England was free, and that he had no control over *The Times* or over any other newspaper. When he spoke to me full of apologies, the second time, it was to say that the King would now be satisfied, and leave the Prime Minister alone, if the latter would read the leading article for him. Could I possibly let him see it for the sake of peace? By this time, as I told him, the paper was just going to press; but towards midnight I sent a proof of the leader by messenger to Downing Street and heard no more about it."[52]

He heard no more about it because Baldwin was in bed when the article arrived, and his biographer admits that he did not read it.

The next morning was one of the few since World War I that the weather was replaced as the chief topic of public discussion.

The headlines read: GRAVE CRISIS.

The Times editorialized:

"There are many daughters of America whom the King might have married with the approval and rejoicing of his people. It would have been an innovation, but by no means an unwelcome innovation in the history of the Royal House . . . The one objection, and it is an overwhelming objection, is that the lady in question has already two former husbands living from whom in succession she has obtained divorce."

The *Daily Express:*

"Let the King speak . . . Let the King give his decision to the people . . . Are we to lose the King or are we to keep him? He knows the answer that the people want to hear. But it must not be goodbye, for the citizens of these shores would hear him say it with their hearts loaded with grief and their heads bowed with sorrow."

The *Daily Telegraph:*

"Queen Mary, Queen Alexandra, Queen Victoria—these have been the Queens of England whom this country and empire have known for a full century and they will not tolerate any other or different standard of Queenship."

The *Daily Mail:*

"Abdication is out of the question because its possibilities of mischief are endless. The effect upon the Empire would be calamitous. It must never happen. The King and his Ministers must find a way out . . . The people want their King."

Most unusual and unexpected comment came from the *News Chronicle*, most staunch of the pro-Baldwin papers. It advocated the plan of a special marriage whereby the King would marry as the Duke of Cornwall, making his wife a king's consort instead of a queen. Dawson called the idea "particularly mischievous." Baldwin, however, must have been most pleased with the support of the opposition Labour Party paper, the *Daily Herald*, which insisted that the King must take the advice of his ministers.

Dominion newspapers were even more dogmatic on the issue. They all stressed the King's "high sense of duty," his need to "make a supreme sacrifice" and that his happiness was "a small price to pay for the devotion of empire."

The King was quoted as saying, "They don't want me."[53] But the more he read, the angrier he grew. Most belatedly, he decided to fight, and tell his story. He worked hard, finally completing the draft of his proposed radio speech. While he was still working on it, Wallis entered his room, carrying a newspaper, the agitation obvious in her face and voice.

He said he was sorry she had to see them at all and she said how sad she was that she had done this to him. Then she added, "I cannot stay here another day . . . I must leave England this afternoon."[54]

Again, he didn't argue.

That evening the King was to dine with his mother and his sister at Marlborough House and he had persuaded them, finally, to let him bring Wallis so that they might meet her and make their own judgment. Weeks before, it might have been most important. Public approval of Wallis Simpson by Queen Mary could have been critical. Or, as John Gunther put it, it would also have made a difference if Wallis went shopping with Mrs. Baldwin.

However, even if the Queen Mother had met Wallis, and liked her, she would have found it almost impossible to approve the marriage. Her feeling against divorce was basic. Her respect for royalty was unlimited. Nor would she ever have gone against the "advice" of the government. It could have had meaning only if it had happened at the beginning, before any government opposition could crystallize.

Perhaps this meeting was another thing Wallis couldn't face, perhaps this was another reason she wanted to leave that very day. Things were quickly arranged. The King called his friend Lord Brownlow.

"I got a call from the King about 11 o'clock," said Lord Brownlow. "He asked me to take 'W'—that was his code word for her—out of the country, come with my own car to The Fort that afternoon and bring clothes for a fortnight. I didn't know where we were going until I got there."[55]

Walter Monckton came to help organize things. With him was his seventeen-year-old daughter, Valerie, who had often acted as messenger for her father between The Fort and 10 Downing Street. Her vivid memory of the luncheon on that day was the fact that Wallis could be so kind to her at such a tense time, and even try to keep her involved in the conversation. Valerie noticed how careful she was to call the King "Sir," because she was there. She marveled, too, at the King's thoughtfulness. He had once seen her drinking beer, and made sure that there were several bottles set for her at lunch.

This was a day of frenzy, a fury of packing and arrangements, and yet these two people in the eye of the hurricane remained courteous, considerate human beings. Good manners came with the training for kingship; with Wallis they were more instinctive.

Lord Brownlow arrived in his Rolls at dusk. It was time for tea. The King explained that Wallis was going to Cannes to stay with her friends Herman and Katherine Rogers. He had made the arrangements himself and they were complicated. Instead of traveling by train in a sealed compartment, which would have been simple, they unexplainably were going by car, under assumed names. He was sending along his personal chauffeur George Ladbrooke and a Scotland Yard detective.

Before they left, Lord Brownlow asked the King:

"And what are you going to do, Sir?"

"He told me he was going to Switzerland until the situation quieted," Brownlow remembered. "I was very angry with him afterwards because there was no need for him to lie to me."[56]

It was hard to say good-by because neither the King nor Wallis had the vaguest idea of when they would see each other again. Wallis left her dog, Slipper, with the King—Slipper had been his first present to her.

For Wallis now came a time of loneliness and of fear. She couldn't escape the gnawing worry that perhaps—despite all his assurances—

this might be the end. It had the feeling of finality, like the will she had just written. Somewhere within her she felt that she might never see him again. Suddenly they both seemed small pawns in a series of events that would overwhelm them. And yet, despite all this, she found herself caught up in a kind of exhilaration, as if she were part of a great adventure.

21

AUNT BESSIE was right about Wallis: she was afraid. Fear was an unusual companion for Wallis. With her remarkable quality of ease, she stood in awe of no one. She had the further courage to accept any exciting challenge, and a natural aggressiveness, an honest bravado.

But never, in her wildest imagination, had she ever dreamed that her affair with the King would reach such dimensions. Prominence was one thing, and celebrity another. She liked having both. Now, however, she was one woman against a world. Those headlines that morning reported the condemnation of a whole country.

The letters she received were full of hate and murder. Her friends in Britain were pleading and sneering. The man she loved was being pilloried and disgraced.

If she feared for herself, and felt the shame of it, she now feared even more for him. It was only on that last day that all the pressures and forces seemed to converge on her. Many years afterward, she confided to him that it was only then that she truly realized what abdication really meant for him.

She later said that when she left him that day she was certain that she would never see him again.

Wallis and Perry Brownlow drove through the darkness, the fog settling in, the drizzle starting. The ferry to France left at ten, and Wallis' Buick was already there, with the King's chauffeur. Now, in Perry's Rolls Royce, they could talk.

"We were about halfway down to Newhaven," said Lord Brownlow, "when I asked her if she knew what she was doing. She gave me all her reasons for leaving the King, saying that her situation had become untenable, but I said I wasn't talking about that. I was talking about her influence on the King. I asked her if she realized that as soon as she left the country, she would lose the major influence she had over him, and there was no telling what he might do. To tell the truth, I wasn't even thinking of Abdication. The word Abdication wasn't even in my head. But I was worried what else he might do. I knew how emotional and unpredictable he was."[1]

Brownlow earlier had wanted her to renounce the King, but now he realized that she had an impact to exercise within his orbit before she broke away. This would be a transition.

"What I said startled her," Brownlow continued. "She seemed confused and bewildered and asked me what I thought she should do. I told her she should come to my country place at Belton, where nobody would expect her to be, nobody would know she was there. The place was all ready, fully staffed with servants."[2]

Brownlow ordered the chauffeur to pull over to the side of the road and he and Wallis discussed the situation in more detail. Brownlow, of course, was not privy to the true situation, the full intent of the King to abdicate rather than surrender Wallis, the dangerous turn the situation had taken with Baldwin and the Dominions. But his intuition about Wallis' influence on the King was absolutely right. Wallis' argument was that the King had taken great pains to arrange this trip to France, and that he would feel double-crossed if she did otherwise.

"She also thought that he would leave the Palace and The Fort and come directly to her in the country. I argued with her, but she was firm on this, and felt we ought to continue our plans as scheduled."[3]

Wallis was wrong, and later admitted she was. Had she stayed on in England, she might well have swayed the King to stay on the throne. She would have given him the strength to fight and maneuver, more than he was then willing to do.

Discouraged at his failure to convince her, and unwilling to sit alongside her in silence or recrimination, Brownlow took the wheel from the sleepy Ladbrooke. He soon heard a police siren and looked at his speedometer. He had been going over seventy miles an hour. The detective showed the police his identification and they were off again.

On the ferry to Dieppe, they were listed as Mr. and Mrs. Harrison.

"It was all very silly," said Brownlow, "because we fooled no one. Our passports were still in our real names, and the French were on to us in a minute, as soon as we arrived. French officials must have tipped off the reporters, because they were soon on to us. We never escaped them, all the way down to the south of France."[4]

The first stop was Rouen, the Hôtel de la Post, at three o'clock in the morning. Wallis was exhausted, went to her room, stretched out on her bed without undressing. A maid awakened her at daylight with tea and rolls sent up by Perry. By the time they came downstairs, there were people there.

Ladbrooke had the dark blue Buick waiting with a license plate, CUL 547, that soon became world-famous. At the hotel that day there was a touring company of the Comédie Française. A young, blond French actress, Nadia Dauty, recognized Wallis, even then impeccably neat in a rust-colored traveling suit. She took a photograph of Wallis, but the detective rushed in, pushed her aside, knocking her camera and hat to the floor. The girl screamed, and Perry pulled Wallis into the car, and it raced away.

The burly Ladbrooke had brought a large pile of road maps, which he read, and he gave directions as they took a side road to try to avoid the reporters. Wallis wanted most of all to call the King.

They stopped in Evreux in Normandy for lunch. Wallis had remembered a hotel with a large courtyard. The phone was in a booth near the bar. Perry put through the call to The Fort. The King's code name was "Mr. James."

"He must have given orders to clear any communication to him from France, because it would never take more than four or five minutes to get through."[5]

The phone connection was so bad that Wallis ended up screaming, trying to be heard, repeating the same things over and over.

"She was giving him streams of advice about consulting Churchill, the Aga Khan, Lord Derby, telling him not to abdicate, not to do anything rash. I think she thought, even then, that the King's threat of abdication would force the Government to accept a morganatic marriage. Anyway, she was shouting so loudly·on the phone that Evans, the detective, and I were worried that the people in the dining room would hear her and so we made a lot of noise, too, trying to cover up her screaming."[6]

Wallis hung up, depressed, knowing that she had not been heard.

En route, again, Wallis suddenly remembered that she had scribbled notes of the things she had wanted to tell him, and left them in the phone booth.

Brownlow was terrified what reporters would do with those notes if they found them. But they decided it was too late to turn back and they must take the chance and continue.

The secret was already out. Reporters had found Wallis' maid arriving in France with her luggage, all of it addressed to Cannes. Even in Evreux, she had been identified. "We all recognized her," said the daughter of hotelier M. Julio Pacciarelli, "but we pretended not to know her."[7] Pictures of her had appeared in every French newspaper.

In the concern and confusion about the notes, Ladbrooke took a wrong turn, and they found themselves heading for the coast. It was almost dark before they were back on the right road. Again they stopped to call, this time from an antique phone in the lobby of a small hotel. They spent an unsuccessful hour trying to reach Buckingham Palace.

When they at last reached the Loire Valley town of Blois, all of them weary and unhappy, it had started to snow, and they decided to spend the night at the Hôtel de France and de Guise. Brownlow discovered that the hotel already was full of reporters.

They had adjoining rooms, and Wallis was so worried about the newsmen that she couldn't sleep and they kept the door ajar between them and talked.

"Wallis, I've been through a good bit of bother with your affairs," said Brownlow, "and I think I deserve an account of how the whole thing really happened and built up. Did he go on his knees to propose?"[8]

"I think you're entitled to know," Wallis answered.

"Just at that moment," said Brownlow, "I dozed off, and when I woke up, she was saying, 'and I think you must admit I've been very candid with you . . .' After that, I couldn't ask her to repeat it!"[9]

To try to fool the reporters, Brownlow had left orders at the hotel desk for a morning call at nine o'clock. Secretly he had bribed the porter to bring them coffee at three, then lead them out through the kitchen.

A clever reporter, the night before, had blocked their Buick with his own car. Ladbrooke, however, managed to push that car out of the way, and they were again on their way, the snow making the driving hazardous.

They breakfasted at Moulins and Brownlow sent two telegrams, one to the Rogerses about their delay and the other to Beaverbrook, in code, that read:

"W. M. Janet strongly advising the James Company to postpone purchase of Chester shares to next autumn and to announce decision by verbal methods, thereby increasing popularity, maintaining prestige, but also the right to reopen negotiations by the autumn."[10]

Translated, this meant that Wallis wanted the King to forget about the marriage for at least a year, and go through with the coronation ceremony.

There was almost never a good phone connection, and it always seemed to be a shouting match between Wallis and the King. Brownlow noticed two important things: the word "abdication" was used more often, and the realization of its possibility now hit him hard. There were also constant annoying clicks on the line. Brownlow, months later, confronted the head of British Security, M-5, "and I told him I thought it was disgraceful for his people to record the King's private conversations for the Prime Minister. 'We did no such thing,' he told me, but then I reminded him, 'I myself heard the intercepts on the phone.' He couldn't deny it after that."[11]

Wallis seemed to have the feeling that she no longer existed as far as the King was concerned, that she simply wasn't getting through to him.

"I must say this for her," Brownlow afterward recalled. "As tired as she was she was a gay companion all the way. She could be absolutely charming."[12]

Wallis' chatter during all this must have been a kind of protective coating to stop her from thinking. The gift of small talk during crisis is often a therapeutic one. But at several points she felt she would break.

At one stop, a newsman from *Paris Soir* asked a few questions and she answered in "very bad French":

"You French people are very sympathetic, but very bothersome. I've not been able to get any sleep for two days. I want rest, lots of rest."[13]

The reporter had one more question: What did she think of the situation?

"I can't make any statement," she answered. "The King is the only judge. I have nothing to say except that I want to be left quiet."[14]

At the Lyons outskirts, Ladbrooke stopped to get directions and a man nearby noticed Wallis and yelled, *"Voilà la dame!"*

Their Buick now headed a caravan of cars, filled with reporters. Early that afternoon they arrived at Vienne, south of Lyons, at the world-famous restaurant Café de la Pyramide. The owner, Madame Point, knew Wallis and took her to her own room. She looked "very tired and very nervous," Madame Point afterward reported, and she maintained their privacy by putting them in the private banquet room, big enough for forty. Wallis had *pâté de fois gras,* shrimp salad and some fowl, but only nibbled at it. She sipped some white wine.

While the reporters were busy eating, Madame Point suggested they climb out through a back window into the alley. Wallis later told a friend it was the toilet window.

"I wish Baldwin could have seen that," said Brownlow.[15]

The rains came again, along with sleet. Wallis now had too much time to think and remember. Her gaiety was gone. Her future seemed as bleak as the weather. She felt numb with exhaustion. Close to midnight, they stopped in town to call the Rogerses from a street telephone. Brownlow's loud French bluster, trying to get through to the operator, struck Wallis as so funny that it broke her tension, and she laughed and laughed, almost hysterically.

Despite the late hour, when they reached the Rogers villa, Brownlow saw a large crowd in front of the gate.

"I told Wallis to get down on the floor of the car and I covered her with the robe and we raced into the courtyard."[16]

British and French detectives outside told the waiting people "that they might as well go home because she's tired and wants to sleep."[17]

It seemed as if she had come a long, long way, but where was she?

22

WHEN WALLIS MOVED OUT of The Fort and headed for Cannes, Walter Monckton moved in. Monckton could see that the King was under great strain and felt that he ought not to be alone, that if the King ever needed a friend close to him, he needed one then.

Monckton soon realized why the King wanted Wallis for his wife and queen. His physical resilience and endurance were extraordinary, and so was his courage, but there was still a fundamental weakness and uncertainty in him that needed constant bolstering. Wallis would have anchored him and given his power a real force. The two complemented each other in many distinctive ways. The King supplied the background, the heritage, the training for kingship, a phenomenal memory and curiosity, a willingness to discard the old and try the new. Wallis brought him a complete understanding and sympathy, a relaxing love, a lively spirit, a practical sense and an ability to instill confidence to an exceptional degree. He got these things from no one else and he needed them; he needed them badly. Tom Jones afterward recorded a breakfast meeting with Prime Minister Baldwin at 10 Downing Street on November 25, in which Baldwin reported that the King had told him he could do nothing without the woman.

The King was coming to count more and more on the proposed radio speech. In drafting it he tried to explain Wallis' importance to him. He wrote of how long it had taken him to find the wife he wanted, and how much he wanted to marry her. Then he added:

"Neither Mrs. Simpson nor I have ever sought to insist that she should be Queen. All we desired was that our married happiness should carry with it a proper title and dignity for her, befitting my wife."[1]

Out of the speech, the King evolved a new plan: he would make his speech, then go to Belgium and wait for public opinion to swing in his favor. In that event, a council of state could substitute for the King, as it did during a monarch's serious illness.

Shortly after Wallis left, he hurried to Buckingham Palace to meet the Prime Minister with a draft of his speech. Beaverbrook had urged him to read it to Baldwin, but not to give him a copy. Again, the King ignored the advice. The speech startled the Prime Minister and he would only say that he would call a special Cabinet meeting to discuss the subject. To one thing, Baldwin did grudgingly agree: the King could consult Churchill.

After leaving, Baldwin told a Cabinet member about Churchill, and said, "I have made my first blunder."[2]

Baldwin always had been fearful of Winston Churchill, sensing a hidden power in the man, the ability to stir a nation with rousing words. Churchill had broken with his Conservative Party colleagues on their stand on India, and resigned from Baldwin's shadow Cabinet in 1931 on that issue, declaring against Gandhi's release from prison. Neville Chamberlain had been delighted: "It would be an immense accession of strength to us to get rid of Winston."[3]

Churchill then became a party gadfly, prodding again and again on the military rise of Nazi Germany and the dire need of the British to rearm. One critic described Churchill's position as "the best-hated man in British politics."

It was Beaverbrook who later told a depressed Winston Churchill, who had regarded his political career as finished:

"What nonsense! A man in your position may be in the depths of despair one day and the next raised to the heights and appointed Prime Minister."[4]

No one knew this better than Baldwin. He feared Churchill because he saw in him the one man who might still save the situation for the King by forming a King's Party, blended from the dissidents in all three.

That day Churchill was making a speech at Albert Hall. He repeated his urgent plea for rearmament, his defense of the League of Nations, and then added:

"There is another grave matter that overshadows our minds tonight. In a few minutes we are going to sing 'God Save the King.' I shall sing it with more heartfelt fervour than I have ever sung it in my life. I hope and pray that no irrevocable decision will be taken in haste, but that time and public opinion will be allowed to play their part and that a cherished and unique personality may not be incontinently severed from the people he loves so well."[5]

At the end of his speech there was a resounding "Three cheers for the King."

Churchill afterward went to see Beaverbrook. They discussed the King's proposed radio speech, and Churchill suggested some changes. The King was visiting his mother that night, but asked Churchill to come to dinner on the following evening.

The Queen Mother had written him a note saying that she had not seen him for ten days, and was upset by the news, and couldn't he come that night. She signed it: "Ever yr loving Mama, Mary."[6]

She had gone that afternoon to see the smoking ruins of the burned-out Crystal Palace, and it only added gloom to her day. The Duke and Duchess of York were dining with her that night and the King saw them all, tried to explain that he hadn't visited earlier because he didn't want to bring the family into his crisis. He told them that he felt he had to resolve it alone. The Duke of York later recorded that the King had told his mother "that he could not live alone as King & must marry Mrs. Simpson. When David left after making this dreadful announcement to his mother he told me to come & see him at the Fort the next morning."

The King then hurried back to The Fort to await Wallis' first call. From then on he stayed there, almost never leaving for fear that he might miss a call from her. Traveling through the night with little sleep, Wallis brooded over the thought that she had cut herself out of his life. As they moved closer to Cannes, most of her thinking and much of her conversation with Brownlow was a further detailing of what she would say to the King in her next call. The King, on the other hand, was equally concerned about what he would say to her so that she wouldn't feel so desperate. Each was only worried about the other. To each, the other was the only person who mattered. Each phone call was another emotional peak.

"Those telephone calls with a bad line at a long distance will never be forgotten by any of us," Monckton confided in his diary. "The house is so shaped that if a voice is raised in any room on the ground floor it can be heard more or less distinctly in the whole house."[7]

What intimacies could the King tell when he had to yell them, when he knew the whole household was listening? What he really wanted to say, he could only whisper.

Out of the crisis came a whole crop of new rumors. A prominent peer was reported to have said that the King was so drunk one night that a stomach pump had to be used.

"Nothing could be more ridiculous," recorded Monckton. "Life was for all of us disorganized, a series of interruptions with snatches of sleep. I certainly drank more than the King, but among all the great men who saw us constantly throughout those days I never heard of one who thought either of us had been drinking."[8]

On Friday, December 4, Baldwin spoke in the House of Commons, making it plain that British law did not recognize morganatic marriage and that His Majesty's government was "not prepared to introduce such legislation" to change the law. Furthermore, he added, the Dominions agreed with the government. The House cheered.

From across the floor, Churchill shouted at Baldwin, "You won't be satisfied until you've broken him, will you?"[9]

The accusation did nothing to deter Baldwin, who had further bad news for the King. The Cabinet would not permit him to make his radio speech.

Beaverbrook, however, was still hopeful. He saw the public tide gathering force in favor of the King. If Wallis now would withdraw from the marriage, Baldwin might still be beaten. "The future was bright with promise," he afterward wrote. "Victory seemed to be within our grasp."[10]

There was, indeed, a great wave of sympathy for the King. A crowd of 300 young men and women paraded to Buckingham Palace unfolding huge banners:

> LET THE KING KNOW YOU ARE WITH HIM—
> YOU CAN'T LET HIM DOWN.
> WE WANT EDWARD. PERISH ALL POLITICIANS.[11]

At the Prime Minister's home at 10 Downing Street, they massed and chanted: "We want our king . . . We want our king . . ."

Then, in between, they sang, "For he's a jolly good fellow" and the national anthem.

Other signs read:

> GOD SAVE THE KING FROM BALDWIN.
> STAND BY THE KING.
> THE KING CAN DO NO WRONG.

Other crowds elsewhere were shouting: "We want Eddie!"[12]

In Liverpool, T. J. Hodgson, general secretary of the Post Office Workers' Union, summoned a mass meeting, declaring: "The whole civil service is solidly behind the King."

At Hyde Park, a speaker said: "Let 'im marry who he likes . . ."

Harold Laski, however, spoke for many of the labor leaders when he stated: ". . . out of this issue no precedent must be created that makes the royal authority once more a source of independent political power in the State. The Labour Party is a constitutional party . . . Pivotal to that conception is the principle that a Labour government with a majority in the House of Commons is entitled to have its advice accepted by the Crown . . . He [the King] may advise. He may encourage. He may warn. But if the Cabinet stands firm in its advice, the King must in our constitutional system necessarily give way."[13]

Novelist Hugh Walpole said: "Queen Wally? Why it's absolutely ludicrous." Lady Mary Elizabeth Burton added: "Any woman but Mrs. Simpson for Edward—but Edward at any price, even Mrs. Simpson!" And British actress Pamela Stanley: ". . . If I had to choose between love and the Empire, I'd choose the Empire."[14]

The *Evening Star* in London editorialized an appeal:

"His Majesty needs your most earnest attention and immediate support. He has dared to follow the courage of his convictions. He wants to marry an American lady. His Cabinet Ministers say 'No!' You will lose this great Englishman unless it is at once shown that the British people would welcome such a union. Think well what it would achieve for the two largest English-speaking nations in the world."

Crowds angrily mobbed the car of the Archbishop of Canterbury coming out of a meeting with Baldwin.

George Bernard Shaw was stirred to write "a fictitious dialogue," a fantasy about a king who wanted to marry an American divorcée, Mrs. Daisy Bell. Shaw has the Prime Minister and Archbishop visit the King, the Prime Minister threatening to resign and the Archbishop refusing to officiate at the coronation. The King tells the Prime Minister that he will form a King's Party and reminds the Archbishop that only 11 percent of the 500 million people in the British Empire are Christians and he would gladly dispense with the religious part of the coronation altogether.

Shaw offered the interesting suggestion that "an American who has been married twice before was therefore likely to make an excellent wife for a King who has never been married at all."[15]

And in the Bronx, New York, Borough President James J. Lyons introduced a resolution: "It is with keen regret that we read of the attitude of Prime Minister Baldwin toward Mrs. Wally Simpson, an American citizen. His policy is an affront to American womanhood."[16]

A poll in the Illinois State Penitentiary listed 321 for the King's abdication and marriage to Wallis, and 127 for renunciation of Mrs. Simpson and retention of the throne.

Even the British fascists and communists found themselves on the King's side:

"How would *you* like a Cabinet of old busybodies to pick *your* girl?"[17] British fascist leader Sir Oswald Mosley asked a crowd of his Blackshirts.

Communist MP Mr. William Gallacher added: "We Communists certainly should not worry about it. If he wants to marry her, as far as I am concerned I will say, 'Good luck to him and good luck to her.' "[18]

But, more negatively, there was a Reverend Paxton who told Harold Nicolson, "I never dreamt that I should live to see the day when my congregation refused to sing 'God Save the King.' "

Author Jessica Mitford, then in her teens, later described the mood of her young friends in *Daughters and Rebels*.

"Something closer to home, seemingly more foreboding, more threatening to the established order, than any of those rows abroad dominated the thoughts and conversation . . . Now the British monarchy itself was threatened—and, of all things, by an American woman with the unlikely and extraordinarily unprepossessing name of Wallis Simpson.

" 'Her Christian name can't *really* be Wallis. The papers must have got it wrong. You know how inaccurate they are about everything.'

" 'Children! [said her mother] You are not to mention that dreadful woman in front of the servants. And I don't want you to bring any of those American magazines into the house.' "

The magazines were uncensored copies of *Time* that Jessica Mitford got from a young friend who received them from the States by mail. All newsstand copies had the accounts of the Simpson affair scissored out. One of her friends suggested a demonstration in front of Buckingham Palace.

"Can't you visualize the scene?" he said. " 'Down with Baldwin!' will be their cry. The papers tomorrow will be full of pictures and stories about this great throng. Like wildfire, news of our demonstration will reach the provinces. Next day the Tory government will fall . . ."

"I didn't especially care one way or the other what the outcome might be," wrote Mitford. "The romantic aspects seemed to me intensely dull; two middle-aged people with nothing in particular to recommend them, a good deal less interesting than the average film star—besides, Edward had recently shown signs of being impressed with the Hitler regime."

But she went. "We held aloft our homemade banners painted with such slogans as 'EDWARD'S RIGHT, BALDWIN'S WRONG,' 'BALDWIN RESIGN!' . . . We were an oddly assorted little group. Peter had gathered a few young men in polo-necked sweaters, a few society girls, a few unpublished poets. After hanging around for about an hour or so waiting for others to show up, stamping our feet to keep warm in the chilly winter air, we marched toward Buckingham Palace. Rather to my surprise we actually did attract . . . about fifty of the curious who fell in behind us."[19]

At Buckingham Palace, they shouted, "We want Edward," but the King was at The Fort. They then started for Downing Street, lost their way and finally asked directions from a mounted policeman. But Downing Street was blocked off. "The demonstrators, murmuring that it was time for tea, gradually dispersed."[20]

Public confusion was still considerable. Geoffrey Dawson accused "the Simpson press" of "a regular barrage of pleas" for delay, for reference to the people, for anything that would keep a popular sovereign (and, it was not obscurely hinted, get rid of a bad prime minister).

Churchill that night, at dinner with the King, insisted that there was still no constitutional issue at stake and there would be none until the King's marriage was imminent, and certainly not until Wallis' divorce decree became absolute in April. Hereditary principles must not be left to the mercy of politicians, he said.

"His advice was that the King should ask for time," said Monckton, who was also at the dinner. "He said that he could not say that the King was through if he stood and fought, but that he ought to take time to see what measure of support he received. His presence was a great encouragement to the King who liked him, and mimicked his mannerisms superbly without the slightest malice.

" 'We must have time for the big battalions to mass. We may win; we may not. Who can tell?' "[21]

Churchill's zeal had impact on the King. "When Mr. Baldwin had talked to me about the Monarchy," noted the King afterward, "it had seemed a dry and lifeless thing. But, when Mr. Churchill spoke, it lived, it grew, it became suffused with light."[22]

Wallis was still en route to Cannes that night. She had called him earlier and they had shouted at each other, hardly hearing, but he did have some encouraging news this time and he was happy to shout it.

And Wallis was shouting, "Don't give up. Fight! Fight!"

23

FRIDAY WAS THE FATEFUL NIGHT for the King. It was the night he searched his soul. It was the one night, more than any other, that he needed Wallis. It was the night of final decision.

In a sense, he had made that decision long before. This, though, was the time for confronting it.

He had talked to Wallis, talked to Churchill, talked to Beaverbrook, talked to Monckton. They all had urged him to wait and fight. But he was too impatient, too stubborn and too much in love.

Earlier that evening, Churchill's spirit had buoyed him with fresh hope. He had momentarily made everything seem possible. The King knew that there were strong stirrings for a King's Party. A declared group of sixty members of Parliament were ready to side with him against Baldwin. Wallis' cousin Newbold Noyes had gone to a secret meeting where leading members of the King's Party went so far as to discuss possible members of the new Cabinet of their new government.

If the King refused to accept Baldwin's "advice," and Baldwin's government resigned, then Churchill was the ideal man to form a King's Party and head a new government.

At the same time, he could "unleash" the "Simpson press" and let them whip up and shape up public opinion in his favor. Crowds demonstrating for the King numbered as large as several thousand in some areas. Kingsley Martin quoted a working woman as saying, "He's a naughty boy, but we don't want to lose him."[1]

The religious question troubled him very much. As king, he was also Defender of the Faith. He could have withdrawn his suggestion of morganatic marriage, gone through the coronation, then, eventually, married Wallis anyway. This he could have done without anybody's permission. But, during the coronation he would be anointed with holy oil, take the sacrament and swear to uphold Church of England doctrines. Since these doctrines disapprove of divorce, it would have meant that the King would be crowned "with a lie on my lips."[2]

In view of this, there was also the question of whether the Archbishop would even perform the coronation service. The Archbishop's official biographer, however, felt this: ". . . if, with the consent of Parliament, the King had been able to have his way, the Archbishop, despite the heaviness of his heart, would neither have refused his services nor himself have resigned. He might have pointed to the complicating relationship of Church and State, arguing that in clearing himself from complicity, he would merely be passing on the burden to someone else."[3]

The Archbishop's further thought was that this "someone else" might be "more complaisant" about the claims of the establishment and the law and the church and could critically hurt the church, putting it "in fumbling and suspected hands."[4]

Therefore, according to his biographer, he would have performed the coronation.

If an archbishop would perform such a ceremony, knowing the meaning of the oath and knowing the result, how much could a king be blamed for accepting it?

The Archbishop, supposedly, was "extremely annoyed" by Bishop Blunt's speech, "since it looked as though the leakage had come from Lambeth."[5] However, he had been a breakfast host at Lambeth Palace for Anne and Christopher Fremantle. An American paper on the side table had the headline: WILL DAVID WED WALLY?[6]

"The Archbishop, seeing Anne's and her husband's concern, told them the marriage must and would be stopped. 'It would be the end of the monarchy in England,' he told them. He added that next day editorial silence on the subject would be broken—at his instigation— by a leader [editorial] in the Yorkshire Post which would alert the country. It did."[7]

It was, then, not too presumptuous of the King to see the shadowy figure of the Archbishop in the background maneuvering among the King's enemies.

After talking to Churchill that Friday night, the King had called Beaverbrook to say that Churchill was coming to see him. "I also concluded," wrote Beaverbrook afterward, "that he had changed his mind and was ready to fight for his Throne after all."[8] After talking to Churchill, Beaverbrook had more hope than ever.

But by then it was long after two in the morning and by that time the King again had changed his mind.

The King's Party was waiting for his word. Pacing his bedroom floor, he felt unable to set the necessary forces in motion. If he unleashed the King's Party and unshackled the friendly press, it would cause political chaos in the country, divide the people in a kind of civil war. This, in turn, could only cripple the monarchy. Instead of symbolizing unity, the crown would cause only division and hate. If he then married Wallis, how could they hope for happiness?

Were Wallis with him that night, she might have had a hundred arguments to counter him.

Even on the religious issue, which he stressed so strongly, the King himself had told Brownlow "that the Archbishop of Canterbury had said to him, almost in so many words, that he should keep Wallis as his mistress, and in the background."[9] Wallis would have preferred to be his morganatic wife or his queen, but she would have been happy to stay in the background and still be with him. Then, with the passage of time and the gradual public acceptance, they could have married and had it all. This would have been her persuasive argument, and such was her strength that she might well have convinced him. She called him "the Mule,"[10] and he was undeniably stubborn, but such was his love that he could deny her little that she truly wanted. And more than anything else, Wallis truly wanted him to stay on the throne, not only for himself but for herself.

Without Wallis on that night of decision, we do not know how much the King paced the floor, how many cigarettes he smoked, how much liquor he drank, how many times he cursed his fate. We can guess at the confusion of his soul. When you are young, you know all the answers; when you get older, you realize you don't even know all the questions.

He had created his own urgency, his own crisis, and now he resolved it in his own way. When he saw Monckton after breakfast the next morning he told him his final decision. It was no surprise. He asked Monckton to invite Prime Minister Baldwin to The Fort that evening and warn him that the King planned to notify him formally of his decision to abdicate.

Even as he heard it and expected it, the unflappable Monckton listened with shock. As a trained diplomat, bred in the tradition that facial expression is almost a sort of sin, Monckton maintained his composure. Beyond all else, the events of the past weeks had sapped all his reserve energy and emotion. He was too tired for tears, even within himself. He knew the King was beyond argument and he didn't even attempt it.

Now, though, he had a new flicker of concern. "I was desperately afraid that the King might give up his Throne and yet be deprived of his chance to marry Mrs. Simpson."[11] The possibility was real. Until the divorce decree was made absolute in April, the King's proctor could claim collusion or illegalities and stop the proceedings. The proctor could not cite him in the case while he was still king; once the King abdicated, he was as vulnerable to court action as anyone else.

Another potential difficulty was a pending divorce reform bill proposed in the House by A. P. Herbert. If this bill, at this time, became a subject of parliamentary discussion it would again stir up the whole subject of rigged divorces, with perhaps disastrous repercussions for the King. To eliminate all possible pitfalls and give the King the peace of mind he so badly needed, Monckton suggested coupling the bill for abdication with another bill to make Mrs. Simpson's *nisi* divorce absolute and final immediately. "This would have cleared up a grave constitutional position affecting the whole world and left no ragged ends or possibilities for further scandal," he said.[12]

The King was enthusiastic. What it meant was that he would not have to be separated from Wallis until April, but that he could marry her immediately.

That evening at The Fort, Baldwin was in a highly charged mood. The climax had come and he had won, and yet he tasted ashes in his mouth. Beneath the pragmatic politician, there was a man whom his first cousin Rudyard Kipling had called "the literary member of our family." He was a cauldron of sensitive imagination and hard fact. He saw before him a younger man in trouble, and his fatherly feeling came to the fore. He not only bought Monckton's proposals, but untypically volunteered the emotional statement that he would resign as Prime Minister if the Cabinet turned down the proposal for the divorce bill.

The Prime Minister's son, Oliver, afterward told Harold Nicolson how his father and the King walked around and around the garden discussing the abdication that night. Back in the library of The Fort, his father felt exhausted and asked for a whiskey and soda. Then he raised his glass and said, "Well, Sir, whatever happens, my Mrs. and I wish you happiness from the depth of our souls."[13]

"At which the King burst into floods of tears," Nicolson noted in his diary. "Then S.B. himself began to cry. What a strange conversation-piece, those two blubbering together on a sofa!"[14]

Baldwin had a special Cabinet meeting to discuss bills planned for Sunday as well as a meeting with the Archbishop of Canterbury.

The King, meanwhile, was keeping his abdication plans secret, even from Churchill and Beaverbrook. Churchill had written the Prime Minister that he thought it would be "cruel and wrong" to force the King to make an important decision in his present condition. To the newspapers, Churchill issued a statement:

"I plead for time and patience . . . There is no question of any conflict between the King and Parliament. Parliament has not been consulted in any way . . .

"The question is whether the King is to abdicate upon the advice of the Ministry of the day. No such advice has ever before been tendered to a Sovereign in Parliamentary times . . . No Ministry has the authority to advise the abdication of the Sovereign . . . If the King refuses to take the advice of his Ministers, they are, of course, free to resign . . . Again, there is cause for time and patience . . ."[15]

Elsewhere in the press, Labour MP Colonel Josiah Wedgwood (of the Wedgwood china family) wrote:

"Don't bully the King! The thing we have got to avoid more than anything else is abdication . . . The King is beloved. Any change will tear the country in two."[16]

Massing in front of Buckingham Palace that weekend, thousands of citizens demonstrated for the "Poor Man's King." Some of their placards read:

HANDS OFF OUR KING. ABDICATION MEANS
REVOLUTION![17]
WE WANT EDDIE AND WE WANT HIS MISSUS.[18]
EDWARD'S RIGHT AND BALDWIN'S WRONG![19]

From Emporia, Kansas, William Allen White, editor of the *Gazette*, prepared a statement that he urged the King to broadcast from Buckingham Palace:

"You are all a bunch of white-livered hypocrites, for if I was to carry this gal on the payroll as a *sub-rosa* cutie instead of taking her in through the front door and giving her a good name, you would all wink and snicker and say 'Oh well, boys will be boys,' but anyway she is not that kind of a girl and I am not that kind of a fellow."[20]

Novelist Sinclair Lewis pleaded in the press:

"David Windsor, come over here! We are a funny people because we believe in righteousness. We believe that a man must have his own conscience, his own wife. We believe that perhaps the most important thing that has happened in the last hundred years is whether David Windsor should have his own life or not."[21]

Beaverbrook got word of the special Cabinet meeting called to discuss the King's decision to abdicate and went to Churchill to tell him "my miserable news."[22]

"Our cock won't fight," insisted Beaverbrook.[23]

But Churchill, who had just seen the King and felt the fight in him, refused to believe it.

That night at dinner with Sir Edward Peacock, Monckton's colleague, a different king discussed Churchill's suggestions. Peacock remembered him saying that "Winston had been very amusing, but quite wrong in what he suggested, and that such a course would be inexcusable."[24]

Peacock even remembered the King speaking "with gratitude of Stanley Baldwin's kindness and help."[25] Possibly, he was still enjoined by their mutual tears.

The King was not a man of guile, but he would not tell even Wallis that the deed was done. He was still awake in the early morning hours of Sunday, December 6, when the entourage arrived in Cannes.

Wallis slept the sleep of exhaustion that first night. When she awoke, it was almost noon, and the sun was blazing. Her bedroom had a balcony overlooking the orange, fig and palm trees, the brilliant beds of flowers and the spectacular view of the valley to the sea. She flung open the doors and stood there in her pale pink negligee, her arms outstretched, forgetting the sleet and snow of the night, the harrowing thirty-six-hour drive, forgetting everything for a fraction of a second. Then, as she opened her eyes, she remembered who she was. Down the road, in front of the villa, were crowds of Wallis-watchers, waiting for a glimpse of the most famous woman of the world. Perched in the trees surrounding the villa were the photographers with their long-range lenses. She hurriedly backed into her room, shut the doors and kept them shut.

Wallis Simpson had become Public Figure Number One. Her pale pink negligee became part of a story on the front page of *The New York Times*. The world wanted to know absolutely everything about her. Who was this woman who had so captured the heart of a king? What did she eat, what did she wear, what did she think? Was her friends' yacht in the harbor ready to spirit her away to some rendezvous? Was the King's private plane being warmed up to fly to her? Did she look more like Hollywood actress Miriam Hopkins or like the Mona Lisa? If she married the King, would women really have to curtsy to her? Would that make her a Royal Highness? Was it true that the King had given her a million dollars' worth of jewels?

One New York newspaper thought it important enough to fill a good part of its front page with close-up pictures of the eyes of Wallis and the eyes of the King, with the caption: THEIR EYES GAZE INTO THE FUTURE.[26]

What was their future? Neither of them really knew. Their life had become a matter of day-after-day living with the unexpected and the unpredictable.

Wallis knew the stark fact that she was a prisoner. The gawking, noisy crowd outside the courtyard seemed willing to sleep there and the dozens of scattered photographers never seemed to sleep at all. Besides the Scotland Yard detective, there were French Sûreté agents and gendarmes. She could never take an unseen walk in the garden or open the window for a deep breath of the sweet-scented air. And her telephone was surely tapped.

She learned only later that Herman Rogers, who slept alone in the room adjoining hers, put a pistol under his pillow the day she arrived.

"Wallis was the great love of his [Herman's] life," said Herman's second wife, Lucy. "But it was purely a platonic relationship. He was such a straightforward man that he would not have had it any other way—and he would never have divorced Katherine, who knew how he felt about Wallis but put up with it. But if Herman had become a widower earlier, before Wallis met the Duke, I'm sure he would have married her. In fact, he told me so."[27]

Herman gave Wallis what sympathy and tenderness he could at this time, but there had to be limits to it. Katherine Rogers, a head taller than she was, and not as attractive, was an old friend from her California days, and they genuinely liked each other, but Herman must have been an invisible barrier between them. Perry Brownlow was wise and wonderful and honest and she could always count on him for a straight answer, but his heart and mind were elsewhere, at The Fort with his king.

She could completely confide in any of them, but it's doubtful that she did. She was not the confiding kind. Beyond that, misery was something she did not like to share. It reflected a weakness she did not like to admit.

Her mother had once told her that loneliness had its uses, that it helped one to think, but she didn't want to think. Her private torture was her memory and her imagination. What had she done wrong? And when? And why? What could she do now? What should she say to the King? Did she have any options at all?

She always insisted she loved to live life with a heedlessness. Now, more than ever, she wanted to see the coming pattern of her life laid out before her with the detail and directions of a road map. She saw herself, instead, caught in a maze, wandering in and out of rooms, with nowhere to run, nowhere to hide.

The joke of it for her was the graphologist, examining her handwriting, who had written, "not much 'inner conflict' in that even and confident hand." She did write in bold strokes, and it did have the look of confidence, but her whole being was a mass of inner conflict. A variety of astrologers had publicly analyzed her horoscope, many of them contradicting each other. She was a Gemini in conjunction with the planet Venus, which meant favorable love, wrote one of them. Another noted the influence of Neptune, which meant "grandiose power" rather than love. A third observed that the sun had eclipsed on her previous birthday and that she must not consider any marriage in the coming year. Then, too, there was always the memory of the fortune teller who had told her long ago that she would marry a king.

The astrologers all agreed on one thing: she was a Gemini with two faces and two lives. Wallis was determined to show only one of them.

The servants at the villa saw her as a woman who maintained a sort of mindless chatter. But her friends knew her torment.

"Wallis then was no longer the cool, confident Wallis I had known," Brownlow remembered. "In Cannes, she was at her most different. She was worried, frightened. And, frankly, I wasn't there to calm her fears. My concern was with the King."[28]

That was also Wallis' concern. What frightened her most was that she was no longer in control of anything. It was all happening elsewhere and she got only trickles of the truth over the telephone. That first day she listened to the King trying to be soothing and hopeful and she knew he was only spoon-feeding her pap, so as not to worry her. She could sense his weariness, but she could only guess at what he was really doing and thinking. She kept insisting that he should fight for his rights, that he was the King, that he was so loved by the people that this popularity could carry anything and everything. She was thinking of the sweeping democratic power of the American people and not the great determining force of a secret British Cabinet meeting. She felt her insistence and enthusiasm buoy him a bit, but she didn't know how long it would last. She knew how he waited for her calls, how he longed for them, because he told her so, but she no longer knew what force she had with him.

She knew she could no longer tell the King what he must do. The wire connecting them now was tapped by British M-5 Security, and also overheard by underpaid French telephone operators who promptly passed on everything to the many generous newspaper reporters. Knowing this, the King and Wallis tried to talk in code:

The King was still "Mr. James," Churchill was "W.S.C.," Beaverbrook was "Tornado," and Baldwin remained "Crutch."[29]

Every so often the double-talk complexity of their code would confound her and she would break through, emotionally, telling him that he must not make any rash decisions, that he must listen to the advice of his friends, that nothing would be harmed by waiting.

The King's only answer was that he had to deal with the situation in his own way.

There were several phone calls that first day but the connection was always bad.

It was a handsome cage, this stone villa set at the top of a narrow, winding road. Cypresses hemmed in the back of it and the front overlooked the sea. "Lou Viei," the name of the villa, meant "The Old One." One of the historic houses of Cannes, it was once a twelfth-century monastery that later became a pirate's hideout. The local legend said it had been haunted by the spirit of a beautiful woman, disappointed in love, waiting for her unfaithful lover. The Rogerses had bought it in 1927, greatly modernized it, installed six bedrooms and bathrooms, badminton courts and a tea pavilion, and lit the pink stucco courtyard with their Chinese lanterns.

Looking at the lanterns that night Wallis felt an added unreality. Peking had been the romantic fantasy of her life. The peace there had been complete, the forgetfulness full, the contentment absolute. A different handsome man each night, if she wanted it, as she often did. It was Shangri-La, and why had she ever left it?

Now she was a world headline, a public face, a figure for finger-pointing; now she was "that woman!"

Now she was even a part of a jingle.

> The King is in his palace, fighting many foes
> Mrs. Simpson rests in sunny France, thinking
> of her woes...[30]

The irony of it was that to many millions she was the most envied woman in the world.

Of the many thousands of articles written about the crisis, imagining every possible alternative, the most wildly improbable one was written for Wallis' hometown newspaper, the Baltimore *Sun*. The headline read: EDWARD'S ARDOR BELIEVED FADING.

"Despite the prevailing impression . . . that the King is madly in love with Mrs. Simpson," the article continued, "he is, as a matter of fact, it was said, beginning to grow just a little bit tired of her, and it is but a question of time before this affair goes the way of others . . ."

The most optimistic note came from Keith Prowse & Co., Ltd., which continued to advertise in *The New York Times* that they still had tickets for the Coronation Procession of His Majesty King Edward VIII. "*You* want the best seats; *We* have them."

One of the most forthright writers was Walter Pitkin, author of *Life Begins at Forty*. "All his life Edward was raised to be a model dummy . . . Now he can live his own life . . ." Dr. Thaddeus Bolton, head of Temple University's Psychology Department, claimed that the King was "in the throes of a belated love trance." He added: "The King and Mrs. Simpson are in the third stage of that little bacillus called love which finds many women reaching the period of richest attractiveness only as they approach forty."[31]

The most neutral note came from Mayor William Hale "Big Bill" Thompson of Chicago. In 1927, he had threatened to "crack King George on the snoot." Now, he said: "The King's lady friends are no business of mine, or anyone else's."[32]

Sir Stafford Cripps was more querulous: ". . . I cannot help feeling that if the lady in question had been a member of the English aristocracy, under precisely similar circumstances, a quite different decision would have been come to by the government . . ."[33]

Cripps had a point, but it was a point silently agreed to by the English aristocracy itself, not by the masses of British people. The ugly root of the matter for the middle-class Briton, and even a large segment of the working class, was the existence of two living divorced husbands.

The public mood that weekend of December 5 in England had started to turn. Members of the Cabinet and Parliament had gone home to their constituencies, and returned filled with this public animosity against a divorced woman. The British Mothers' Union, of which Queen Mary was a patroness, representing 577,000 mothers in 13,000 branches, made public its "anxious concern."[34]

Baldwin's Cabinet ministers met for their special Sunday morning session, and the debate was long. Despite Baldwin's pressure for approval of the two bills, the Cabinet refused. Neville Chamberlain later told Monckton that "the two bills smacked of a bargain where there ought to be none; that the second bill [for Mrs. Simpson's quick divorce] would affront the moral sense of the Nation and that it would be resisted and debated, and that in the course of the debate unpleasant statements and suggestions would be made."[35]

Sir Edward Peacock further added that this bill could not possibly be passed in Parliament. He pointed out the danger that the King's proctor would note this intervention "and none of them could interfere with the law."[36]

Several of the more immediate reasons given by the ministers for turning down the divorce bill was that "it would lose votes" and that the church would consider it "an abomination."[37] Informing Monckton of their decision, they then asked him how the King would react. Monckton said he felt the King would be bitterly disappointed and would now want more time to consult other advisers. Monckton measured this time in weeks rather than days. The ministers were plainly unhappy. Baldwin insisted the affair "must be finished before Christmas."[38] Neville Chamberlain mentioned the bad effect of the crisis on trade and Christmas shopping.

That Sunday in churches all over England the clergy offered prayers—without sermons—for the King and the royal family. It was a woman preacher, Maude Royden, conducting a nondenominational service in Guild House, who said: "I ask everyone to pray for the

King and also not to forget the woman he loves, who also needs your prayers."

The Archbishop of Canterbury arrived at 10 Downing Street for his meeting with Baldwin, added his opposition to the "abomination" bill of divorce and received Baldwin's assurance that the King would abdicate. Police had to force through the crowd to get the Archbishop to his car. The crowd kept chanting, "The King Can Do No Wrong." A caption under the Archbishop's picture in the paper the next morning read: THE MAN WHO OBJECTS. In the public mind, the prelate's meeting with Baldwin only heightened the talk of a conspiracy against the King.

Baldwin also went to see Queen Mary that day. "I see the world around me being shattered," she told him, "the world which took me so long to build up."[39]

Her husband had been "the solid worth of England"[40] and his creed was that the king must be "the fountain of honour." Tradition of kings was stamped into every British schoolboy's mind, along with the Battle of Hastings and Magna Charta. The king's head appeared on every letter, every coin, every bill. Royalty stood for the pageantry of magnificence and Queen Mary now saw it as mucked with mud. The Queen's official biographer, James Pope-Hennessy, reported she had told her family that "no single event in the whole of her life . . . had caused her so much real distress or left her with so deep a feeling of 'humiliation.' "

Baldwin managed to hurt the image still further that Sunday afternoon. Having tapped the King's phone, he knew of the daily conversations with Wallis Simpson, and was worried about her plans. He had Acting Head of the Treasury Sir Horace Wilson call in Wallis' divorce solicitor, Theodore Goddard. Acting for Baldwin, Wilson asked Goddard to visit Mrs. Simpson and find out "her real intentions." Goddard agreed.

The King was bitter at Monckton's news. They had refused his compromise on a morganatic marriage. They had denied him the right to make his radio talk to the people. He was willing to leave the kingship quietly, and with dignity, but not without firm assurance that he would have no problem in marrying the woman he loved. They now wanted his complete surrender.

Monckton did mention that Baldwin had repeated his willingness to resign because he could not deliver the divorce bill and that Monckton had assured him, on behalf of the King, that they did not wish this. It would only have meant that Neville Chamberlain would have become prime minister and his attitude against the King was almost vehement.

The King now found himself caught in a corner and squirming.

Wallis was still more frightened. She felt she was no longer reaching the King. He was her only source of information and he was letting little seep through. She was bewildered. She still kept insisting to him over the phone, again and again, that he should fight for his rights, that his popularity with the people would carry anything. The British people themselves barely knew what was happening. The Cabinet sessions were secret. Parliament knew only what Baldwin told them, and he told them only driblets.

Lord Brownlow saw the trend clearly. "I told Wallis that she had to issue a statement renouncing the King. I didn't think it would work but I felt we had to do something."[41]

Wallis finally agreed and he and Herman Rogers prepared a statement for the press. She read it and watered it down. It read:

"Mrs. Simpson, throughout the last few weeks, has invariably wished to avoid any action or proposal which would hurt or damage His Majesty or The Throne.

"Today her attitude is unchanged, and she is willing, if such action would solve the problem, to withdraw forthwith from a situation that has been rendered both unhappy and untenable."[42]

Wallis knew it wouldn't work. Everything had gone too far. At least, though, it stated her position to the people. Maybe they would despise her less now. Everything seemed so hopeless. She should never have left England, never have left him alone.

The distance between Wallis and the King was now more than physical. He was wrestling with his confusions and she with her ignorance, each in a separate world with nothing connecting them but an incoherent piece of tapped wire. He was trying to save her from worry and, instead, only multiplied it. She was trying to get him to fight a battle when the war was lost. It was no longer a romance; it was a tragedy.

The tragedy deepened on Monday, December 7. Wallis called the King in the morning and read him the statement she planned to release that afternoon. She recalled that he was at first unbelieving, then hurt. Finally he told her to go ahead and issue it. "It won't make any difference."[43]

Their weekend sampling had convinced a great many members of Parliament that the British voters wanted the King, but they did not want Wallis. "It wouldn't have done," a taxi driver said.[44]

Baldwin informed the House of Commons that afternoon that the government was still waiting for the King to make up his mind. Winston Churchill then made his final, forlorn stand.

Before he stood up, Sir George Lambert, who sat next to him, pleaded with him, "My dear Churchill, I beg you from the depths of my soul, don't intervene in this. Don't you sense the feeling of the House?"

Churchill's answer was "I am not afraid of this House, and when I see my duty, I go straight ahead."

He launched a strong attack, saying the government had no right to force the King to abdicate without consulting Parliament. Four days before, the Commons had cheered him for making the same request. Now the public was changing its mind, and so were they.

"Sit down!" some of them shouted. "Shut up!" And more of them booed.

"Winston suffered an utter defeat," Nicolson recorded. He almost lost his head, and he certainly lost his command of the House. It was terribly dramatic.

"First we had Baldwin—slow and measured. Then Winston rose to ask a supplementary question. He failed to do it in the right form and was twice called to order by the Speaker. He hesitated and waved his spectacles vaguely in the air. 'Sit down!' they shouted. He waved his spectacles again and then collapsed. It was almost painful."[45]

The Times of London later described it as "the most striking rebuff in modern parliamentary history."[46]

Describing how "Winston collapsed utterly," Nicolson wrote his wife, Vita Sackville-West, "Bob Boothby was so funny about it. 'I knew,' he said, 'that Winston was going to do something dreadful. I had been staying the weekend with him. He was silent and restless and glancing into corners. Now when a dog does that, you know that he is about to be sick on the carpet. It is the same with Winston. He managed to hold it for three days, and then comes up to the House and is sick right across the floor.' Which is literally true. He has undone in five minutes the patient reconstruction work of two years."[47]

There was no longer time for his "battalions to march."

Most political observers agreed that Churchill had gone into this royal battle not simply to fight for the King but to fight against Baldwin. Churchill's great concern was the growing danger of Nazi Germany and Baldwin's revealed record on British rearmament was pitiful. Like Beaverbrook, he hoped that this issue would oust the current prime minister. Out of power too long, Churchill wanted back in. Instead, everything had crumbled around him, shattering his political hopes, severely damaging the needed push for more rapid rearmament.

A generation later, Churchill was busy painting at Beaverbrook's villa on the French Riviera. The two men talked of their early political struggles, how they had always seemed to differ. "Except once," said Beaverbrook, mentioning the abdication crisis.[48]

"Perhaps we were both wrong that time," answered Churchill.[49]

When Churchill stormed out of the House, "a look of thunder" on his face, Lambert arose and said, "Does the Prime Minister realize the deep sympathy which is felt for him [Baldwin] in all sections of the House?"[50]

There was a wild burst of applause.

The King's Party was dead. The sputtering rocket had fizzled. With it seemed to ebb the great vitality of the King. He had driven himself beyond endurance. Despite this, he had insisted on seeing Theodore Goddard and forbidding him to visit Wallis. In Great Britain there were few things more sacred than the relationship between a solicitor and his client, but such was the King's intense desire to keep Wallis away from worry that he had no hesitation even in interfering in this. Goddard remained noncommittal as the King helped him on with his coat and escorted him to the door. Goddard's next stop was the Prime Minister.

Wallis, meanwhile, was ready to release her statement of renunciation. At this point she was ready to release anything. Even during Spencer's drunken days, she had had a remarkable endurance, an ability to cope. Now she felt herself floundering in a whirlpool, and Brownlow and Rogers were the only anchors she could reach. Having lost all her self-confidence she needed minds and shoulders stronger than hers. She sent the two men to the Majestic Hotel in Cannes, where Brownlow read her statement to the press.

Brownlow himself had not been happy with the statement. He felt it was too weak. "I wrote it, but I myself didn't know what it meant."[51] Wallis had altered it, weakened it. She was afraid of hurting the King too much. She was torn.

She knew better than anyone how he would weigh every word. She knew how he was suffering, how lonely he was, how sensitive. She already felt too responsible for all the hurt he had and she didn't want to add to it. Consequently, she softened the sharp statement into something much less than forthright. Besides, it seemed like too final a plunge and she had the lingering hope that her king might somehow still manage the miracle.

"I made the statement at five P.M. In London at six P.M., the newspapers were full of headlines that Wallis was giving up the King."[52]

Most of this optimistic reaction came from the Rothermere-Beaverbrook newspapers. Rothermere's *Daily Mail* placed its emphasis on the two words "unhappy" and "untenable."

"In the first, she records the verdict of her heart, in the second, that of her head. In both she is right."

Beaverbrook's *Daily Express* had the biggest headline:

END OF CRISIS.

The *Daily Express* declared:

"Let's say this of Mrs. Simpson. Her name has been thrown about by gossips in some parts of the world for a long time and in our part for long enough. By her word printed yesterday she answers the whole pack of them."

But what did the statement itself mean, what did it do?

Brownlow, who wrote it, admittedly didn't know. Wallis was equally unsure. As a true renunciation, it rang "somewhat hollow." The King had approved its issuance reluctantly, perhaps realizing that it would, to some extent, "divert criticism from her to him, the very thing he wanted."

People read into it what they wanted.

The *Express* was the most optimistic:

"Can we rejoice? Yes we can rejoice. The crisis has passed into history, and the King is still with us. The deadlock has been broken by the act of renunciation by a woman."

Answering its own question, LOVE OR THRONE?, a New York newspaper replied firmly: EDWARD WILL KEEP THRONE.

When the headlines hit the streets, the King called Wallis, and exploded, "You're ruining my plans. You're making me look like a fool."[53] He still didn't tell her, however, what his plans were.

Wallis saw fit not to argue with him then. She might well have reminded him that he had agreed to let her issue the statement. He had not expected the newspapers to react as they had. He had seen it only as a statement that might minimize the animosity toward Wallis. Since he already had told Baldwin that he would abdicate, the new development was an unwanted wrinkle. Though she did not say so, Wallis was delighted with the headlines. Perhaps they *would* let her ease out.

But the King's pain agonized her. In the meanwhile, she had other problems. The photographers had been most troublesome. Several of them had managed to get into the garden, hide in the shrubbery until she finally appeared, and then their flashbulbs popped. Detectives rushed on the scene, smashed cameras and made arrests. In the hope of forestalling any such future incidents, Wallis agreed to pose for a single photograph. She arrived in a black sports suit with a blue jersey and high-heeled shoes. She had a sad expression when she posed, and the photographer asked her to smile.[54]

"Why smile?" she asked.

Goddard had gone to see Prime Minister Baldwin at Downing Street to report on the King's reaction to his proposed trip to Cannes. Baldwin showed Goddard the afternoon headlines and asked him what he knew about the Simpson statement. Goddard, of course, knew nothing of it. Baldwin then said that it was Goddard's duty to go to Wallis Simpson and find out what was going on, regardless of how the King felt about it. Goddard then said he would "certainly go," and Baldwin made a private government plane available.

The King soon learned of this and again called Wallis. He told her Goddard was coming and ordered her not to see him, listen to him or talk to him. Wallis bristled. He not only sounded strong enough for her to argue with, but she resented his imperious tone. In most of their calls she had kept her tone pleading and conciliating, trying always to reason with him. Now she was angry. She had kept too much welled in her for too long. She had had it. Who did he think he was anyway? She didn't like to be ordered to do anything by anybody. She had her own mind. There was also a simple question of courtesy. Goddard *was* her solicitor. She certainly would meet him and listen to him. Who knows, she might even agree with him.

The King backtracked, quieting quickly. The most he could get her to say was that she would consult with him before she made any final decision based on what Goddard would have to say.

Geoffrey Dawson decided that the Simpson statement meant "exactly nothing." He simply printed Wallis' statement on top of another new item, which read: "Thelma Viscountess Furness arrived at Southampton on the liner *Queen Mary* yesterday from New York."[55] It was the kind of coupling that caused snickers in certain social circles, but it was criticized as "feline malice and vulgar frivolity that can scarcely have been paralleled in the worst of the gutter press."[56]

On Tuesday, December 8, Dawson correctly gauged that "there was little kick left in the opposition by this time, and we were all simply waiting for the crisis to end at Fort Belvedere and not at Cannes."[57]

Goddard, meanwhile, arrived in Cannes late that night. Bad weather and a broken engine had delayed the flight.

"I was awakened at four A.M. and handed a message from the press," Lord Brownlow said, "and it was the news that Theodore Goddard and a clerk and gynecologist were at Marseilles, en route to Cannes. I told the press I knew nothing about this and they would not get into the villa."[58]

Wallis had neglected to inform Brownlow about Goddard.

"Then Goddard called me and asked for an interview with Wallis, on family affairs," Brownlow continued. "I told him he could see her, if he got out of the car a hundred yards in front of the gate, came in without a briefcase, without the clerk and without the doctor."[59]

The reporters had made much of the doctor's presence. He was Dr. W. Douglas Kirkwood, formerly house surgeon at Queen Charlotte's Hospital for Women, one of London's largest maternity and gynecological hospitals. The quickest rumor was that Wallis might be pregnant. A more reasoned one was that the six months' delay for the *nisi* decree to be made absolute was provided mainly in case a child should be born in that interim to the wife of the divorced husband. Therefore, if this doctor could establish that no child was expected, it could expedite the divorce.

Goddard's explanation was that he had a heart condition and this was the first time he had flown in a plane, and he therefore thought it advisable to bring along a doctor friend.

Rather than expedite the divorce, Goddard had a private idea, one which, if successful, might indeed have made him the hero of the hour—not to the King, not to Wallis, not to Baldwin, but to the royal family and the British people.

Goddard's proposal was absolutely simple: Wallis should withdraw her divorce action and the crisis would be over. Since the King would not then marry her, there would be no point in his abdication.

Wallis was delighted with the idea. It sounded sensible and plausible, a perfect solution. She knew Ernest Simpson would go along with it, because she knew how seriously he felt about the abdication, how willing he was to do anything to stop it, and because he had earlier made overtures about the same subject. At that time she passed it on to the King; now she was more ready to listen. She wasn't exactly sure how deeply he was committed to Mary Kirk, but it would all resolve itself in a matter of time. She felt Churchill and Beaverbrook were right on this. Let him go through with the coronation and this tempest would resolve itself in a typical British afternoon tea. Then they could marry, and so could Ernest and Mary.

If she could be with the King at that moment, she knew she could convince him of this. It was so simple, so right. But he would have to agree to it. Why had she run away? She should never have left him. Now they could still have everything, and each other. How could she explain all this to him in that stupid code? The telephone was just no good for this sort of thing. It needed a quiet night, just the two of them, with a few drinks, in front of a fire. She was so certain she could make him see it.

Goddard filled her in on the changing British reaction to the whole affair. "She definitely said she was quite prepared to give him up," Goddard recalled, and added that it was essential to get the King's agreement or else, "wherever she went, the King would follow her."[60]

Wallis wanted Brownlow's judgment, and invited him in to consider Goddard's proposal.

"I thought about it for five minutes," Brownlow remembered, "and then I said she shouldn't do it, because if she did, and the King kept after her, as he would, then the divorce would ultimately take place some six months later in Reno or Mexico or elsewhere, and it would cause an even stronger stink in Great Britain. Besides, she knew the King wouldn't stand for her being his mistress until they could marry. He wanted her with him always and he was bourgeois about it: he wanted to make an honest woman of her. Wallis listened to me, but she knew I was not representing her; I was representing the King."[61]

Wallis hesitated. What should she do? To whom should she listen? She trusted Brownlow completely. But what Goddard said seemed like a way out, the only way out she could see. Perry Brownlow had known the King ever since they were young men together. And nobody knew better than herself how stubborn the King could be. But the price was right. It was worth making the full try to convince him.

Wallis called the King. Goddard remembered the connection as being "a very bad one . . . there were continual interruptions."[62] Add to that the frustrations of the shouting and the code and the tension.

Wallis told him that she had decided to withdraw her divorce petition. The King, in his effort to dissuade her, put his legal adviser, George Allen, on the wire.

Allen told her not to withdraw the petition because the King had already set the machinery for abdication in motion.

Wallis hung up. He had decided and gone ahead without even discussing it with her, without even telling her about it afterward. And, even now, he couldn't bring himself to tell her; he had to let Allen do it. Why?

Suddenly she felt too emotionally drained even for anger. It was all over, the drama was over and the tragedy had begun. As pale and broken as she was, somehow she managed to say good-by to Goddard and leave the room without any overt display. Inside, she never felt more dead.

No matter how the King felt that evening, he still had a dinner guest, Prime Minister Baldwin.

"He must wrestle with himself in a way he has never done before," Baldwin confided to a friend, "and if he will let me, I will help him. We may even have to see the night through together."[63]

Speaking later to another friend, Baldwin added, "Only time I was frightened. I thought he might change his mind; but I need not have been. He had given his word, and that was enough."[64]

Baldwin arrived at The Fort with his suitcase, prepared to spend the night. The King felt he could not deal with the Prime Minister all that time and asked Sir Edward Peacock to gently tell Baldwin that he was welcome to dinner but that the King was too worn out to discuss anything more that night.

The talk they did have before dinner was short and fruitless. Baldwin gave him a copy of the Cabinet message, a polite, formal note asking the King to "reconsider an intention which must so deeply distress and so vitally affect all Your Majesty's subjects."[65]

281

The King well knew the hypocrisy of it, how anxious the Cabinet was for him to abdicate quickly and quietly.

Among the dinner guests that night were the Duke of York and Walter Monckton. For the Duke, it was the end of that "awful and ghastly suspense of waiting."[66] The King told his brother, who would succeed him, of his irreversible decision.

Knowing how absolutely exhausted the King was, Monckton suggested that the two of them dine alone, and let the other guests eat in the dining room. But for the King it was a test of strength.

"When we were settled down for dinner, he walked in and sat at the head of the table between Mr. Baldwin on his right and Sir Edward Peacock. This dinner party was, I think, his *tour de force*. In that quiet, panelled room he sat at the head of the table with his boyish face and smile, with a good fresh colour while the rest of us were pale as sheets, rippling over with bright conversation and with a careful eye to see that his guests were being looked after. He wore his white kilt. On Mr. Baldwin's right was the Duke of York, and I was next to him, as the dinner went on, the Duke turned to me and said: 'Look at him. We simply cannot let him go.' But we both knew that there was nothing that we could say or do to stop him."[67]

Wallis had the same feeling. At that distance, he was a different man. He was a king and an emperor and he wanted to act out his last hour to the full. The way he had told her not to see Goddard— he didn't ask her, he commanded. He had never ordered her to do anything before.

Wallis, though, was worn to a frazzle of taut nerves. He had told her so little and countered her so much, vetoing all her ideas as if they were nonsense, and only his plans were the perfect ones. When she was with him, she knew his unsureness. When she was this far away, she could only sense his metamorphosis. He had made his decision; he would act his part.

The fault was hers, not simply for leaving him, but for freely putting her life and her fate in his hands, for his decision and his disposal, without consultation.

She had done this the day she agreed to marry him, the day she had agreed to divorce Simpson. The succession of events then had its own momentum, its own multiplying speed and force, all beyond her control.

"Wallis was getting increasingly terrified as the situation intensified," said Brownlow, "and I helped to terrify her, trying to explain the enormity of the decisions.[68]

"During my stay at Cannes, we made only one trip outside the villa. Lord Rothermere's son, Esmond Harmsworth, an old friend of Wallis' and mine, was staying nearby and asked us to come for tea because he had something important to tell us. It was Harmsworth who had first proposed the morganatic marriage idea. This time he told us about the proposed set-up of a Council of State to govern while the King was away, but we found it hard to believe it was even being considered.

"On the drive home, I told Wallis that if she let him abdicate, and married him, she would be the most hated white woman in the world."[69]

Wallis cringed. She knew deep within her that what Perry Brownlow said was absolutely true. She had felt it a long time ago. She had read it in the daily flood of mail.

All her life she had wanted people to like her, and they had, they always had. She believed in fun and she made people laugh, and they loved it. And they loved her for it. She was always a welcome guest at any party. She radiated charm and cheerfulness. It was a great gift, and she had it. And she had a pride in it. She wanted to be liked; she wanted to be loved.

Now, suddenly, there was hate. There was more hate than she had ever known. And it was only the beginning. Not only couldn't she handle it, it was too enormous for her even to think about.

What's more, there was nothing she could do. Her David had pulled the rug from under her without even alerting her. He had kept it as his own private secret, as if it involved only his life. It involved her more than him. People would pity him and hate her. They would blame her for everything. And maybe they were right. At least he could have consulted her after he had made his decision. He at least had had a choice; she had had none.

"She started crying," said Brownlow. "She really broke down. I had never seen her cry before. No matter how worried she was, or how exhausted, she always somehow had managed a sense of calm and dignity and control. But that was all gone now. She just couldn't take it any more. She was just crying and crying. I tried to comfort her and finally she quieted and she looked at me and she asked me: 'What should I do?' "[70]

24

"SHE ASKED ME what I would do if I were in her place. I told her we should leave immediately, that very night. I would arrange for a train to Rome, then on to Genoa and we would get on a ship to Ceylon. She said, 'All right, let's do it.' She was ready to do anything, she really was. However, my loyalty was still to the King and I felt she should call him first and tell him what she was doing. You see, I knew him, and I knew what he was going through, too. I felt he had to know. She called him, and he gave her a terrible bawling out, said that it would upset all his plans, that she was 600 miles away, and couldn't possibly know what was going on, that if she did go to Ceylon, or anywhere else, he would simply follow her immediately. He then told her that the only conditions on which he could stay would be if he renounced her for all time, and that he could never do. Did she want him to do that?"[1]

She had told him earlier that anything was better than abdication, but this "anything" was too much. They could give each other up for a while, for an interim until things quieted, but they could not give each other up forever.

That ended it. Her fight was over.

The British public sensed it, too. They had begun to realize more fully the heart of the conflict: their king had to choose between them and a woman, and he wanted the woman. Even in South Wales, where the King was most loved, the people were bitter and disapproving.

Even Wallis' old friend and social sponsor Lady Emerald Cunard turned traitor. Harold Nicolson overheard her say to a friend, "Maggie darling, do tell me about this Mrs. Simpson—I have only just met her."

"What is so tragic is that now people have got over the first sentimental shock, they *want* the King to abdicate," Nicolson wrote in his diary. "I mean opinion in the House is now almost wholly anti-King. 'If he can betray his duty and then betray the woman he loves, there is no good in the man.' Thus although he may keep his throne if he 'renounces' Mrs. Simpson, he will have lost the respect of his subjects.

". . . Two things emerge, I think. First the supremacy of Baldwin. A leading Labour man said to me yesterday, 'Thank God we have S.B. at the top. No other man in England could have coped with this.' And, secondly, how unanimous the House really is in time of crisis. There has been no hysteria and no party politics. One really feels that at such moments the House is a Council of State. What a *solid* people we are under all our sentimentality."[2]

The switch from the sentimental to the "solid" found a dramatic sidelight that day in the small seaside resort town of Lancing, England, when the Parish Council decided not to name a new street "King Edward Avenue," and instead called it "Power Road."

That street was well named. The kingship had become a power road. The British king was not supposed to do much or say much; he was just supposed to be there. The only trouble came when there was a show of power, any kind of power. Regicide came only with the flouting of rules. Showing an open sympathy for impoverished workers made him seem like a populist king. Picking a wife they did not want made him seem a willful king.

As emotionally torn as Wallis was, the King was now almost at the end of his tether. He still had another meeting with his mother that day at the Duke of York's study at the Royal Lodge in Windsor Park. It was his first trip outside The Fort in six days.

The Dowager Queen listened to his account of the past week, bewildered, distraught, but always maintaining her dignity. She simply could not understand. As she later told Monckton, "To give up all *this* for that!"[3] But she did have something tender to say to him that day: "And to me, the worst thing is that you will not be able to see her for so long."[4]

There was no sleep for the King that night. The lights at The Fort were ablaze through most of the night, as they were at 10 Downing Street. The chimes of Big Ben boomed at 2:30 in the cold, foggy morning when a dispatch rider came out of the Prime Minister's historic house with a long, narrow, black metal box, just big enough to hold a scroll. It had a great red seal on it, and reporters and the small

285

crowd correctly guessed it was the abdication decree being rushed to the King for his signature.

So little did Wallis know about British history and tradition that she had asked the King, "Even if you give up being King, can't you still be Emperor of India?"[5]

It was her last desperate attempt to salvage something for both of them. Was it just fate that the two men she really loved both had to make crucial choices between her and a career? Espil had chosen a career and her king had chosen her. Deep within her, she may have wished that each of them had made a different choice.

She was always frail-looking, but now she looked like a wisp of herself. Her big eyes looked bigger and more haunting. She had lost almost ten pounds, a tenth of her normal total weight.

She felt beaten. Katherine Rogers tried to cheer her, telling her she had done everything she could, that nobody could fault her. Wallis knew that it wasn't true. She had done everything wrong. She had done everything too late. Always before she had had the resilience to take things as they came, but not now. Partly, it was because she never even knew what was coming. In trying to insulate her from all concern, the King could not have been more wrong.

Lord Brownlow, too, felt this sense of uselessness and hopelessness. The press kept badgering him constantly and he couldn't tell them anything because he didn't know any more than they did. "I'm going gradually mad with all this," he said.[6] But the worst of it was the defeat. The king he loved was abandoning his throne and he could do nothing.

The Prime Minister had told Monckton that he wanted the abdication completed by Friday night. He and his ministers also emphasized that if the King delayed or went to Mrs. Simpson or did anything different from the plan before the Civil List Bill was passed, he would not get a penny, because Parliament would refuse to pass it.

The Civil List Bill detailed the financial allowance for the royal family out of which would come the settlement the King could expect after his abdication.

Monckton had worked that night at Downing Street along with the Home Secretary, Sir John Simon, and Major Hardinge, among others. Hardinge, still on the King's staff, had visited the Archbishop of Canterbury the previous day to inform him of everything and assure him that the King would abdicate.

Monckton brought a copy of the draft of the abdication message to the King at The Fort. Sir Edward Peacock had arrived before him to give the King the further news that the Cabinet insisted he must not return to England for at least two years. Peacock then suggested that since there was nothing more they could do that night, they all go to bed. The King walked Peacock to his room, continued talking. "I begged him to go to bed," said Peacock. "As he went away I heard him say to poor Walter Monckton, who was dead beat: 'I just want a word with you.'"[7]

The King's three brothers arrived the next morning to witness the signing of the instrument of abdication. It read:

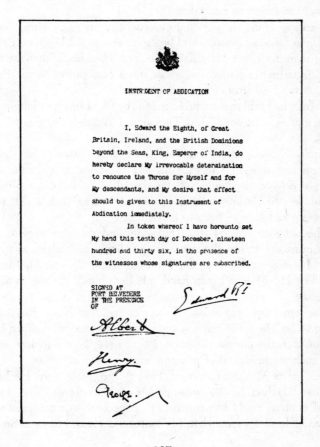

INSTRUMENT OF ABDICATION

I, Edward the Eighth, of Great Britain, Ireland, and the British Dominions beyond the Seas, King, Emperor of India, do hereby declare My irrevocable determination to renounce the Throne for Myself and for My descendants, and My desire that effect should be given to this Instrument of Abdication immediately.

In token whereof I have hereunto set My hand this tenth day of December, nineteen hundred and thirty six, in the presence of the witnesses whose signatures are subscribed.

SIGNED AT
FORT BELVEDERE
IN THE PRESENCE
OF

He signed seven copies of the instrument of abdication and eight of the King's Message to the Parliaments of the Empire. Then, as his brothers signed their names, the King stepped outside to the garden.

Monckton followed him, apologized, then said the Prime Minister had asked whether there was anything the King wanted him to include in his message to Parliament the next day.

The King thought it was "nice of S.B." to make that gesture.[8] He scribbled two notes on separate small rectangular slips of paper. One referred to his confidence in his brother as his successor and noted that they had always been the best of friends.

The other note declared how "the other person most intimately concerned" had consistently tried to the last "to dissuade the King from the decision which he had taken."[9]

Instead of taking the signed documents directly to Downing Street, Monckton followed protocol and brought them to Buckingham Palace, giving them to Major Hardinge to deliver. How ironic that the man whose initial letter started the whole storm now carried to the Prime Minister the final fruit of his work.

Baldwin had said that he preferred to "be silent in seven languages" rather than talk in one.[10] But Thursday, December 10, was his day to talk.

Harold Nicolson described the House of Commons that day as "nervous and noisy." The galleries had filled up in a double row, people sitting on the gangways. He described Baldwin, fumbling to find his key to his box, extracting sheets of paper with a red, royal monogram and some of his own flimsy notes.

"The old man collects them hurriedly and the next minute . . . walks hurriedly to the Bar, turns round, bows, and advances to the Chair. He stops and bows again. 'A message from the King,' he shouts, 'signed by His Majesty's own hand.' He then hands the papers to the Speaker.

"The latter rises and reads out the message of abdication in a quavering voice. The feeling that at any moment he may break down from emotion increases our own emotion. I have never known in any assemblage such accumulation of pity and terror.

"The Prime Minister then rises. He tells the whole story. He had a blue handkerchief in the breast-pocket of his tail-coat. The 'Hear, Hears!' echo solemnly like Amens. His papers are in a confused state . . . and he hesitates somewhat. He confuses dates and turns to Simon,

'It was a Monday, was it not the 27th?' The artifice of such asides is so effective that one imagines it to be deliberate. There is no moment when he overstates emotion or indulges in oratory. There is intense silence broken only by the reporters in the gallery scuttling away to telephone the speech paragraph by paragraph. I suppose that in after-centuries men will read the words of that speech and exclaim, 'What an opportunity wasted!' They will never know the tragic force of its simplicity. 'I said, to the King . . .' 'The King told me . . .' It was Sophoclean and almost unbearable. Attlee felt this. When it was over, he asked that the sitting might be adjourned until 6 P.M. We file out broken in body and soul, conscious that we have heard the best speech that we shall ever hear in our lives. There is no question of applause. It was the silence of Gettysburg."[11]

What was so tragic and unbearable was not simply the speech, alone, but the scene and the deed.

With Baldwin's speech, the House of Commons saw these scenes in their intimate detail for the first time. Baldwin talked of the King as an old and dear friend, and he was not. He talked of himself as trying desperately to keep the King on the throne. The truth of this is much mixed. Indeed, at the start, he did try to persuade the King to do that by giving up Wallis. When the King flatly refused and Baldwin saw how such a marriage would divide the country, then he was plainly eager to see the King abdicate. And, years later, when Brownlow gave Baldwin Wallis' handwritten renunciation of the King, and told him what plans and hopes he had had then to prevent the abdication, Baldwin told him, perhaps not so jokingly, "If you had succeeded I would have put you in the Tower of London for the rest of your natural life."[12]

Yet, at that final dinner at The Fort—the last time they would ever see each other—Baldwin argued even more persuasively than ever "for the sake of the country and for all the King stood for" to abandon his decision to marry. The weary king then asked to be spared any more advice on the subject, but the Prime Minister was slightly deaf and didn't hear him. "To my astonishment," remembered Monckton, "Mr. Baldwin returned to the charge with renewed vigour and, I thought, put the position even better than before."[13]

So there was the truth, mixed as it so often is. The practical, political Baldwin wanted the King out as soon as possible; the emotional, sentimental Baldwin wanted to keep the King.

None of this, of course, was in his speech to Parliament.

He did, however, include the King's requested reference to his brother, but there was no mention of the thing the King wanted even more, his statement of how Wallis had fought to prevent abdication.

The King had called her to tell her about the abdication. She was numb then, but she did tell him what a fool he was.

"We heard the abdication news on the radio," said Brownlow. "We were expecting it. She was stretched out on the couch. She started crying again. The two of us were alone and I tried to comfort her. I don't know how successful I was. She cried for a long time."[14]

The King's dinner at The Fort that night was not the most pleasant. George and Kitty Hunter were there, with Aunt Bessie. The Hunters had been with Wallis at Felixstowe while she waited for her divorce hearing at Ipswich. Kitty Hunter later described the dinner to Monckton.

"The poor King must have had a pretty difficult time," Monckton recalled, "because apparently George and Kitty wept into their soup and everything else during that meal in spite of the King's heroic efforts to carry off the dinner cheerfully."[15]

Monckton still had the King's business to do. He talked to the Duke of York about Edward's title after abdication.

"I pointed out that the title 'His Royal Highness' was one which the Abdication did not take away, and one which would require an Act of Parliament for its removal. The King, for himself and his successors, was renouncing any right to the Throne but not to his Royal Birth which he shared with his brothers. The Duke saw the point and was ready to create his brother Duke of Windsor as the first act of the new reign."[16]

The question of title became more complicated when applied to Wallis, but that was later.

The King had told Baldwin that he planned to make a farewell radio speech to the people after the abdication became official. As a private citizen, he would no longer need Baldwin's permission.

BBC scheduled the speech for that night, Friday, December 11, and arranged for proper cables at Windsor Castle. The whole world asked to be tuned in by relays. Even though there was a civil war going on in Spain, with Madrid being bombed and shelled, Radio Madrid telephoned to request permission to relay the abdication speech.

The King and Monckton worked on the preliminary draft. "On the same day," noted Monckton, "Churchill came down to Fort Belvedere and greatly improved the form of the proposed message, although he did not alter its substance."[17]

Almost as if there were no end to the bad news, Home Secretary John Simon, whose men had been monitoring the King's telephone, notified him that "in the changed circumstances"[18] British detectives protecting Mrs. Simpson at Cannes would now have to be withdrawn.

The King exploded in anger. Everything he had done had been primarily motivated to keep worry or problems or publicity away from Wallis. And now, this. The Home Secretary quickly reversed his decision, and the detectives remained.

Wallis needed all the protection she could get. The crowds were always there, always watching, always waiting. They counted how many boxes of orchids the King had sent her each day. They identified anybody who might be walking in the courtyard. They watched every window, staring inside every exiting car. H. L. Mencken had called it the greatest story since the Resurrection, and they all wanted to feel themselves a part of it.

What made the story so monumental was not simply that the whole world loves a lover, but that most people's lives were so filled with daily drabness that there was a hunger for this kind of romance.

All through Friday as the Abdication Bill was going through its final stages at the House of Commons, all the members seemed to be in a self-congratulatory mood, while making the usual speeches of sympathy to the King.

Independent Labour Party member George Buchanan cut through some of the hypocrisy, saying he had heard more cant and humbug about the King than he ever had in his life. "If he had not voluntarily stepped from the Throne, everyone knows that the same people in the House who pay lip service to him would have poured out scorn, filth and abuse . . . if he is a tenth as good as you say, why are you not keeping him?"[19]

The King and Churchill had lunch together that day at The Fort. Churchill asked for a photograph of the King and the King sent for it. Churchill then took out his watch, and just as Parliament was scheduled to take its final vote on the abdication, he asked the King to sign his name on the photograph. The King signed it "Edward, R.I." and said, "This is the last signature I shall sign as King."[20] The abdication was official at 1:52 P.M. He had served 325 days, 13 hours and 57 minutes.

At the door when he said good-by, the former king heard Churchill recite, almost as if to himself, the lines of Andrew Marvell on the beheading of Charles I:

> *He nothing common did or mean*
> *Upon that memorable scene.*

There were tears in Churchill's eyes as he walked toward the waiting car. Just as the car was ready to leave, the former king came rushing out of the door, shouting, "Hey, Winston, you forgot your picture . . ."[21]

His brother Bertie, the Duke of York, the next king of England, came into his room while he was in the middle of his final packing. Both men felt strange and uneasy. The former king told the future king that the job wasn't that difficult, not to worry about his stutter because it had improved a great deal.

Monckton arrived with the final copy of the speech. Baldwin had indicated to Edward that he would appreciate it if there were some friendly mention of him in it. Edward was not feeling very friendly toward Baldwin because he had not used the requested mention of Wallis. Still, he did include a warm reference to the Prime Minister. He later explained it by saying that he didn't want to be mean. Quite possibly, his subconscious thought was that Baldwin still could quash Wallis' final divorce by use of Edward's proctor. Baldwin also held other things in his power: a proper title for Wallis, the amount of government allowance, Edward's future relationship with his country.

It was a quiet dinner that night at The Fort, just the former king and a few of his faithful. En route to Windsor Castle, they stopped at the Royal Lodge to see the Duke of York and Queen Mary. Then, to the castle for the broadcast.

"We went up to the room where the broadcast was to be given," Monckton recalled, "and Sir John Reith [director general of the BBC] talked to us about Spain and other subjects for a few minutes, then left the King and me alone.

"The King ran through the draft broadcast rapidly in the last five minutes before he was due to begin. He also tried his voice on the microphone and was told that everything was in order. At 10 o'clock Sir John Reith came in and stood over the King, who sat before the microphone, and announced 'His Royal Highness, Prince Edward' and left the room."[22]

It was the largest listening radio audience in the world. At the Villa Lou Viei in Cannes, Wallis had been chatting nervously only five minutes before when Brownlow reminded her that it was time to turn on the radio. She stretched out on the couch and stared at the radio as if she were seeing him speak:

At long last I am able to say a few words of my own.

I have never wanted to withhold anything, but until now it has not been constitutionally possible for me to speak.

A few hours ago I discharged my last duty as King and Emperor, and now that I have been succeeded by my brother, the Duke of York, my first words must be to declare my allegiance to him. This I do with all my heart.

You all know the reasons which have impelled me to renounce the Throne, but I want you to understand that in making up my mind I did not forget the Country or the Empire, which as Prince of Wales and lately as King, I have for twenty-five years tried to serve.

But you must believe me when I tell you that I have found it impossible to carry the heavy burden of responsibility and to discharge my duties as King, as I wish to do, without the help and support of the woman I love, and I want you to know that the decision I have made has been mine, and mine alone. This was a thing I had to judge for myself. The other person most nearly concerned has tried, up to the last, to persuade me to take a different course. I have made this, the most serious decision of my life, only upon the single thought of what would in the end be best for all.

This decision has been made less difficult to me by the sure knowledge that my brother, with his long training in the public affairs of the Country and with his fine qualities, will be able to take my place forthwith without interruption or injury to the life and progress of the Empire, and he has one matchless blessing, enjoyed by so many of you, and not bestowed on me, a happy home with his wife and children.

During these hard days I have been comforted by my Mother and by my Family.

The Ministers of the Crown, and in particular Mr. Baldwin, the Prime Minister, have always treated me with full consideration. There has never been any constitutional difference between me and them and between me and Parliament. Bred in the constitutional tradition by my Father, I should never have allowed any such issue to arise.

Ever since I was Prince of Wales, and later on, when I occupied the Throne, I have been treated with the greatest kindness by all classes wherever I have lived or journeyed throughout the Empire. For that I am very grateful.

I now quit altogether public affairs, and I lay down my burden. It may be some time before I return to my native land, but I shall always follow the fortunes of the British race and Empire with profound interest, and if, at any time in the future, I can be found of service to His Majesty in a private station, I shall not fail.

And now we all have a new King.

I wish Him, and you, His people, happiness and prosperity with all my heart.

God bless you all.

God save The King.

"The King began, I thought, a little anxiously," Monckton remembered, "but with the sentences his confidence grew, and the strength of his voice, and the final sentence 'God save The King' was almost a shout. When it was over the King stood up and, putting his arm on my shoulder, said: 'Walter, it is a far better thing I go to.' "[23]

Wallis later said that the entire household staff as well as the Rogerses were in the room to listen to the abdication speech and left her alone immediately afterward. One of the staff afterward insisted that Wallis had said as she listened, "The fool. The stupid fool."[24]

On that couch in that sitting room in Cannes, after they left, Wallis was sobbing as if the world had ended.

"This time I couldn't console her," said Brownlow, "and I didn't try. At that moment, I felt that she had destroyed my king. I left the room without saying goodnight."[25]

The former king returned with Monckton to say good-by to the royal family. Queen Mary masked any feelings she had and maintained a magnificence "and took leave of the King cheerfully. I shall always remember the car starting and the King's bow to his mother when she left," said Monckton.[26]

For almost an hour, the brothers then talked about everything but what was uppermost in their minds. Finally, the Duke of Kent, the youngest and favorite brother of the former king, said, "This is quite mad!"[27]

Later, George VI wrote: "When David and I said good-by we kissed, parted as free masons and he bowed to me as his King."[28]

In their car on the way to Portsmouth, the former king reminisced with Monckton about old times and places and mutual friends. They entered the wrong gate at the docks and wandered all over the yard before they found the HMS *Fury,* the new destroyer that was taking him to France. He had insisted on crossing without any official friends, but only with a few of his staff.

It was four o'clock Saturday morning when Monckton returned to London and immediately sat down and wrote a letter to Queen Mary. "I left him on the destroyer," he wrote; "he was still full of the same gay courage and spirit which have amazed us all this week . . . There is still and there always will be a greatness and a glory about him. Even his faults and follies are great . . ."[29]

Monckton said he had gone "like a great gentleman."[30] Baldwin

* In the original draft of the first speech of George VI, he supposedly had a phrase, "Through the abdication of our dear beloved elder brother," which was dropped from the final version of the speech.

later told his biographer, "Whoever writes about the Abdication must give the King his due. He could not have behaved better than he did."[31]

As the HMS *Fury* slipped away quietly and alone, the former king stood on the deck and stared in the dark at the shadow of his England. He had not only given up his throne: he had given up his country.

"I knew now that I was irretrievably on my own," he later commented. "The drawbridges were going up behind me. But of one thing I was certain; so far as I was concerned love had triumphed . . ."[32]

PART III

25

Most men dream of empire they would gain;
May this man never dream of one he lost;
Pray God I may be such a chatelaine
That he will never say, "I rue the cost."

No smallest wish shall go unheard,
Lest he remember—and regret—those ties;
An English flower, a song, a flag, a word
That bring lost lands before nostalgic eyes.

One woman must be all, and I that one,
To answer each demand of man and King,
Bring to each day a benison
And turn the Winter of his life to Spring.

To all the women who now envy me
I say: Covet not Gethsemane![1]

WHETHER OR NOT Wallis ever read that poem, it was at the center of her soul. There were no more tears. The walls were up again.

She would need all her defenses, all her control.

The incoming letters now numbered thousands, from all over the world, so many filled with hate. Out of her natural curiosity, and perhaps as a form of penance, she insisted on reading a great deal of it.

If there was an overriding tone, it was plaintive.

"Why did you take away our king?"

Police denied reports that her food was tested daily for poison. They did not deny that several people had been arrested for their threatening letters.

One of the letters, she opened quickly, the handwriting as familiar as her own. Part of it read:

". . . And would your life have ever been the same if you had broken it off? I mean could you possibly have settled down in the old life and forgotten the fairyland through which you had passed? My child, I do not think so."[2]

The letter was from Ernest Simpson.

How understandable that he felt so paternal toward her at that time, although he was really slightly younger than she was. It was as if he knew her so well, he realized the collapse of her confidence, the depth of her self-reproach. In another letter he wrote that he wanted to believe that she had done everything in her power to prevent the final catastrophe.

Her staunch defender in the United States, Upton Sinclair, wrote a long article upbraiding the British. About Edward he added: "You have, by one magnificent gesture, done more to dignify womanhood and give woman her rightful place, than many great people have been able to do by long and laborious effort."[3]

One of the published replies to Sinclair was a cablegram: "You consider Mrs. Simpson the flower of American womanhood. We don't." Signed, "Londoner."[4]

Virginia-born Lady Astor also put down Wallis, repeating that the British people had rejected her because of "her previous history." She added, "Those who will not obey the rules, can't rule."[5]

Wallis spent that first day after the abdication secluded in her room. This was too overwhelming to talk about yet, even to Rogers or Perry Brownlow. She simply stayed in bed until the middle of the afternoon. How much she slept is another question.

The radio stayed on most of the day and Wallis may have marveled at how undemonstrative the British were at the abdication news. If they were stirred, they smothered it in their famed British reserve. There were few crowds. Some talked of their king "letting the country down." Lloyd George in Jamaica had tears in his eyes, and so had many millions of women throughout the world.

"Nobody who heard this ruler speak will ever forget his words," noted actress Ina Claire. "The whole abdication has made our dramas seem tame and uninteresting. It out-Hollywooded Hollywood. It makes Greek tragedy seem trivial. The theater must learn a lesson from this historic broadcast."

Philip Gibbs described the reaction to the abdication speech at a Royal Air Force dining room: "He has let us down . . ."[6]

Even that anger was a contained anger. The greater mood was regret, sadness, shame.

Queen Mary set the mood in her message to the people.

". . . I need not speak to you of the distress which fills a mother's heart when I think that my dear son has deemed it to be his duty to lay down his charge, and that the reign, which had begun with so much hope and promise, has so suddenly ended.

"I know that you will realize what it has cost him to come to this decision; and that, remembering the years in which he tried so eagerly to serve and help his country and empire, you will ever keep a grateful remembrance of him in your hearts. . . ."[7]

In a letter to *The New York Times*, a Londoner tried to explain this reaction to Americans.

"Let the American people despise us, if they must, that we did not smash windows, lynch politicians and bring down in ruins the whole structure which our ancestors had so laboriously built up; but let not the foul lie be spread that we approved and applauded the disgraceful manoeuvre by which powerful interests removed from public life one of the most courageous, sincere, and straightforward of living Englishmen . . ."[8]

Wallis did not understand this. She had believed from the first that the King's strength was in the people, who loved him and would not let him down. She did not realize that the people did not know, until it was too late; then, when they knew, they did not fully understand; and then, when they understood, the majority turned against him.

In a confidential memo to the Secretary of State, the American consul in Plymouth tried to sum it up.

It was not a question of her being an American or even "the inherent distaste for divorce" that turned the people against the marriage, "but the people here consider the proceedings leading up to the second divorce were too much of a farce for them to endure." The "solid front" of great objection, he wrote, came from "the middle class, which includes the dyed-in-the-wool non-conformists and the greater part of the Church of England adherents . . ." Many of the latter "stated openly that it would be quite all right if the King were to

301

follow the example set by some other Kings in the past, and make Mrs. Simpson his mistress. They appeared incapable of realizing the hypocrisy of this view, and find no difficulty in saying, almost in the same breath, that the King must set a moral example for his people."[9]

"How could he choose against his people? they ask."

This moral hypocrisy grated on Wallis. Her bitterness toward the British grew even deeper in later years.

Perry Brownlow could no longer stay at Cannes. His grief for Edward was so deep that he could no longer pretend a compassion for Wallis that he did not feel. More than all this, he wanted to be with his friend who needed him.

His only comment to the press on the abdication speech was: "The King's voice was heard at the villa, as it was heard everywhere else. There is nothing further to say."[10]

26

Wallis was depressed because she was trapped; the newly made Duke of Windsor was exhilarated because he felt free.

Aboard the destroyer HMS *Fury*, the captain's report noted, "His Late Majesty looked as might be expected, as if he had passed through a very trying experience, but his manner betrayed no weariness, his voice had animation."[1]

He quickly busied himself aboard ship sending cables of farewell and thanks to all his friends. Told that the wireless could not be used when the ship reached territorial waters, the Duke ordered the *Fury* back to sea until he had finished with his list. He later gaily confided to Lord Brownlow how much money he had saved because all those cables were free.

One of them went to Prime Minister Baldwin, who still held a few vital keys to the Duke's future.

HMS *Fury* had a 6,000-mile cruising range and one of the many rumors was that it was headed for the Riviera, where the Duke and Wallis would rendezvous. But his legal advisers had warned that he would jeopardize Wallis' divorce if they were even in the same country before the decree *nisi* was final.

The *Fury* docked at Boulogne, and it was still dark when he boarded the special railway car waiting for him. When he said good-by to the few friends whom he had permitted to come along, he made a remark that summed up his tragedy, "I always thought I could get away with a morganatic marriage . . ."[2]

"Amid all his great qualities, there was also something lacking in himself . . . What seems almost incredible is that any man who was born and trained to such high responsibilities, who had clearly the capacity to undertake them, and who had in fact begun to exercise them with the complete good will of the nation, should sacrifice it all through a personal preference for another way of life. It can hardly have been a better verdict upon the Emperor Galba than it is upon King Edward that all men would have judged him worthy of the Throne if he had never ascended it.''[3]

Despite the winter weather and the early hour, a large crowd of people, including the mayor of Boulogne, were awaiting his arrival. But he was no longer an official figure and refused to receive anyone. They saw only a glimpse of a man in a dark coat and a derby, and four truckloads of Mobile Guards kept them back. Five French Sûreté agents joined the Duke, his equerry and Wallis' dog, Slipper. Four big trunks and twenty-six pieces of hand luggage were loaded, and the train was on its way.

Originally he had made plans to stay at a small hotel in Switzerland, but Wallis would not hear of it. She called their friends Baron and Baroness Eugene Rothschild, who promptly invited the former king to stay at their Castle Enzesfeld in Austria.

The Baron was a handsome, elegant man and his wife was one of the most distinctive women in Europe. The Baroness was the former Kitty Wolff, daughter of a Philadelphia dentist, and this was her third marriage. A tall, graceful woman with an elegant figure, she usually made the list of the best-dressed women of the world.

The castle was close to a small village overlooking a flat plain, bleak and dreary in winter. The Duke, however, still felt buoyant enough after the overnight trip to pose for the photographers. At the castle, he made a long phone call to Wallis and was later reported "singing in his bathtub."

When the Baron visited the Duke in his bedroom he found him unpacking his own clothes. The Duke had come without a valet and apologized for the disarray. "I'm not very good at this," he admitted. "You see I've never done it by myself."[4]

By the next morning, his freedom felt flat. He tried putting on the golf links but it was too gloomy and cold. The Baroness invited him to use their bowling alleys in the basement, but she beat him. And the news was bad.

The Archbishop of Canterbury had kept quiet during the crisis. Now, with the controversy over, he found it necessary to speak against the marriage. That Sunday he talked about the former king who left these shores "in the darkness."[5] He mentioned his "craving for private happiness"[6] that caused him to surrender his trust.

"Even more strange and sad is that the should have sought his happiness in a manner inconsistent with the Christian principles of marriage, and within a social circle whose standards and ways of life are alien to all the best instincts and traditions of his people . . ."[7]

Then he ended by saying, ". . . The pity of it, O, the pity of it."[8]

The Duke of Windsor was angry enough to consult Monckton about a possible lawsuit. He also kept the phone busy to his brother the King and his mother. It took long, persuasive, soothing calls from Wallis to cool him. The Archbishop's speech had been broadcast and published in full by all the leading newspapers to an audience of millions.

Reaction was mixed.

Prime Minister Baldwin, in a handwritten letter of praise, called the speech "the voice of Christian England." It was a strange action coming from a man who called himself Edward's "old friend," and who wrote him afterward: ". . . you ran dead straight with me, and you accomplished what you said you would do; you maintained your own dignity throughout; you did nothing to embarrass your successor."[9]

More critical and more typical was the quatrain:

> *My Lord Archbishop, what a scold you are!*
> *And when your man is down, how bold you are!*
> *Of Christian charity, how scant you are!*
> *And, auld Lang Swine, how full of cant you are!*[10]

The Archbishop of York followed the leader and also referred to the "sad, humiliating story" of King Edward's decision to give up his throne for "another man's wife." Then he added, "A man of honour would have acted differently."[11]

The comments of both archbishops, seeming to kick the former king when he was down, brought a typical English reaction calling for "fair play." In this sense, it softened the public censure.

Labour leader Ben Tillett expressed a growing sentiment in the country, saying, "Whatever he's done, he's been punished enough. Mrs. Simpson has suffered enough, too."

The Duke's loneliness now became physical and acute.

He talked to Wallis more often on the phone, and for longer periods. He complained of headaches, earaches. "The Duke is not especially ill," the Baron told the press. "He cannot be entirely well, under the circumstances."[12] The indisposition was described as "a nervous, emotional letdown."[13]

Lord Brownlow's arrival could not have been more timely or more welcome. He brought with him a stack of letters from Wallis, as well as photographs of Riviera villas that they might want to rent.

"I remember talking to him until three o'clock in the morning. I was catching a plane that morning to be home with my family for Christmas. He said he wanted to see me before I left and I woke up late. I knocked on his door and he didn't answer my knock, so I walked in. And there he was in bed—a typical bachelor's room, his golf clubs, camera and everything else all scattered. But then, all around his bed, propped up on chairs and tables, were pictures of Wallis. I counted sixteen of them. It was as if he were in a crypt.

"And there he was, fast asleep, hugging a small pillow of hers with the initials 'WS' on it. All around him were souvenirs of all their good times together, everything from rocks to heather. I wanted to bawl! I left the room stunned, found his newly-hired German valet and told him to wake the Duke and when I walked in, everything—all the pictures, all the souvenirs—had been cleared away.

"I can still close my eyes and see that room!"[14]

27

WALLIS FINALLY FELT FREE when the detectives left, along with the crowds. Jean Rouré, in charge of the special French detectives guarding her, told a reporter: "Everything Mrs. Simpson did was done on orders from London, right up to the time Baron Brownlow left Saturday night. She is now free and can appear publicly."

One detective still stayed with her, a special request from London. But her chauffeur, George Ladbrooke, wearing a tight beret, left her the Buick and took the train for home. She could open the window now and go for a walk. In one of his many calls, the Duke had urged her to abandon her self-confinement and shop, play golf, attend parties.

Wallis then called Pierre, one of the leading *coiffeurs* of France, to come and shampoo and arrange her hair. He brought an assistant and they spent three hours practicing their art.

She may have been beaten, but she was not totally defeated, and she wanted to look her best. She also invited couturiers to show her some new clothes, and alter the ones she had to fit her lighter weight.

The newspaper *Parisien* tried to smooth her way, and editorialized: "In coming here, Mrs. Simpson gave our country a mark of confidence and friendship which we must answer, gentlemen. Let us allow a young woman who can only be broken in emotion to rest in peace, security and liberty."

Her first visit to Cannes, however, was not pleasant. She was recognized and forced to return abruptly home.

Mayor Pierre Nouveau of Cannes sent her a note with flowers, expressing regret for the incident with the hope that the rest of her stay would be more pleasant. Even this simple gesture brought repercussions. Some of his constituents, particularly the British ones, publicly complained about the mayor spending taxpayers' money for flowers for "that woman."[1] They noted that many regular British visitors were boycotting the city that season because Mrs. Simpson was there. She was ruining the tourist trade, they said.

From Villa Lou Viei came the plaintive word: "Everything that happens in these parts now seems to be connected with me."

Probably on Herman Rogers' advice, Wallis decided to try to improve her image. In answer to some of the questions she wrote, "There has been no disagreement between Mrs. Simpson and His Royal Highness of any kind." She added, "Mrs. Simpson is not in a position to make any plans, and did not expect to see His Royal Highness within the next few weeks, and would not express an opinion on the unfairness of the recent comments on the Duke in England by the Church."[2]

Then came a more public press conference at the villa. She appeared on the steps wearing a checked sports coat thrown over her shoulders like a cloak, and no hat. She stood near a bed of daisies while reporters waited at a bend in the driveway.

She carried a large, dark brown leather bag. Her only ring was a half-inch jewelled band on her engagement finger. On her left wrist, barely showing, was a delicate gold charm bracelet set in emeralds and amethysts.

Her only sign of nervousness was the frequent dabbing at her lips with a tiny handkerchief. A newsman noticed also that her lips were scarlet but that there was no tint on her fingernails.

Was the world really interested in the color on her nails? The answer was yes. The world wanted to know everything.

Herman Rogers acted as spokesman and adviser at that press conference, but Wallis was described as "vivacious," "a winning conversationalist," "a good listener." "When she asked courteous questions, as she did frequently," wrote a reporter, "she waited for the answers as though intensely interested."[3]

She had little news for them. She talked about the weather, the beauty of the Riviera scenery, the dangers of mountain roads, and she expressed amusement that she had been reported in Egypt and Rome during the past few days.

Her future, she said, rested in the hands of the man who gave up his throne for her.

Cervantes had said, "Everything disturbs an absent lover." Normally restless, the Duke called Wallis as often as three times a day.

He was depressed and jumpy. His ear still hurt. The weather was too icy for golf. The Baroness continued to beat him at bowling.

The Enzesfeld burgomaster wanted to have a torchlight parade complete with folk dances for their honored guest, but the Duke excused himself. The village choir arrived accompanied by school children and the village band, all set to serenade the Duke, and he said thanks anyway, but please, some other time. He even appeared unexpectedly for lunch at the British Ministry in Vienna, an hour's drive away, and seemed startled by the hostess's use of napkin rings. "Do you mean to tell me," he asked, "that people don't get a fresh napkin at each meal?"[4]

Official papers still arrived from London, but they were now few and inconsequential. He was bored enough to read the clippings that came in the mail, and even a leaflet called "Solution of the Austrian Problem,"[5] proposing him as the new king of Austria.

He was not amused by an editorial in *The New York Times* referring to his "dereliction of duty" because of his "one mad surge of passion for a woman."

Nobody seemed to understand. It was not a question of passion; it was a question of his life. Wallis was the heart of it. It was that simple.

He no longer seemed interested in his clothes. He was most comfortable in his checked riding breeches, a gray flannel shirt and gray sweater. He still insisted on having his privacy respected. The grounds were patrolled by detectives, gendarmes and gamekeepers armed with shotguns. Some gendarmes on duty even had fixed bayonets. The Austrian government mobilized two police planes to keep away enterprising news photographers. A description of police dogs chasing some half-frozen photographers in the adjoining wood gave the Duke one of his few hearty laughs.

Otherwise he settled down to watch Mickey Mouse movies, drinking hot red wine spiced with cloves, sugar and cinnamon—an Austrian folk remedy prescribed for his cold and headaches.

Word circulated that the Duke was interested in either renting or buying a castle, and almost seventy of them were soon offered to him for inspection. He did visit a number of them, and even selected one for his honeymoon.

He called London often, talking to his brother the King, giving him all kinds of unasked-for advice. He did his Christmas shopping, looked at fur coats for Wallis. He bought little for himself, some hunting knives and suitcases, always careful to compare prices. He had never handled his own money before. In buying a Tyrolean coat for himself he reflected a long time, then chose the cheapest lining to save fifteen dollars. Putting it politely, local tradesmen said of him, "He is watchful of money."[6]

His chauffeur arrived from London with his ski clothes and equipment and the Duke sent him back with a carload of presents for the royal family. For Christmas, his mother had sent him a large portrait of George V. Although probably meant to inspire him, his father was the one man who never had.

It might have been his mother's suggestion that he take part in the local Christmas church service. It would, indeed, be an answer to the archbishops of Canterbury and York. He read the story of the nativity from the lectern of Vienna's English Church. "I was very nervous," he remembered afterward. "But strangely, when I got into the pulpit to read from one of the Gospels, a great peace came over me and I felt comforted." He then read it in a clear, assured voice. At the end of it he sang, with the rest, "God Save the King."[7]

Then, once again, more lonely than ever, he called Wallis.

The surest sign that Wallis was beginning to adjust and recoup was that she had sent to London for all her clothes, and for Aunt Bessie.

She also packed a box of tangerines, gathered from the Rogerses' trees, to be shipped to the Duke.

And she had a Christmas message for the archbishops of Canterbury and York; she authorized a news service to say on her behalf that she believed the prelates and all other critics of the Duke did not really know him, and if they truly knew him, they would have no reason to criticize.

To her cousin Newbold Noyes, Wallis cabled answers to more questions: No, it was not true that her divorce was being hurried so that she could marry the Duke earlier; no, it was not true that the Duke had given her many of the crown jewels and she was forced to return them; no, it was not true that they had bought homes either in northern Africa or in Green Spring Valley, Maryland.

Some of the articles Wallis read during those weeks must have pleased her. The novelist Gertrude Atherton had written: ". . . Look out Britain, you have seriously affronted not only one American woman, but all American women. And we count in this country."[8] And noted British novelist Rebecca West added a provoking thought, "It may be unwise for Mrs. Simpson to be Queen, but I am sure the

British Empire would be safer than it is if Mrs. Simpson were Prime Minister."[9]

Something that pleased Wallis much more than the proposed elevation to prime minister was the news that somebody had bought her old Baltimore home at 212 East Biddle Street and turned it into a museum, almost a shrine, full of her pictures, opening it to the public at fifty cents a look.

A representative of the so-called museum made the mistake of trying to buy the train and feathers "that Wally wore at the coronation." Lady Furness was out but her sister Gloria met the man, told him Wallis had not attended the coronation, and they had no intention of selling the train. "Please, Mrs. Vanderbilt," said the man, "think how the shrine is going to suffer!"[10]

"Shrine? Shrine, indeed!" shouted Mrs. Vanderbilt. "Now look here, I'm a very religious woman. I only put God and His saints in shrines, and believe me, Mrs. Simpson is neither!"[11]

Nor did she ever pretend to be.

Wallis was surely emerging from a state of shock, and if she thought of anything, she relived all her trials and telephone talks, and tried to imagine what the Duke was doing. She later said she spent a lot of time alone in her room, staring into space.

A friend who saw her then described her as "a little girl who had grown up and grown wise—a little girl from whom they had taken a doll. They were breaking it into pieces before her eyes."

Then as the new year started, Wallis was seen more frequently. A party at Somerset Maugham's nearby, a visit to a perfume factory at Grasse, a tour of the Riviera at twilight wearing a smart white ermine coat and a Russian-style casque to match. In February, there was a party given for her at a Cannes night club by friend Henry Clews, Jr., of New York. Wallis slipped in the side door wearing a black lace dress and a pearl necklace, looking vibrant and acting vivacious. She danced twice with Nicholas Zagraphos, head of the famous Greek syndicate which controls the baccarat tables at French casinos. That was enough to start a whole series of rumors about her and Zagraphos.

The world was waiting for the Simpson story to climax. Would the Duke marry his Baltimore belle? Would the American princess desert her king for a Greek gambler? Who would ever live happily ever after?

The fact was that Wallis was again exuberant because she and David had been detailing their marriage plans. She had spent a great deal of time inspecting Riviera villas as a possible home, and also as a place for their marriage. Herman Rogers was also busy on the project and was in contact with a friend who owned a beautifully secluded chateau some three hours from Paris.

The Duke was again heard singing in his bathtub. Somebody now reported to somebody else that he wore flaming orange pajamas and his mood had similarly brightened.

He posed for photographers, happily played more golf, no longer had any more problems with his ear. He was most comfortable in the forty-room castle. He had his own suite of rooms: a bedroom, a small library, a smoking room, a drawing room and a bathroom. Slipper seemed delighted with the run of such a large place, had considerable fun catching mice and only once got into a fight with the larger Rothschild dog.

The great and only trial was being away from Wallis.

According to the strict, technical terms of the law, there was no need for Wallis and the Duke to stay physically apart during the coming five months before the divorce decree was made final. But to avoid any conceivable claims for complaint the Duke's legal advisers insisted that the two must not only avoid seeing each other in this interim, they must not even be in the same country.

Into all this came a note of mystery and complication. A solicitor's clerk, Francis Stephenson, went to the Divorce Registry, insisting the Simpson divorce must not be made final. He said he had "new facts." No one knew whom he represented or why, and he wouldn't tell.

The mystery deepened when he suddenly withdrew his intention to file affidavits, "because I was asked to."[12]

The seventy-four-year-old Stephenson went to his grave without unraveling the mystery. The King's proctor afterward made it plain that he also had no plans to intervene.

The Duke tried desperately to speed up the divorce. He called all the important people he knew who might have some weight in the matter, particularly the King.

The new King always had looked up to his older brother. But now the establishment had put the freeze on the Duke and pressured the King to do likewise. They stressed the point that the Duke was giving the King all kinds of advice that often ran counter to that of his ministers.

"I'm afraid, David, that I can't go on telephoning to you anymore," the King said, finally.

"Are you serious?" asked the Duke.

"Yes, I'm sorry to say that I am," the King answered. "The reason must be clear to you."[13]

To make it clearer, the King sent Walter Monckton to Austria to explain. He had knighted Monckton, who now served him in the same capacity in which he had served the Duke when he was king.

The Duke later said that his father and his brother were members of the establishment, and he wasn't. He explained that his father detested change, that he would have repealed the twentieth century if he could. His brother fitted more fully into his father's mold, willingly accepting the status quo. Had he been king, David said, he would have been more independent. He would not have rebelled against the establishment, but he would have collided with it. The collision would have been inevitable, marriage or no marriage. The result, he felt, would have been helpful, not hurtful, to the country.

The establishment could not only be cutting; it could be cruel. Shortly after his brother had abdicated, King George had gone to a small dinner party. The hostess, Lady Maureen Stanley, had invited comedian Stanley Holloway to entertain her guests. Holloway gave his popular recitation of "Albert and the Lion." Not thinking of the implications, he came to the part "There was one great big lion called Wallace, whose face was all covered with scars . . ." The instant analogy caused the King and his guests to explode with laughter.[14]

When David Lloyd George returned to England, the former prime minister was made the Earl of Dufor, and he lunched with King George. They were soon discussing Wallis Simpson and the King said:

"She would never dare to come back here."

"There you are wrong," said Lloyd George.

"She would have no friends here," said the King.

"She has friends," Lloyd George insisted.

"But not you or me?" inquired His Majesty anxiously.[15]

This was the woman who had made him king, and he did not want to be king. This was the woman who had destroyed his brother. He had no wish to quicken her divorce, even if he could, and he couldn't. David knew this, and yet what concerned King George was the urgency and persistence of his brother's calls on the subject.

The King similarly found it embarrassing to discuss David's financial arrangements over the telephone. The Duke never before had had to think much about money. His private fortune was said to be considerable. As Prince of Wales, he had received all revenues from the Duchy of Cornwall, estimated at $1 million a year. In addition, he had received a bequest of an estimated $5 million from his grandmother Queen Alexandra. He also still owned Sandringham and Balmoral castles. The consensus of knowledgeable people put the Duke's annual lifetime allowance—which would come out of the Duchy of Cornwall income—at about $125,000 a year. The sale of Sandringham and Balmoral would bring at least another $500,000. To escape public discussion, the plan was to keep the arrangement within the royal family, and not subject to the approval of the Civil List.* Princess Mary, the Duke's sister, confirmed these financial arrangements when she and her husband visited the Duke. Money was not a major concern, but the Duke persisted in making it one. His persistence on this lasted his lifetime.

The Duke now had much time to ponder his future. John Grigg, the distinguished son of Sir Edward Grigg—a close friend of the Duke —had a suggestion. John Grigg had surrendered his title, so that he could serve in the House of Commons. Taking a cue from his own life and from George Bernard Shaw's *Apple Cart,* a play which deals with a constitutional monarch who threatens to resign and run for election as a commoner for a seat in the House of Commons, Grigg suggested that the Duke give up his title and enter politics. He proposed that if the Duke absorbed Lloyd George's home policy and Churchill's foreign policy, he would become a "well-nigh irresistible force."

It was an exciting idea, too exciting for the Duke at this time. The future he now longed for was out of the limelight, puttering in the garden, golfing in the afternoon and doing something that might be considered useful.

As much as he and Wallis talked on the phone, there were still so many practical things unsettled. Where should they live? What should he do? Where were they going?

* At the beginning of each reign an act called the Civil List is passed by Parliament providing a schedule of annual grants to be made to the royal family.

28

WALLIS WAS GETTING her bearings again. The tumult was quieting. She was going to be forty-one years old and perhaps it was too late to change, and maybe she didn't want to anyway.

Besides, she *was* getting married. Nothing now would stop that. Her divorce decree was still several months away, and she was restless. She was not a gardener like the Duke, and golf was not her game. No exercise really was. A leisurely swim easily satisfied her. Otherwise, though, she liked to move and go and do.

It was spring and the yellow mimosa had come back to Cannes and Aunt Bessie returned to the United States. Aunt Bessie had been a full warm heart and a sympathetic pair of ears and a wise mind that relaxed her niece more than anyone else could. Aunt Bessie had the Montague tongue too. She had the ready wit to make Wallis laugh, and laughter was the medicine Wallis needed most. She could also tell Wallis things that even the Rogerses wouldn't, critical things to keep Wallis from getting off course. It was a wrench to see Aunt Bessie go.

The Duke called more often now but conversations with him were still difficult. Connections were bad but now they could at least speak on a more scheduled basis, often for as long as an hour. He urged her to change her scene.

She did like to scout the nearby villas. The one she liked most was La Croe at Cap d'Antibes, belonging to Sir Pomeroy Burton. A white house on a small rise overlooking the sea, it had a swimming pool cut into the rocks, a tennis court, a beautiful garden and a bathtub in the shape of a swan. It offered a perfect setting for a wedding. Herman Rogers also had found the Chateau de Candé, the country house in a wooded park near Tours belonging to Charles Bedaux. Bedaux offered his home free as long as necessary.

The Duke felt it important to consult his brother. The King felt the Candé setting was preferable, considering the rather wild reputation the Riviera had acquired in recent years.

Wallis was now anxious to see it. The day she visited, it was rainy, but once Fern Bedaux showed her over the elegant castle, her spirits rose. She quickly chose the music room for the wedding. Visualizing the projected scene heightened her impatience.

Spring also made the Duke more restless than ever. He climbed mountains, drove cars, went skiing, hiking, golfing, but stayed away from any night clubs. Once a week he motored to Vienna to have his hair trimmed at the Hotel Bristol, while the barber gave him the local gossip. He wandered around the Schoenbrun Castle and the State Museum.

Unauthorized persons caught on the chateau grounds were fined two shillings (about thirty-seven cents), fifty were caught and paid. Most townspeople, however, respected his wish for privacy. They brought him gifts of fresh trout, which he loved, and poems. Local chimney sweeps even let him touch the snout of their traditional pig, the ancient belief being that it would bring him luck in both love and material things. From elsewhere in the world came hundreds of turkeys, eighty fountain pens, sixty cakes, twenty cigarette cases and a variety of dogs. He returned the dogs and distributed the food and other gifts among the town's needy.

He was not an easy guest, and the Baron and Baroness tried hard to please him. When he wanted privacy, they let him alone. When he got restless, they arranged small dinner parties with interesting people. They even ordered films for his private viewing. Nothing pleased him too much or too long. Someone reported that the Baroness finally said, "Anybody can have him anytime."[1]

In the end, the Rothschilds told the Duke that they were soon leaving, and the Duke decided that he too would leave. Just before he did, Lord Brownlow arrived with a barrel of the Duke's favorite oysters, and a credit at Coutts (Bank) for £4,000. The Duke was delighted, especially with the money, and asked Brownlow to pay his telephone bill. The bill was £900 ($4,500). "Nine hundred pounds for love," Brownlow said many years later, still incredulous.[2]

The Duke rented a simple house nearby at St. Wolfgang. He kept only his butler and his detective-bodyguard.

Without the Rothschilds to entertain him, he was more and more impatient for May 3.

The Chateau de Candé sat on a thousand acres in the Loire Valley, the heart of the chateau country where so many of the French kings had built their private marble palaces for their pleasant seclusion. It's a lush land of moors and meadows, full of partridge, pheasant and deer, the weather seldom extreme and the air almost luminescent at twilight.

Candé itself had more than fifty rooms. From a distance, its high towers and pointed turrets looked like witches' hats. The land had been deeded to a Roman family at the time of the Crusades, then became the seat of the dean of the Abbey of Saint Martin. The imposing chateau was built in 1508 by the dean of that abbey, who was also the first mayor of Tours and the minister of finance to Louis XII. Three hundred years later, another large wing was added. Charles Bedaux, the ninth owner, bought it in 1927 from a British-Cuban family, then modernized it with an eighteen-hole golf course, tennis courts, a game preserve and a swimming pool. The changes required that sixty tons of pipes be put through the ancient stone walls.

An underground tunnel connects the house to the game room, but local legend has the tunnel winding under four miles of countryside to a neighboring chateau. Under part of the golf course are the former dungeons of the monastery.

Most of the rooms were paneled, high-ceilinged and enormous. Wood bins were heaped with logs along all the passageways for the countless fireplaces. The room Wallis had picked for the wedding ceremony was a small music salon off the library with pale paneled walls and antique furniture.

Fern Bedaux insisted Wallis have the bedroom with cream-colored walls, a beautiful view, and boiserie carved in Louis XV style. The ceiling was soft rose beige with touches of gold and the bathroom had pink marble, blue walls, gold fixtures and a chandelier of china flowers. What pleased Wallis most was her dressing room with a mirrored armoire. Her bed was large, pale pink with a headboard covered in Alençon lace, the spreads in pale pink silk. Adjacent to it was a sitting room, and Herman Rogers slept there. Katherine slept in another bedroom upstairs. A guest suite elsewhere in the chateau was reserved for the Duke.

Fern Bedaux, formerly of Grand Rapids, Michigan, was a gracious woman of exquisite taste. When Wallis and the Rogerses arrived, Fern greeted them with a house full of flowers, and her English butler, V. J. Hale, had lined up the twenty-two servants in their uniforms under the soft red glow of the chandeliers to meet their new mistress. It was to be Wallis' house as long as she was there.

"She and Madame Bedaux were very different," said Hale. "Madame was more reserved and more formal than the Duchess, and I think the Duchess admired her aristocratic airs. After Madame left, I asked the Duchess if she wanted any changes and she told me, 'Do things just as you did when Madame Bedaux was here.' "[3]

The days passed slowly for Wallis. She had two months to mark time. Katherine Rogers made occasional trips to Paris, but Wallis never left the chateau and Herman Rogers never left Wallis.

She needed him, too. He had given up his own way of life, with all its freedom, to give her someone to lean on and she leaned on him hard.

Fortunately the telephone connection to Austria was clear here, for she and the Duke had a hundred details to resolve about their wedding. Should it be religious or civil, or both? Whom should they invite? What about his family?

Wallis found herself too excited to sleep much. Sleep, and its recuperative powers, had always escaped her. The Duke, on the other hand, always slept like a child.

Wallis had her afternoon walks. The nearby woods were thick with violets and wild strawberries and lilies of the valley. She was so bored and desperate that she played some golf with the Rogerses. She even permitted an occasional interview. Since the day after her arrival, a group of reporters had parked outside the courtyard gate.

She told them little. She thought the Spanish Civil War "will be the ruin of beautiful Spain."[4] She hoped to learn French, she had no plans to ride any horses, she didn't know where they would live, she always hoped to live in the United States again. She wanted to know whether America was still a country of gadgets. "Here they won't have anything to do with them," she said. "You rush down to the kitchen and distribute the dearest little gadgets—and find them in the wastebasket the next day."[5] Her dog had gotten all wet and she had been drying him with her hairdryer as she spoke.

Was blue her favorite color?

"Yes, and my favorite mood, these bleak, rainy days. You know, we keep a rowboat out there," she explained, pointing out of the window. "When it's submerged, we know it's a very bad day. If it shows its nose, we venture out."[6]

A young woman reporter noticed that Wallis' hands always had to be busy, that she kept constantly clasping and unclasping them, and also patting her hair every few minutes.

"What about your future?" the reporter asked.

"Who knows? I'm a fatalist."

"And a gambler?"

"And a gambler."

Before the young woman left, Wallis asked her wistfully, "Is Paris gay?"

"Very," said the reporter.[7]

As it came closer to May, and the divorce decree, the Duke sent Slipper back to her, delivered by Chief Inspector Storier of Scotland Yard. Slipper had been his first important present to Wallis, and she had loved the dog. He had taken it with him to Austria because it meant taking some more of her love with him. He had sent it back because he felt that her need now was greater than his, and because he wanted to send more of his love to her.

Wallis and Slipper were overjoyed at their reunion. But then one afternoon, the two of them were on the golf course, following the Rogerses, when Slipper broke away to chase a rabbit. When he didn't return, Wallis searched for him. She found him thrashing from a viper bite. She carried him, running, to a car, and raced to a hospital, but they could do nothing, and the dog died.

Slipper's death was a terrible trauma for Wallis.

"They had a regular funeral service," said Hale. "I've never seen her so sad and broken."[8]

The weather stayed bad that spring, cold and damp and rainy. Toward the end of April, the skies brightened and so, finally, did Wallis. Cecil Beaton arrived to photograph her. The chateau had taken on an air of suppressed excitement. More and more people were coming and going, involved in arrangements for the wedding, even though nobody yet knew the date.

Beaton described the dinner that night. "The women had dressed to the nines, all in red. Wallis sported a new jewel in the form of two huge quills, one set with diamonds, the other with rubies. Her dress shows to advantage an incredibly narrow figure, narrower since the abdication."

After the Rogerses went to bed, Beaton and Wallis talked until dawn.

"I was struck by the clarity and vitality of her mind," he said. "When at last I went to bed, I realized she not only had individuality and personality, but was a very strong force as well. She may have limitations, she may be politically ignorant and esthetically untutored; but she knows a great deal about life."[9]

From their talk, Beaton felt that Wallis did not have any clear intentions of marriage until the final conflict with Parliament, and that she was as surprised as anybody by the abdication. She was determined that she and the Duke would "work things out."[10]

"She obviously has great admiration for his character and his vitality and loves him, though I feel she is not *in* love with him. In any case, she has a great responsibility in looking after someone who is temperamentally polar to her, yet relies utterly on her."[11]

He watched her twist her hands, laugh a square laugh "protruding her lower lip." He listened to her talk about how lonely she had been so much of her life, and how, perhaps, this isolation had helped her.

"She confessed that it had been difficult for her not to give way and hang herself on one of the many antlers in the room in which we sat. But her control surprised her. She was, she said, very like a man in many ways; she had few women friends. Katherine Rogers, the most intimate among them, has likewise, I think, a man's mentality."[12]

The days finally began to pass with speed.

Then, at last, there was a call from London on May 3. Her divorce decree had become absolute. She was free to marry anytime.

She called the Duke and told him, "Hurry up!"[13]

29

The Duke already was packed and waiting when Wallis called. The next train out that afternoon was the Orient Express, and he was on it. He arrived, almost on the run, hatless, looking thinner, but radiating happiness. "Darling, it's been so long," he said.[1]

He carried two packages for her: a colorful Austrian peasant costume called a dirndl, and some edelweiss, a mountain flower he himself had picked.

His exile away from her had been twenty-two weeks. For him, certainly, it seemed longer.

After a while they took a long walk together. She knew how much he had hoped for some representative of the royal family to attend their wedding, particularly his youngest brother, George, whom the Duke wanted to be his best man. That was no longer possible. The government would not approve. Nor would the Queen Mother.

He also had wanted a religious ceremony performed by a British minister of the Church of England. But the bishops had virtually forbidden all their ministers to perform such a ceremony. Furthermore, the Duke decided they must postpone the ceremony because it could not compete with the coronation, now scheduled for May 12.

Wallis understood all these things, and they concerned her mostly because they were vital to David. She was willing to adjust to any necessary situation now. Her only wish was to please this man in every possible way. He had given up his whole world for her.

They settled on a simple wedding at Candé, with only a few friends. They would arrange for the local mayor to perform the ceremony. The wedding date was set for June 3. Wallis, who was "terribly superstitious, having been brought up in the South," believed the unlucky things in life were "hats on the bed, things hung on doorknobs, number 13, breaking mirrors" . . . and May weddings.[2]

There was some other distressing news. A number of close friends whom they wanted at the wedding shied off. The simple truth was, the King was dead, long live the King. The royal family set the pattern by refusing to attend the wedding, and the aristocracy fell into line. One of those who reveled in this "slap in the face" for Wallis was Mary Kirk Raffray, who was then in England trying to settle her own divorce. But for Wallis herself, the reaction simply "has shown me *who* among my friends *are* my friends."[3]

The Duke was obviously more hurt by the fact that the establishment turned thumbs down on the wedding. No recognition, no representation, no publicity. Geoffrey Dawson already had ruled that *The Times* would treat the Windsor wedding as an ordinary event and give it minimal space.

Rumors persisted in the press that the Duke had given Wallis Queen Alexandra's jewels, and that she had refused to return them. Wallis decided to present more of her own image to the world. She granted an interview to a distant kinswoman and practicing barrister in England, Helena Normanton, to deny flatly that she had ever been given any jewelry from any member of the royal family.

"It is true, I have a few nice pieces, but not anything to compare in quality or quantity with what really rich women possess."

She chatted easily, informally, as if exchanging confidences. "I am ordering just my usual spring outfits. I like to have a half-dozen good things at a time, and wear them straight off, until they are finished with."

No, she had not ordered any coronet-embroidered pajamas. "I even dislike seeing women walk at seaside resorts in them, and, as far as coronets go, I've never even seen one."

Normanton's final comment was that Wallis had met the right man too late.

That seems highly questionable. Would she have preferred Felipe Espil to the Duke in earlier years? Espil had been to Wallis what Count Charles Kinsky had been to Lady Randolph Churchill—the man of all men; the former Edward VIII was to Wallis what his grandfather Edward VII had been to Lady Randolph Churchill.

Here at Candé, though, the love shone in both their eyes. The difference was only in degree.

The Duke's new equerry, twenty-four-year-old Dudley Forwood, who had come with him from Austria, many years later still had a vivid memory of the Duke's feelings at that time.

"When she was out of the room, he moped. When she was with him, it was as if the sun had come out. It was almost terrifying to me that a man could so worship another person."[4]

The butler, V. J. Hale, noticed how restlessly the Duke played solitaire while he was waiting for her to appear. Then when she arrived on the scene, "the way he padded after her, it was hard to believe that he had once been king."[5]

Strictly from a distance, Havelock Ellis, world-renowned authority on the psychology of sex, had his own analysis of why the Duke acted as he did. "I have always had the opinion due to Edward's quite boyish appearance, that he is in some way different from most other men . . . to me it is obvious. Edward's face is more boyish than his younger brothers, who seem to me to have a much more normal look. If Edward is slightly different than most men it may be much harder for him to find a woman who suits him than it would be for a perfectly normal man. Mrs. Simpson is evidently a very unusual woman . . . she seems highly intelligent. She seems a distinctive personality. She is an attractive woman. I think it is possible for Edward to find real happiness with the woman he loves. They are both persons of experience."[6]

"He always relied on her," said Hale afterward. "He would say, 'Don't you think so, darling?' on anything in which he wanted her judgment, and it seemed to me he wanted her judgment on everything."[7]

On May 12, though, he needed nobody's opinion. He told Wallis that he intended to listen on the radio to his brother's coronation ceremony.

It was hardly the happiest time of Wallis' life, sitting there with him, and their friends, in utter silence as they listened to the description of the ancient ceremony. Wallis could only look at the former king and into herself. If it were not for her, he would be in Westminster Abbey, the ceremony would be for him, he would be proclaimed king and emperor. If it were not for her . . .

The Duke sensed the trauma within Wallis. He could see the guilt and the questions and the sadness in her eyes. As for himself, it was easier for him to mask everything; he had been bred to it. Even so, listening to the ceremony caused some twinges, but primarily he had come to terms with himself when he had made his decision. In that respect, he was not a complicated man.

For Wallis it was not so easy.

The news now turned good. Despite the bishops' prohibition, a British vicar had volunteered to perform the ceremony. He was Reverend Robert Anderson Jardine of Darlington, an industrial parish in the north of England. When he read an article stating that there would be no religious ceremony for the Duke of Windsor's wedding, "I went into the garden and entered my old army tent in which I used to do much of my preparation work for Sunday. I knelt in prayer of deep earnestness, and rose with the clear conviction that, here is a man who needs something; and I must give it to him."[8]

"The Duke desperately wanted his marriage to be a highly religious one, and blessed by the Church," noted his equerry, Dudley Forwood. "And when the news reached him that the Reverend Jardine had offered to bless the union, he was overjoyed. . . . You have no idea of the tremendous idealism and dedication with which the Duke approached his marriage. In his mind, it was to be the wedding of all weddings. He felt extraordinarily deeply about the sanctity of marriage."[9]

It was natural. The royal marriages he had seen were always awesome in their religious ceremony. Besides that, he had never been married before.

Though Wallis hovered around with a businesslike, organized air, her face showed the strain of the situation, and her friends who saw her then claimed "she looked far from her best."[10]

There was so much to do. It took time to create and produce a wedding gown, and a trousseau. The designs, the selections, the fittings. Then, too, she was a perfectionist about everything. The arrangement of flowers, the use of color, the menu, the wines, the vintage of the champagne, the seating of guests, the timetable and logistics of the two ceremonies. The world was watching and everything was such a far cry from what it could have been. But, most of all, she wanted to look superb.

Mainbocher arrived with sketches for her wedding gown and trousseau. Designer Edward Molyneux had said of Wallis that "she had a distinct flair for clothes . . . There is a clear-cut individual air to all her things."[11] Schiaparelli had commented, "Her taste was good, and quiet."[12] Rudolf de Wardener added, "She is interested in clothes that are becoming to her, easy to wear, simple and practical . . . doesn't try to set styles, but dresses to suit her own taste."[13]

Mainbocher was an American, born in Chicago, a short, stocky man who was christened Main Rousseau Bocher. He reworked his name and gave it a French pronunciation when he opened his Paris salon. For her wedding dress, he sent a fitter to Candé on six successive Saturdays and went himself on the Saturday before the wedding for a final inspection.

The color of the silk crepe dress was somewhere between a medium and a pastel blue. "I named it Wallis blue, a blue of which there was never a sample available to anyone," he later recalled.[14] The closely guarded secret of the color and design, however, was somehow spirited to the United States and put into instant mass production, almost at the same time as it was worn at the wedding.

The dress itself was devised as a two-piece gown with a long, clinging skirt, and the first of the tops where the jacket was not supposed to be removed. The lines were severely simple, cut high at the neck. The jacket's corseted insert and closing used nine tiny covered buttons.

Designer Schiaparelli, who had designed so many of her clothes in London, now did a trousseau. Most of the dresses were in blue, the Duke's favorite color, and classic in design. None of her dresses had deep necklines because of her protruding collarbones, and she preferred the effect of form-fitting lines. Her selections included a negligee of sapphire-and-silver lamé. She also chose an exotic waltz dress of snow-white organdy, printed with two fiery-red lobsters; a dinner dress of form-fitted black, embroidered with colored-glass flowers and gold paillettes; some black crepe dresses printed with turtles and flowers; two fitted suits and jackets made of light-blue tweed; an afternoon ensemble of a blue tweed redingote, with dolphin buttons and a butterfly on the lapel, worn with a crepe dress printed with white morning glories.

Her Paris hairdresser made the mistake of revealing to the press that she planned to tint her hair blue to match the dress. She promptly denied it, and brought in a new hairdresser. Herman Rogers, her liaison to the reporters, also told them that she now had a platinum and emerald engagement ring. Local bars offered a new cocktail, a concoction of gin and cordial which they called "My Blue Heaven."

Restaurants and hotels nearby all had featured dishes "à la Mme Simpson." Photographers and reporters waited along the fence for any glimpse of the two of them taking their daily walk arm in arm. They also ran along the golf course fence while the Duke played and "upset his concentration."

Reporters, though, generally agreed that the Duke looked considerably younger now, the pouches under his eyes no longer so pronounced, his ruffled gold hair and sunburned complexion heightening his radiance and the excitement in his transparent blue eyes. The Duke let it be publicly known that he was "on top of the world."

Then, a "terrible moment."[15]

Word came from London that Walter Monckton was coming to Candé with bad news. No one was more aware than Monckton how passionately the Duke felt about the question of his wife's royal title. Given the ultimatum that she could not share his royal status as queen, he gave up his crown; he could not, however, give up his royal birth or his right to be called "His Royal Highness," which came with it. To him it was a minimal courtesy for her to share that title.

Ancient custom called for the Duke's wife to take his same rank and social precedence. As the Duchess, Wallis should logically rank just behind her two sisters-in-law, the Duchesses of Gloucester and Kent, and similarly be referred to as "Her Royal Highness." Like Wallis, two of his brothers' wives had been commoners, and both were accorded this privilege, which automatically bestowed the right to receive bows and curtsies. These courtesies went against the grain of many in high places throughout the British Empire who were not just bitter about Wallis; they hated her.

King George was upset, but he knew his brother would regard it as a deadly insult if the proper titles were denied her. It would make Wallis a second-class wife, as far as the Duke was concerned. The King did not underestimate the intensity of his brother's feeling in this, and would not have crossed him on it, but it was a Cabinet decision and one strongly based on the insistence of the Dominions. Canada and Australia particularly felt that this woman must not be called Her Royal Highness. So it was decreed in the so-called Depriving Act of 1937. Printed in the official *London Gazette,* it said that the Duke was "entitled to hold and enjoy for himself only the title, style or attribute of Royal Highness, so however, that his wife, or descendants, if any, shall not hold said title, style or attribute."

"Only" was the key legal word. The Duke saw it as a mean, petty gesture, a hard slap in the face, which he would never forgive or forget. There was no British precedent for this. *Burke's Peerage*, the British bible of social rank, later called it "the most flagrant act of discrimination in the whole history of our dynasty."[16]

"There had been no disillusionment in his mind up to that time," remembered his equerry, Dudley Forwood. "He was completely blind to the fact that the woman he loved and felt so perfect might be imperfect to others. It was incomprehensible to him that anyone should feel anything but admiration for her. Thus the Duke found it difficult to comprehend that a brother to whom he was devoted could be forced to deny his wife-to-be that which he considered so essential to their marriage and future happiness. It was a terrible blow to him. He felt deeply hurt. . . . It caused him a great deal of sadness for his family meant a lot to the Duke."[17]

"This is a nice wedding present," David said when Monckton brought him the news.[18]

"The Duke was inclined to give up his own royal title rather than take one different from his wife," wrote Monckton, "but I persuaded him, with her help, against this course. It would have been openly offensive to the King, and would have meant giving up something for very little."[19]

Many of those who were not involved thought the decree was absolutely contemptible, but still trivial. They were surprised that the Duke should attach such enormous importance to it. They saw it as a weakness in him, and thought that if he were really as emancipated a monarch as he was supposed to be, he shouldn't have cared about this panoply of royalty. But then, some of them had never been kings.

What they did not understand was that the Duke saw it for what it was, a slur on his wife-to-be, the one woman he loved beyond all else. From then on he was bitter about Baldwin, bitter about his brother, bitter even about his mother. It became a kind of Berlin wall between him and his family.

Wallis tried hard to mollify him. But she herself felt deep within her the resentment of being so blatantly labeled a social outcast. She knew that a large part of the court circle was delighted with the ruling, and that this delight was shared by the new queen, and approved by the Queen Mother. Royalty was very sharp and clear on rules and she had broken the rules and must pay the price of it. She could understand some of this, but why oh why had they done this to the Duke only a week before the wedding? Couldn't they have waited? That was the ugliest thing of all.

And why did they blame her so much? Had she wanted to, she could have caused considerable trouble. She was the one who had first urged on him the idea of a morganatic marriage. She was the one who had begged him not to abdicate. She had offered to withdraw. She would have been prepared to give him up. She was constantly pleading with him not to cause needless trouble. Had she played the part of a devastated woman demanding revenge, she might have roused him to a hate that might have divided the country and destroyed the monarchy. They could fault her for accepting his love and proposal and for initiating the divorce, but they could not fault any of her actions afterward. She could not have been more correct, more impeccable, more dignified.

She now had more immediate concerns. Aunt Bessie's arrival was a blessing for Wallis. She took over the preparation of ten guest rooms, deciding on the seating arrangements, planning the decorations and wedding breakfast. Constance Spry moved in from London and was soon in overalls and a large picture hat arranging flowers. The three-story organ in the library had to be repaired and the grand piano was removed to make room for more seating.

Reporters kept the phones ringing. While Wallis never answered them, she hovered to find out who was calling and might tell whoever answered, "Be careful and be nice. So-and-so is very important."[20] One of the more important reporters was socialite Cornelius Vanderbilt, who parked outside the courtyard in his own trailer, but even he was not permitted to enter the courtyard.

Herman Rogers met the press outside twice a day, spending much of his time denying rumors: no, the Duchess was not dead; no, she would not wear a diamond tiara for the ceremony, but she would wear a blue straw cap with a halo brim of tulle; yes, Wallis had legally dropped the name "Bessie" as well as the name "Simpson"; no, the Duke was not knitting a blue sweater for Mrs. Warfield; no, he did not know if Mrs. Warfield had had her underwear embroidered with "HG" ("Her Grace").[21]

Rogers also arranged for a special dispensation from the mayor of Monts to permit the ceremony to be held inside the chateau instead of in the mayor's office. The mayor, Charles Mercier, was a modest forty-six-year-old country doctor, bespectacled, mustached and somewhat nearsighted, but very friendly. Two weeks before the marriage, the Duke and Wallis signed the French marriage contract, providing for separate ownership of property.

Some American friends of Wallis, Mr. and Mrs. Grafton Minot of Boston and New York, lived in a nearby chateau and invited the Duke and Wallis for dinner. The host toasted their happiness. Just at that moment, lightning struck the chateau's electric plant, plunging the dining room into darkness. Wallis saw it as still another in the series of omens.

Then she was caught up in the frenzy of the final week. Her famous energy did not desert her. Every time she entered a room, her butler felt she made everyone else look exhausted.

Antonio Magnagnini arrived from Paris to do her hair, setting it in a new way, with the waves flowing up instead of down. The wedding ring, made of Welsh gold, arrived from the Paris jeweler. It was the kind worn by British queens. Her lingerie came, rose pink and almost every shade of blue. The pale peach table linens and sheets were delivered, decorated with the ducal coat of arms.

They signed their names on the wood paneling beside the library fireplace: "Edward-Wallis-1937." And they finally posed for photographers, who asked them to look happy. "We are always happy," she answered.

Aside from the jobs assigned to Aunt Bessie, Wallis herself handled the details of her marriage, keeping them away even from the eager Katherine Rogers.

The Reverend Jardine arrived, the "poor man's pastor," the rebellious priest who told the press he would listen to no one but his own conscience. Reporters hailed his arrival as "the miracle at Monts."[22]

The Duke shook Reverend Jardine's hand firmly, smiled broadly, then asked, "Why don't they give us a religious ceremony? We are both Christians."[23]

"What could I answer?" Jardine recorded later. "I am afraid a lump came to my throat at the pathos of this ex-King denied what is the right of every man, king or commoner, the blessing of God on his wedding day.

"Seeing I did not answer, he went on to tell how they had sought for someone to perform the ceremony and had failed."[24]

"Pardon my language, Jardine," the Duke said, "but you are the only one who had the 'guts' to do this for me."[25]

When the Duke began discussing the wedding, Jardine said, "Sir,

329

we cannot discuss that matter in the absence of Mrs. Warfield. It is her wedding as well as yours."[26]

In meeting Wallis Warfield, Jardine could not help remembering an old contest in a London weekly paper. The question asked was "What sport has woman not yet conquered?" The winning answer was "His Royal Highness, the Prince of Wales."[27]

Later, after dinner, the Duke and Wallis gave Jardine a pair of gold cufflinks with their joint crest on each link, and again expressed their deep gratitude.

The vicar needed an altar, and they brought the chest from the hall, an ornately carved piece faced by a row of fat female figures. Wallis worried about an altar cloth to cover the female figures and remembered a tea cloth already packed at the bottom of her linen trunk. Her maid complained about all the trouble involved in getting married, and said she would never do it, and Wallis reassured her, saying, "Oh, it isn't always as bad as this—only if you're marrying the ex-King of England."[28]

As the cloth was spread, one of the guests, the Duke's solicitor, George Allen, brought in two candlesticks he had found in another room.

"Hey, you can't put those up," Wallis told him. "We want them for the dinner table tonight."[29]

In the confusion someone knocked over an Italian lamp and cracked it. The Duke was most disturbed and tried, himself, then and there, to repair it.

The mayor of Monts insisted on a wedding rehearsal because Wallis had a difficult time understanding French and he wanted to impress every word on her mind so that she would know when to make the proper answer. The Duke's French was scarcely better.

Some of the guests started arriving: Winston Churchill's son Randolph; Major Edward D. Metcalfe, known to the Duke and his friends as "Fruity." The major was an Irishman who had served the Duke in India and Japan, when he was Prince of Wales, and later became his equerry. Fruity was to be the Duke's best man. With him was his wife, Lady Alexandra, the daughter of the late Marquis Curzon of Kedleston—a former viceroy of India who had lost out to Baldwin as prime minister. Others en route included the Rothschilds; Mr. and Mrs. W. C. Graham, the British consul at Nantes; Lady Walford Selby, wife of the British minister to Vienna; and Hugh

Lloyd Thomas, first secretary of the British Embassy in Paris. The total number of guests was sixteen.

It was indeed a remarkable wedding for a man who, only six months before, had been the king of England and the emperor of India, the ruler of 500 million people living on 13 million square miles of the earth.

The crowds outside the courtyard had begun to increase. The old woman by the gate wearing the traditional peasant lace cap told reporters, "No outsiders will see the ceremony, not even I."[30]

Policemen wore new uniforms and polished boots. On every road were motorcycle patrols. Food stands did a thriving business in coffee and bananas. All the nearby houses had French and British flags, and one of the signs read: HAPPINESS TO WINDSOR AND MRS. WARFIELD.[31]

Early on Thursday morning, June 3, a truck and car pulled out loaded with suitcases and trunks to be put aboard the train for Austria.

There was scarcely a cloud in the soft blue sky and reporter Inez Robb wrote, "There must be a nugget of truth in the old adage that 'happy is the bride the sun shines on.' "[32] The wedding ceremony was scheduled for 10:30 and the crowd soon swelled to several hundred, including a Chinese peddler unsuccessfully trying to sell suspenders and belts. One British woman arrived with three cases of champagne ready to break open as soon as the couple had said their vows. Robb wrote that the scene began "more and more to resemble an Elks picnic in any town west of the Hudson."[33]

Inside, all was ready. Large vases of pink and white peonies flanked both sides of the marriage table, and before it were four chairs for the bride, bridegroom, Herman Rogers and Major Metcalfe. On another table were more flowers and a string of American flags. On the walls hung three paintings of horses and a large oil of the Resurrection. The room was forty feet by twenty, the carpeting of red, green and blue in small patterns. On the south side was a big stone fireplace, above it stood still more peonies. Flowers were arranged on a third table under the window, bouquets of red, yellow and white, with a large bunch of lilies. The windows had yellow silk curtains and a brass chandelier hung from the center of the ceiling. The guests were seated on several rows of chairs, some reporters seated on the side. The room was flooded with sunshine.

While the Reverend Jardine was putting on his robe, someone knocked on the door and asked if he had seen Mrs. Warfield.

"'The papers reported she was three minutes late at the civil service," noted Jardine afterward. "She was not. While they were searching for her, she was quietly sitting in a corner, unaware that they were looking for her."[34]

First came the civil ceremony in the grand salon, conducted by the self-conscious mayor of Monts, who nervously kept adjusting his red, white and blue sash with its gold tassels. He read the short service, informed the bride that she must obey her husband and told the groom that he must provide for his wife's needs. They both said, *"Oui,"* agreeing to the marriage, then signed the Marriage Register and the British Councillor Record. The Duke rubbed his chin thoughtfully, then clasped and unclasped his fingers behind his back, his eyes twinkling with excitement.

"I waited quietly for them to come for me after the civil ceremony was over," Jardine recalled. "When the time arrived, I walked through the library in which the servants of the Chateau were standing by their chairs, through the open door that framed their view of the ceremony, into the Music Room now filled with guests and up to the Holy Table where I bowed in prayer for the man and the woman about to receive the full rites of the Church of England."[35]

Marcel Dupré, the leading French organist, softly played some Bach and Schumann and a fugue of his own composition. Then came the march from Handel's "Judas Maccabaeus," and the Duke and his best man walked to the altar. Two minutes later, Dupré played his own wedding march, and Wallis walked in on the arm of Herman Rogers. It was only fitting that he should give the bride away—she had been his responsibility for so long.

Wallis' gown touched the floor. Her "something old" was a piece of antique lace stitched into her lingerie; "something new" was a gold coin minted for the coronation of Edward VIII, with his profile, which she put in the heel of her wedding slipper; "something borrowed" was a handkerchief from Aunt Bessie; and "something blue" was her wedding dress.

Positioned on the improvised altar were two old silver cups filled with lilies of the valley and a plain gold cross, two feet high, borrowed from a nearby Protestant church. Behind the altar stood two candelabra, each holding five candles. On the altar were two large candlesticks, one on either side of the cross. Flowers framed the whole altar, including trails of a rare clematis of creamy-green that filled the air with a sweet perfume.

In front of the altar lay two white satin pillows on low stools, on which the couple knelt.

The Reverend Jardine read the service in a strong voice. The Duke, in his morning coat and pin-striped trousers, seemed absolutely at ease. His nervousness was gone. He looked remarkably young and incredibly happy. At the appropriate time, though, he answered, "I will," in a tone so high pitched and loud that it startled the quiet of the room. Wallis' voice was contrastedly low when she promised to "obey, love, honor and serve" the Duke.

One of the observers said she then gave the Duke "a fleeting shy smile." Another said the smile on her face was most strange, as if she were saying, "Well, I made it."[36]

The only French press representative, Maurice Schumann, who later became French foreign minister, remembered "the slight tremor which ran through the small groups of guests" when the vicar asked, "Whosoever has any objection should speak up now or be silent for eternity."[37]

Jardine then asked those present to pray to the Almighty to "bless this man and woman," and added his own prayer, "May they remain in perfect love and peace together."

At the organ, Dupré played "O Perfect Love."

The bride and groom did not kiss.

The guests lined up to congratulate them. Each had to resolve his and her own dilemma on whether or not to bow and curtsy to the Duchess. Monckton had no problem. "I bow easily," he said.[38]

After the ceremony, Wallis asked the reverend to inscribe something in her prayer book. Jardine went to a nearby table, followed by the Duke.

"Turning to the Duke," recalled Jardine, "I said, 'What shall I write —Her Royal Highness, the Duchess of Windsor or just the Duchess of Windsor?' "

"Write," he replied, "the Duchess of Windsor."

"I still hesitated," Jardine remembered, "and seeing it the Duke said, 'Write Her Royal Highness.' "[39]

And so he did.

After leaving the salon, they gathered in the main dining room for the wedding breakfast. The butler later recalled that the Duchess had decided on a buffet instead of a sit-down meal so that the guests would not linger too long. There was a six-tier wedding cake, about three feet high, perfectly plain, without fruit, "and did not remind one of Christmas puddings."

3. 5. 37

Déjeuner

Caviar - Blinis

Langouste - froide

Homard - américaine

Bavarois aux légumes

Fricassée de Volaille

Jambon d'York

Parfait de foie gras

Salade Russe

Coq en Pâte

Gateau Breton

Bayonnaise

Fruits Rafraichi

Fraises des Bois

Omelette Norvégienne

The best man, Major Metcalfe, toasted "Long life and happiness to His Royal Highness, the Duke of Windsor, and his Lady."[40] Everybody drank to their health in champagne and then Wallis cut the cake. The first slice went to Aunt Bessie, the only relative there, from either family.

"Unlike most brides who simply cut through the cake and leave it to others," said Jardine, "the Duchess continued for all of a quarter of an hour cutting pieces for her guests and absent friends. My portion was a fairly large one because the Duchess wished me to take a piece home to my wife and family."[41]

"We had Lawson 1921 champagne," said Hale, "but not for the Duke. He just wanted his cup of Earl Grey tea."[42] It was all very informal and friendly. The terrace had a large sunshade and Wallis asked that it be lowered. The Duke himself jumped to adjust it, while the servants stared.

Eight years earlier, when he was Prince of Wales, he had said, "During twelve hours every day, I have to be what other people want me to be. The rest of the time I can be myself. If I married, I should spend the rest of my time being what my wife wanted me to be."[43]

And so he would.

Most of the guests were gone by early afternoon. Before he left, Walter Monckton took Wallis aside. "I told her that most people in England disliked her very much because the Duke had married her and given up his Throne, but that if she made him and kept him happy all his days, all that would change; but that if he were unhappy nothing would be too bad for her. She took it all very simply and kindly, just saying, 'Walter, don't you think I have thought of all that? I think I can make him happy.' "[44]

30

Wallis knew the climate of her future. As long as they lived, the world would wait with the smoldering question "Will they be happy?"

The drama of their story would diminish, fade and brighten in varying degrees at different times. Still, theirs was a story unique in history, etched into the emotional bedrock of all those who had lived through it, all those who had listened and read and wept or sneered. And, always, there would be that hidden question, "Will they be happy?"

"Many people like to think the Duchess made a good bargain because she married England's former King," remarked the Duke's equerry, Forwood. "They little realize this intelligent woman, in turn, dedicated herself to making the marriage a success. She went into her marriage with the supreme thought that this was for keeps, no matter how apprehensive she might have been."[1]

She was most apprehensive. She knew that their marriage would be under a perpetual microscope, and that millions were waiting with gleeful anticipation for an announced breakup. They had enjoyed the Prince Charming romance and now they wanted the Greek tragedy. She also knew that there were an equal number of supporters who wished them well. Among them was a whole generation of middle-aged women for whom Wallis represented a new hope in life. In every language, there were articles being written with the headline CHARM BEGINS AT FORTY. Essentially, they all said the same thing: "She has made the love affair of a woman of forty-odd years a dignified and an important thing."

A leading Japanese woman philosophized, "If a woman be loved, hated and envied, her life was worth the living."[2]

Wallis qualified.

What this marriage had more than most marriages was love and determination. It also had the full willingness of both partners to adjust to each other.

Marriage, according to Ambrose Bierce, is "The state or condition of a community consisting of a master, a mistress and two slaves, making in all, two."[3]

The Duke and the Duchess would indeed be slaves to each other. Perhaps it made their marriage a desperate thing, "so joined together no man shall ever put asunder." Theirs was a marriage resembling a pair of shears, cutting anybody who came between them. In the Hindu marriage ceremony, the bridegroom hangs a ribbon on the bride's neck and ties it in a knot. In this marriage, the knots were on both their necks. It was a marriage that could not fail. The price had been too high.

When they left Candé after the ceremony, Herman Rogers vainly pleaded with the press, "Don't follow them."

Just before their departure the mayor of Monts rushed back to his office to get something. He had forgotten the indispensable *livret de mariage*. This was the French family identity card with the names of the couple, and the place and date of the ceremony. It also contained twelve blank spaces to record the names and birth dates of any children, spaces which both the Duke and Duchess must have known would remain empty.

Their first train stop was Venice, but only for a few hours. They fed the pigeons in St. Mark's square and drifted in the gondolas, and then were off again for Austria. It was almost midnight when they arrived, but the local prefect was still waiting in Alpine costume, with a bouquet of red and white roses and a short speech of welcome. So were fifty boys and girls in peasant costume, followed by reporters and photographers. Police had warned that all those taking pictures would have their cameras confiscated for a week. It was not a deterrent.

Finally, the Duke and Duchess were in a car racing up a winding mountain to an ancient castle set high among the Alpine lakes and surrounding mountain peaks. The honeymoon had begun, the ancient custom of drinking honey for the time of a full moon. For Wallis, it seemed like such a long time since the two of them had been completely alone like this.

Wasselerleonburg Castle was a thirteenth-century building with a wide, cobblestone courtyard, a beautiful garden, a tiny chapel. Although the forty-room castle actually dated from A.D. 1250, it had been rebuilt in 1747 and now even had a tennis court and a swimming pool.

For those who cared, somebody counted 266 pieces of luggage, including 186 trunks, much of which arrived before the couple did.

It was also recorded that the Duke properly carried his bride over the threshold without stumbling. That was particularly important to the superstitious because the no-stumbling meant that their days here would be happy.

And they were. They took long walks, although the Duchess let the Duke do his own mountain climbing. When he reached the summit of the rocky peak called the Dobratsch, he signaled to her from the top, using a small mirror. Most of all they rediscovered each other.

"I believed with all my heart that married couples should, as early as possible, promise each other never to discuss a problem about which nothing further can be done," later confided the Duchess. "Otherwise, such a problem can well become a ghost which can haunt a marriage to its very end."[4]

Of course they did rehash the abdication crisis during their honeymoon, to the point of distress. Of course they made the decision never again to discuss it with each other. And of course it haunted their marriage to the very end.

It had to. It was the heavy stone to which they would be chained forever.

The Duke had asked the press to let them alone on their honeymoon, and the press did. There was a small item in *The New York Times* of June 6 about what they did on their first Sunday of married life. "Attired in Tyrolean leather breeches, white hose and a short-sleeved shirt, he watered flowers in the garden. In the morning he surveyed the tennis court and looked for grass he might mow . . . the Duchess supervised preparation of an Austrian dinner." The article noted that they both drank Austrian beer.

Still the Duke and Duchess led very English lives. The Duke had his British equerry and the ever-present Scotland Yard detective David Storier. Storier often substituted for the Austrian valet, bringing the Duke his morning tea and helping him dress. He could even supply a homemade version of the Turkish bath that the Duke had enjoyed on Jermyn Street in London. Storier did so by boiling an electric kettle full of water, placing it under a chair, seating the Duke on the chair, then wrapping him up in towels until he was happily perspiring. Storier was also known as the Duke's "walking wardrobe."[5] Out of his coat's two enormous inner pockets he produced on request anything from an apple or an aspirin to a wide variety of clothing.

The Duke and Duchess learned without pleasure, but without surprise, that newsreel film of their wedding day was not shown in England.

The *Daily Express* commented:

"You will have to go to France or America—or maybe to Russia—to see them, thereby proving that a large-sized piece of humbug is talked over here about freedom, no censorship, no dictatorship and what not, yet the imperial British people still are treated as a mentally-deficient race . . ."

The Reverend Jardine also found trouble when he returned to his church in Darlington. His local parish council resigned. People looked the other way when they passed him. It was the establishment, grinding the screws. In the end he moved to Los Angeles.

Prime Minister Stanley Baldwin also retired, saying, "I have had my hour. I pass soon into the shade."[6] To the British people he had been the man who deserved the fullest credit for knowing what they wanted during the abdication crisis, for doing what they wanted him to do, and for saving the principle of constitutional monarchy. They would leave it to history to remember that this was the man who had failed to prepare England for the coming war with Germany.

After his speech to Parliament on the crisis, he had told a friend, "I had a success, my dear Nicolson, at the moment I most needed it. *Now is the time to go.*"[7]

During the pageantry and parade of the coronation, the cheers for Baldwin were at times greater than the cheers for George VI.

Preparing his Christmas card list that year, Baldwin confided to Lord Monckton that he was sending one to the Duke of Windsor, writing on it, "I don't want our old friendship to die on my hands." Then he added, "Of course, she will look over his shoulder and say: 'That old b—! (Or whatever may be the Baltimore equivalent!) Pitch it in the fire!'

"But I must take the risk of that."[8]

He had guessed right about risk. The Duke would forgive Baldwin much, but would never forgive his refusal to give Wallis the Royal Highness title she deserved.

On the day of the Windsor wedding Ernest Simpson had dined unobserved at a famous London chop house. A mutual friend mentioned casually that he had talked to Wallis the previous day.

"Oh, did you?" said Simpson with a smile. "And how is she—all right I hope."[9]

While the Duke and Duchess were in Austria, Simpson won a slander suit against a prominent British society woman who had been overheard at a party saying, in effect, that "a sum of money had been accepted by Simpson as price for his silence."[10]

And in San Diego, California, Commander Earl Winfield Spencer said of his first wife, "She is a lovely person, intelligent, witty, and good company. 'Stimulating' is the word which best describes her charm. In whatever future she may choose—into whatever places it may take her—I wish her my very best. She will always hold my respect and admiration. . . . She is a most attractive woman and has one of the strongest characters I have ever known any person to possess."[11]

Not many women divorce two husbands and yet retain such affection and respect.

During the abdication, the Duke was reported to have told Baldwin, "I am now happy for the first time in my life and I wish you would let me alone." Whether or not he ever said it is not as important as the fact that this is what he truly felt. He *was* happy for the first time and he really *did* want to be left alone.

So did Wallis. She later described love with such words as "unselfish devotion," "contentment" and "happiness." And she added, "You see, I don't think love ever dies. It changes its course, it softens, it broadens. It may be blunted temporarily by a row or misunderstanding. But if it was genuine to begin with, it has a soul."[12]

The only test of real love, she said, was time.

Time is what she would have.

31

THE FALL OF 1937 was not a honeymoon year for the world. Japan had invaded China in July and "was eating it," as Churchill put it, "like an artichoke, leaf by leaf."[1] Despite the pious agreement for nonintervention, the grinding civil war in Spain had become a battleground for Germany and Italy on one side, and Russia on the other. Nazi planes practically obliterated the Basque city of Guernica, but a British training manual that year still noted: "The principles of training in field operations given in Cavalry Training (Horsed) are, in general, applicable to armored car regiments."

British diplomatic maneuvers followed the same line. The shy Arthur Neville Chamberlain, a Birmingham businessman, had succeeded Stanley Baldwin as prime minister and felt he could do business with Hitler. France was more fearful of the growing Nazi threat but relaxed in the supposed omnipotence of its intricate Maginot Line of connected pillboxes. They also continued to rely on their cavalry, rejecting Major Charles de Gaulle's prescient proposal for a mobile force of tanks, saying, "Oil is dirty, dung is not."

The people of France and England seemed to feel that any war was unthinkable, and, largely, refused to prepare for it. The British were much more excited about the Lambeth Walk, a dance craze that swept through every level of society.

Chamberlain's policy was appeasement, and the people were for it. Another individual practitioner of appeasement was Charles Bedaux, the man who had lent the Windsors his chateau for their wedding. The restless Bedaux was a short, stocky man, of some personal charm, a French-born American citizen who had made millions all over the world with his time and motion studies for utilizing labor in a "speed-up stretch-out"[2] system. When the Nazis came into power, they had closed his business offices in Germany, and Bedaux was most anxious to have them reopened. His best friend and contact in the German government was Dr. Robert Ley, the leader of the Nazi National Labor Front.

Bedaux now proposed that the Duke make an inspection tour of labor and housing conditions in Germany, and the Duke was automatically intrigued.

Bedaux, who also owned a castle in Hungary which he used as a lodge for shooting parties, invited the Windsors to stay with them. Wallis and Bedaux's stately, sophisticated wife, Fern, had become good friends. Charles Bedaux informed the Duke that he had contacted his German friends about the proposed tour, and that they were very excited about his coming.

Bedaux was fully aware of the propaganda possibilities of such a trip, and hoped that the Nazis would be properly appreciative in his future negotiations with them for business concessions—as indeed they were. The Duke, however, saw the trip mainly in terms of a diversion, a change of scene. He loved Germany, loved to speak German, always had had a marvelous time there. There was also always the possibility that he might get involved in a career in housing. As for the Nazi business, how could it concern him any more since he was no longer a British official? Bedaux indicated, furthermore, that the visit would be private, and not sponsored by the Nazi government.

After three months of sitting in a silent castle, Wallis too was ready for a change. Her political naïveté matched the Duke's, and she saw no harm in such a trip. Her husband was, after all, a private citizen, and he keenly wanted to go. Even if she had had doubts, she would have hesitated in discouraging him from doing the first thing he had wanted to do since their marriage.

The Duke told Bedaux to go ahead with his plans. Meanwhile, the Windsors went to Paris, taking a suite at the Hotel Meurice while they went house hunting.

Their nine-room hotel suite overlooked the Tuileries Gardens. They were the same rooms he had had as Prince of Wales. Still, it made them the more impatient to find their own home.

Bedaux, meanwhile, went immediately to Berlin to arrange final details with his friend Dr. Robert Ley.

"Kings not only live in glass houses," wrote Walter Monckton, "but have constant access to the best advice in every sphere. It was hard

342

to convince people at home how much more difficult it was for the Duke, because of the position he had held and the advice which had been available to him, to keep an even and temperate judgment when responsible ministers never went near him, and instead he was surrounded by friends who, for one reason or another, lived abroad largely divorced from English society and interests. With someone so quick to take a point, and so impressionable as the Duke, this was a constant anxiety to me."[3]

The Duke had felt it unnecessary to discuss his forthcoming trip with his brother, or the British government, but he did meet Beaverbrook in Paris and told him about it.

Beaverbrook was appalled. He told the Duke that he would be accused of interfering in foreign affairs, that such a visit at this time would stir up bitter public feelings against him for having any dealings with Hitler and Nazis. The resulting publicity could only further the fascist cause, not the cause of British democracy. If the Duke wanted a trip, why not go to the United States first? Finally he urged, "My private plane is here in Paris. Let me send it back to pick up Churchill and bring him here."

The Duke refused. Abdication had not changed him. He still only wanted advice that confirmed his own opinions.

The Duchess was determined not to be a negative influence at this time, and so she sided with her husband. Even during the pleasure of their honeymoon, she had sensed within him the seeds of boredom and discontent. He needed to feel a sense of usefulness and she was not going to crimp it now, even if she had wanted to. The fact was that she saw no reason to counter him on this.

The Windsors left for Berlin early in October. Waiting for them on the railroad platform was Nazi labor leader Robert Ley. Also there was the third secretary from the British Embassy to tell them the ambassador had left Berlin unexpectedly and would not see them, and that the chargé d'affaires had been informed by the Foreign Office not to take any official recognition of their arrival. The chargé d'affaires, Sir George Ogilvie-Forbes, who had known the Duke well when he was prince, later unofficially offered to help "behind the scenes . . . in any way I can."[4]

The Nazis had everything scheduled and wanted no help.

The Nazis also knew their man. They had a fat folder on him, and almost all of it was favorable.

Hitler had been so impressed with the Duke's suggestion (when he was Prince of Wales) that British soldiers visit Germany to fraternize with the men they had once fought that he himself met the first British contingent. In return, the Prince, on the day before his father's death, informed the German ambassador that he hoped to have a dinner party for the arriving German soldiers.

After Edward had become king, the German ambassador, Hoesch, had reported to the Foreign Ministry:

"You are aware from my reports that King Edward, quite generally, feels warm sympathy for Germany. I have become convinced during frequent, often lengthy, talks with him that these sympathies are deep-rooted and strong enough to withstand the contrary influences to which they are not seldom exposed . . . I am convinced that his friendly attitude toward Germany might in time come to exercise a certain amount of influence on the shaping of British foreign policy. At any rate, we should be able to rely upon having on the British Throne a ruler who is not lacking in understanding for Germany, and in the desire to see good relations established between Germany and Britain."[5]

More directly, Hitler had heard from Ribbentrop in 1936, "If the King were to give his support to the idea of Anglo-German friendship, his great popularity might well help to bring about an understanding."[6]

Ribbentrop also claimed credit for telephoning Hitler and advising him to keep the Simpson affair out of the German press—and this was done.

Ribbentrop later explained to Hitler that the real reasons for the recent crisis were not those constitutional and moral considerations which had been publicly announced. On the contrary, Baldwin's real motive was a purely political one, namely, to defeat those German-ophile forces which had been working through Mrs. Simpson and the former king with the object of reversing the present British policy and bringing about an Anglo-German entente. The report also quoted Herr Woermann as saying that Ribbentrop "had based the whole of his strategy on the role that Mrs. Simpson was expected to play in Anglo-German affairs. Her disappearance has completely disconcerted him and he now views the future with considerable anxiety . . ."

Ribbentrop had gone on to say that "the Führer himself was very distressed at the turn affairs had taken in this country, since he looked upon the late King as a man of his own heart and one who understood the Führerprinzip and was ready to introduce it into this country."

Most revealing to Hitler was an earlier report marked ONLY FOR THE

FÜHRER AND PARTY MEMBER V. RIBBENTROP.[7] It came from the Duke of Coburg, a grandson of Queen Victoria, who had been born in Britain. He was educated at Eton until he inherited his German title at the age of sixteen. The Duke of Coburg was head of the House of Saxe-Coburg-Gotha, which had intermarried with almost every royal family in Europe. The first cousin of George V, he wore a Nazi uniform and was known as the Nazi Duke. His report concerned three conversations with his second cousin when he was still Edward VIII.

Coburg's report on the conversation claimed that the King had said that a German-British alliance was an urgent necessity for safeguarding a lasting European peace, that the League of Nations was a farce and that he hoped to concentrate the business of British government on himself.

"To my question whether a discussion between Baldwin and Adolf Hitler would be desirable for future German-British relations," Coburg reported, "he replied in the following words: 'Who is King here? Baldwin or I? I myself wish to talk to Hitler, and will do so, here or in Germany. Tell him that, please.'"[8]

When the Coburg report was made public a generation later, Sir Harold Nicolson commented, "Coburg was an awful snob who was very concerned to impress Hitler with his high connections. Edward certainly felt his role in life was to help his country to reach an understanding with Germany, and I often argued with him about the practicability of this, considering the nature of the regime. What he dreaded was war.

"Perhaps he believed more than he should have in German integrity, and perhaps he exaggerated his chances of influencing the course of events. But so did many other people. He was always perfectly frank with everyone about his views, and there was nothing discreditable or unconstitutional about it."[9]

One can question the details of the Coburg report, but few quarrel with the existence of the sympathy and intent. Edward VIII had been undeniably pro-German.

Now almost a year later the Duke of Coburg gave a dinner at the Grand Hotel in honor of the Windsors and became the first European royal personage to recognize the Duchess' claim to the title of "Her Royal Highness."

Coburg's gesture was the place-card at her dinner table—it bore the German equivalent of "HRH." He also made certain that both the

Duke and the Duchess understood what he had done. It meant more to the Duke than it did to the Duchess, but she was properly pleased. What impressed her more was the fact that she was the only woman at that Coburg dinner, and the men were flatteringly attentive.

An official of the Saxon State Chancery also volunteered the information that Berlin had informed all local authorities to address the Duchess as "Your Royal Highness."

The Nazis knew that the best way to the Duke's good graces was through the woman he loved. They knew of the Duchess' particular interest in fine china and they made sure her itinerary included a visit to the Meissen Porcelain Works, where Dresden china is made. Guards of honor and carefully arranged crowds were always at the railroad stations chanting, "We want to see the Duchess."[10]

The only black marks in the Duke's Nazi folder were his friendship with the Rothschilds and the use of a Jewish otologist to treat his ear trouble. Julius Streicher, the high priest of anti-Semitism in Nazi Germany, and editor of *Der Stürmer,* had made the expected diatribes about it in his paper at the time. It was now thought prudent for him not to be present at official functions for the Windsors. The Duke, however, denied that he had made any objections to meeting Herr Streicher. Nor did he make any objections in Leipzig, when it was explained that they were not staying in the city's best hotel because it was owned by a Jew.

As guests, they felt they could not complain even if they had thought about it. American reporters, however, observed that the Duke responded to the crowds and the cheers by giving them the Nazi salute.

Both the Duke and the Duchess were visibly impressed with what they were seeing. The red carpet tour did not include any of the brutalities: the persecuted minorities, the wholesale arrests, the concentration camps, the burnings and beatings. The Windsors saw only the highly organized energy and industry of a people driven by fanatic leaders. They saw the ends and made no inquiry about the means.

The Duke told one of Ley's German Labor Front meetings in Leipzig, "I have traveled the world and my upbringing has made me familiar with the great achievements of mankind, but that which I have seen in Germany, I had hitherto believed to be impossible. It cannot be grasped, and is a miracle; one can only begin to understand it when one realizes that behind it all is one man and one will."

This did not make the Duke a Nazi. He was a man who admired power and results. He had been a king and an emperor who had reigned but did not rule. He would have loved to have ruled. He had the wish for it, and perhaps the will. He certainly had the dream of it. Here in the Germany he loved he saw his dream of power put into action, and it dazzled him.

This is not to say that he could never have become a Nazi or a fascist. It had stirred him, and the potential was there. But he was, basically, a decent human being, with natural sympathies for the depressed and the deprived. The more he learned about specific Nazi methods, the more they repelled him. This is exactly what later happened.

At the time, however, he was emotional, naïve, and let himself be used. It was a sadness because his name and his cause had had a ringing sound, and now it was harsh and clanging, and out of tune.

William L. Shirer, a correspondent in Berlin, joined the Windsor party, as did Winston Churchill's son Randolph. Shirer noted their escort, "one of the real Nazi ruffians, Dr. Ley." Shirer also wrote, "Had my first view of Mrs. Simpson today, and she seemed quite pretty and attractive . . . A curious thing for the Duke to do, to come to Germany where the labour unions have been smashed, just before he goes to America. He's been badly advised."[11]

Wallis did not like Ley. She thought him unpleasant and crude, and she disliked the way he paraded them through the streets, sitting between them in the back of an open Mercedes.

Wallis much preferred Field Marshal Göring. He invited them for tea at his baronial country home and greeted them effusively in his white uniform, crowded with medals. The Görings gave Wallis the house tour including the gymnasium with an Elizabeth Arden massage machine.

Still wearing his bemedaled uniform, Göring "forced his generously proportioned body between one of the pairs of rollers to show the smiling Duchess how they worked."[12] Afterward, he demonstrated some of the toys in the attic. One of them was a toy airplane attached to an overhead wire, flying across the room, dropping small wooden bombs.

Wallis saw one thing that particularly intrigued her, and she asked the Duke to query Göring about it. It was a map which treated Austria as part of Germany. The Duke did ask, and Göring grinned and said that it was a new map, and that since he was certain that Austria would soon want to be part of Germany, it simply saved him the bother of getting a new map made when it happened.

The Windsors' most enjoyable night was in Munich at the Platzl, a favorite beer hall. The place was packed. The Duke downed three pints of beer, jumped onto his chair to make a speech in German, saying how much he loved the city. A crowd of several hundred, many of them in Bavarian leather shorts, pounded their stone mugs and roared in approval as he put on a false mustache. They all sang German songs and the Duke joined in. At the end, the Duke received "the kind of applause that only the old Kings of Bavaria could expect."[13] The Duchess took away with her from that place the memory of "those delightful little white sausages."[14]

Hitler sent word that he wanted to see them at tea the next afternoon at Berchtesgaden. He put his special train at their disposal, and afterward they were taken up a steep mountain road to his lodge.

The house had a great hall with a spectacular view of the Austrian Alps. Foreign reporters were surprised that the Windsors had not been invited for lunch, although they had arrived at one and Hitler kept them waiting more than an hour before he greeted them. He first called in the Duke, and Rudolf Hess stayed with Wallis. She thought Hess good-looking and charming. The interview lasted over an hour, and then Hitler walked out with the Duke, Hitler still doing most of the talking.

"The Duchess joined in only occasionally in the conversation," later reported the interpreter Paul Schmidt, "and then with great reserve, when any social question of special interest to women arose. She was simply and appropriately dressed, and made a lasting impression on Hitler," who told Schmidt, "She would have made a good Queen."[15]

"I could not take my eyes off Hitler," Wallis herself later wrote. She noted his long slim hands, and felt the impact of a "great inner force." What most affected her were his eyes, "truly extraordinary—intense, unblinking, magnetic, burning with the same peculiar fire I had earlier seen in the eyes of Kemal Atatürk."[16]

When they left, Hitler gave them the Nazi salute, which the Duke returned.

Afterward, Wallis tried to learn what Hitler and the Duke had talked about. The Duke said little, only that Hitler had done most of the talking, discussed mostly what he had done for Germany and how he hated Bolshevism.

The Duke also later described Hitler's eyes as being piercing and magnetic.

"I confess frankly that he took me in. I believed him when he implied that he sought no war with England . . . I acknowledge now that, along with too many other well-meaning people, I let my admiration for the good side of German character dim what was being done to it by the bad. I thought that . . . the immediate task . . . of my generation . . . was to prevent another conflict between Germany and the West that could bring down our civilization.

"Well, I was wrong about that . . ."[17]

Assessing the Windsor visit, foreign diplomats agreed that it had been more of a triumphal procession than an informal inspection tour. The Nazis had widely publicized the Duke's reputation as a friend of the working man, intimating that he had been driven from his throne because of this. Their propaganda emphasized that the Duke had found in the Third Reich a system which he liked.

There were reports afterward that Hitler had told intimates that if he had had an hour with the Duke during the abdication crisis, he would have been able to persuade him not to give up the throne. Hitler felt that, as king, with his views, he had responsibilities not only to his country but to Europe.

32

THE DUKE AND DUCHESS refused to believe that their German trip had been a fiasco, that they had been "taken in" and "used." They refused to understand the new stir of resentment against them in England, and, indeed, throughout the world. They still brimmed with the excitement and enthusiasm of the tour.

The Duchess had thrilled to it because never before had she received such red-carpet treatment. There had been the short visits to assorted kings during the *Nahlin* cruise and her reception in Turkey had been most impressive, but those now seemed like teasing intermissions. The German greetings had been overwhelming, fully orchestrated with crowds and cheering and guards of honor and parades, and everybody trying desperately to please. It gave her an enormous sense of power, and she loved it. She later told a friend that she had hoped to meet Hitler's mistress, Eva Braun, but never did.

The Duke had been through a thousand such state visits. Only a year before he would have accepted it with little emotion. Now he was no longer a royal personage. He had just spent some restless months in Austria considering his future. In an interview, he confessed, "By withdrawing from the great position which my birth had destined me to fill, I had become something alien, something apart."[1]

The result was that the German trip had assumed an importance beyond itself. It gave him a taste again of what he was. Even more, the German recognition of Wallis as a royal highness, with full courtesy and honors, was a matter of enormous satisfaction. To his mind, it restored him in her eyes.

What was incredible was that he could not or would not accept the disastrous propaganda engendered by their trip. How could he not have known of the brutalities of Nazi Germany and its potential menace to the world? How could he have conceivably believed that the carefully programed show of energy and efficiency represented the whole truth? Why had he no curiosity to try to balance what he had seen by probing for some of the more obvious rot and disease in the fascist system and society?

And, above all, why were he and Wallis so completely captivated by Hitler?

The Duke was hungry to believe what he wanted to believe. Germany and its people formed the largest part of his family heritage. He loved the country and the people, and he felt comfortable there. As for the Nazi doctrines of race and hate, he probably knew little of them, and believed less. His social set had neither the fear nor the understanding of the threat of Nazi Germany. Churchill was one of only a few aware but lonely voices, and how many listened to him?

Wallis' reaction was even more understandable. Politically, she was even more ingenuous than the Duke. Her formal education had stopped at Oldfields, where students were then more concerned with manners and religion than they were with ideas. She had soaked in her knowledge of the world from newspapers and magazines and cocktail party conversation.

The truth was that Hitler had overwhelmed the Duke because he was the more magnetic personality and that he had fascinated Wallis because men of power always had fascinated her. With the Duke, she was in command, and she knew it. Her wish was his law. It was perhaps not a role she deliberately chose, but one that he seemed to prefer. Therefore, when she met a man of immense sweeping dominance, she tingled. Atatürk of Turkey had made her feel that way, and Atatürk had ruled only a pimple of land compared to Hitler. Her reaction was predictable. Her mind was not filled with facts she did not know or principles she did not understand: her response was primarily emotional.

Still ebullient about Germany, they tended to ignore any criticism. Their trip had caused a cooling with Beaverbrook, a silence from Churchill. The American columnist Westbrook Pegler wrote that the Nazis had led him around "by a nose ring" and that the Duke "just doesn't know how to run his own show when thrown on his own resources."[2]

A new note came from Dr. William E. Dodd, Jr., son of the United

States ambassador to Germany, who warned that the Duke was "deeply impressed with the glories of fascism," during his visit to Germany, and might "try to convince Americans of the achievements of National Socialism."

The British were more caustic. Herbert Morrison, MP, leader of the London County Council, angrily noted, "The choice before ex-kings is either to fade out of the public eye or be a nuisance. It is a hard choice, perhaps, for one of his temperament, but the Duke of Windsor will be wise to fade."[3]

Fading was not the Duke's style. Fading was boring. The Duke and Duchess both wanted involvement. He wanted, somehow, to carve for himself some position of importance. He wasn't quite sure what it would be, but he wanted to keep searching until he found it.

Wallis was equally determined to help him find himself. She may well have been the one who had suggested a trip to the United States. It would ostensibly have the further purpose of inspecting housing and labor conditions. When they had discussed the German trip in Hungary with Bedaux, they had told him to plan the American tour, too. The highly organized Bedaux had promptly informed the American Embassy in Budapest that the Duke and Duchess would arrive on the *Bremen* in New York on November 11 and that the Duke would appreciate being received by the President to discuss social welfare. The Duke, he said, would also make a fifteen-minute broadcast to the American people from Washington, and they would travel by private Pullman.

Bedaux wanted to know, promptly, whether the President would receive the Duke and whether the American government would provide police protection. Bedaux also noted that the Duke was visiting Germany at Hitler's invitation and that the German government had placed two airplanes and eight automobiles at his disposal.

Wallis was overjoyed by the programed five-week visit. Baltimore, of course, was on the itinerary. It would be her triumphal tour. She had left the United States with little money, heartbroken by a frustrated romance, and she would return one of the most envied women in the world. She could hardly wait.

Arrangements moved ahead quickly. President Franklin D. Roosevelt invited the Duke and Duchess to tea at the White House. George Summerlin, chief of protocol for the State Department would welcome them on their arrival and stay with them until they left, and the government offered its full cooperation and facilities for the proposed tour.

The Duke's equerry even issued a seven-page memorandum to the staff of the German ship *Bremen*, outlining the Duke and Duchess' requirements. It included service in the Red Room, a separate dining room set aside for them on the Sun Deck, provision for a special English blend of tea, a barrel of London drinking water. The memo informed chefs that the Duke liked plain food, steaks and cutlets and chicken for dinner, preferred French dressing without mustard, only drank mineral water before cocktail time. He also enjoyed canapes of liver paste, Wesphalian ham and rarebits. With dinner he liked claret, but not white wines or champagnes, and had an after-dinner brandy with his coffee.

The Duchess had no specific dining desires that differed from her husband's, the memorandum continued, but she did like to have flowers at her table and in her room—any flowers but roses. The Duke preferred dark red carnations for his lapel.

Everything seemed settled and then the conflicts began.

Bedaux himself was the initial stumbling block. His name had become anathema to American labor. They saw his management-consultant companies as disguised efficiency systems which, in effect, would convert human labor into practical automatons. His Nazi connections convinced them of his fascistic intent. Bedaux was appalled.

Sensing danger, he hurried off to the United States. Coincidentally sailing on the same ship with him was Ernest Simpson, completing plans for his own future. Within three weeks, on November 19, Simpson would marry Mary Kirk Raffray in a quiet ceremony in Fairfield, Connecticut.

The Duke and Duchess meanwhile busied themselves in Paris. The two were seen taking long walks in the Fontainebleau Woods, once a royal preserve of the kings of France. They had piles of mail, all of which would be faithfully answered, even those who wrote "Dear King." They liked their quiet drives in the country with their two cairn terriers. And they packed their bags for the five-week trip.

The Duke decided to put in an appearance at the Anglo-American Press Association lunch in Paris. He had originally accepted with the stipulation that he would not have to make a speech but the heightened reaction to the Germany trip prompted him to defend himself.

"Some of the recent misstatements concerning the Duchess and myself have caused us considerable concern and embarrassment, and might well lead to dangerous consequences. . . . Our visit to Germany has been very interesting, and we are now looking forward to our tour of America, and to further opportunities of making a study of the methods which have been adopted in the leading countries of the world in dealing with housing and industrial conditions."

The Duke then felt it necessary to add, "I am now a very happily married man, but my wife and I are neither content nor willing to lead a purely inactive life of leisure. We hope and feel that in due course the experience we gain from our travels will enable us, if given fair treatment, to make some contribution, as private individuals, toward the solving of some of the vital problems that beset the world today."[4]

It was a large hope. Hannen Swaffer, London columnist, mocked it quickly. "It's nothing but a publicity stunt. I traveled with the Duke when he was studying housing in Wales, and if he were there for fifty years he wouldn't know anything more about it than he knows now."

At the same time the scheduled Windsor visit to the United States created consternation in Great Britain. The British ambassador to the United States, the Honorable Sir Ronald Lindsay, returned from London with fresh instructions and soon talked with Undersecretary of State Sumner Welles. Welles' confidential report to the Secretary of State was explicit.

The Ambassador said that before his departure from England he had been summoned to spend a few days with the King and Queen of England. He said that, as I probably knew, the relationship between the present King of England and the Duke of Windsor had been throughout their lives particularly close and that during the present King's earlier years when he had suffered from an impediment in his speech, the then Prince of Wales had taken it upon himself to shield and to support his brother and that the present King for that reason had a very natural and particular sense of gratitude and affection for the Duke of Windsor. On the other hand, they both felt that at this time when the new King was in a difficult situation and was trying to win the affection and confidence of his country people, without possessing the popular appeal which the Duke of

Windsor possessed, it was singularly unfortunate that the Duke of Windsor was placing himself in a position where he would seem constantly to be courting the limelight. The Ambassador went on to say that he had found on the part of all the governing class in England a very vehement feeling of indignation against the course of the Duke of Windsor based in part on the resentment created by his relinquishment of his responsibilities and in even greater part due to the apparent unfairness of his present attitude with regard to his brother, the King. The Ambassador said that in Court circles and in the Foreign Office and on the part of the heads of political parties, this feeling bordered on the stage of hysteria. The Ambassador said rather significantly that there recently had been a widening of this sentiment of indignation because of the fact that the active supporters of the Duke of Windsor within England were those elements known to have inclinations towards fascist dictatorships and that the recent tour of Germany by the Duke of Windsor and his ostentatious reception by Hitler and his regime could only be construed as a willingness on the part of the Duke of Windsor to lend himself to these tendencies. The Ambassador expressed the personal opinion that the Duke of Windsor himself is probably not cognizant of the state of feeling in this regard and that it is being exploited without his knowledge.

. . . What the British desired he said was to prevent any action on the part of the authorities of the British Government which would permit the Duke of Windsor to appear in the light of a martyr . . .[5]

Soon after the meeting with Welles, the British ambassador announced that he and his wife would give a dinner at the Embassy for the Duke and Duchess the night after their arrival in Washington.

Bedaux, meanwhile, found himself in deeper trouble. The entire American labor movement suddenly seemed to erupt in a national outcry of vituperation. It became so critical that the top officials in the four American Bedaux management-consultant companies demanded that Bedaux ease himself out of these companies and withdraw from the Windsor tour.

Bedaux did both. His nine days in America had proved devastating. ". . . apparently being called a Fascist in forty-eight states had not sickened him," wrote Janet Flanner in *The New Yorker*, "but failure had—failure for the first time in his career. He had lost . . . his pride;

success was his natural element and vanity was essential to his state of well-being."

Bedaux cabled the Duke.

"Sir, I am compelled in honesty and friendship to advise you that because of a mistaken attack upon me here, I am convinced that your proposed tour will be difficult under my guidance . . ."

It was an understatement. The tour had become impossible because of his guidance. President William Green of the American Federation of Labor announced that labor would welcome the Duke now that Bedaux was no longer associated with the trip. But it was too late. Too much damage had been done. The Duke sent a telegram of regret to the President of the United States. The last time he had been in the White House he had had lunch with President Calvin Coolidge, and the time before that he had visited the sick President Woodrow Wilson.

So strong was the press reaction that the former king felt compelled to issue a statement: "The Duke emphatically repeats that there is no shadow of justification for any suggestion that he is allied to any industrial system, or that he is for or against any particular political and racial doctrine."

The public affront was difficult for the Duke to take, but the fault was his own. His judgment had been bad. For Wallis, the cancellation of the American trip came as a crushing blow. She had counted on it so much. She had felt hemmed in for so long and she had looked forward to her homecoming as a chance to feel free, laugh and gossip with old friends, enjoy her position to the hilt. Now it all had turned inexplicably ugly.

"The best advice that the Duke's friends can tender him is to step outside the public arena," warned Beaverbrook's *Daily Express*.

Wallis read that editorial with wonder and worry. If her husband did indeed step outside the public arena, where could he go? What could he do? And, unless he were happy, how could she be happy?

33

A HOTEL IS NOT A HOME, and Wallis now saw this as her primary job: to find one, and to make one. Since the Duke wanted to live in the country, and she preferred the city, she began her house hunting in a considerable quandary. In the interim she tried to create some feeling of coziness and order in their hotel suite.

"She had a small gold book in which she wrote comments and complaints about meals," recalled her butler, Hale, whom she had borrowed from the Bedaux. "She was always correcting different things such as the fact that the footmen should run to the door. She couldn't stand seeing too much food served on a table anywhere.

"She and the Duke each had their own bedrooms, and they breakfasted separately. He liked kippers and eggs but she didn't have any favorites. They stayed apart in the mornings. She enjoyed her privacy then. If he popped into her room, she made him pop right out again."[1]

Wallis spent much of her mornings on the mixed business of beauty and the house. After the masseur and the hairdresser, she conferred with Hale on the dinner menu, the guest list and staff problems. Hale was the funnel for complaints. There were not many because the Duchess was a careful, considerate employer.

"She was always very kind and generous to the staff," Hale reported. "Whenever we traveled anywhere, she always made sure we had the best accommodations, the best rooms. The staff always knew what she wanted and we knew what we had to do. And she was quick to compliment. She would tell me, 'The dinner went off very very well, Hale.' "[2]

The Duke and Duchess averaged two dinner parties a week at home, with almost never more than sixteen guests. Most of the week they were invited out.

357

"They ate almost nothing at lunch," said Hale, "and when they dined alone, they ate most simply. Dinner was always promptly at 8:30, preceded by a short cocktail time."[3]

Besides two chauffeurs and Hale, they had two footmen, a chef and two kitchen helpers, a personal maid and valet and two housemaids. There were later additions such as another maid to care only for the fine china and a pastry cook. There seemed to have been little turnover among the staff.

If no man is a hero to his valet, the same is surely true of a butler and the other servants toward the mistress of the house. Women cannot fool their servants. Their wages were no higher than wages in other houses, and, in some cases, less. They stayed because her charm was not skin deep, her naturalness was not phony, her interest in them was a genuine interest. This must be an important touchstone in any description of her character.

While still in Paris, Wallis had another taste of what might have been when she was invited that November 1937 to open a sale on behalf of the British Episcopal Church of Christ at Neuilly. When she and the Duke arrived the initial applause was meager. The British colony had come *en masse* really out of curiosity. What pleased Wallis, and particularly the Duke, was that after her short speech, their applause had an enthusiastic ring.

Making her first public speech, the Duchess read from a note, "We appreciate the welcome which you have given us. We are glad to be here at your community gathering and wish it every success. In declaring this sale open I wish to congratulate all those who have worked for it and contributed to it, and I am sure they will meet with a generous response."[4]

Three short sentences, neither profound nor literary, and yet very important to both of them. It broke the ice. The delighted Duke congratulated her, for it was the first time he had had an opportunity to show his bride off to a very British audience.

And the general consensus was that the Duchess was "sweet," "clever looking," "a pleasant mixture of humor and kindliness in her eyes," and her voice was "soft and pleasant, not a bit like the usual American accent."[5]

The Duke and Duchess toured the stalls with laughter and good humor, bought marmalade and homemade pickles and went home delighted with the pleasant impression. After so many public fiascos, this fractional success seemed all the more marvelous.

About this time someone had asked Wallis how she would feel if the royal crown had been placed on her head.

"Just like a forced landing," she answered.[6]

Foremost among their loyal friends who returned often to see them was Walter Monckton. He easily sensed that the Duke was "beating against the bars," increasingly irritated at "the ambiguity of his position."[7] Monckton felt, too, that Wallis was subconsciously unreconciled to the fact that the Duke had become a less important person by marrying her.

Part of the problem was that many of their British friends were avoiding them because any visit to them "might be misunderstood by the royal circle at home." Monckton persuaded many of them to come. "Their visits were welcomed, and improved the atmosphere."[8] One guest at their Hotel Meurice suite was that shy, bird-watching fly fisherman Prime Minister Neville Chamberlain.

Since the Duke no longer represented a threat to him Chamberlain now could be condescending, and even kind. Indeed, the two men were enthusiastically tied in their attitude toward Nazi Germany, both men fully in favor of appeasement to avoid war. Hale noted how careful the Prime Minister was in his conversation. As soon as Hale entered the room, the Prime Minister stopped talking, almost in the middle of a sentence, and didn't begin again until the butler left.

What the Duke wanted most from Chamberlain and the British government was its permission for him to return home with his wife. He wanted roots again, an English home with an English garden, and a job of some responsibility. But he would not return unless his wife received her due honor as "Her Royal Highness."

Chamberlain promised to consider and discuss these things upon his return.

In the meantime, Wallis' public case was not improved when a rumor was reported in the press that a visitor to her bedroom had observed five photographs on her mantelpiece—one of the Duke and Duchess, another Queen Mary and three of Adolf Hitler. Even more incredible than the Hitler photographs was the one of Queen Mary. Intimates who knew of that relationship were highly amused. Had the false report not included the Queen Mother, it would have had many more believers.

The decorations she did have on her dressing table were mementos of her courtship: a bouquet of flowers along with a royal-crested card, a fan, fragments of a letter, the first formal invitation she had received when David was prince, a pair of white evening gloves and a pair of golf socks that he wore on one of their country weekends.

Then in February 1938 the Duchess received added publicity when named one of the world's best-dressed women for the second consecutive year. As if to prove it, she attended the farewell reception for American ambassador William C. Bullitt wearing a simple white crepe gown with a barely décolleté square neck. It skimmed the floor with straight paneled folds. The dress was trimmed with only two bands of gold embroidery, starting at the waistline and coming down in a curve over her hips. She wore the Duke's most recent gift, a tiara of diamonds and emeralds. Completing her costume was a thin strand of diamonds and emeralds at her throat.

That winter Wallis had found a house in Versailles that finally suited the Duke, the Chateau de La Maye, luxuriously furnished, with extensive grounds, tennis courts, a golf course and a swimming pool. They increased the staff to a dozen servants, besides four cooks, and the French Sûreté again cooperated with Scotland Yard on security. After their six-month lease expired, they returned to the Riviera and took a ten-year lease on La Croe—the villa that Wallis originally had wanted for the marriage ceremony. Wallis had it painted blue and white and began collecting assorted furniture from storage.

They spent Christmas of 1938 there, giving their first big party. It was a gay affair, even though the Duke lost the money Wallis gave him to pay for the band. She thereafter handled most money transactions herself.

Christmas morning provided the Duchess with a story she liked to retell about the Duke. They had gone to church that morning and, in the middle of the service, the Duke whispered, loud enough to be overheard, "Darling, how much did we give these people?"

Wallis could have been happy at La Croe. It had serenity, the terraces stepping down to the sea. It had a luxurious comfort, the most pleasant climate, a group of entertaining neighbors. Despite this, she felt his brooding, his unease, and reacted accordingly, but was aware of her helplessness. She could give him herself, but how could she give him an importance in the world? He had been trained only to be a king. She knew, too, that he saw France as an intermission, a stopping place. He still was firmly determined to go home to England.

One of their neighbors who welcomed them often was novelist Somerset Maugham. His Villa Mauresque at Cap Ferrat was surrounded by red and white oleanders and faced a view of winking lighthouses. When the Windsors came for dinner, Maugham prepared his other guests carefully. "He said the Duke gets cross if the Duchess is not treated with respect," remembered one of the guests in his diary.[9]

"In they came. She, I must say, looks very well for her age. She has done her hair in a different way. It is smoothed off her brow and falls down the back of her neck in ringlets. It gives her a placid and less strained look. Her voice has also changed. It now mingles the accents of Virginia with that of a Duchess in one of Pinero's plays. He entered with his swinging naval gait, plucking at his bow tie. He had on a *tussore* dinner jacket. He was in very high spirits. Cocktails were brought and we stood around the fireplace. There was a pause. 'I am sorry we were a little late,' said the Duke, 'but Her Royal Highness couldn't drag herself away.' He had said it. The three words fell into the circle like three stones in a pool. Her (gasp) Royal (shudder) Highness (and not one eye dared to meet another).

"Then we went in to dinner. There were two cypresses and the moon. I sat next to the Duchess. He sat opposite. They called each other 'darling' a great deal. I called him 'Your Royal Highness' a great deal and 'Sir' all the time. I called her 'Duchess.' One cannot get away from his glamour and his charm and his sadness, though I must say he seemed gay enough.

"They have a villa here and a yacht, and go round and round. He digs in the garden. But it is pathetic the way he is sensitive about her. It was quite clear to me from what she said that she hopes to get back to England. When I asked her why she didn't get a house of her own somewhere, she said, 'One never knows what may happen. I don't want to spend all my life in exile.' "[10]

Her real feeling toward La Croe is perhaps best revealed by her butler at the time. "Never in my life have I worked so hard. The Duchess, I soon discovered, regarded the villa, not so much as a home, but as the stage on which to present an unending show of hospitality and entertainment. She was the producer; I was her stage manager. On my arrival . . . I found house telephones not only in the butler's pantry, not only in my bedroom—but in my bathroom and lavatory as well. It was clear that when the Duchess insisted on instant communication with the staff at all times, she meant, *at all times*."[11]

Monckton had visited them at La Croe that fall, and witnessed how unhappy the Duke was in his new role. He was tense, irritable, quick to show his temper. To Monckton, he could only talk of returning to England. The two would climb to his room at the top of the house, which looked out between the trees across the garden to the Mediterranean. There the Duke would compose letters with Monckton addressed to the Prime Minister, the King and his mother.

Upon his return, Monckton stayed at Balmoral with the King and Queen and the Prime Minister. He brought up the Duke's plea, first to Chamberlain.

"The Prime Minister thought that the right course was for the Duke of Windsor to be treated as soon as possible as a younger brother of the King who could take some of the royal functions off his brother's hands. The King himself, though he was not anxious for the Duke to return as early as November 1938 (which was what the Duke wanted), was not fundamentally against the Prime Minister's view. But I think the Queen felt quite plainly that it was undesirable to give the Duke any effective sphere of work. I felt then, as always, that she naturally thought that she must be on her guard because the Duke of Windsor, to whom the other brothers had always looked up, was an attractive, vital creature who might be the rallying point for any who might be critical of the new King."[12]

Monckton relayed his bad news to the Duke and suggested he delay his return. A more formal letter from Prime Minister Chamberlain, wrapped in diplomatic language, expressed the concern that such a visit might "provoke heated controversy." Chamberlain suggested that the right time was "not yet" but when the time was ripe, he would "flash a friendly signal."

It was then that Wallis decided they needed a more permanent home in Paris. She found one on the Boulevard Suchet, with windows facing the Bois de Boulogne, and she took a long lease. It was a bright, cheerful house with a pleasant courtyard, marble floors and a small elevator. Like La Croe, it also had a gilded bathtub. It was not the country home the Duke had wanted, but again her wish was his wish.

Wallis kept a weather eye out for the depressed Duke's growing irritability. He was more apt than ever to say whatever he felt like at a party and Wallis would move over to him and say, "Now darling . . ." and he would then quiet very quickly.

One of the more rampant rumors at this time was the insistent item that Wallis was pregnant. Before long she even received gifts of baby socks and other knitted infant clothes. It reached the point where crowds began to cheer her whenever she left the house.

Opera singer Grace Moore created a small teacup storm when she was photographed curtsying to the Duchess. Returning to the United States, Miss Moore told reporters, "I certainly do consider the Duchess as royalty. The Duchess would have been considered royalty long ago if she had been English and not American-born. After all, the Duchess gave happiness and the courage of his convictions to one man, which is more than most women can do. She deserves a curtsy for that alone."

Wallis also managed to maintain her gaiety at parties. A young Englishman who had seen her at several told a New York reporter that sometimes a remark of the Duchess "makes you want to give back wisecrack for wisecrack in the Baltimore manner."[13]

At a bridge game with Somerset Maugham, who stammered when excited, the famous novelist once said, "D-D-Duchess, why d-d-didn't you s-s-support me with three k-k-kings in your hand?"

"My kings don't take tricks," she answered, smiling, "they only abdicate."[14]

Wallis was forty-three years old in June 1939, and the Duke gave her rubies and emeralds in modern clasps, with a bracelet to match. Earlier he had given her a newly created platinum fox skin from Molyneux.

But it was no longer a world of jewelry and fox skins and wisecracks. The Nazi blitzkrieg was moving across Europe. The Germans had absorbed Austria the previous spring, as Göring had so confidently predicted. When Hitler next ordered the capitulation of Czechoslovakia, Prime Minister Chamberlain made his first plane flight, an umbrella serving as his olive branch. Returning from Munich, Chamberlain said, "I have no doubt, looking back, that my visit alone prevented an invasion for which everything was prepared." The Duke of Windsor was among those who approved and applauded. And the Duke's friend Lord Castlerosse enthusiastically wrote, "Thanks to Chamberlain, thousands of young men will live. I shall live." He was right about himself but not about the rest.

Not all Britons agreed. Anthony Eden had quit the government saying, "We must not buy goodwill." And *The Week* asked why Chamberlain had "turned all four cheeks" to Hitler. After absorbing Czechoslovakia, Germany now looked toward Poland.

The Duke and Duchess took a trip away from their unreal world of parties and pleasure and visited the battlefield sites of World War I at Verdun. The Duke decided to make a speech appealing for peace, broadcast it from Verdun and aim it primarily at the United States as the strongest power in the world. The Duke may not have forgotten the faceless soldier whose forehead he had kissed.

"I speak simply as a soldier of the last war, whose most earnest prayer it is that such cruel and destructive madness shall never again overtake mankind."

He urged national leaders to bury their "jealousies and suspicions," to negotiate by mutual concessions.[15]

The Duchess sat beside him as he broadcast in a strong clear voice. He later admitted that she had helped him write the speech, just as she had helped him with some speeches when he was king.

Wallis was enthusiastic about the idea because it made her husband again feel he was a man with some meaning, involved with the world powers. The speech, however, had the impact of a feather in the wind. In England, there was bitterness about it. At that particular time the King and Queen were en route to the United States, and many Britons saw the Duke's speech as a ploy to move into stage center.

Adela Rogers St. Johns later gave the Duke her explanation for the sour reception of that speech: "To us, Sir, your brother King George VI was, in our eyes, a pinch hitter. When you left the game, he came in as a *substitute*. All American hearts go out to someone who is, let us say, pinch-hitting for Babe Ruth . . . We felt it wasn't right for *you* to appear in an heroic role and speak from a battlefield in France when he was trying so hard to bat in your place . . ."[16]

The Windsors' poor timing was further underlined when it was learned that they were dining that week with the Count Johannes von Welczek, the German ambassador. It did not help matters when the Duke added that the Welczeks had been their friends "for years."

Late in August came the almost unbelievable news for the Duke that Germany had signed a nonaggression pact with Russia. He and Wallis returned to La Croe at Antibes, where the world seemed even more unreal. He was now in almost daily telephone communication with Monckton, whom George VI had made his legal adviser and liaison with the Prime Minister.

"The Duke was strongly against the waste and horror of war, and felt it ought somehow to be avoided," Monckton recorded. "Neither of us saw that it was inevitable. Almost on the last day the Duke sent a telegram to Hitler which I have never mentioned, in which, as a citizen of the world, he asked him not to plunge the world into war. Hitler replied that he never wanted a war with England, and that if it took place it would not be his fault. During the last day or two before war was declared I had a troublesome time speaking constantly to the Duke from 10 Downing Street and urging him to come back, making elaborate arrangements for the purpose."[17]

The Duke somehow saw this as a time when he could dictate new terms. He would not come to England unless he and his wife were accommodated either at Windsor or one of the royal castles. This could not be done and Monckton canceled the plans.

The Nazis attacked Poland at dawn on September 1. Hitler remained confident that Great Britain would again backtrack. He was wrong. After thirty-six hours' delay, the British government issued an ultimatum demanding withdrawal of German troops from Polish territory within two hours. World War II had begun.

That was September 3. The Duke was no longer dictating terms. He simply wanted to serve.

Now it was Prime Minister Chamberlain's turn to talk terms. The Duke could return to England only if he were willing to accept one of two posts, either deputy regional commissioner in Wales or liaison officer with the British Military Mission No. 1 in France.

The King offered to send his plane for his brother, but Wallis refused to fly. They then received instructions to go to the channel coast. Wallis packed her valuables in brown paper and cardboard boxes, filling the station wagon, joined by their three cairn terriers, Preezi, Detto and Pookie. After some secret and complicated instructions, they proceeded to Cherbourg, where the destroyer HMS *Kelly* was waiting, under the command of the Duke's cousin Lord Louis Mountbatten. With him was Winston Churchill's son Randolph, representing his father, the new first lord of the Admiralty.

They left after ten, the night as dark as it had been almost three years before when he had left his throne and his country. In their small cabin there was silence. His memories were mixed, and his hopes were small. He told Wallis that he didn't know how things would work out.

Wallis had her own rush of doubt. This was not the way she had hoped to return to Britain. She had hoped to arrive with her head high. This was like sneaking back as a recalcitrant sinner. The royal family had made no preparations to receive them or house them. She was still the outcast. She had made her husband happy for a while but she knew the torment that was now in his mind, and she knew that she had caused it. How could he now not have regret? How could he now not blame her? In the dark silence of that night, she had no great expectations.

34

Fʀᴜɪᴛʏ Mᴇᴛᴄᴀʟꜰᴇ and his wife, Lady Alexandra, whom the Windsors called "Baba," journeyed to Portsmouth to greet their friends. They boarded the destroyer to discover that no orders had been issued for the Windsor reception, no accommodations made available. There was a naval guard of honor, which Churchill had arranged, and the admiral had invited them to spend the night at the Admiralty House. But there was no royal emissary to greet them, no further plans arranged. Wallis felt that the greeting of the admiral and his wife was "almost desperately polite."[1]

The Duke and Duchess went with the Metcalfes to their place in South Hartfield Manor in Sussex. The Duke's first desire was to see the King.

"Long and rather boring discussions took place in order to bring about a meeting between the King and his brother," Monckton recorded, "which I finally achieved by excluding women, as I explained to Alec Hardinge that it would save trouble if it was a stag party."[2]

The total royal rejection of Wallis made the Duke angry. Anything that hurt her enraged him. It was the one wish of his life to keep her on a pedestal, and here she was shamed and rebuffed to his face and he was helpless to counter it. If the Duke wanted to do anything in this war, he would have to go to his brother and to his government, like a small, bad boy, hat in hand. Monckton pleaded with him not to discuss Wallis with his brother, or any other controversial issues. The Duke grudgingly agreed.

Wallis had it within her to upset everything. The royal family had snubbed her and she could have made a scene, perhaps even cried a little. If she had, the aroused Duke would have disowned them all and left the country with her immediately. Wallis, however, knew how vital it was that her husband serve his country in some capacity. If not, he would be a defeated man and their future life together would be a shambles. She therefore wore the Wallis smile, laughed the Wallis laugh and kept the air bright with the Wallis wit. It made everything possible.

"I motored up with the Duke to Buckingham Palace," Monckton wrote. "Commander Campbell met him at the Royal Entrance, and took him up to his brother's room. I went into the Equerry's room, and waited for an anxious hour. Then the brothers came down together; the King came over to me and said, 'I think it went all right.' The Duke watched him with a wary eye, and asked afterwards what he said. I told him, and he said that it had been all right because, on my advice, he had kept off contentious subjects."[3]

Of the two jobs offered, the Duke had decided he preferred the job of regional commissioner of Wales, rather than the military liaison in France. Perhaps he felt he could do more good with civilian groups, perhaps he was simply anxious to live again in England, and perhaps he felt that the military job might separate him and Wallis whereas the Wales position would keep them together. The King had agreed with his choice and promised to discuss it with the government.

The government saw it in another light. The presence of the Duke in England during wartime would distract public attention from the King. The King needed no popular competition from his brother. Chief of the Imperial General Staff Field Marshal Sir Edmund Ironside informed the Duke of his assignment to the British Military Mission in France.

Wallis stayed behind in Sussex with Baba Metcalfe when the Duke made his excursions to London in preparation for his new post. Some people recognized him and greeted him, but many didn't.

Before leaving, the Duke went to see Winston Churchill to thank him for sending Mountbatten with a destroyer to ensure his return in some style.

He knew Churchill was against his visit to Hitler and against his Verdun speech, but they still had a strong bond of personal feeling for each other.

The Duke had one more pilgrimage to make. He wanted to pay a final visit to his beloved Fort Belvedere. It had to be painful no matter what he saw there. He was a gardener and he knew what an untended garden looks like. He was a romanticist, and his imagination would fill the emptiness with poignant memories.

Before returning to France the Duke wanted to tour the British army commands, and take his Duchess along. Secretary of State for War Leslie Hore-Belisha personally passed on the Duke's request to the King.

"He [the King] was in a very distressed state. He felt that if the Duchess went to the commands she might have a hostile reception, particularly in Scotland. He seemed very disturbed, and walked up and down the room."[4]

Hore-Belisha then persuaded the Duke how much more impressed the public would be if he took up his appointment in France at once.

Since the Duke was still a field marshal of the Army, and this caused some military embarrassment, he voluntarily accepted the lesser rank of major general. Military Mission headquarters was with the French General Staff at Vincennes, outside Paris. The Windsors decided not to reopen their house and Wallis stayed at a hotel in Versailles.

The Duke was now away part of the time, and Wallis felt a loneliness that she had not experienced for a long time. She felt cut adrift, away from friends, no longer part of the social mix. Beyond that, she felt frustration. Here was a people facing war and she hardly knew them and barely knew their language. She was involved neither with them nor with anyone else, not even a part of what her husband was doing. She felt useless.

Once again to the rescue came Lady Mendl, the former Elsie de Wolfe, wife of the British press attaché in Paris.

Lady Mendl had been one of Wallis' first friends in London during the Simpson days, and it was she who taught Wallis much about style and clothes. Lady Mendl, an energetic seventy, was the kind of woman who could still turn cartwheels, and did. She had started the Trianon War Charities to distribute kits of clothes and sundries to French troops, and she invited Wallis to be its honorary president. At a press conference, the Duchess explained, "We have obtained large quantities of wool and are opening workrooms in both Versailles and Paris. Some paid employees are working for the committee, but thousands of women without means come to the committee room and receive wool, which they take home and later they bring us sweaters, scarves and socks.

"Other articles are purchased, and a standard package will be sent from our committee, which is known as the Colis de Versailles Trianon. This package includes one knitted sweater with roll collar and knitted hood, two pairs of socks, two large handkerchiefs, soap, woolen gloves, toilet paper, flea-powder, aspirin, quinine, laxative, cigarettes and chocolate."

The Duke did some crochet work for the soldiers, but the Duchess passed it on as her own to save explanation. The Duchess also created a new type of trench mitten with a zipper attachment, permitting a soldier to use his trigger finger in an emergency. She also suggested that women might limit the colors of their clothes in view of wartime chemical needs.

The important thing was that she was now a tiny part of the war effort. She spent much time in the actual work of collecting and packing, and it filled her days and gave her satisfaction.

The Duke's satisfaction was much less. His job was mainly a showcase title with minimal importance. He did make some tours of the front, but it was hardly a front because it was still hardly a war.

The French had built along the German border a series of the most expensive forts in the world, interconnected by underground trains and equipped with everything from sun-ray rooms to movie theaters. Named after the French war minister at the time, it was called the Maginot Line. The forts were supposed to "halt the Hun"—if he came that way. The Maginot Line psychology of invincibility lulled the French people and the French generals. They had only to sit and wait, and destroy. Like the British, the French war command, led by General Maurice Gustave Gamelin, still planned war in terms of 1914 rather than 1940. The French, after all, had more than a hundred divisions in readiness and even Winston Churchill had said, "Thank God for the French Army."[5]

The German Army on the western front, on the other hand, was stripped. Their Siegfried Line was still incomplete. Facing France were no more than twenty-five reserve divisions, with enough ammunition for only three days' battle. The Nazi Luftwaffe had a small reserve of bombs left, half of their original supply already used over Poland. Had the French attacked in force at that time they could have reached the Rhine within a fortnight, and possibly have won the war. But Gamelin kept his huge army stretched out and sitting. It was reminiscent of a campaign plan once brought to Napoleon, showing the French Army neatly and evenly lined up from one end of the frontier to the other. Napoleon looked at it and asked curtly, "Are you trying to stop smuggling?"[6]

Years later Paul Reynaud remarked about Gamelin, "He might be all right as a prefect or a bishop, but he is not a leader of men."[7]

"Gamelin had no guts" was the way one French general put it. He maintained his headquarters in a French chateau without radio or telephone, sending messages by motorcycle. He was primarily a political general who confined himself to short memos. He was content to wait years for an allied army to arrive before taking any major offensive. His prime interest was to preserve the territorial integrity of France with the minimum loss of French lives. He relaxed with the full confidence that he was sitting behind an invulnerable Maginot Line.

Gamelin's attitude reflected the public sentiment. A former soldier who had fought well in 1914 told French senator Lémery, "This time I'm going to lie low. I'm not going to get myself killed for Poland."

In one of his frontline tours, the Duke of Windsor stopped at a Maginot fort. The officers fired four artillery shells and then joined him in a champagne lunch.

The phony war lasted almost nine months with hardly a shot fired. A British correspondent touring the so-called front noticed a young German soldier, in plain view, naked to the waist, washing himself. He asked the French sentry why he did not fire at him. The sentry seemed surprised, and answered, ". . . if we fire, they will fire back . . ."[8]

With the threat of air raids gone, Paris came alive again. Maurice Chevalier starred in *Paris Reste Paris* and the more chic refugees returned to complain about the lack of entertainment. "What a mad, twittering world they inhabit," wrote novelist Simone de Beauvoir in her diary. "What does the word 'war' really mean? A month ago, when all the papers printed it boldly across their headlines, it meant a shapeless horror, something undefined but very real. Now it lacks all substance and identity."[9]

Wallis also returned to Paris. She reopened her house on the Boulevard Suchet and joined the French Red Cross. Volunteer organizations had more women than they needed, and Fabre-Luce wrote cynically, "Twenty thousand nurses and more were demanding the wounded. Some of them gave the impression of believing that the military authority was failing in its duties by not providing them."[10] Many of Wallis' friends, "in simple black dresses," stood in the Ritz Hotel lobby collecting money in tin cans for refugee relief and soldier canteens. When collections came too slowly they adjourned to the Ritz dining room for lunch and drinks. *Le Jour* revived its World War I program of "wartime godmothers," each of whom adopted a French soldier and sent him special packages.

Wallis was assigned the job of delivering blood plasma and bandages to hospitals behind the Maginot Line, at ten-day intervals. For this she had a driver, the Countess de Ganay, known as "Pinky." It was a long ride, as they started at daybreak and returned at dark, but the actual work was not arduous.

Paris had air raid alerts but Wallis refused to go to any bomb shelters. She explained, "I suffer from claustrophobia." Then she added, "Anyway, if you are at war, you must accept your chances. Being killed by a bomb is something like being killed in an automobile accident if you are a careful driver. A sort of act of God. It is unpredictable and there isn't much you can do about it."[11]

Wallis still kept up her other job, the collection and distribution of comfort kits. She and Lady Mendl had made an appeal to the United States for wool and woolen products and the response was overwhelming. Wallis also announced that she and the Duke would convert their home at Antibes into a convalescent home for Canadian and American officers. She had lined up a doctor and six nurses, including Katherine Rogers. Herman Rogers would be in charge of transportation. That plan, however, never materialized. Something that Wallis did help to organize was a fund-raising group which converted the Bal Tabarin night club into a giant mess hall serving hot meals to needy people in the Montmartre.

That winter in France was the coldest in fifty years. The English Channel froze at Boulogne. The war had become a battle against boredom. Railway stations had special rooms called "disethylation rooms," which were simply drying-out places for drunken soldiers. More and more soldiers disappeared on weekends for "French leave."[12]

The Duke made a quick trip to London, alone, desperately trying for a more significant assignment. Britain, too, seemed paralyzed by the phony war. The children had been sent out of London and blackouts were faithfully observed but many questioned their necessity since at the moment England's only war casualties resulted from automobile accidents in the blackout. British planes flew over Germany but only to drop propaganda leaflets.

The Duke received no encouragement and returned to Paris more resentful than ever.

Among the later captured German documents was a report from the German minister to the Hague, Count Julius von Zech-Burkersroda. In it, he described the Duke of Windsor as disgruntled with his relatively minor post as liaison officer, making statements about the Allied plans for meeting a German invasion in Belgium.

The Count also claimed that "there seems to be something like the beginning of a *fronde* [an opposition group] forming around W. [the Duke], which for the moment, of course, still has nothing to say, but which at some time under favorable circumstances might acquire a certain significance."

The Duke was later accused of having "babbled carelessly or deliberately in Paris . . . and on at least one occasion he babbled on about urgent plans."

The Duke denied everything.

To brighten his mood, Wallis had a Christmas Eve party with Noel Coward playing the piano and singing "Tropical Heat Wave." The Duke did his bit by wearing his kilt and coming downstairs playing his bagpipes.

The Duke started playing more golf again. The Duchess tried to immerse herself in the details of her various jobs, convincing herself that she was busier and "more useful" than she had ever been. She had never lived through anything like this before. Her chef was called into service and so was her butler, and even her maid left to be with her family. These would have been yesterday's crises, but now they were matters of no moment. It was a time of uncertainty and Wallis thrived on it.

The French had forgotten that war is a storm. It was so easy to forget because the cold winter had turned into a splendid spring. Chestnut trees on the Champs burst into leaf, the gray buildings became opalescent in the sunlight. The Grand Palais had a crowded calendar of art shows in April and there was still racing at Auteuil. It was true that Paris patisseries were now closed three days a week and there were meatless days and sugarless days and even days without liquor. Nor were the superb chocolates always available. But the windows of Cartier and Van Cleef and Arpels sparkled with their jewels. And the people promenaded at their pleasure.

For nine months the French had sat silent and motionless behind their Maginot Line in their smug security pretending the war was a bad dream that would go away because "time is on our side." They waited, unthinking and uncaring, while the Nazi troops wiped out and absorbed Poland.

"The relatively passive attitude of the French during the winter of 1939–40," Nazi general Guderian wrote later, "incited us to conclude that the adversary had little inclination for war."

The Germans had more than inclination. They had their timetable and their detailed tactics of surprise.

Then the storm broke, and World War II really began.

The French and British had concentrated their troops on the frontiers of Belgium and Holland, expecting the Nazis to make the classic enveloping movement from the north across the Belgian plain. Instead, the German panzer troops thrust through the supposedly impenetrable and therefore undefended Ardennes forest. Nazi tanks smashed through Luxembourg and the wooded hills to seize the Meuse River crossings at the weak center of the Allied line.

While German parachute troops dropped on Holland and drew French reserves northward, the Nazis massed seven tank divisions supported by hundreds of dive bombers, plus several dozen infantry divisions, ignored the Maginot Line on the east, and swept west toward the English Channel over ideal tank country to outflank the whole Allied Army.

Within a week, the front had been broken beyond repair; within three weeks the French Army "was in rout and ruin" and the British Army hurled to the sea with a loss of all its equipment.

The French were shocked into a national paralysis.

Notified of the intended withdrawal of the French government from Paris, Winston Churchill flew to France to confer with General Gamelin.

"I then asked 'Where is the strategic reserve?'" wrote Churchill afterward, and, breaking into French, which I used indifferently (in every sense): *'Où est la masse de manoeuvre?'* General Gamelin turned to me and, with a shake of his head and a shrug, said: *'Aucune.'*[13]

"There was another long pause. Outside in the garden of the Quai d'Orsay clouds of smoke arose from large bonfires, and I saw from the window venerable officials pushing wheelbarrows of archives onto them.

"'NO STRATEGIC RESERVE,'" repeated Churchill. "I was dumbfounded. What were we to think of the great French Army and its highest chiefs? It had never occurred to me that any commanders having to defend five hundred miles of engaged front would have left themselves unprovided with a mass of manoeuvre . . . What was the Maginot Line for? It should have economized troops upon a large sector of the frontier . . . enabling large forces to be held in reserve. I admit this was one of the greatest surprises I had in my life. Why had I not known more about it?"[14]

It was an appalling failure in liaison.

Pointing to the red bulge on the war map where the Germans had broken through the Ardennes at Sedan, the new premier Paul Reynaud twice said, "I assure you that in this bulge there is at stake not only the fate of France but also that of the British Empire."[15]

Churchill asked Gamelin about a counterattack on the flanks of the bulge and, again, Gamelin shrugged his shoulders helplessly, saying, "Inferiority of numbers, inferiority of equipment, inferiority of method."[16]

The French military was bankrupt and beaten.

Paris was in a panic. The Duke's only concern was Wallis. He wanted her away, somewhere in safety. As for himself, his job was with the Military Mission in Paris, and he would have to return. But he wanted her neither exposed nor involved. The Duchess was not prone to argue. They decided on Blois, where Wallis and Brownlow had spent the night on their flight to Cannes in 1936. She would have the same chauffeur, George Ladbrooke. The Windsors left so hurriedly that they didn't even notify Fruity Metcalfe, who had joined the Duke as his equerry.

Some 12 million refugees were on the road in France. They employed almost everything that could move—buses, ice cream carts, furniture vans, baby buggies and ancient wagons. Many walked without direction like frightened cattle. André Maurois remembered the pathetic scene of a refugee mother camouflaging the top of her baby carriage by picking up four leaves and spreading them evenly along the top of it.

At Blois, the patron put up two cots in a sitting room for the Duke and Duchess. The next morning they went on to Biarritz, just over the border from Spain. The Hôtel du Palais was as packed as Blois, but again a room was found for Wallis.

When the Duke returned to Paris, Wallis found herself a most undesirable guest. The German radio not only announced her arrival in Biarritz, but even revealed the number of her hotel room.

Hardly a week passed before the Duke and Ladbrooke returned. His job was finished, and so was Paris. The Germans would soon be goosestepping down the Champs Elysées. The French Army had collapsed; the British were preparing their brilliant evacuation at Dunkirk. As Churchill would tell them, though, "Wars are not won by evacuations."

The Windsors arrived at La Croe on May 29. The news remained bad. On June 10, the French government left Paris. On that day, Italy declared war on France, and President Roosevelt said, "The hand that held the dagger has stuck it in the back of its neighbor." The catastrophe was complete. The disintegrating French Army in retreat now resembled a funeral procession. From their villa, the Duke and Duchess could hear the big guns. Italians were reported fighting on the edge of the Riviera.

It was time to run again. The British consul at Nice had papers of permission to cross the frontier into Spain, and he invited the Duke and Duchess to join him. The Duke accepted.

Again they were on the outside, going nowhere.

Wallis said good-by to her friends, to her servants, to her home. Her life had been a collection of things, of mementos, all of them evoking memories. They had packed what they could in a trailer but the rest of it would stay behind. She stared at it all, her calmness gone, her tears ready to flow. Then the gardener handed her a big bouquet of flowers. It was June 19. Her birthday.

35

Hitler, whatever his shortcomings, was a man of great imagination. Foreign Minister Ribbentrop often managed to match his master's flights of fancy. However, in 1940, the impossible looked very real. Hitler's Nazis had swept through Europe in juggernaut fashion and with unbelievable speed. Their invasion of Great Britain seemed imminent. Dunkirk had been a British miracle but it also represented a massive defeat. The ringing prose of Churchill soon promised to fight the enemy on the beaches ("and with broken bottles if we have to"), but the fact was that Britain did not seem to have the military strength to withstand the full assault of what the Nazis called "Operation Sea Lion."

Hitler and Ribbentrop really believed in the quick German conquest of England and saw a need to install their own puppet king and queen. Both seemed certain that they had their perfect candidates in the Duke and Duchess of Windsor.

Hitler had timetabled the "Sea Lion" invasion of England for the middle of September 1940 and was therefore anxious to get his royal puppets packaged as quickly as possible .

On July 11, 1940, the following conversation was recorded between German foreign minister Joachim von Ribbentrop and Gestapo counterespionage chief Walter Schellenberg.

My dear Schellenberg, you have a completely wrong view of these things—also of the real reasons behind the Duke's abdication. The Führer and I already recognized the facts in 1936. The crux of the matter is that, since his abdication, the Duke has been under strict surveillance by the British Secret Service. We know what his feelings are: it's almost as if he were their prisoner. Every attempt that he's made to free himself, however discreet he may have been, has failed. And we know from our reports that he still entertains the same sympathetic feelings toward Germany, and that given the right circumstances he wouldn't be averse to escaping from his present environment—the whole thing's getting on his nerves.

We've had word that he has even spoken about living in Spain and that if he did go there he'd be ready to be friends with Germany again as he was before. The Führer thinks this attitude is extremely important, and we thought that you with your Western outlook might be the most suitable person to make some sort of exploratory contact with the Duke—as the representative, of course, of the Head of the German State. The Führer feels that if the atmosphere seems propitious you might perhaps make the Duke some material offer. Now we should be prepared to deposit in Switzerland for his own use a sum of fifty million Swiss francs—if he were ready to make some official gesture dissociating himself from the maneuvers of the British Royal Family. The Führer would, of course, prefer him to live in Switzerland, though any other neutral country would do so long as it's not outside the economic or the political or the military influence of the German Reich.

If the British Secret Service should try to frustrate the Duke in some such arrangement, then the Führer orders that you are to circumvent the British plans, even at the risk of your life, and, if need be, by the use of force.

Whatever happens, the Duke of Windsor must be brought safely to the country of his choice. Hitler attaches the greatest importance to this operation, and he has come to the conclusion after serious consideration that if the Duke should prove hesitant, he himself would have no objection to your helping the Duke to reach the right decision by coercion—even by threats or force if the circumstances make it advisable. But it will also be your responsibility to make sure at the same time that the Duke and his wife are not exposed to any personal danger.

Now, in the near future the Duke expects to have an invitation to hunt with some Spanish friends. This hunt should offer an excellent opportunity for you to establish contact with him. From that point he can immediately be brought into another country. All the necessary means for you to carry out this assignment will be at your disposal. Last night I discussed the whole matter again thoroughly with the Führer and we have agreed to give you a completely free hand. But he demands that you let him see daily reports on the progress of the affair.[1]

Schellenberg asked for fuller details about his possible use of force. "Well," answered Ribbentrop, "the Führer feels that force should be used primarily against the British Secret Service—against the Duke only insofar as his hesitation might be based on a fear psychosis which forceful action on our part would help him overcome."[2]

Ribbentrop also explained that the "fifty million Swiss francs by no means represents the absolute maximum. The Führer is quite ready to go to a higher figure."[3]

Ribbentrop then placed a phone call to Hitler and gave Schellenberg a second receiver to listen in.

Hitler listened to Ribbentrop's report then replied curtly, "Yes—certainly—agreed." Finally he said, "Schellenberg should particularly bear in mind the importance of the Duchess' attitude and try as hard as possible to get her support. She has great influence over the Duke."[4]

The Duke and Duchess had had a wearing trip to Spain. The French put up barricades at key roads to check credentials. France had fallen and this was simply another meaningless bit of bureaucracy. The Duke circumvented them by announcing in French that he was the Prince of Wales, and would they please let him pass. They did. At the border, though, they were refused admittance because the Spanish consul was afraid they might become charges of the Spanish government. After refusing them, the consul then asked the Duke for his autograph. Fortunately the Duke's memory did not fail him. He knew the Spanish ambassador to France, and a telephone call later they were in.

Wallis discovered for the first time how helpless her husband was without his valet—who had left for England from Cannes. She found his clothes in complete confusion, and he was embarrassed when she tried to start sorting them out, indignantly refusing her help.

The British ambassador to Spain was Sir Samuel Hoare, whom the Duke still regarded as a friend, although he had been of little help during the abdication. Hoare settled them at the Ritz Hotel in Madrid, gave them a big Embassy party and told them what was happening.

The Duke made no secret about his feelings regarding the war. He told American ambassador Alexander Weddel that the important thing was to end it "before thousands more were killed or maimed to save the faces of a few politicians."

"In the past ten years Germany had totally reorganized the order of its society in preparation for this war," the Duke told Weddel. "Countries that were unwilling to accept such a reorganization of society and its concomitant sacrifices should direct their policies accordingly and thereby avoid dangerous adventures. He stated this applied not merely to Europe but to the United States also," Weddel reported.[5]

Winston Churchill knew exactly how the Duke of Windsor felt about the war. He knew that the Duke believed that Britain's natural ally was Germany and not France. He knew the Duke's sympathies for the German people and the German nation. He had been thoroughly briefed on every detail of the Windsors' trip through Nazi Germany as well as the personal impact Hitler had on them. Churchill knew, too, how shabbily the Duke had been treated by the British establishment, and how angry he was about it. As much imagination as Hitler had, Churchill had more. He fully saw the dangers of the upcoming scene. Franco's Spain was more than friendly with Nazi Germany. In Spain the Duke was highly vulnerable for a quick kidnap by the Nazis. The Duke was a highly emotional man, and his Franco friends, acting as Nazi agents, might be enormously persuasive. It was difficult to predict how they might tempt him or what he might do. In Hitler's hands, the Duke of Windsor could be a propaganda tool of tremendous leverage.

As the new prime minister of Great Britain, Churchill felt the situation was of paramount importance. He wanted the Windsors back in England, and fast. He notified Ambassador Hoare to tell the Duke that he was sending two flying boats to Lisbon to take them back to Britain. Churchill also added that he had arranged for them to have the home of the Duke of Westminster.

Wallis was ready. As much as she hated flying, she was willing now. She was tired of fleeing from one place to another, packing and unpacking, everything scrambled and uncertain. She wanted to settle somewhere, with some finality. She knew how desperately the Duke wanted to return to England, knew that he would never be truly happy unless they did, and so they might as well start now. Once they were there, things might resolve into some kind of normalcy, some kind of acceptance. With Churchill as prime minister, they had their best chance for a renewed entry into British life. He would surely give the Duke some important war work. With that settled, the problem of her proper title would come more easily. And perhaps as the King became more popular and no longer feared the Duke's rivalry, even the royal family might soften and accept.

The Duke, though, was in a different mood. Before he agreed to return, he wanted to know two specific things: what kind of job would they give him, and how would they treat his wife?

Hearing of the proposed departure plans, the German ambassador to Spain, Eberhard von Stohrer, sent a "Strictly Confidential" cable to the Nazi Foreign Ministry saying that the Spanish foreign minister "requests advice with regard to the treatment of the Duke and Duchess of Windsor." The Spanish foreign minister had received "certain impressions . . . that we might perhaps be interested in detaining the Duke of Windsor here and possibly in establishing contact with him."[6]

The prompt reply queried, "Is it possible in the first place to detain the Duke and Duchess of Windsor for a couple of weeks in Spain before they are granted an exit visa? It would be necessary in all events to be sure that it did not appear in any way that the suggestion came from Germany."[7]

Spain in June was expectedly hot, but the Duke was too restless for siestas. Wallis found herself on an energetic sightseeing tour and social whirl that seldom seemed to stop. While they were waiting for exit visas and cables from Churchill, they saw many of their Spanish friends, most of whom were now high officials in the Franco government. They dined one night with a Spanish Air Force general and the Infante Alfonso, the Duke's cousin, both of whom spent the evening emphasizing the invincibility of the Germans, citing statistics on tanks and planes, and one night the Duke of Alba's sister Doña Sol greeted them with the fascist salute.[8]

The Nazis even had inveigled the Spanish government into offering the Windsors free use of the Palace of the Caliph at Ronda in Spain for an indefinite period.

By this time the cables between the Duke and London were taking on a more querulous tone. Churchill had a war to win and here was the Duke of Windsor worrying about the social reception of his wife.

Wallis could change her husband's mind and opinions about many things, but she could do nothing with him on the specific issue of herself. On this, he was adamant. He wanted his wife to have social equality with the wives of his brothers. And perhaps Wallis did not fight him too hard on this issue, because she herself felt she deserved that recognition.

"Windsor told the Foreign Minister that he would return to England only if his wife were recognized as a member of the royal family and if he were appointed to a military or civilian position of influence," another report to the German Foreign Ministry noted.[9]

The report added that there seemed no likelihood that the British would agree to the Windsor conditions. In this, they were correct. It further added that the Duke had strongly expressed his feelings against the war with Germany to the Spanish foreign minister. There is little reason to disbelieve this, either. The Duke had few inhibitions in saying what he felt, and he felt this deeply.

Did this make him disloyal? However much he liked the Germans and Germany, he was still British. He was impetuous, he was sometimes silly and often wrong, but he had been born and bred in English history and English traditions, and it was part of his spirit and his being.

Furthermore, he was a military man, and an order was an order. On July 4, 1940, Churchill cabled his appointment as governor and commander in chief of the Bahamas, and added, "Personally I feel sure it is the best open in the grievous situation in which we all stand. At any rate, I have done my best."[10]

The cable cut short the Duke's plan to fly directly to London to fight personally for his own cause. The Duke now answered that he accepted the appointment "as I am sure you have done your best for me in a difficult situation. I am sending Major Phillips to England tomorrow and will appreciate your receiving him personally to explain some details."[11]

A "most secret" cable also went from Churchill to Roosevelt noting the difficulties that the Duke of Windsor's recent activities on the Continent had been causing His Majesty and His Majesty's government. "Though his loyalties are unimpeachable there is always a backwash of Nazi intrigue which seeks to make trouble about him."[12] The cable then mentioned the appointment, which the government felt "might appeal to him and his wife." Before the cable was sent, the phrase "and his wife" was cut out.

The Duke and Duchess, meanwhile, had gone to Lisbon to await further arrangements.

The Duke, of course, knew the British ambassador to Portugal, Sir Walford Selby. Sir Walford had arranged for them to stay with a Portuguese banker, Dr. Ricardo de Espirito Santo e Silva, at his pink stucco home on the sea, outside Estoril at Cascais. The flying boats were ready, Sir Walford said. They could leave in the morning. The Duke again made it plain that, war or no war, he was not leaving unless his terms regarding Wallis' status were met.

The heated interchange of coded cables meant a nightly session for the Duchess helping the Duke phrase his replies. Since the Duke was committed and determined, and since she secretly agreed with him, she gave him the benefit of her suggestions. She later admitted, however, that his timing was wrong: his point of pride was a picayune thing at a time when his country was fighting for its life.

Churchill in particular saw it as an incredible pettiness. The controversy not only cooled him toward his former king, it practically destroyed their friendship. Never again would they feel the same warmth toward each other.

On July 9, the Spanish foreign minister told the German envoy "that the Duke of Windsor had asked that a confidential agent be sent to Lisbon to whom he might give a communication for the Foreign Minister."[13] On that same day, the British made public the Duke's appointment to the Bahamas.

The Duke and Duchess made little attempt to disguise their displeasure. "It's not an appointment," said the Duchess, "it's a disappointment." She further quipped to a friend, "St. Helena—1940 model." And when correspondent Walter Kerr congratulated the Duke, saying how important the islands of the Bahamas really were, the Duke stared at him and said, "Name one."

The open Windsor dissatisfaction spurred the Nazi intrigue.

From his minister in Lisbon, Ribbentrop received another report: "As Spaniards from among those around the Duke of Windsor have informed us confidentially on visits to the Legation the designation of the Duke as Governor of the Bahama Islands is intended to keep him far away from England, since his return would bring with it very strong encouragement to English friends of peace."

The report speculated on the possibility of the Duke's arrest on his return to England—an idea as unlikely as it was imaginative. It added, however, that the Duke planned to postpone his departure for the Bahamas as long as possible. This was true. The Duke still wanted royal agreement on his wife's status. "He is convinced that if he had remained on the throne war would have been avoided, and he characterizes himself as a firm supporter of a peaceful arrangement with Germany. The Duke definitely believes that continued severe bombing would make England ready for peace."[14]

The last statement is most difficult to believe. In fact, given his personality, it is impossible to conceive.

But he was angry with the British establishment. Ribbentrop knew it. He cabled the German Embassy in Spain of the need to bring the Duke back to Spain out of the hands of the English agents "who will try to get him away from Lisbon as soon as possible, if necessary by force."

"In our opinion, haste is accordingly required," wrote Ribbentrop. "From here it would seem best if close Spanish friends of the Duke would privately invite him, and of course his wife, for a short one- or two-week visit to Spain on pretexts which would seem plausible both to him, to the Portuguese, and to the English agents. That would mean, therefore, that the Duke and Duchess, as well as the English and the Portuguese, must believe that Windsor in any event is going to come back there. . . . After their return to Spain, the Duke and his wife must be persuaded or compelled to remain on Spanish territory. For the event of the latter alternative we must reach an agreement with the Spanish Government to the effect that by reasons of the obligations of neutrality the Duke will be interned, since the Duke as an English officer and a member of the English Expeditionary Force must be treated as a military fugitive who has crossed the frontier. . . . At any rate, at a suitable occasion in Spain the Duke must be informed that Germany wants peace with the English people, that the Churchill clique stands in the way of it, and that it would be a good thing to hold himself in readiness for further developments. Germany is determined to force England to peace by every means of power and upon this happening would be prepared to accommodate any desire expressed by the Duke, especially with a view to the assumption of the English throne by the Duke and Duchess . . ."[15]

It was at this point in time that Ribbentrop contacted counter-espionage chief Schellenberg. Schellenberg soon met with German ambassador Stohrer in Madrid. Stohrer reported that he had talked with Spanish interior minister Ramón Serrano Suñer, a brother-in-law of Generalissimo Franco, and asked "his and Franco's personal support" for the Windsor project. They arranged to send the Marqués de Estella, Miguel Primo de Rivera, "a friend of the Duke for a long time," as the agent the Duke requested in Portugal.[16] Rivera would invite the Duke and Duchess to the hunting trip in Spain. He left for Lisbon "following a meeting with Franco."[17]

In the meantime Schellenberg hurried to Lisbon to make his own plans. He recruited a Japanese friend to get precise information about the Windsor residence—how many entrances, what floors were occupied, what kind of security, all about the servants.

"Within two days, I had drawn a close net of informants round the Duke's residence," said Schellenberg. "I had even managed to replace the Portuguese police guard with my own people. I was also able to place informants among the servants, so that within five days I knew of every incident that took place in the house and every word spoken at the dinner table."[18]

Portuguese parties provided a third valuable source of remarks by the Duke and Duchess.

Spurring the Schellenberg effort was Britain's worsening position. England was all alone in the summer months of 1940. Spain was expected to demand Gibraltar or else invite the Germans to help her attack it. Pétain's Vichy France was being pressured to declare war on England. The Germans had taken over what was left of the French fleet. Nazi invasion seemed imminent. In all of England there were barely 500 field guns and scarcely 200 medium or heavy tanks. The Home Armies were practically unarmed except for rifles.

With all this pressing on him, Prime Minister Churchill had to cope with cabled queries from the Duke of Windsor insisting that his former servant Fletcher should be released from the Army to accompany him to the Bahamas. Churchill cabled, "I regret that there can be no question of releasing men from the Army to act as servants to Your Royal Highness. Such a step would be viewed with general disapprobation in times like these, and I should ill serve Your Royal Highness in countenancing it."[19]

British Secret Service had intercepted Nazi reports and cables and Churchill was now aware of the Nazi interest in persuading or kidnaping the Windsors. There were now two cats in the cat-and-mouse game, British agents and Nazi agents desperately trying to keep close tabs on each other. The Nazis never had changed their original plan involving a hunting lodge invitation to lure the Windsors but they had to alter details and refinements to keep the British agents off the track.

Wallis and the Duke spent much of their time discussing the

Bahamas. The Duke saw the appointment in terms of exile, an insignificant post far away from the war, in the middle of nowhere. Wallis had read all of Churchill's cables and sensed that Churchill had reached the breaking point. There would be nothing more they could expect from him at this time. Being more practical than her husband, she began adjusting to the idea of the islands. The post did have advantages—the climate, the closeness to the United States, the chance to do something interesting. It was not worthy of her husband, but it was better than a do-nothing job as a liaison officer in a military mission. She tried to mollify the Duke with her reflections, and partly succeeded, but he was not yet willing to surrender.

Rivera arrived and he and the Duke had some long talks, all of which were faithfully passed on to the Germans.

"His designation as Governor of the Bahamas was made known in a very cool and categorical letter from Churchill with the instruction that he should leave for his post immediately without fail. Churchill has threatened W. with arraignment before a court martial in case he did not accept the post (this appears to have been communicated orally only to the Duke)."[20]

Rivera next reported that the Duke had received a postponement since he was awaiting some of his effects and objects from his house in Paris. Although he had given up all his military offices "the Duke sees in the appointment recognition of the equal status of his wife."[21]

Rivera soon had further reports for transmission to Ribbentrop:

> The Duke expressed himself very freely. In Portugal he felt almost like a prisoner. He was surrounded by agents etc. Politically he was more and more distant from the King and the present English Government. The Duke and Duchess have less fear of the King, who was quite foolish [reichlicht töricht], than of the shrewd Queen who was intriguing skillfully against the Duke and particularly against the Duchess . . .
>
> The Duke was considering making a public statement and thereby disavowing present English policy and breaking with his brother . . .
>
> The Duke and Duchess were extremely interested in the secret communication which the Minister of Interior promised to make to the Duke . . . The Duke and Duchess said they very much desired to return to Spain and expressed thanks for the offer of hospitality. The Duke's fear that in Spain he would be treated as a prisoner was

dispelled by the confidential emissary, who in response to an inquiry declared that the Spanish Government would certainly agree to permit the Duke and Duchess to take up their residence in southern Spain (which the Duke seemed to prefer), perhaps in Granada or Malaga, etc.[22]

When he [Rivera] gave the Duke advice not to go to the Bahamas, but to return to Spain, since the Duke was likely yet to be called upon to play an important role in English policy and possibly to ascend the English throne, both the Duke and Duchess gave evidence of astonishment. Both appeared to be completely enmeshed in conventional ways of thinking, for they replied that according to the English constitution this would not be possible after the abdication.

When the confidential emissary then expressed his expectation that the course of the war might bring about changes even in the English constitution, the Duchess especially became very pensive.[23]

This was understandable. The idea was not outside the realm of her imagination. It was not inconceivable. She and the Duke often had discussed the power they saw in Germany. The swiftness of the Nazi sweep over France had shocked but not surprised them. They knew Britain's unpreparedness. The English Channel seemed to grow smaller every day. The Nazis had done everything they said they would do. It could happen. It almost seemed probable. Was it possible that she still might be the queen of England? Could she accept it under such circumstances?

Hitler was becoming impatient. "The Führer orders that an abduction is to be organized at once," Ribbentrop cabled Schellenberg.[24] Using a second confidential emissary, this time a woman, Schellenberg outlined his plan for the Duke and Duchess: they would set out officially for a summer vacation in the mountains at a place (providing opportunity for hunting) near the Spanish frontier. Schellenberg would send forces to guarantee safety on the Portuguese side, while Rivera would wait on the Spanish side with similar forces. Since the Duke and Duchess had surrendered their passports at the British legation, the Portuguese frontier official would have to be "won over." In event of an unexpected action by British secret agents, "preparations are being made whereby the Duke and Duchess can reach Spain by plane."[25]

How carefully the Duke and Duchess considered the German proposals is difficult to say. The Duke later admitted having discussions with Nazi emissaries, and added, "At no time did I ever entertain any thought of complying with such suggestions, which I treated with the contempt they deserved."[26] The British Foreign Office added further, "His Royal Highness never wavered in his loyalty to the British cause."[27]

The German offers certainly must have heightened the Duke's sense of his own importance and independence, if nothing else. He had arranged his own transportation on an American ship which stopped at New York. This was something Wallis obviously wanted. Before settling in Nassau she longed for a return to the familiar peace and memories and friends in the United States.

This caused a considerable flap in the British Foreign Office and a flurry of messages between the Prime Minister and the British ambassador to the United States, Lord Lothian.

Lothian cabled, "The more I think of it the more I am convinced that it is very undesirable that His Royal Highness should come to the United States at all en route to the Bahamas . . . If he visits New York there will inevitably be a great deal of publicity much of which will be of an icy character and which will have a most unfortunate effect at the present juncture."[28]

Lothian forwarded some negative American press comments on the Windsor appointment, including a Cleveland *Press* editorial, which described the Duke as "the manager of a high class winter resort" and hoped he would not do any intriguing under the Nazis.[29]

The Duke rebelled angrily at the British government's refusal of his transportation plans and cabled Churchill, "Have been messed about quite long enough and detect in Colonial Office attitude very same hands at work as in my last job. Strongly urge you to support arrangements I have made as otherwise will have to reconsider my position."[30]

Schellenberg, meanwhile, tried to exert his final influence on the Windsors. Knowing the Duke's strong aversion to his secret guards, "I therefore arranged for a high Portuguese police official to tell the Duke that the Portuguese guard would have to be strengthened because they had information that the Duke was being watched . . . That same night I staged an incident in the garden of the Duke's villa; stones were thrown at the windows, and as a result an intensive search of the whole house was made by the Portuguese guard which

388

caused a considerable disturbance. I then started rumors among the servants at the villa that the British Secret Service had been behind the incident. They had orders to make the Duke's stay as uncomfortable as possible and thus make him readier to leave. . . ."[31]

Schellenberg also had a note delivered with a bouquet of flowers to the Duchess, warning her: "Beware of the machinations of the British Secret Service—a Portuguese friend who has your interests at heart."[32]

In addition, he informed the police and the Duke—through mutual friends—that the British secret police had planted a bomb on the Duke's ship, planning to explode it before his arrival and blame it on the Germans, in an effort to speed his departure. Through Rivera, Schellenberg again pressed the accusation that the British secret agents planned to kill the Duke in the Bahamas, or en route, because the government feared his return at the head of a new peace movement. Rivera dramatically urged him again not to endanger his life but to stay in Spain.

"It sounds fantastic," Monckton later said of the plot, "but he managed to impress the Duke and Duchess. They considered him their friend, they knew his status in the Franco Government, his access to all kinds of sources."[33]

Schellenberg had another of his own "dirty tricks" ready. His plan was to have shots fired at the Duchess' bedroom window but he finally decided against it "since the psychological effect would only have been to increase her desire to depart."[34] What he did do was to send her another anonymous note of warning that their lives were in danger from the British.

Churchill was worried. British secret agents were piecing together more fragments of the Nazi kidnaping plan. Earlier, he had cabled the Duke, "His Majesty's Government cannot agree to Your Royal Highness landing in the United States at this juncture. The decision must be accepted. It should be possible to arrange if necessary for the Duchess either to proceed from Bermuda to New York for medical reasons, or alternatively it will always be easy for her to go there from Nassau by sea or land."[35]

As a sop, Churchill added that he had succeeded in overcoming the War Office objection to the departure of Fletcher, "who will be sent forthwith to join you."[36] Similar arrangements were made to send Wallis' maid from London to Lisbon.

The official British excuse was that since the Duke was also now commander in chief of the Bahamas, his presence on an American ship might violate the American Neutrality Act. The compromise was that the Windsors would sail the American ship to Bermuda, disembark and then take a Canadian ship to Nassau. Special payment was made to the ship company to make the detour.

The Duke agreed to the new arrangements but added testily, "Regarding not landing in the United States at this juncture, I take it to mean that this only applies until after the events of November. May I therefore have confirmation that it is not to be policy of His Majesty's Government that I should not set foot on American soil during my term of office in the Bahamas? Otherwise I could not feel justified in representing The King in a British colony so geographically close to the United States if I was to be prevented from ever going to that country."[37]

Churchill agreed that the Duke could visit the United States in the future.

To expedite matters, Churchill sent his own emissary to the Duke and Duchess, their friend and adviser Walter Turner Monckton. His mission was to persuade them to leave for the Bahamas at once. Monckton currently was the director general of the British Ministry of Information. His arrival greatly relieved the Duke and Duchess. They finally had a friend they could trust without any reservations. They confided everything that Rivera had said about the possible kidnaping and murder.

Monckton asked to see Rivera, then confronted him with a demand for documentary evidence. If Rivera could produce such evidence, Monckton agreed not to let the Duke proceed to the Bahamas. Rivera said he could not produce it then, that he would need at least ten days. Monckton refused to postpone the Windsors' departure that long. Meanwhile, at the Duke's request, Monckton had cabled London to send a Scotland Yard detective to accompany the Duke on his voyage. Rivera suggested that this was not enough: what if the British secret police were awaiting the Duke in the Bahamas and planned to kill him there, blaming it on the Germans? After consultation, the Duke and Duchess insisted that Monckton have Scotland Yard send a second detective to meet them upon their arrival in the islands. Monckton agreed and in addition promised the Duke he would wait in Portugal after their departure while Rivera tried to document the plot. If real evidence emerged he would have the ship stopped at Bermuda.

Finally Monckton told the Duke and the Duchess that Churchill had found enough information to convince him that there was, indeed, a kidnaping plot, but that it was of German origin.

This was too much for Wallis: the spies and counterspies, the threats, the fear. She trusted Rivera, but she believed Monckton more. She was ready to go.

So was the Duke. Monckton had presented his message well. Britain was fighting for its life and the Duke had to do his duty.

"Duty" was an important word to the Duke. It had been the motivating word in his royal world. Except for the tortuous decision of his abdication, duty had ruled his life. His stubborn insistence on persnickety points may have seemed ridiculous to the Prime Minister— and during Britain's battle for survival, they were ridiculous—but to the Duke they were points of pride. They made him more important to himself, and he may have felt they made him seem more of a man to his wife. His concern, always, was Wallis. Her opinion, her reaction, her wishes. If he listened to the Nazi agents for any reason, it was probably because it fed his ego and, again, made the Duchess realize once more the international importance of her husband.

This reflected a weakness in him, perhaps even an emotional instability. It is difficult, however, to conceive his participation in all this intrigue as something inherently evil. Evil requires a more complex man. The Duke was basically simple, warm, direct.

According to Rivera though, "the Duke had hesitated even up to the last moment. The ship had to delay its departure on that account. The influence of the legal adviser of the Duke, Sir Walter Turner Monckton, was again successful, however, in bringing him around to leave."[38]

Schellenberg's final act was an attempt to sabotage their luggage car to delay its arrival before sailing. Like the entire intricate intrigue, the maneuver was not quite effective.

Rivera reported that the Duke had told him that no prospect of peace existed at the moment, but that the situation in England at that moment was still by no means hopeless. "Therefore he [the Duke] should not now, by negotiations, carried on contrary to the orders of his Government, let loose against himself the propaganda of his English opponents, which might deprive him of all prestige at the period when he might possibly take action. He could, if the occasion arose, take action even from the Bahamas."[39]

The German minister in Lisbon, Baron Oswald von Hoyningen-

Huene, filed his own report to the Foreign Office. It was the Duke's reply to a Ribbentrop message that once Germany forces Britain to make peace, Germany "would be willing to cooperate most closely with the Duke and to clear the way for any desire expressed by the Duke and Duchess." The Duke's answer according to Hoyningen-Huene was a tribute to the Führer's desire for peace, "which was in complete agreement with his own point of view. He was firmly convinced that if he had been made King it would never have come to war . . . He was also convinced that the present moment was too early for him to come forward, since there was as yet no inclination in England for an approach to Germany. However, as soon as this frame of mind changed, he would be ready to return immediately. Either England would yet call upon him, which he considered to be entirely possible, or Germany would express the desire to negotiate with him.

"In both cases he was prepared for any personal sacrifice and would make himself available without the slightest personal ambition. He would remain in continuing communication with his previous host and had agreed with him upon a code word, upon receiving which he would immediately come back over."[40]

One must automatically assume that the Nazis exaggerated their reports, that a great deal of what they said was simply self-serving. But even if one believes only part of all this, then the Duke could no longer be considered a political innocent, but still could be classified as a political amateur. The Duchess, though, was probably still both. This maneuvering was beyond her education, her experience or her background. Her instinctive trust was in Monckton, and so was the Duke's, determining their final move. Had he not come, the result would have been more questionable. Again, at the root of it, was the former king's pride and his love for his wife.

Just before they sailed on an American ship, the *Excalibur*, the Duchess' maid, Mrs. E. V. Fyrth, arrived from London to accompany them. The Duchess was pleased with their set of six cabins and their veranda, an outer deck space set apart from the rest of the ship.

The Duke felt defeated. The Battle of Britain had begun. While he and the Duchess sat in their deck chairs on the ship's veranda, Hitler had issued Directive Number 17 authorizing an intensified air war against England. For this, the Nazi Luftwaffe had 1,015 bombers, 346 dive bombers, 933 fighters and 375 heavy fighters. The air bombardment would precede Operation Sea Lion. Out of a total of a thousand British pilots, almost one-fourth would be killed or wounded in a single fortnight. London would be blitzed and blitzed and blitzed again, a city in flames.

During this time of home front courage and chaos, the Duke would be moving into the life of ease of an Empire salesman. He felt shunted aside.

The Duchess felt otherwise. Great Britain was not her country. It had treated her badly and her husband worse. She liked the British people but she didn't love them. She was sorry about their plight and about their war, but it wasn't her war. The United States was still neutral. She had helped the war effort in France, but then the French had been kind to her. If she grieved at all, it was only in sympathy with her husband. Now she could only think of tomorrow.

PART IV

36

It was Love, Love alone
Cause King Edward to leave the throne.
It was Love, Love alone
Cause King Edward to leave the throne.

We know that Edward was good and great
But it was Love that cause him to abdicate.

Take my crown and take my throne
Just leave me and Mrs. Simpson alone.

Let the organ play, let the church bell ring;
Mrs. Simpson took our bachelor king.

Being a victim of circumstance
They now live in the south of France.
              —Bahamian folk song
                 by Blake Higgs

THE *Excalibur* had smooth sailing under clear skies, just what the Windsors needed to try to forget the frenetic past few weeks. The Bahamas began to look better long before they got there. They soaked up the sun, strolled the deck and tried to imagine their future.

The official announcement from Downing Street read: "The King has been pleased to appoint his Royal Highness the Duke of Windsor, K.G., K.T., K.P., G.C.B., G.C.S.I., G.C.M.G., G.C.I.E., G.C.V.O., G.B.E., I.S.O., M.C., to be Governor and Commander in Chief of the Bahama Islands."[1]

397

His "subkingdom" was actually composed of 29 islands, 661 cays, 2,387 coral reefs and sandspits and approximately 80,000 people. It was a far cry from being king and emperor of almost a quarter of the world's population on almost a fourth of the planet.

The Windsors disembarked at Bermuda, along with their three cairn terriers, three truckloads of baggage, a sewing machine, a trailer, two golf bags with clubs, two cases of champagne, two cases of gin and two cases of port, a total of fifty-seven pieces as well as their staff and servants.[2]

Bermuda was more of a spree than an interval. They even did some shopping (golf balls, polo coat and fabric shoes—size 6—for him; bathing suits—size 10—and sweaters for her). At one shop Wallis admired a set of expensive china painted with Bermuda fish, but told the shopkeeper, "I have to ask my husband's permission first."[3]

They did not go to Church of England services that Sunday. The presiding bishop was the man who had gone to a newspaper office to tear their picture from the wall. The caption under it had read, "They are happy now," and the bishop said, "It is disgraceful that they should be in such a public place."[4]

During their short stay the Windsors gave their first joint press conference. The Duke did not want to give his opinion on the war, because "the moment is not propitious," but Wallis was willing to speak personally: "When you live in this war, you get used to anything. You never know anything, and it's not knowing that's the worst. When you're told to move, you move and move very quickly."[5]

They were both looking forward to visiting the United States very soon, they said: the Duke's last visit there had been sixteen years earlier, and the Duchess had not been there for eight years. "I have a family to see," she added.[6]

Neither had ever visited the Bahamas before, but the Duke remembered, "When I was King . . ." that the Governor had sent him a Christmas card of his new swimming pool in which he had printed on the tiles "E.R. VIII." "It's rather funny that I am going to use that swimming pool now," said the Duke, without smiling.[7]

The practical Wallis had a parting statement to the press. "We hope a great many Americans will come to the Bahamas."[8] She was already working.

Bahamians were busy planning a "rejoicing day" for the Windsor arrival; parades with floats and costumes of elephant, cat, peacock, mermaid and voodoo together with rumba, tap and jitterbug dancing. Local citizens were particularly excited about seeing "Mrs. Simpson," because "She made him happy."[9]

After a zigzagging trip from Bermuda, escorted by a British cruiser to protect them from any lurking German ships, they docked at Prince George Wharf. Waiting for them was the Guard of Honor, the Bahamian Executive Council, streets bedecked with flags and flowers, and crowds of the curious, some of whom even perched in the casuarina trees in Rawson Square. One of the homemade signs read: COLUMBUS 1492; WINDSORS, 1940.[10]

The Duke wore the khaki uniform and insignia of a British major general, and Wallis carried a bouquet of miniature pink hibiscus presented by the young daughter of a Nassau Garden Club member.

The temperature was over 95 degrees and the Duke's shirt was soon wet with sweat as the two walked across the square to the Legislative Council Chamber for the oath of office. It took all his breeding to maintain his composure in that heat. His mood was more of resignation than exhilaration.

For Wallis, despite everything, it was a dramatic day. A governor's lady wasn't a queen and these islands weren't an empire, but the girl from Baltimore now was the most important woman in this realm. Her status was proclaimed that first day when she received an honor never before accorded the wife of a Bahamian governor. Until then, governors' wives had sat alongside other colony officials. At this inauguration, a special platform had been built halfway between the general floor and the governor's throne. Her dais was covered with a heavy red cloth and had a heavy chair upholstered in red leather.

The Duke's dais, a step higher, was under a canopy bearing a golden crown. Hatless and nervous, the Duke fidgeted with a handkerchief he kept in his left sleeve. The traditionally bewigged and berobed chief justice administered the oath of office and the Duke promised to "well and truly serve His Majesty King George." As he formalized his acceptance by signing the document, he was perspiring so heavily that Wallis saw the dripping sweat blob his signature into something unrecognizable.

In his speech, the Duke made pointed reference to his wife. "How delighted I am that the Duchess is with me to share the pleasure of my first visit to these islands."[11]

The upper social circle in the Bahamas was white and tight. Specific instructions had come from the British government that Wallis was not to be called "Your Royal Highness" but "Your Grace," and that she did not merit the curtsy. At the formal reception following the swearing-in, only one woman curtsied. Another seemed about to do so, but changed her mind.

At the end of the ceremony, when they played "God Save the King," the Duke saluted. Some of those who saw the Duchess' face at that moment said it was very sad.

One of the black leaders at the reception was Etienne Dupuch, editor and publisher of the Nassau *Daily Tribune*. A thin, wiry man with sparkling eyes, blunt and forceful, Dupuch later said that his people were of two minds: they felt the Duke should have stayed on as king and not married, but they were delighted to have them in the Bahamas because it meant more tourists and more dollars.

When Dupuch heard the Duchess complain of the sweltering heat and the mosquitoes, he told her that it was much hotter in many parts of the United States that day than it was in the Bahamas. As for the mosquitoes, "I told her that the mosquitoes in Virginia were far worse."[12]

After the reception the Duke and Duchess made their first official social appearance at the Emerald Beach Club. In his speech of welcome, the club's president, Sir Frederick Williams-Taylor, omitted any reference to the Duchess. Icily containing his anger, the Duke rose and responded by saying that the president had submitted his speech to him earlier, and it contained a reference to the Duchess then and he wondered whether Sir Frederick had overlooked it because the light was so dim.

It was an oversight that he, the Duke, could not overlook. The Duke then gave his own speech, making a most gracious reference to Sir Frederick's wife, "Lady Jane," the recognized social leader of the colony.

To magnify the embarrassment at dinner that evening, a toast was proposed to the Duke, again not mentioning the Duchess. Wallis started to rise with the rest of the guests when the toast was made, and the Duke said, "You don't have to stand up for me, darling."

"It's a pleasure to stand up for you, darling," she answered, smiling.[13]

To make up for the gaffe, a separate toast was proposed to the Duchess. In her short response, she apologized, explaining she was not accustomed to making such speeches as she was usually toasted with her husband and he answered for them both.

After that night the Bahamian social leaders would make no further mistakes. They soon learned that the Duke frowned on his wife being called "Your Grace" and that servants and staff had been discreetly instructed to call her "Your Royal Highness." The British on the islands would not do this but compromised by referring to her as "Duchess." Even the photographers who had requested pictures of the Duke posing alone were curtly told that he preferred posing with his wife. "We are a team," he told them.[14]

Wallis herself made one final move that emphasized who was now the official mistress of the islands. She inspected the newly redecorated governor's mansion. The local elite waited expectantly for her comment and she said it was "lovely." But her tone indicated that she was not impressed.

The grounds were beautiful, a ten-acre garden in the heart of Nassau, three blocks east of Bay Street, but facing the water and surrounded by thick hedges of purple bougainvillea, with enormous rubber trees and an avenue of giant royal palms. The mansion itself had been built in 1801. There were seven bedrooms, six bathrooms and twenty-four other rooms, including the Executive Council Chambers, private secretary's office and a grand ballroom. Taken on a more complete tour later by a staff member, Wallis maintained an expressionless face throughout, saying nothing until the end and then commenting, "But how primitive!"

Actually the house had been restored several times, once after a hurricane, and again just before their arrival. The House of Assembly had appropriated $7,000 to redecorate but the bathrooms remained antique both in appearance and in performance. Closets were few and tiny. The small kitchen had a wood-burning stove. There was no laundry room—clothes were washed and beaten on the rocks beside a stream. There were also termites. The interior painting that had been done was in blue enamel "so shiny you could see all the shadows on the walls." Her own bedroom had been done in white organdy which she considered "too girlish."

The Duchess' deep displeasure with both Government House and the intense heat spurred the Duke into instant action. He cabled the Colonial Secretary proposing that he and the Duchess leave for his ranch in Canada for two months until Government House could be repaired. Lord Lloyd replied that "it would not only inevitably create a sense of disappointment but also possibly some misgiving and anxiety among the public as well" if the Windsors left so early after their arrival. He suggested they postpone their departure for several months. "There is of course no reason why, if the Duchess feels the heat, she should not go away for a few weeks."[15]

The issue was dropped. The Duke and Duchess did not plan to go anywhere unless they went together.

The Duchess quickly imported her Baltimore decorator friend, Mrs. Winthrop Bradley, and an American architect, Sidney Neil. Her first act was to take down a ten-foot-high portrait of Queen Mary from the dining hall. It was not something she wanted to look at every evening at dinner. She did, however, eventually replace it.

While the renovations were in progress the Windsors moved into one of the finest homes on the island, the Sigrist house. Owned by Mr. and Mrs. Frederick Sigrist, it was in the fashionable Prospect Hill area, on the highest point of Nassau, with a magnificent view of sea and garden. Although a Spanish colonial of white stone with an old tiled roof and large patios, its interior was typically English—English Chippendale furniture, English paintings, English antiques—and there was even an English garden cut out of the bush. The Duke felt immediately at home.

The two most important duties facing the Duke were the development of the islands' agricultural resources to make them more self-sufficient, and the need to increase tourist trade. The House of Assembly was in session from October through March, but the Governor could only veto legislation, not initiate any. He did, however, have a nine-man Executive Council, the white leaders of the island, and the Duke governed with their guidance.

The energetic Duke absorbed himself quickly with his work. He could pardon criminals but he could not follow through his natural sympathy for public welfare plans. Royal instructions strictly limited his initiative; nevertheless, he carried considerable weight among community leaders who could initiate and execute.

He began his morning dictating correspondence. His letters were no longer restricted to the heads of state on points of protocol but more likely to local experts about the serious decline of the Bahamian sponge industry or a sisal crop failure. He checked his daily appointment schedule and sent it with his secretary to the Duchess for her approval and comment. Most of his meetings were with government officials concerning budget or policy. He had reports to write to his boss, the Secretary of State for the Colonies. When he inspected the guards during ceremonials he wore his white-helmeted colonial service uniform.

To help him, he had a staff of two aides, three clerks, a private secretary, a valet, a butler, ten servants and a Scotland Yard detective who followed him wherever he went—even cycling.

The Duke's great problem, according to a prominent black Bahamian, was that he had not been trained as a colonial governor. One of his red leather dispatch boxes was imprinted with "The King." And he used his gold and red velvet field marshal baton as a map pointer. When he was king, things happened quickly on his command; as a colonial governor the gap between command and action seemed forever. Small details became large hurdles. Inaction frustrated him. At the suggestion that a new golf course be named "Windsor Downs," the Duke said, "Why not call it Windsor's Ups and Downs?"[16]

The Windsors kept their mornings private, and apart—as they always had—she in her suite, he in his. "The Duchess is the only person who can speak to me before breakfast," he once said.[17] And she seldom did.

They both rose early. The Duke needed little sleep and the Duchess never could get much. Nassau weather is best in the mornings, particularly in the summer, before the heat comes. The trade wind varying northeast to southeast gives the eastern Out Islands some of the most perfect year-round weather in the Western world. But Nassau, the capital, is on New Providence Island, an "In" island. While the weather there is ideal in winter, it is much less than that in summer, surrounded as it is by the warm shoal waters of the Great Bahama Bank.

To escape the heat the Duke bought a small motor yacht, which he promptly named *The Gemini* after Wallis' zodiac sign. Together they visited the many Out Islands hoping to produce useful programs. Somebody at Hatchet Bay had successfully raised Guernsey cows, another in Governor's Harbor had started reviving native crafts. Miss Jo Carstairs, a woman who preferred pants to dresses, successfully used fish as fertilizer and built some very good roads on Whale Cay. "Damn it," said the Duke, "why can't all the Out Islands make roads like these?"[18]

During their tour the Duke and the Duchess were intrigued to find three kinds of outhouses on Cat Island: WOMEN, MEN and GENTLEMEN.

While on the island they met the visiting doctor, whose specialty at his base hospital was plastic surgery. He introduced himself to the Duchess by saying, "I lifted Mrs. McLean's face three times."

The Duchess looked at him unsmilingly and said, "I wonder that you didn't lift the Hope Diamond." Mrs. McLean, of course, owned the famous stone.

It took time for Wallis to make her presence felt and accepted. The snide joke that still circulated Bahamian society was that the former king, once first lord of the Admiralty, was now third mate on an American tramp. They embellished all the shadows of her Baltimore background and they waited impatiently for her to make any wrong moves.

Wallis was careful to disappoint them. She redecorated Government House in the best of taste. Since most of the items she ordered came from the States, she called it "shopping by mail order." The tiling in the downstairs hall was attractive and durable. The rustic French wallpaper converted the library into a most peaceful refuge. Color schemes of rooms were interrelated to overcome what the decorators called "biteyness." A local firm dyed the dining room rug to a soft shade of green. Chairs were upholstered and recovered, to help carry out the soft tones. The Duke wanted a portrait of Wallis by Gerald Brockhurst to be the focal point in the drawing room. It has lovely flesh tones, but hardly flatters the Duchess.

Wallis' bedroom suite on the second floor had three rooms—a bedroom, a dressing room and a porch workroom—all decorated in her favorite blue. Her initials, "WW," were intertwined in raised rope carving on her blue-painted wood bureau. Her curtains were white with blue fringe. Around the room were some fifteen pictures of the Duke and a sampler sent by an old woman, embroidered with a crown and the words "The Lad That Was Born To Be King."

Across the hall was the Duke's suite, a recessed bed surrounded by a bamboo frame, all the furniture bamboo including a big desk. The comfortable curved sofas were covered in bright chintz. The windows had a circular layout and the walls were painted lime to carry out the tropical feeling, though one area had been hung with paper that had a skiing motif. There were large hanging maps of the Bahamas, and sixteen assorted photographs of the Duchess.

The kitchens and bathrooms had been modernized and Wallis had ordered two large refrigerators. A French chef was also on his way to Nassau.

"Don't you see," Wallis told Adela Rogers St. Johns, "I must make a home for him. That's why I'm doing this place over, so we can live in it with comfort as a home. All his life he has traveled and a palace to come back to is not always a home. The only one he ever had he made for himself at Fort Belvedere, he had to leave it, you don't know what that meant to him. I must make him a home . . ."

They had fun, too. Margaret Case Harriman described a stout American tourist walking along a Nassau road when she saw the Windsors' chauffeur-driven blue Buick coming down the road with the Duke and Duchess in the back seat. The noises coming from the car sounded "like cows dying," reported the American woman. "These sounds were broken by a feminine voice crying, 'No, darling! No more, no *more*!'

"The Duchess of Windsor was pleading with the Duke, who, with rolling eyes and cheeks distended, was stubbornly serenading her on a bagpipe."[19]

The woman tourist afterward remembered that she walked along the tire tracks of their car humming a tune called "Here's to Romance."

They had imprinted that kind of memory on the world.

"Together he and she are the best act in public today," a Broadway manager told Janet Flanner.

Another American visitor saw them the night after a ball at the Emerald Bay Club.

The Duke was saying how much he enjoyed dancing with his wife. "Of course when I waltz with her I have to reverse so often I don't know where I am—and in a waltz you're supposed to keep on twirling and twirling."

"But twirling makes me dizzy," said the Duchess.

"Not dizzy, darling," said the Duke, "*giddy*."

"It may make you giddy," she said, emphasizing her Southern accent, "but it makes me dizzy."

"Oh quite, quite," he said, "but either way one can twirl, can one?"

"No, darling," she interrupted, "one can't."

The visitor watched them while they laughed and laughed.

Anybody who dined with them mostly heard them call each other "Darling" and "Dear." A secretary who worked for him remembered how he would be dictating to her and suddenly hear the Duchess's car drive up. He would immediately tell his secretary that was all for the day and he would then call out, "Darling, darling, I'm here," or "Darling, darling, come in here . . ." But it would always be "Darling, darling . . ."[20]

Among their many American visitors was a radio executive with a proposal that the Duke make some international radio broadcasts. While the Duke reflected on it, the executive approached the Duchess, who was staring silently out of a window. He asked her opinion.

"The Duke can be extremely moving on the radio," she said softly.

"I heard him, Ma'am—once," he said.[21] As he later declared, his eyes were wet when he remembered.

Perhaps the greatest small problem the Duchess faced were the insects. They were everywhere and she hated them. A friend once asked her whether she had measles. "There isn't room on my ankles for even one more welt," she said. She was simply covered with bites from sand flies, which were tiny enough to move through mosquito netting. She had an even greater horror of cockroaches and lizards, which thrive in wet heat. A staff member visiting her in the morning when her face was covered with cream and her hair still in curlers heard the pain in her voice when she exclaimed, "There's an ant in my forty-dollar cold cream!"[22]

"All my life I've disliked hot weather," she told a reporter, "and coming to Nassau has been like taking a permanent slimming cure."[23]

She held up a finger and smiled. "Soon I'll be as big as this. But how I would like to draw just one cool breath."[24]

Her weight had gone down from her normal 110 to 97, and a dressmaker reported her most recent measurements were 34″ bust, 25″ waist and 34″ hips, a size 8 figure. "She could live on lettuce leaves," said a friend.

Wallis' eagerness to return to the United States was fulfilled sooner than she expected. She had an impacted wisdom tooth and she and the Duke sailed to a Miami hospital in December 1940. They were met by thousands at the pier. Despite her painfully swollen jaw, Wallis looked "fresh and lovely" and she chatted and laughed "like a trooper." It was the fourth anniversary of the former king's abdication, but none of the waiting reporters remembered it.

The operation turned out to be more serious than expected, with the worried Duke pacing the waiting room like an expectant father. Accompanying them on this strictly nonsocial visit were their three cairn terriers—Pookie, Preezi and Detto—his equerry, two servants, a Scotland Yard detective and twenty-seven pieces of luggage.

The trip served a double purpose. For many months the Duke and Wallis had agreed how logical it would be for him to serve as British ambassador to the United States. Since they were both enormously popular in America, Wallis could have been more of an asset to him there than anywhere. The timing was now unique: the British ambassador had died just the day before.

As soon as Wallis was feeling a little better, the Duke contacted President Franklin D. Roosevelt, who was fishing nearby on the cruiser *Tuscaloosa*. The President agreed to the meeting and sent a plane for him. The last time they had met was in 1919 when the Duke was Prince of Wales and Roosevelt, "my gay and witty companion," was assistant secretary of the Navy. Now the two men discussed naval bases and the war, and the Duke surely was not coy in putting forth his proposal.

Roosevelt obviously could make no commitment of support. Back in Florida the Duke also dropped a hint to the press, indicating that he would certainly accept the ambassadorship "if I thought it was in the interest of our two countries."

It was all of no avail. To begin with, the Duke's chances for the job were dim. His too-much-publicized visit to Hitler's Germany, his controversy with Churchill about the Bahamas, all combined with the real reluctance of the British government to put the Duke in any position of international prominence. More adamant than the King on this subject was his wife, Queen Elizabeth, who bore an unrelenting grudge against both the Duke and the Duchess.

When the Duke's visit with the President was revealed, Foreign Office spokesmen expressed pithy, but private, indignation. The Duke they said, was now the governor of a small British colony and had no more authority than any other petty official to speak for the British government.

The appointment of Lord Halifax as the new ambassador to the United States quickly followed.

After Wallis' recovery, the Windsors stayed on long enough for her to buy several day dresses, ranging in price from $12.50 to $25, and the Duke found time to play golf with top professionals Sammy Snead and Gene Sarazen. The Duke played consistently, but not well.

On the Windsors' departure, the University of Miami band gave them a rousing sendoff. They both needed all the cheering they could get.

The Windsors' transportation on the trip back was luxurious. They had the 338-foot yacht *Southern Cross* of their new friend, Axel L. Wenner-Gren. Wenner-Gren's wife was from Kansas City, but he was a much more controversial figure. A Swedish multimillionaire and one-time friend of Field Marshal Göring, he was heavily involved in armaments and had many close Nazi ties. He was later blacklisted by both the British and the Americans. Wenner-Gren, who had set up a canning factory at Bimini, once told Etienne Dupuch that he was such an international industrialist that he would be "considered a spy in whatever country he was in."[25]

Whether the Duke favored him because of his background or despite his background is not known. But he did favor him. He also favored Harold Christie, the colony's biggest real estate developer, who also sat on the Duke's Executive Council. Christie once brought the publisher of the Chicago *Tribune*, Colonel McCormick, to meet the Duke and Duchess. No American publisher had been more vociferous against Britain and the British than McCormick, so Christie telephoned to inquire if the Windsors would see him.

"The Duchess knew all about him," remembered Christie. "She concentrated on him, charmed him so completely that he went away beaming."[26] The colonel afterward told Christie that it wasn't British royalty that he disliked, just some British policies.

One thing Christie always remembered was something the Duke said when he invited them to a picnic: "Talk to the Duchess about it. If it pleases her, it will please me."

If any phrase epitomized their marriage it was that: "If it pleases her, it will please me . . ."

At a party, when the Duke got up to leave, everybody got up to leave. But if Wallis was having a good time and didn't want to go home to bed, she simply sat down—as one English hostess remembered —and then the Duke sat down, and everybody sat down.

That same hostess said, "You could always see the emotion in the Duke's eyes as he followed his wife around the room with his eyes . . . the Duchess never showed any such emotion in her eyes. She was always very self-contained."[27]

"The only time the Duchess ever lost her facial composure, that I can remember," said an Englishwoman, "was at a dinner when the

Duke had to make a speech. He had had too much to drink, and when he was introduced, her face had an agonized expression that I had never seen. He got through the speech all right, but her face maintained that expression until he finished."[28]

Does patience make women beautiful in middle age? She was then forty-five years old. An important man in the shipping business, who happened to visit the Duke on business early in the morning, caught a glimpse of Wallis that he will never forget. She was wearing a robe, without make-up with her hair falling loosely, "and she looked lovely, absolutely lovely." There was a light coming onto her from a window and her eyes "were cerulean blue and sparkling, like the water on the west side of the island."[29]

"You couldn't be mad at the Duchess, if she didn't want you to be mad at her," remembered one woman who was not particularly her friend. "She *was* a charmer."[30]

"At dinner she talks well and constantly," reported Janet Flanner. "Like most good talkers, she likes to have her say which is usually personal and outspoken. Her most ardent admirers say she is so honest she will say first what she thinks, even if on second thought she has to regret it. She gets in trouble because what she says is usually right to the point."[31]

A friend called her "La Belle Jolie." Another commented that the Duchess was more fascinating than the Duke because the Duke's life had been predictably patterned, and you usually knew how he would react to any situation. "But her background was more unframed, and so you could never be absolutely certain what she would do."[32]

Others disagreed. Except for some parties and dances, the Duchess carefully maintained her front, her dignity, her expected pattern of performance.

A visiting American friend, who had known her in China and had not seen her since, marveled how "completely well-gowned, completely gracious, completely composed, completely complete" she was.[33]

She was not, however, everybody's cup of tea. Some of the more proper local society women felt "We were provincials to her. She didn't warm to us and we didn't warm to her." Another woman added, "She had no airs or pretensions about her, and she was friendly up to a point, but then there was a bridge of familiarity that no one in the Bahamas ever crossed. Nobody was on a first-name basis with her."[34]

They quietly resented, and much envied, her importing decorators from the United States. She also imported her favorite New York hairdresser, Antoine. (Polish-born Antoine Cierplikowski.) He gave her an egg shampoo with two jiggers of rum. It was later discovered that the Duchess even sent her clothes to New York City by steamship to be dry cleaned. One such establishment on East 64th Street received a package marked "Her Royal Highness," with instructions, "Clothes to Be Cleaned."[35] They were dresses. Since they were not on the ship's manifest, the general manager of the steamship line had to post a $500 bond before the package could be released.

Wallis had all the attributes and problems and liabilities of a strong-minded woman. She knew her duty and she did it without complaint. But she insisted on certain rights of privacy and preference, and even indulgence. She would tolerate some Bahamians for her husband's sake, but she would not cultivate them. She preferred Americans.

Regardless of the satisfaction and even the pleasure of her work, she was in fact homesick for the United States.

"Be sure you say hello to New York for me," she shouted at a departing American guest.[36]

37

WHEN WALLIS FIRST ARRIVED in the Bahamas she scratched out "Government House" and inserted "Elba" when she wrote to her friends. Her mood changed when she became fully absorbed in the work and responsibility of her position, but she never felt completely at home. And she was forced to watch her husband grow increasingly unhappy as the war progressed.

He read stories of the Battle of Britain; his brother the King working in an aircraft production plant; Germany smashing into Russia with a massive blitzkrieg; Nazi general Rommel moving against British troops in North Africa. The world was in turmoil while he played his daily afternoon rounds of golf.

Wallis urged a change of scene for both of them, a trip to the United States. The Duke excitedly agreed, and they planned an itinerary that included Washington, Baltimore, New York and the Duke's 4,000-acre ranch in Canada. Their visit to Miami had whetted her appetite for a longer return trip. As she told a Miami reporter, she planned to replace her "refugee rags" and "We hope not to stay in Nassau during the heat of this summer."[1]

It wasn't until September 1941 that the Duke was able to get the necessary official permission.

Because of the war, a ship was not available, and Wallis survived her first plane trip. In Miami they boarded a private Pullman train provided by one of their new friends, Robert Young, president of the New York Central Railroad. Accompanying them, as usual, were their servants, their three cairn terriers and 146 pieces of luggage. Their private car had adjoining bedrooms, each with a three-quarter bed, a private dining room, a lounge and another compartment. A connecting car had bedrooms for everyone else. As usual, too, they brought along their own silk sheets.

From Miami they went first to Canada by way of the Midwest. A railroad official passing through their car saw the Duke in their private lounge kissing the Duchess on the ear and patting her gently on the rear.

Even with his attention focused on his wife, the Duke still observed everyone around him. A railroad staff man had a sty on his eye, and the Duke hurriedly got his "Windsor Medicine Kit," as he called it, a musette bag filled with "absolutely every kind of medicine you could think of."

The Windsors changed clothes on the train several times a day, dressed for dinner, showed cordiality and consideration for everybody, but maintained their absolute privacy.

The Duke loved the trip because it gave him more time alone with her. In Nassau, he had to share her with her dozen activities. Here, it was almost another honeymoon. For Wallis, it was the change of scene she wanted and needed. She had been a good governor's wife in the Bahamas. She had made herself available to many, but always to him. In his melancholy, she was his spirit; in his boredom she was his reserve and his resource. Now she wanted to unwind. No duties, no responsibilities, no worry about watchful eyes.

The Duke's Canadian ranch was a working one near the foothills of the Rocky Mountains and he immersed himself in its business. He had not been there for almost fifteen years. He didn't have time to go horseback riding, but he did visit two air training centers and got in some duck shooting.

Wallis' closest touch with civilization was twenty-five miles away, the tiny frontier town of High River, bleak and barren with a yellow brick city hall built shortly after the turn of the century. Someone there asked what size shoes she wore and she replied that the size of her shoes was of no conceivable interest to anybody, but that she would be only too glad to talk about the two infant welfare clinics in Nassau.

Ranch life was not for Wallis. She disliked horses and hated hunting. She appreciated the worth of the rough-cut people but she preferred the witty and the bright and the sophisticated, and she was eager to return to the States.

Aunt Bessie and a crowd of 10,000 people were waiting for them when they arrived at Union Station in Washington, D.C. They were scheduled to have lunch with the President and his wife at the White House, but Mrs. Roosevelt's brother had died only hours before their arrival, and the luncheon was canceled. The two of them saw the President alone for a half-hour after being barraged by photographers. "No more waves," they laughingly said.[2]

The Duke went on his rounds of official calls while Wallis stayed with Aunt Bessie and visited Mrs. George Barnett, the Rogerses, and other assorted friends, at the British Embassy. She had much to tell them. She could tell them about the Bahamas. She could tell them about her work on the islands, and she would tell this with great pride. Whatever frustration and pain she had, she would keep within herself. She did not tell them her feeling of being under a microscope with everybody watching to see whether she had one cocktail or two at a party, how many servicemen she danced with at the canteen. She may have told them of her intense longing to return to the United States on a permanent basis.

The time was a pleasant one. So many crowds of people everywhere the Windsors went, some of them perching precariously in windows and on roofs. So many of them wanted to see *her!*

The Baltimore visit was next, the long-awaited feather in the cap, the girl from Biddle Street coming back with a former king and emperor. A close family friend gave another explanation. "One of the reasons she brought the Duke to Baltimore in 1941 was to show that she also had good breeding and a good family.[3]

"It is true that Wallis had a lot of relatives in Baltimore," the same woman continued, "and they all liked her, and treated her well when she came, because she was of their kin, but none of them that I know really loved her."[4]

Looking at some old pictures of Wallis as a young girl, her cousin Mrs. George Barnett told a guest, "Oh, she's never been a beauty. Too much jaw, don't you think? And then all the Montague women were known for their hands and feet. Her mother, Alice, had the most exquisite ankles. I've always thought Bessie Wallis got hers—and her hands—from her father's family. They were in railroads."[5]

Although her Baltimore return made national headlines, the Bel Air (Md.) *Times* dealt with it as just another local social item:

GENERAL WARFIELD'S NIECE IS WEEKEND GUEST

General Henry Mactier Warfield of Salona Farms in the Harford hunting country between Fallston and Timonium will have as his

413

guests this weekend, his niece the former Miss Wallace (sic) War-field and her husband. They are passing through from their ranch in Canada to Washington, D.C. and the Bahamas.

General Warfield's niece married the Duke of Windsor who was formerly the Prince of Wales and the King of England. The Duke is an enthusiastic horseman and has an important position with the British Government in Nassau, an island in the Bahamas off the east coast of Florida.

One of her Baltimore kin, a Mrs. Zachary Lewis, the general's daughter, earlier had said, "We'll probably take them to the races. Wallis likes the races, of course. Edward does, too. I don't know what else we'll do with them.

"The way they refer to this house as a great mansion amuses me. It's only a big barn with lots of dogs and horses. That shack they photographed as the place Wallis and Edward will stay at was just a joke. And I wish when they took a picture of the bedroom they had taken one with double beds instead of the one with the single bed."[6]

En route to Maryland, Wallis confided her growing excitement. "That's going to be quite an experience for me."[7]

Their train came directly to the small Timonium station, and wait-ing for them was tall, dignified Uncle Warfield, with his silver-white mustache, looking very much like the general he was. Wallis was "tremulous" when he kissed her gallantly on the cheek.

"With a gesture that spoke more loudly than her words," wrote Inez Robb, "drowned out by huzzahs of the crowd, she presented to her uncle and her cousin the man who gave up his heritage to be her husband. The Duke seemed almost boyishly eager that the general like him . . ."[8]

Reporters observed that the Duchess wore a fitted tweed reefer of Wallis blue over a slim black dress, a felt skullcap, also of Wallis blue. Her shoes and bag were of black suede and she carried a sable scarf of three skins.

Salona Farm was a big, white rambling farmhouse, set on 400 acres, only several miles from Oldfields school and her grandmother's summer home at Manor Glen near Little Gunpowder Falls and Uncle Emory's house at Pot Spring.

To please photographers, she posed four separate times shaking hands with her uncle. "We will wear out our welcome," she said jestingly to them, and then smilingly asked photographers, "Please don't use the picture with our mouths all open with smiles or conversation, and our feet halfway up a step."[9]

As emotional as the moment was, she was as practical as ever. It was the trait that some of her hometown friends, even those who liked her, called "calculating." She knew how much "appearance" meant in Baltimore, and she wanted it to be the most proper. For the same reason, with convincing firmness, she told another photographer, "Not through the screen, please."[10]

At Salona, Wallis proudly pointed out to the Duke the evidence of her own heritage, the portraits of her ancestors that lined the walls. Her relatives observed that her speech had changed slightly, but not her movements. She still gestured with her palms upturned at her sides, sometimes with an extended arm.

The State Department and the British had bothered General Warfield with all kinds of instructions about protocol, but he decided to let them do as they pleased. His daughter made certain that they lacked little, and that the dinners included the traditional Maryland foods such as fried chicken and crabcakes.

It seems surprising that Wallis did not make time to go back to Oldfields; she never ever did go back. Had she left it so far behind her? Was it now something too simple to show her royal husband?

Or was it simply that there was nothing to show? Oldfields to her was not the place, but the people, and the people were gone. The closest of them, Mary Kirk, who had married and given birth to a son, died that October. Simpson had sent them to the States, away from the war, and Mary Kirk then discovered she was fatally ill. With a Churchillian gesture, a reward for Simpson's earlier grace and sacrifice, the Prime Minister arranged for Mary and her son to fly to London to rejoin her husband during the last months of her life. She died while Wallis was in Baltimore.

All Wallis' memories returned with a rush. After a quiet family weekend, the mayor of Baltimore put them on parade, a slow-moving procession of cars from City Hall to the Baltimore Country Club. Police estimated the cheering crowd at 200,000 people.

"This is *her* party," remarked a woman. "It must be wonderful to have this many people waiting to take a look at you."[11]

It *was* her party, her moment of absolute triumph. Baltimore had never seen anything comparable. It was a hero's parade, complete with confetti. As someone said, "Our little girl from Baltimore not only brought home the bacon, but the side meat as well."[12]

The procession passed the intersection of Calvert and Biddle Streets. She got a quick glimpse of the house in which she had spent her teenage years. The glimpse was all she wanted. It was shabbier now, the neighborhood not what it had been.

Police were much in evidence. Pennsylvania state troopers had warned earlier of a former mental patient who had once wanted to bring flowers to the Duchess in Europe.

At the country club she and the Duke stood on the veranda, and no receiving line was ever more regal. More than 800 people waited to bow, look, shake hands, gasp, smile, say a few words. A woman started to ask Wallis if she remembered her, and before she could finish, Wallis embraced and kissed her. "She was my first school-teacher," Wallis told the Duke. "Miss Ada O'Donnell. She conducted a kindergarten here." To a listening reporter, she added, "Get it right. *Ada O'Donnell*."[13]

"She can't possibly greet this many people," a voice cried out of the crowd. "Some of us will have to say we shook hands when we didn't."[14]

The band played "There'll Always Be an England," and the mayor's daughter-in-law, former Metropolitan Opera singer Rosa Ponselle, sang "Home Sweet Home." The Wallis watchers said she listened intently and her eyes were misty.

They might have been. Among the many well-wishing strangers, there were old friends reappearing like ghosts from the past. She found herself joking, laughing, remembering stories and names. One heard her refer to former friends as "boys and girls," as if they were all children again. She kept saying, "Please forgive me if I don't recognize all my old schoolmates." And she kept repeating over and over again, "I'm so glad to be back."

One of those who didn't have an invitation but waited outside for a glimpse of her and finally wrote her a note was Josephine, who wanted to say, "Miss Wallis, do you remember Josephine, who used to make your sandwiches every day for your lunch for you to take to school."[15] In her answering note, Wallis said she certainly did remember.

For the ceremony Wallis wore a short white dress edged at the neck with black, and on one of her gloved wrists rested a magnificent diamond link bracelet. She also wore diamond earrings, a sable scarf and two orchids from the mayor.

"She has what it takes," murmured an onlooker.[16]

Could she have dreamed that the boyish Prince of Wales she put in her schoolgirl diary would one day be sharing her pillow and her heart? Could she have dreamed that this formidable city would be at her feet? Could she have dreamed that even though she couldn't quite make it as Queen of the May at Oldfields, Maryland would accept her as the uncrowned Queen of the World?

She and the Duke had been vibrant, warm, vivacious all afternoon. Then the orchestra played "God Save the King" and the radiance went out of their faces for a moment. The Duke stood stiff at attention. Then, gradually, they both smiled and laughed again.

After Baltimore New York was an anticlimax. They stayed at the Waldorf Astoria, visited the British War Relief Society and Bundles for Britain. Crowds gaped at them, and some cheered. But if Wallis was "bright-eyed and gay," it was still the Baltimore glow.

A bartender at the hotel, Ray Swanson, had a lingering memory. "I could see them as they sipped their drinks, one of them always touching the other on the hand, arm or back. It was obvious to me how much they cared for each other."[17]

A cousin visited Wallis afterward, listened to her laugh in the shower. The cousin wanted to know what the joke was.

"Oh, nothing," Wallis answered. "I'm just thinking of my old existence in Baltimore—and now look at me!"[18]

38

THE DUKE AND DUCHESS flew back to the Bahamas in a heavy rain early in November 1941. It had been a happy tour, but it was not a happy time. A Baltimore doctor had diagnosed that the Duchess had stomach ulcers and asked her to return within a month to determine the question of possible surgery. It was the medical cost of keeping so much within herself.

The world had a natural sympathy for the Duke because of all he had surrendered for a woman's love. But comparatively few people realized how much of a cross Wallis carried, how steady and unrelenting was the strain. Few people realized the full price she paid for this marriage. The Duke never got ulcers; the Duchess never lost them.

After eighteen months of renovations, Government House was almost ready. The Windsors, meanwhile, had moved from Sigrist House to "Westbourne," the mansion of the island's wealthiest and most prominent entrepreneur, Sir Harry Oakes.

They both knew Sir Harry as a crude and generous man. Originally he had been a teacher and surveyor in Maine. He left to search the world for gold and found his mother lode in Ontario, Canada, the second largest gold mine in the western hemisphere. His net worth was more than $200 million, enough to make people tolerate his primitive manners and language. Harold Christie had persuaded Oakes to settle in Nassau and he soon owned almost a third of the island. He built an airfield, a golf course, bus lines and hotels and he loved to operate a bulldozer, clearing his own land. He became a British citizen, donated generously to many charities, and then "the Cinderella prospector" became a British baronet, the richest in the British Empire.

The Duke liked him enormously. He liked his naturalness, his energy, his ideas. Sir Harry helped make their stay pleasant.

Then Pearl Harbor changed everything on December 7, 1941. When Prime Minister Churchill called President Roosevelt that night, Roosevelt told him, "Well, we're all in the same boat now."

America's entry into the war meant that the Bahamas were no longer a pleasure place for American tourists. The increased tourism alone had earned the Duke his $12,000-a-year salary. With tourism dead, unemployment increased. Poorly paid workers rioted early in 1942, and the Duke felt compelled to make a show of force. Wages then edged slightly upward, restoring peace.

The one thing the Duke made no effort to change was the color bar in the Bahamas, where no colored man could be in charge of anything. Etienne Dupuch recalled that the Duke, as Prince of Wales, once had commended the Australians for maintaining an all-white immigration policy. But Dupuch also admitted a contrasting incident in his home. The Duke, who had been visiting him, suddenly disappeared. Dupuch found him in the kitchen cutting bread for his young son.

The Duke was conscious of some of the resentment against him on the part of native leaders. When one of his secretaries showed him the daily batch of clippings, he said, "But where are all the stinkers?" The secretary explained that she did have the unfavorable articles but she had not thought he would want to see them. "You must put them in," he said, "they're the most interesting ones."[1]

On the other hand the Duke would not tolerate any criticism of his wife. He wanted no "stinkers" about her.

During their trip to the States, Wallis had made a remark about the dress of native Bahamian woman which Etienne Dupuch felt was unflattering. She also had endorsed a brand of American cigarettes, with the stipulation that her payment go to the Red Cross in the Bahamas. Dupuch felt this endorsement, too, was improper, and so wrote an editorial mildly critical of her.

Up until this time Dupuch had believed himself in line for a knighthood. He had been responsible for organizing a massive effort of fund raising, food canning and scrap-metal accumulation for the war effort in England, and Bahamians fully expected Dupuch to be rewarded royally. Indeed, the Duke told him that he would "soon have something for him." This was the typical remark indicating an upcoming honor.

Dupuch knew that if he printed the critical editorial, the Duke would cancel any honor. His vanity vied with his integrity and finally his integrity won. He published the editorial.

When it appeared, the Duke called in Dupuch and in the Duchess' presence said that in Great Britain the press never criticized the royal family.

Dupuch simply answered, "I am not criticizing you as a member of the royal family; I am criticizing the governor of the Bahamas and his wife."[2]

At that point the Duke became so agitated that he left the room ". . . and the Duchess politely showed me through the small door on the eastern side of the Government House."

"You don't catch flies with vinegar, Mr. Dupuch," she said drily as she closed the screen door behind him.

"Duchess, I am not trying to catch flies."[3]

Dupuch freely admits that the Duchess worked hard during her five years in the Bahamas. Besides being an active president of the Red Cross she also built an infant welfare center on Blue Hill Road with money from a private fund controlled by the Duke. There had been much talk for a long time about such a center but it was the Duchess who made it happen. So successful was the first center that she soon built another, at the other end of the island, even providing the nurses with bicycles and automobiles. Nor was she a figurehead; she was there, and often. Each clinic cared for almost a hundred babies a day.

Wallis' work in the infant clinics stirred an old memory, her supposed disinterest in children. Perhaps it had been true, for a while; but she disproved any public comment on the subject in the Bahamas. She liked these children. She knew their names and their histories. She spent a great deal of time with them. She could have spent that time in a thousand different ways, but this was something she wanted to do.

Sometimes the most unlikely women can make the most wonderful mothers.

When the Duchess once again had been selected as one of the best-dressed women of the year, she said, "You know, I'm not as interested in clothes as I'm given credit for. I'm more interested in my work in the Bahamas.

"It's been so long since I've bought any new clothes, or, in fact, thought much about them. I could not order anything from Mainbocher or from anyone else in the United States if I wanted to, because we are not allowed to take or send money out of the islands now. And the stock in the shops here is quite limited. I did pick up a few little simple dresses in Miami and a couple in a shop here in Nassau. Outside of these I have bought nothing since I arrived. I think I may try to get my Aunt Bessie to get me a dress or two."

As a side project, Wallis started a class for a hundred native women in needlepoint, to try to spur a native needlepoint industry. She also directed the Dundar Civic Center, operating as a nonprofit vocational institute and placement bureau for Bahamians.

In addition she found time to help the YWCA and the IODE (Independent Order of Daughters of the Empire), which she also headed, as well as the Nassau Garden Club. She was involved in a program funding "Meals-on-Wheels," delivering meals to needy families. The Duke also created a Duchess of Windsor Fund to provide nurses, canned milk and medical supplies for the sick and poor of the Out Islands.

When Wallis made her first tour of welfare facilities, she was nervous, although she did not show it. She urged a friendly staff member, "Don't leave me . . . don't leave me . . . don't leave me."[4] Inspecting the two-room Red Cross setup, she told one of the officers, "You are not going to make a committeewoman out of me." She wanted action, not titles. The Red Cross then was a bandage-wrapping operation with limited space. Wallis approached her various wealthy friends and soon had offers of houses and supplies and money. Bonwit Teller even offered to put on a fashion show and donate a handsome watch for an auction.

The war made Wallis' life still more active. Within a few months after Pearl Harbor, Nazi U-boats destroyed five ships within ten days near Nassau. The Duchess and her Red Cross worked overtime to provide hundreds of survivors with clothes, food, shelter and personal comforts. Shortly afterward, during a widespread Bay Street fire, Wallis rushed to the Red Cross building to find it in flames. She hurriedly formed a bucket brigade with some co-workers and managed to save most of their supplies before the building was completely gutted. That's the kind of thing that stirred native admiration for her. "She didn't warm to us and we didn't warm to her," said one native leader, "but she worked hard while she was here and she did a lot of good things."[5]

War brought in thousands of Royal Air Force officers and men in training for the Coastal Command. The U.S. Army Air Force also sent a group and there were even American Rangers completing commando training. Wallis persuaded Frederick Sigrist to donate the Bahamian Club, a former gambling casino, to the canteen she had organized.

She raised money at bazaars and cocktail parties, volunteered her services to the canteen as a short-order cook, concentrating on eggs. After three years on the job, she later estimated that she had cooked some 40,000 servings of eggs and bacon. She worked hard. One of her most caustic critics agreed that "Anybody who did any cooking at that canteen deserved a Victoria Cross because it was so unbearably hot there."[6] Not only was there no air conditioning, but the cooking area was very badly ventilated and had no windows. And nobody hated heat more than Wallis Windsor.

It was here that her determination, aggressiveness, toughness paid large dividends and earned high praise.

She spent mornings at the infant clinic and the Red Cross, afternoons cooking in the canteen, and some evenings dancing with the servicemen.

At the service canteen dances, Wallis was at her warmest, loosest, most relaxed. There was no need for airs or dignity or control. If she was older than most, few noticed or cared. She was lively. She could do a marvelous Charleston, and she kept the air crackling.

The Duke was jealous of the time she spent there, but it was not something he could complain about. He was simply jealous of any time she spent away from him. Among the steady stream of American visitors and celebrities came actor Sterling Hayden, tall, blond and extremely handsome. There is a revealing photograph of Wallis staring up at him, almost enraptured, while the Duke stands alongside, absolutely glowering.

In those segregated days she founded a separate canteen for the native members of the Bahamas Defense Force. She started a first aid detachment, where every volunteer was a businesswoman. At the canteen, her 150 volunteers alternated as waitresses, cooks and hostesses.

"I never worked harder in my life," Wallis said afterward. "I never felt better used." She said she was exhausted but exhilarated. "I have to keep busy. I couldn't stay here if I didn't."[7]

It was probably true. Life had been hairdressers and manicurists and couturiers and parties and fun. Now she had purpose, now she had people who depended on her, now she saw buildings that would not have been there but for her, now she saw children every day who would not have been cared for were it not for her.

There was more. In addition to the Red Cross she was also automatically president of many other civic, welfare and social organizations. She gave more time to some than others, but she paid attention to all.

The Duke's day was not as busy as Wallis'. Nor did his work seem as important to him. He felt himself to be a figurehead with limited authority. Besides golf every afternoon he went bone fishing at Andros Island, sailed and toured and inspected. As the war worsened, his resentment grew at being sidetracked and ignored. Downing Street had not forgotten him completely. They became concerned that the Nazis might land a submarine in the Bahamas and kidnap the Duke and the Duchess. To forestall this, they sent a company of Cameron Highlanders as an available guard. This seemed to depress the Duke even more.

Then his favorite brother, George, the Duke of Kent, was killed in an air crash.

Despite his animosity toward most of his family, the Duke still could not destroy the early attachment, still had photographs of his family in his room. The Duchess could not always hide her own feelings about them. When a photographer posed the Duke alongside a picture of his mother, the Duke asked the Duchess, "Can't we get a better picture of Mother, dear?"

Wallis kept her voice flat and dry when she answered, "No. That is the best one, dear."[8]

Wallis knew how much the break with his family had hurt her husband, and one day she wrote the Dowager Queen. It must have been a wrench for her. Had the Queen Mother given her David the early love he needed, he would have been a stronger man. Had she given him the sympathy and understanding he needed during and after the abdication, his hurt would have been minimized. Had she made the simplest recognition of her son's wife, she would have made him boundlessly happy.

Wallis forced herself to write partly because she felt herself to be the source of that breach, but mostly because she loved her husband. If he were happier, she would be, too.

Her letter was courteous and deferential, expressing her regret that she had come between mother and son. She informed the Queen

Mother that the Bishop of Nassau would soon be in London, and perhaps the Queen might want to talk to him about her son.

Queen Mary did send for the Bishop to discuss David. She never replied to the Duchess but she wrote a letter to her son, including "a kind message to your wife."[9] The Duke was surprised. He would have been even more surprised and deeply touched had Wallis told him what she had done.

The Duke was more impulsive, but the Duchess could be more imperious, if she had to. In many things she obviously had the last word. A local editor had prepared an article with photographs, for an American magazine, showing the Duke and Duchess living luxuriously at the renovated Government House. When he presented the photographs to the Duke, he glowed. "I'll show them to the Duchess," he said, and rushed out. When he returned, his face was solemn. "I'm sorry, but we will not do this."[10]

The Duchess had pointed out to him that the world was at war and it would not do to show the two of them living so lavishly while Britain was burning.

A staff member remembered the time the Duke was busy composing a speech, and having trouble with it. He got on the phone to the Duchess and said, "Darling, please come in here right away." She came in, walking very quickly, rustling her black taffeta-lined robe. "The speech stinks," he said.[11] The Duchess swiftly sat on the floor among his papers, busied her pencil making changes, and then minutes later handed it to him. The Duke read what she had done, approved it promptly and gave it to a secretary to be typed.

"I have rarely seen an ascendancy established over one partner in a marriage by the other to so remarkable degree," a British visitor at Government House observed. The Duke seemed to defer to her in almost everything of any importance, and even in most trivial matters would say to someone, "I'll see what the Duchess has to say about that."[12]

Yet this same observer confessed that he had never seen a man more happy with his wife. "He seemed to revel in being with the Duchess, in sunning himself in her smile, in admiring her appearance, in listening to her conversation."

On one of their trips to the States, a photographer asked the Duke to make the Churchill V-for-Victory sign. The Duke smiled agreeably and started to raise his hand when he saw the Duchess staring at him, shaking her head. The Duke dropped his arm.

It is too simple to explain this by saying she was domineering and he was weak-willed. With anyone else, the Duke could domineer very well. All his life he had been accustomed to instant gratification. Wallis, however, although she was often described as "mannish," could be entirely feminine in adjusting to a man's needs. Her treatment of Spencer was in great contrast to her adjustment to Simpson or Espil.

David Windsor needed her in a particular way, and she fulfilled the need. He never had any real mothering, and she had never had any children. In adult terms, this was partly a transformation of those deep psychological conditions.

While he was dependent on her in one way, he was still highly protective of her.

Aside from his home life, the Duke found himself with less and less to do, and he grew more and more bored. Wallis felt impelled to tell a reporter, "How can one expect the Duke to live here? I, too, wish to do our duty. But is there scope here for his great gifts, his inspiration, his long training? I'm only a woman, but I'm his wife, and I don't believe that in Nassau he's serving the Empire as importantly as he might."

With a world at war, the work of an ex-king was of little relevance. If the Duchess had hoped to stir some action, she failed. The two then found more reason to make more trips to the United States. The aluminum millionaire Arthur Vining Davis made his yacht available to them. The Duchess went to Palm Beach to look at soup vending machines for her servicemen's canteen. She approached department stores in New York about buying native Bahamian jewelry. A store buyer described her as having "a victorious glint in her eye." She and the Duke visited Aunt Bessie, who had fractured a hip, then had lunch with the President and Mrs. Roosevelt. The President surprised them by inviting Herman and Katherine Rogers as well. Roosevelt had known Herman from Hyde Park, where they had been neighbors.

The Rogerses returned to Nassau with the Windsors and it made Wallis realize how much she had missed close friends. She had established rapport with the Bahamian social set, and earned their respect, but she made no real reach for their friendship.

Aunt Bessie arrived later for a short stay, and so did Doc Holden from Palm Beach, along with others. But their most intimate friends, who were always there, were their dogs. As much as she loved them, Wallis never lost her sense of humor about them. The original three terriers had grown to five, four of them pure-bred and one a half-breed. The half-breed liked to bark and always scared one of the mild-mannered secretaries. Finally, one day, the secretary yelled back at the barking dog, "If you bite me, you little bastard, I'll bite you right back."

As the secretary turned, she saw the smiling Duchess watching the scene. "That's right," urged the Duchess, "bite the little bastard."[13]

Unlike the secretary, Wallis had no fear of any dog. What she did fear, with an utter horror, were thunderstorms. And for the Windsors the worst tropical storm was yet to come, one from which there would be no place to hide.

39

JULY 7, 1943, was a wild night, broken by frequent bursts of thunder and lightning. In the very early hours of the morning there was a persistent knock on the door of the Duke's bedroom. Such an interruption was almost unprecedented. The Duke put on his robe and opened the door to find his equerry, Major Gray Phillips. The Duchess was now also awake and strained to hear what the two men were saying, but all she could pick up was the word "murder."

A horrified Duke hurriedly returned to tell her what had happened. Sir Harry Oakes had been found in his bed, beaten and burned.

The night before, Oakes had had a small party at his home. His wife was away and Harold Christie stayed on as an overnight guest. Etienne Dupuch was scheduled to arrive early in the morning to look at Sir Harry's prize sheep. Dupuch telephoned from his newspaper office at about seven in the morning to say he was en route.

Harold Christie answered the phone.

"I'm on my way," said Dupuch.

"Harry's dead . . . he has been murdered," Christie shouted in the phone.

"You are joking," said Dupuch.

"No . . . no . . . no . . . it's no joke. . . . Harry's dead I tell you . . . ! I just found him dead in bed . . ."[1]

Dupuch got more of the story from Christie and quickly cabled the news to the world.

There is no knowing what the Duke and Duchess discussed in their bedroom that morning, but afterward he made two decisions and both were mistakes.

First, he exercised his powers of censorship under the Emergency

427

War Powers Act and forbade any news of the crime to be sent outside the Bahamas. The Duke didn't know it was too late for that. Dupuch already had sent out the story, and the outside world now wanted to know more.

During that morning the Duke also spoke to the local police, Harold Christie and the doctors, and surely had a fairly clear picture of what had happened. His equerry originally had described it as "murder." So had Harold Christie. Even a quick examination indicated extreme brutality. There were four distinct skull wounds above his left ear and the "wet" and "dry" blisters on the body suggested that Oakes had been burned while he was still alive. The grotesque feature was that the burned body was covered with feathers from a pillow, and the feathers had stuck to the blistered body.

A colonial governor anywhere would have called Scotland Yard. Oakes' international stature would seem to have made this decision axiomatic. The Duke, however, then made his second mistake. He called Captain Edward Walter Melchen, chief of the homicide bureau of the Miami Police Department. Melchen had been assigned to him as a police bodyguard during his Miami visits. He told Melchen only that a leading Bahamian had apparently committed suicide and would Melchen fly over and verify the details to eliminate any problems?

He told Melchen neither the name of the man nor any other details.

The Duke later explained that he had called the Miami police because the local police were inadequate to handle the case, particularly the fingerprint detection. Melchen and his associate, Captain James Otto Barker, arrived that afternoon, but without their fingerprinting equipment.

"Santa Claus is dead." That's what Dr. Hugh Quackenbush, one of the examining physicians who reported directly to the Duke early that morning, said. Quackenbush now insists that he originally thought it might be suicide because of the hole behind the left ear and because Oakes was left-handed. He explained the burning as a possible bungling attempt to make the suicide look like a murder. Only after the X rays did Quackenbush realize that there had been four skull fractures and no bullet, and that it had to be murder. At the time, Quackenbush remembered the Duke saying, "For Lady Oakes' sake, I hope it turns out to be murder; for the colony's sake, I hope it is suicide."

Why would anyone want to make a suicide look like a murder?

Why wouldn't the Duke tell the Miami police that it might be murder, and give them more details?

Why did a fingerprint expert arrive without fingerprint equipment?

Why would a British governor call Miami instead of Scotland Yard? And who murdered Sir Harry Oakes?

These were only some of the early questions. The later ones concerned a Mafia connection, stolen gold, faked fingerprints and a local police chief who was transferred to Trinidad almost immediately after the crime. The world press eagerly tagged it "The Crime of the Century."

The Duchess was reputed to have said afterward, "Well, never a dull moment in the Bahamas!"

Many prominent Bahamians quickly blamed the Duke's call to Miami police on the Duchess' influence. Since he deferred to her on the smallest things, he would surely have consulted her. Wallis might have felt a natural preference for American efficiency. If that were true, then why not the FBI instead of Miami detectives? Would an FBI response have taken much longer?

Despite his generosity, Sir Harry had been a ruthless businessman who had made many enemies. "There are so many suspects that I wouldn't know where to start looking," said one Bahamian.[2]

Melchen interviewed witnesses while fingerprint expert Barker stayed at the scene of the crime. To heighten the confusion Barker then revealed that he had forgotten to bring his special camera. Had he consulted the Nassau police he would have discovered that they had a proper fingerprint camera all the time.

The next day the Duke visited the scene of the crime and talked alone with Barker for twenty minutes. Two hours later, police drove to the house of Count Marie Alfred Fouquereaux de Marigny and "charged and cautioned" him with the murder of his father-in-law.

It was no secret in Nassau that Sir Harry hated the Count. The Count had divorced his wife to marry Sir Harry's eighteen-year-old daughter. The two men had had open and violent arguments. Lean, handsome, thirty-six-year-old Count de Marigny pleaded innocent.

The circumstantial evidence was damning. Captain Barker tried to clinch it by hinging his case on a single fingerprint which he claimed to have taken from a Chinese screen in the bedroom where the body was found. The defense attorney had the screen brought into court. The surface of it was covered with a complicated pattern of figures and designs, and the defense conclusively proved that there was not a single place on the screen onto which the fingerprint could fit. The print had been taken off a blank, clean background. The clear suggestion was that Barker had gotten it from a glass tumbler De Marigny had handled while being interviewed *after* the crime was committed. The implication was that Barker had framed De Marigny. There had been bloody handprints on the Chinese screen but they had been washed off by police who said that they were not Marigny's and would therefore "only confuse the evidence."

The collapse of the fingerprint evidence destroyed the case of the prosecution. The jury acquitted Count de Marigny. The case remained unsolved.

Long afterward, Marshall Houts, a private investigator, called it a Mafia murder. A professor of criminal law, former coroner, judge, and FBI agent, Houts based his theory on information from undercover informants. Houts stated that a Mafia representative approached Harold Christie saying his employers would construct a luxurious resort hotel with a casino if the Bahamian government would give them a gambling monopoly. For this they would pay a million dollars or a percentage of profits. Christie saw this as the opening of a new tourist era for the Bahamas and sold the idea to the Duke.

The Duke knew what tourism meant to the Bahamas. Besides that, he and the Duchess both liked gambling. They often had frequented Monte Carlo. The Duchess even had a casino in the service canteen. She, too, would have supported the idea, though neither of them probably knew anything about the Mafia connection.

Backed by the Duke's enthusiasm, Houts said that Christie persuaded Sir Harry Oakes to go along. The deal was made. But Houts believed that Harry may have decided that this new influx would ruin the present paradise, and he changed his mind.

According to Houts, three "button" men then came by cruiser that night and Oakes and Christie met them after their party. One of them hit Oakes with a four-pronged winch lever, then told Christie—who was in shock—that Oakes was only unconscious. They then drove to Oakes' house in a station wagon and dragged the body up the stairway. The stairway was later found covered with mud and debris.

They then undressed the body, put on the pajamas, poured gasoline on a homemade torch, burned the bed, body and mosquito netting, then ripped open a pillow and let the feathers stick onto the burning corpse. They threatened Christie with a similar fate if he ever told the story and ordered him to inform the Duke that they were similarly capable of torturing and mutilating the Duchess before they killed her—and that this was what happened to people who did not keep agreements with the Mafia.

This is the story Houts got from his informants.

If this can be believed, it explains why the Duke hesitated for three hours before he called the Miami police. It would also explain why he did not call Scotland Yard or the FBI, why the local police chief was quickly exiled to Trinidad, even the mysterious death of someone who came to investigate the crime years later.

The Duke, many times, had proved himself a man of great courage. When he was a newly proclaimed king, on parade, and saw a pistol shine in the crowd, he calmly told his accompanying officer, "I suppose that gives us just twenty seconds."[3] This Mafia threat, however horrible, would not have intimidated him, if it were aimed at him alone. But aimed at his wife, it could have thrown him into a panic. Nor would it have been a threat he would share with Wallis.

Houts was not the only one to believe the Mafia theory. Rumors about the gambling negotiations had long been bruited about. Christie had met many Mafiosi during the Prohibition days, when he had made much of his money. And many of the details of the condition of the body, the wounds and the blood, and the trail through the house fitted into the Houts theory.

But there were many other theories. Some claimed Oakes had been killed during a robbery. He had ordered boxes of gold coins delivered to his home several days before his murder and the gold was missing when his body was found. A farm family on a nearby island was later found spending large amounts of money for equipment. They claimed they found the gold in a cave.

Several outside attempts to reopen the case were quickly quashed by authorities. The murderer was never revealed and the case was closed.

There were postscripts.

De Marigny was deported. Years later, Sir Harry Oakes' daughter had their marriage annulled and afterward married the son of the German ambassador to Lisbon, Baron von Hoyningen-Huene.

Captain Barker lost his membership in the American Fingerprint Society and there were many assertions that he was connected with the Mafia. He finally went berserk in his home and was shot and killed.

The Honorable Harold G. Christie continued his life of affluence and eventually became Sir Harold Christie.

The Duke of Windsor decided not to finish his full five-year term of office and resigned in the spring of 1945.

It had been so bizarre, so shocking, that the Windsors decided to leave. They spent the time of the trial making another visit to the United States. They had lived too long in the limelight, and they wanted none of the fire of this court case's publicity.

After the searing experience of the abdication they had hoped for a quiet life, with a good share of pleasure and satisfaction. Instead, the successive crises had made their lives a graph of sharp jigs and jags. The German trip disaster, the Bedaux blunder in the United States, the Spanish spy plots and now this brutal Bahamas murder. Each had revealed errors in judgment and betrayed certain weaknesses. Each had seemed to diminish them just a little. If they had been put on a pedestal by millions, these crises were chipping away at the base. It was one thing for a myth to crash or explode; it was quite another for it to crumble slowly.

As a king, David had the best brains in Britain to advise him. Stubborn as he was, he did listen to their counsel on many matters. Since then, he had had few true friends available whose counsel he trusted. He leaned increasingly on his wife, but such situations in politics and public relations were beyond her. Now everything seemed to have climaxed in this Bahamian nightmare.

Later the Duke seemed to surmount his bad memories of the Bahamas and to remember the time he spent there with affection. An old friend who saw him often in Paris said, "He would always ask me what was going on in the Bahamas. Wallis never did."[4]

PART V

40

"WHEREVER THE DUKE AND DUCHESS GO, the world goes."[1]

It was like that for many years.

Glamour is a fragile, temporary thing that a few people possess at the peak of their lives. But the Duke and Duchess always had it, long after they were no longer headline news. They had it not simply because they were a part of history, not merely because the whole world loves a lover, but because, in addition to all this, they were both very private people. They were friendly, considerate, beautifully well mannered, but they never laid their lives out for public examination. Her need for privacy was even greater than his, and this added to the mystery and multiplied the glamour.

Wallis in fact needed to establish a sense of distance so deeply that it affected her friendships. Even those most loyal never really knew her. They testified that she often made herself available to friends, sometimes at considerable inconvenience and even sacrifice to herself. She worried about them, asked about them, concerned herself about their needs. But though the line between thoughtfulness and warmth may be a thin one, it is real and with Wallis it is always there.

"You can't call her 'warm,' " countered one of her closest friends. "I have my own theory about that, too. I think it's partly a physical thing. She's such a small woman. . . . She can't hug most people. They overwhelm her. If you watched her and the Duke throughout the years, you could see how warm and tender they were to each other. They were both the same size, both small, thin people. I really think that's important."[2]

The Duchess was fifty years old in 1946. It is not an age often associated with fascination, particularly in a woman. But her skin was still magnificent, her style sweeping. A stranger would have guessed her age at ten years younger, but Wallis became angry when anyone mentioned the subject. Once Elsa Maxwell asked her why she devoted so much time and attention to such frivolous things as clothes; she answered, "My husband gave up everything for me; if everyone looks at me when I enter a room, my husband can feel proud of me. That's my chief responsibility."[3]

As she later said, she couldn't help looking at him and remembering and thinking, "What a pity!" Then she added, in a hard voice, "I still think something could have been done."

Such was the persistent air of mystery about the Windsors that the press made much of the fact that the Duke resigned his Bahamas post several months before the five-year term officially ended. Actually the term is an informal one. One serves at the pleasure of the sovereign. Other factors were mentioned. The Duke had resigned partly because he did not want to put the government in a position of wondering what to do with him next, and also because he did not want to put himself in the position of publicly refusing a new post that might be unacceptable to him. Wallis also wanted to avoid another hot Bahamian summer. "We were so bitten by sand flies during the five years we spent in Nassau," she grimly remembered, "that insects no longer have much to draw on, and so they fly away, discouraged."

They had arrived in New York in May 1945, and stayed on until September. It was an unstructured time for them, without any responsibilities. They shopped, visited friends, spent long weekends on Long Island, sunned and swam in the Hamptons, went to the theater and lots of parties. The Duke dropped in at an antique shop, just about teatime, and the store's staff invited him to join them for tea, and he did. The firm's cleaning woman put aside the ordinary china for the occasion and brought out some of the store's eighteenth-century Rockingham china and George III silver. On one of his walks the Duke noticed a long line outside a shop on Madison Avenue and found out it was selling scarce nylon stockings. He joined the line and bought some.

Afterward he told his wife how surprised he had been because the people in line were so intent on the nylons that they didn't even notice him. "And the amazing thing was that I wore a black homburg at the time. After all, one does not usually wear a homburg when one stands in line to buy nylons."[4]

The war in Europe ended on May 8, 1945, with Germany's unconditional surrender but the war in the Pacific still was not over. The world was in a turmoil of change, the directions of the future still clouded. The Windsors' own future looked even cloudier.

"We're right back where we were in 1938," the Duke told Inez Robb. "When we were married, we rented a couple of houses in which to sit down and think. We wanted to find out where we wanted to live, and what we wanted to do."

"Then we were caught up in the war," added the Duchess.

"We're not really thinking of buying a house anywhere at the moment," the Duke continued. "It's very difficult to know where to settle now. But I'm a great admirer of the Duchess' country."[5]

The Duke intimated elsewhere that their future remained flexible in the event that the King asked him to take another appointment. Those close to him observed that the Duke no longer mentioned "my brother the King," but simply said "the King." Shortly after they returned to Paris, the Duke hurried to England. In a general election, the British people had dumped Churchill in favor of the Labour Party. The Duke hoped that the new prime minister, Attlee, might offer him a post of greater responsibility than the Bahamas.

He still wanted to be an ambassador-at-large in the United States, a roving ambassador with the mission of spreading Anglo-American goodwill. It was what Churchill had called "the mixing-up process." He could work within the orbit of the Embassy but not conflict with the diplomatic responsibility of the established British ambassador. He would not necessarily need to be stationed in Washington and would make neither speeches nor public appearances. The King and Churchill both liked the idea, but Prime Minister Attlee did not. Attlee, who had stood by Baldwin during the abdication crisis, did not think it advisable for a relative of the King to be in the British Embassy in Washington.

The Duke insisted he was not going around, "cap in hand, asking for a job," but he was. There were rumors that he might become viceroy of India or else replace his brother as governor general of Australia. Instead, Foreign Minister Ernest Bevin finally offered a position in Southern Rhodesia. The Duke was not flattered by the proposal.

The private nightmare for a wife is to see her husband publicly humiliated and crushed. Wallis' support at this time was more emo-

437

tional than practical. She bolstered hopes where there were none. They had few options. The Duke finally wrote a resentful letter to Churchill saying that since the government obviously didn't need his skills, he would search elsewhere to make a place for himself.

Churchill later tried to console him, saying, "When I left Downing Street, I didn't even have a ration card."

"If his position would allow him to go out and sell refrigerators," Wallis said of her husband, "he'd be terrific."[6]

It did not help his cause at this time for the press to raise old specters. At the French collaborationist trial of Nazi dupe Marshal Pétain, Vichy French premier Pierre Laval testified to a secret conversation between himself and the Duke during the Ethiopian crisis. The Duke denied it. Nor did it help to find himself recognized and cheered by crowds wherever he went in London. "Good old Edward! We want you back!" This again raised the problem of popular competition with the King. An incident that might have clinched the government's attitude, and that of the royal family, was a jewel robbery.

The Duke and Duchess were staying at Ednam Lodge in Sunningdale, twenty miles outside London, as guests of Lord Dudley. While they were away one afternoon, a "cat burglar" climbed the drainpipe and stole jewels belonging to the Duchess reportedly insured for $600,000. Some of them were later found strewn about Lord Dudley's golf course. The robbery was an immediate international headline. Unfortunately Scotland Yard detective Capstick came up with no successful clue. One report intimated that the jewel thief might have dropped in a parachute which was seen near Brest. The French National Office of Meteorology later identified the supposed parachute as a balloon used to carry aloft weather-recording instruments. The publicity convinced the establishment it was right in denying the Duke prominent employment. He was still too "hot" a subject for a serious job.

As disturbing as all these things were, they were more than matched in the Duke's mind by his family's stubborn refusal to accept his wife. He had not seen his mother since the start of the war and he had hoped the years of absence would have stirred some forgiveness in her. It did not. The King was equally unrelenting, supported by his obdurate queen. Their gates were not only bolted against the Duchess, they were barred.

The Duke had said acidly, "We are less interested in curtsies than in courtesies."[7]

In his bitterness, the Duke was indiscreet enough to tell a close friend a story about the King's stammering. It seemed that his brother had a particular difficulty with the sound of "k." When the Duke was king and his brother, the Prince of Wales, had to announce at a party, "Gentlemen, I give you the King," he couldn't complete the word "king."

"I made him see a speech doctor," said the Duke, "and he solved the immediate situation by removing words with the letter 'k.' Afterwards, Bertie would have no problem in saying 'I give you His Majesty.'"[8]

The Duke's guilty feelings about Wallis' rank made him all the more anxious to please his Duchess, cater to her every whim, anticipate her desires. And it made him all the more defensive about their tenth anniversary.

"Ten years have passed, but not the romance," reiterated the Duke, beaming at the Duchess. "It's gone on and on."

"I'm afraid a great deal of wishful thinking went into the predictions that our marriage wouldn't last," said the Duchess, smiling.

"Now we're just a happy middle-aged couple," concluded the Duke.[9]

But they were a couple without a home. Their Paris house had been sold and so they moved their entourage to their rented villa at La Croe. Their staff now included a French maid, a British butler, a French chef and gardener, an English valet and secretary and a boy from the Bahamas, seventeen-year-old Sidney Johnson, who became the most faithful of them all.

That winter they were back again in the United States, and the annual visit to America became part of an established pattern. A columnist observed the Duke at El Morocco not even seeming to notice Lady Furness, who was sitting nearby. It was the year that *Lady Windermere's Fan* was a big Broadway hit, starring Penelope Ward, the daughter of Mrs. Dudley Ward, another of the women from his past.

The Windsors, especially the Duchess, then became prize catches as honorary chairmen of assorted causes, ranging from the advanced medical rehabilitation program for disabled civilians at Bellevue Hospital to heart disease prevention and cancer cure. She was an easy catch for the cancer cause because she herself had had a malignancy in the womb which had been cured. She was also drafted to crown Christina Staguchowicz as Miss Boy's Club of 1947. The Duchess placed a gold paper crown on the girl's curls and told bystanders, "Be careful of her lovely dress. Don't muss it."[10]

In a poll of 100 fashion editors, the New York Dress Institute again voted the Duchess as the best-dressed woman in the world. Editors guessed that she spent a minimum of $30,000 and perhaps closer to $100,000 on her clothes each year. The Duke denied both figures as being extravagant. She cut costs somewhat, according to Schiaparelli, not only by hard bargaining but by doing what many wealthy women did—selling their old dresses to friends.

When the Duchess found herself at a Paris party confronted by two other women wearing the same Givenchy dress as hers, she quipped, "We all looked as if we belonged in the same chorus line."[11] The Duchess also received some unwearable samples, such as an aluminum dress. She frustrated the hat industry by only wearing a favorite beanie, and caused similar consternation among Paris fashion leaders by joining the British female fight against long skirts. She later favored the miniskirt because, she said, it gives you some idea "of what you're getting." Wallis told a fashion writer that her Dior cape was three years old, "and what's more you're going to see it for three years more. Prices are frightful in Paris. You have to buy less and wear them longer and more often."[12]

On her arrival in New York afterward a reporter wondered aloud what kind of fur she was wearing. As she hesitated, the Duke answered, "Rabbit."

Packing for Palm Beach, her maid informed her, "Madame, some of these evening dresses have gone to Palm Beach with you three times." Wallis simply answered, "I hope nobody will remember."[13] Her fashion philosophy, she added, was "A few good clothes at a time, and wear them out." She particularly held on to her suits for several years. On the other hand, she did not have a cocktail dress in her closet.

"Actually," she said, "I have dressed the same classic way all my life. I shop only solid couturiers who avoid fads. Clothes are an investment."

"I know," added the Duke. "I pay the bills."[14]

A reporter interviewed a French owner of a lingerie boutique on 57th Street in New York City. The owner claimed that the Duchess had telephoned asking her to bring her collection to the Windsors' Waldorf suite. The owner refused. A customer who overheard them remarked afterward that she thought the owner would have found it a great honor to serve the Duchess.

"Madame, it is an honor I cannot afford," replied the owner.[15]

An American resident in Paris, who admires the Duchess and shops at the same couturiers, told of arriving for a fitting. Just before her appointment, someone said that the Duchess of Windsor was waiting.

"Well, then, I will leave and you can wait on her," said the American woman.

"No," she was told. "Let the Duchess wait. You pay your bills. She doesn't. She says we ought to be grateful for the publicity that we get because she shops with us."[16]

A friend accompanied her to a New York dressmaker where she ordered several things. The dressmaker afterward mused aloud to the mutual friend, "I wonder if I'll get paid," and then quickly added, "Not that it matters."[17]

The friend replied, "I think that you will get paid, but, as you said, 'Not that it matters.'"

Rumors circulated that the Windsors paid for neither their transatlantic steamship travel nor their suite at the Waldorf Towers. The Duchess herself insisted that they did pay at the Waldorf, although they received a "diplomatic discount." Even if they paid nothing, the publicity value of their presence was well worth the cost. They were photographed at every arrival, and the newspaper reports always mentioned where they were staying.

As for the small shops, a large number of them, including a picture-frame maker on 63rd Street, agreed with jeweler Olga Tritt, who insisted, "The Duchess always paid her bills faster than anybody I know."[18]

At one point, though, the rumors were so widespread that the Duchess felt impelled to declare in print, "We pay our bills."

Commenting wryly on the "special prices" she supposedly got, the Duchess answered, "Always! Windsor prices! They're higher!"

It is unquestionable that a great many things were given to them free of charge and there is also the old-fashioned kingly attitude toward such largesse, "Why not?" It is similarly probable that a number of people didn't even send them bills because they considered the publicity of their purchase or presence well worth the price. All those who knew the Duke generally agree that all those bills which were presented to him were paid.

Hostesses insist that the visiting Windsors would pay their telephone bills and always had gifts for every member of the household staff upon leaving. There is no disagreement, however, that the Duke was an exceptional "pinchpenny." Until the abdication, he had never bothered about money, had never paid a bill or given a tip. An equerry had that responsibility. Until the end of World War II, a royal clerk still handled all his financial affairs. He not only had to learn how to add up a bill in the restaurant, and decide on the proper tip, but also to take care of his own financial records, accounts and checkbooks and investments. This made him persnickety about expenses, even minor items. The Duchess' background of genteel poverty, on the other hand, made her equally conscious of money and value.

Wallis and a friend were discussing another friend who had billions of dollars, both wondering aloud what they would do with that money if they had it. Wallis' friend said that she would spend it as soon as she got it, because she always spent as much as she had. "And I," added Wallis, "would be in debt after I got it."

She always bought only the best, but "she spent money where it showed," emphasized Madame Schiaparelli. "She spent it on food, clothes, her home, but squeezed the money elsewhere." A shrewd shopper, she knew prices and did not like to be fooled. She seldom was. She knew quality and she had taste. She could walk into a strange house, immediately know which was the finest piece in the room, and compliment her hostess on it. A friend laughingly remarked, "She would have made a great buyer at Bloomingdale's."[19]

Two of the few pieces of jewelry she wore most often were bracelets, one on her left wrist of diamond hearts, and another on her right wrist of diamond crosses. "The crosses are crosses I've had to bear," she explained. "Each one stands for something, and so do the hearts. Rather sentimental in this hardboiled world, isn't it?"

One of the crosses could have represented all the never-ending rumors.

Only a few friends were observers in London in November 1946 when the Argentine ambassador and his wife gave a dinner at their embassy in honor of the Duke and Duchess of Windsor. It was a dinner worth admission because the host's name was Felipe A. Espil.

With Wallis Windsor, as with Jennie Churchill, the men in her life once caught, somehow stayed. And like her two former husbands, they had only kind words and tender memories of her until their

442

death. In the case of Espil, he had chosen elsewhere. His wife, the beautiful Courtney Letts de Espil, and Wallis surely had a fascinating evening with each other. Wallis never accounted for her reactions, but Madame de Espil was most generous in hers. She quoted an ambassadress at the dinner who had said, "I always wondered what she had to take the King of England off his throne. Now I know how enchanting she can be." Madame de Espil herself noted more quietly that the Duchess' personality was "beguiling," that she had charm, wit and the ability to enchant those who might be prepared to criticize.

What the ambassador thought of the new Wallis, or she of him, cannot be known. A good guess, though, is that they were both still impressed because the Windsors invited the Espils to dinner in Paris sometime later.

That meeting, however, was not one to attract reporters. An event that stirred up the headlines again was the wedding of Princess Elizabeth and Prince Philip in 1947. The Duke made it plain he would not attend without his wife.

"His attitude is proper, and will be shared by many people," editorialized the London *Evening Standard*, "for any such discrimination against the Duchess would be outrageous. What has the Duchess done that she should be held up to ridicule in this way?"[20]

When the wedding invitation list of 2,200 was revealed, the names of the bride's uncle and his wife were not among them.

Mrs. Thelma Hall Quast of Beggs, Oklahoma, was one of those who declared herself "downright indignant." She felt that the United States should withhold aid under the Marshall Plan until the royal family accepted the American duchess of the former king.

For the Windsors, it was more than just another rebuke. He finally began to realize that family acceptance might never come. It made him all the more insistent that she must be "Her Royal Highness" to the staff. Friends who telephoned often felt awkward in referring to her that way, complained to Wallis. She protested, "It's not me; it's *him. He* wants it that way."[21]

Wallis afterward admitted there was a problem in difference in title. "It is difficult because people are puzzled what to do with me. At parties. At any time. They don't understand being married to Mr. Smith and being called Mrs. Jones."

In defining their relationship, the Duchess reiterated that she had given the Duke all of her affection. To her, this meant "tender, loving care." It meant doing everything to renew his confidence in himself, trying to distract him from his secret concerns, maintaining an ambiance of warmth and gaiety.

This was easier to do in New York, where Wallis almost never said "No" to an invitation.

Ethel Merman sang "Doin' What Comes Naturally" at a party and found the Duke's somewhat squeaky voice joining her in a duet. If his voice was thin, his rhythm was good, and he always knew the words.

He sang "Louise" with Maurice Chevalier, hummed along with Judy Garland. And if the mood was gay enough, the Duke could often be persuaded to do his Sailor's Hornpipe dance or recite, with appropriate gestures, Joe E. Lewis' routine about "being kind to a duck because it might be somebody's brother."

Cole Porter lived on a nearby floor of the Waldorf Towers, which he called "my little boarding house—simple, but good."[22] The Duke and Porter soon found themselves walking their dogs together, meeting in elevators, dropping in on each other for afternoon drinks, going to each other's parties.

Cole Porter was a perfectionist who lived in a world of tight punctuality. When he became crippled, his chauffeur and valet would carry him into restaurants and theaters at precise times. At a dinner party for friends, he timed their arrival at the restaurant exactly at 8:20 and he left them punctually at 9:40 so that he could return home and change and be seated for his private showing of a movie at 10:00 P.M. Cole's friends were all people the Windsors admired: Noel Coward, Beatrice Lillie, Douglas Fairbanks, Jr., Elsa Maxwell, who all came to his magnificent dinner party in honor of the Windsors. Porter reported admiringly on his talk with the Duchess, "It was like playing tennis—back and forth, back and forth."

Someone who met her for the first time marveled at her exuberance and queried a mutual friend, "Is she always like this or is she just putting it on for me?"[23]

She was not. That was her way.

"I love life," she said, "and I love people. I'm never really bored. That gives me the energy to go on."

"New people are very exciting to her," added the Duke. "She enjoys finding out what they think and do. But I've met so many, I've had my share of that."

Except for the entertaining ones, like the Porters and the Cowards. It was at a Porter party that the Duke learned to dance the Charleston. At another party when the conversation became obscene, Mrs. Porter made her classic remark: "My dears, I've heard all those words before, and I've done most of them; but I prefer not having to dine on them."[24]

At still another dinner, the Duchess made a classic remark of her own. When a guest exulted about how much a certain middle-aged matinee idol had done for all the middle-aged men, she replied, "That's nothing to what I did for middle-aged women in 1937."[25]

She still wore very little make-up, just enough rouge to heighten the color of her eyes, but not enough to detract from the pale softness of her skin, then only a faint touch of mascara and only the slightest suspicion of powder and blue eye shadow. The Duchess said she dressed for herself and not for her husband and he added that he would never dare recommend any clothes to her.

Asked how many times a week they went out, she smiled at him and said, "Too much."

But it was never too much for her. And both were filled with the same restless urge to travel.

Lady Mendl invited them to stay with her in Hollywood, and they went. The George Bakers invited them to their 13,000-acre plantation in Tallahassee, Florida, to shoot turkey and quail, and they went. The Arthur Gardners invited them to pleasure at their place in Palm Beach, and they went. The Robert Youngs invited them to Newport, and they went. They went everywhere. Discussing this continual travel, a reporter queried the Duke about plans to settle somewhere permanently in a home of their own.

The Duke seemed somewhat surprised, and answered, "Home is where the Duchess is."[26]

41

"THE DUCHESS OF WINDSOR may be the best wife in the world."[1]

Few women proved it more publicly, or more often. At a party, when the Duke was caught in a corner by someone telling him how he should have run the British Empire, the Duchess was usually the one who first observed his distress and came to the rescue. When they were lunching in Mexico City with the President, she would first tell him, "Now, David, you will be offered tequila and you should not drink it because of the altitude and because it is an unfamiliar drink to you."[2] And he wouldn't. When they had a party, she would brief him on all the dinner guests, what to say to whom, what subjects to avoid.

She was the one who quietly told him to stop speaking German at a dinner because nobody else understood it, except the French generals. She was the one who told an important industrialist, "Please invite him to your plant. He loves to inspect things."[3] And when someone at a party asked her to dance, she answered, "Let's just wait a moment, and see if the Duke dances with anyone else. Otherwise he'll want to dance again with me."[4] She watched him always. When they were being photographed, she whispered, "You're hiding your face with your hat."[5]

When he was tired, she would soothe him. When it was cold, she worried about what he was wearing. When he felt even slightly ill, she immediately called the doctor. She was not only his wife and sweetheart but his sister and mother.

The one thing Wallis wanted most was to make a home for the Duke, a permanent home of their own. The Duke had been asked many times if there was any reason why he should not live permanently in England and he always answered, "No." But after repeated visits, he was sadly reconciled to the fact that he and his wife would never be warmly welcome there. While there was no legal restriction to their return, the establishment had set up an unyielding social bar.

As the 1950s began, Wallis started a serious search for a permanent home. "My husband was a king and I wanted him to live like one," she said. She even considered Comtesse Du Barry's mansion, but the ensuing publicity of owning the home of a French king's mistress— even though eighteenth-century—was not worth the price.

The house they finally found belonged to the City of Paris, and French president Charles de Gaulle once had lived there. The French government was honored to let the Windsŏrs lease it for a token rental, scarcely more than the traditional price of a peppercorn.

The Windsors loved it. It had the air and style of a miniature palace. Faced with stone and great columns, the building had a slate roof and a two-story-high rose and green marble entry hall. It had privacy. A giant gate with a high spiked iron fence surrounded the estate. It had space—a small palatial park of more than two acres with ancient trees.

Sitting at the edge of the Bois de Boulogne, No. 4 Route du Champ d'Entraînement had more of a feeling of a forest than a street. Yet, to Wallis' delight, it was only fifteen minutes' drive to the heart of Paris.

She had a small gold crown hung on the lantern at the entrance, gold spearheads put on top of the railing, old replicas of the royal arms mounted on the walls, and the banner with the arms of the Prince of Wales suspended from the wrought-iron railing above the foyer. Flanking the entrance in the drawing room she hung full-length portraits of the Duke and his mother, each wearing the magnificent robes of the Order of the Garter. On the library table, in jewel-encrusted frames, were pictures of his great-grandmother Queen Victoria, his grandmother Queen Alexandra and, again, his mother, Queen Mary. On another table stood a painting of Windsor Castle.

The footmen wore blue and silver livery with the insignia of the Grenadier Guards and the first thing guests saw as they entered was a battered red leather dispatch box which was stamped "The King."

While she didn't want him to remember too much, she also didn't want anyone else to forget.

She had made the rooms personal. "I play with my house all the time," she once said. She searched everywhere for the exact antique. "I'd rather shop than eat," Wallis told her friend Eleanor Miles, adding that she preferred furniture and china to jewels.[6] For the two-story hall she had a giant German globe, eighteenth-century consoles with flower-filled silver vases, all of it reflected in octagonal mirrors, high-backed Chinese Chippendale chairs with a tall eighteenth-century Chinese screen.

The long, palatial drawing room faced the terrace and parklike lawn. The walls were pale blue, the moldings silver-tasseled and the furniture eighteenth-century French. The tables were covered with an extraordinary collection of gold, vermeil, porcelain and enameled bibelots, including a profusion of Meissen pugs in all positions. The Duchess had a piece of felt under each bibelot, cut to its exact shape so as not to mar the table surface. For the more delicate objects she placed wax impressions under the bases, so they would sit firmly and not jar.

For the dining room, she had found the Chateau de Chanteloup faded blue boiserie and large panels of chinoiserie wallpaper gracefully designed with birds and boats and trees. She had them restored and installed and the ceiling painted with flowers and ribbons. She designed the chairs of blue-green wood with white damask upholstered seats and lit the area with ostrich egg candelabra.

At dinner, they could choose from an eighteenth-century china service that had belonged to Queen Alexandra, a Lowestoft with crown and cipher of George IV, a Lowestoft with embossed gold leaves and royal arms of William IV, or the Meissen "Flying Tiger" service of the Elector Frederick Augustus I of Saxony, king of Poland, which the Duke inherited.

In the library, facing the dining room, she had yellow and gold panels, a yellow silk sofa in an alcove lined with orange-yellow velvet. The paintings were English and historical. On another yellow sofa, which she designed, the Duchess had red velvet cushions made from a cardinal's cape. Over the fireplace hung the Brockhurst portrait of the Duchess in a dark blue dress.

The books concentrated on royal history, and included Churchill's four-volume biography of Marlborough. Churchill autographed the first two volumes to the Prince of Wales, the third to the King and Volume IV to the Duke of Windsor.

The Duke and the Duchess lived on the upper floor, their separate bedroom suites connected by a boudoir. In this boudoir, which served as a study and drawing room, the two shared their newspapers, magazines, letters and scissors. Each had a separate desk. The Duchess had an eighteenth-century secretary lacquered in green, black and gold. On it was a photograph of the Duke as king, mounted on his charger in the Trooping of the Colors. Beside it was a book on the art of conjugating French verbs.

The Duke's suite of rooms was full of the memorabilia of his past, but with pictures everywhere of Wallis. The Duchess quoted Aunt Bessie's description of his suite: "The sort of rooms where everything is hung up on the floor."[7] He had formed an early habit of spreading out his papers in all conceivable corners, but knowing exactly where everything was. He could then sit in a low chair and study them. If she came in he would say, "I'll soon have them cleared away, darling."

Her own rooms were pale-blue, gray-blue and mauve, and her bedroom was surprising. Those who wonder about her warmth can find it there. Instead of the museum look of some of the other rooms, her own had a quiet coziness, the chaise and chairs looking soft and easy, and pillows everywhere. Pictures of pug dogs were crocheted on many of the pillows, but one had the message "You can never be too rich or too thin."

Outside of her room the Duchess "got ulcers if anything is crooked." She detested dust or disorder.

"I'm almost too fussy a housekeeper," she added. "My friends are almost afraid to sit down for fear of disarranging the cushions."[8]

A woman's home is like a man's library. It reveals her personality. However palatial her Paris home, with a strong accent on the formal, there was still classic simplicity about most of the furnishings. Flowers were everywhere, in giant arrangements with a vivid use of color. They gave the home a warmth and an intimacy. Besides their own rooms upstairs there were only two guest rooms, with a bath between them. The dining room seated twenty-six, but there were seldom that many. The Duchess always preferred eight or ten as a perfect number. If she had to have more, she usually set up two tables of eight. More than that, she felt, made conversation difficult.

After choosing the china service for the meal, she conferred with the linen maid about a proper satin undercloth and lace cover to enhance the china, and she made certain that the maid ironed every wrinkle in that lace. She similarly decided on the silver and the centerpiece and the overall color scheme. She might decide this as early as two weeks in advance. The chef sent her sample menus five days before the party and she reshaped them according to the tastes of her guests. Before the Duke's death, if she wanted to have a new dish, they would try it themselves first alone.

One of her specialties was "Avocado Tahiti," halves of avocado filled with rum and brown sugar. It seemed to take some of the starch out of stuffy guests. Another favorite was a jellied consommé, the center filled with caviar, topped with sour cream. Still another was a fish soufflé with curry sauce and Major Grey's chutney heated with butter. She also made a dessert called Montego Bay ice, which consists of lime or lemon sherbet served with hot rum sauce. One of her most popular dishes—a recipe she jealously guarded—was "Camembert glacé," an iced cheese flavored with Camembert, mixed with wine and refrigerated.

"She also was the first to serve champagne with ice," said her friend Edmund Bory. "The ice seems to take out the acid and the gas. My friends who *own* Moët & Chandon and Piper Heidsieck, two of the most important champagne companies in the world, now only drink champagne with ice cubes in it. And so do I."[9]

Bory, who owns a chain of gourmet food shops in Paris, calls the Duchess a *maîtresse de maison;* not just a perfectionist, "but a powerful perfectionist."[10]

Wallis' own view is that "You don't get any original food if you don't work with the cook."

"She knows precisely what she wants," said her chef. "She is very critical. It is good to work for someone to whom only perfection is acceptable. Otherwise, one's standards would fall."[11]

Not only did she classify her guests as to whether they were champagne people or claret people or hard liquor people, and select accordingly, but she actually kept a book listing the menu, wine, table setting, guest list, seating plan and after-dinner amusements for each dinner party. She wanted to avoid any repetition.

When Baron Cabrol and his wife spent a fortnight with the Duke and Duchess, every meal was on a different terrace, in a different setting. Wallis kept them completely at ease. She once confided a secret to a friend, "When you're a hostess, you only sit down when you can't stand up."[12]

One of her butlers, Ernest King, wondered what might have been had she moved to Buckingham Palace. "I shudder to think what a stir she would have caused among the servants, who have not the reputation of being unduly overworked."[13]

In the Duchess' home, the crystal sparkled, the leather gleamed, the furniture shone. During a meal, her eyes worked overtime to keep the butler aware of filled ashtrays and glasses that need refilling. She had a small gold book in which she wrote comments and complaints about meals and other things which she then told the butler. She once explained this need for strict control by saying, "I married a bell ringer."

The Duke was a bell ringer when it came to service. Instant service was a prerogative of kings. It did not seem outlandish to him that a bellhop at the Waldorf in New York flew down to New Orleans to bring him his white tie and tails for a big ball. With food, however, he was not a gourmet. Nor did he like wine. Give him a big breakfast that might include anything from kippers to chicken hash to bacon and eggs, a large glass of grapefruit juice and pots of tea, then he could eliminate lunch entirely. If he were home, he might lunch on some fruit, and his wife often persuaded him to have rice pudding or custard by serving it in a pretty porcelain or pottery dish.

Teatime was never later than five, and Wallis tried to join him then no matter what her other plans. It was the highlight of the day for the Duke. They would relax together either in the garden or in front of a fireplace or in their comfortable sitting room. "High tea" often meant assorted sandwiches, hot squares of melted cheese and bacon, shrimps in their shells, toast, cornbread, petits fours, jam, marmalade, cookies.

"Most Englishmen prefer India's tea," the Duchess told Bob Considine. "The Duke prefers China's. He gets it in New York. It's the same tea that J. Pierpont Morgan used to bring over to England. The Duke carries it with him on trips, even to the golf course."[14]

He drank it from an oversize cup, with milk in it.

For dinner he ate the simplest foods, steaks and chops, couldn't abide onions, and garlic was "death to him." He also liked a haddock soufflé and loved kedgeree shad roe cooked with milk. *Rødgrød* was another of the Duke's delicacies, a dessert of raspberries and currants, served with milk, that his grandmother Queen Alexandria had brought from Denmark. "I also like fattening Austrian and German food and a great deal of American food, too," he once added, smiling at his wife.

Instead of the formal dinners Wallis loved, the Duke preferred their

Sunday night suppers alone. He would set up the card table with china, linen and silver while Wallis created something simple in the kitchen. She had her own way of cooking bacon by heating thin slices, kept in the oven until some of the fat was melted, then coating it with brown sugar before reheating. As the sugar melted, the bacon was turned, the other side sugared and baked until crisp. Sometimes they simply took their food on trays and ate in front of the television set.

Wallis would content herself with tea and toast for breakfast, take along some soup in a vacuum jug or a piece of chicken if she was to be at the hairdresser through lunch. One of her few food phobias was tomato seeds. She would dismiss an entire dish if she saw a single one.

She, too, preferred simple dinners—lamb cutlets and spinach, plainly roasted game or poultry, grilled fish or grilled calves' liver with lemon juice; plenty of salad and fruit but no bread and potatoes. These were typical dishes when they dined alone. As the years went by, both ate less and less.

"He didn't want to be fat and she didn't want to be fat," remarked a close friend. "After fighting fat for forty years, dieting comes naturally."[15]

The house in the Bois gave the Duke everything except the one thing he wanted most—a garden. It did have greenhouses, where Wallis grew orchids in pots, and it had ancient oaks and a close-clipped lawn, but it didn't have an area where he could create and putter.

This he had at The Mill. Le Moulin de la Tuilerie was only a twenty-minute drive from their Paris home, but the feeling of difference was as great as that of St. James's Palace and Fort Belvedere. The Fort had been the single thing he most missed in leaving England. The old Mill would be his new Fort.

"First, there was the quiet and pleasant valley, sheltered by woods of oak, sweet chestnut and Scotch fir," the Duke remembered. "Second, there was the water. The Merentaise separates into two small streams that flow down the valley and meet at The Mill itself. And third, there was The Mill."

The Mill was a tiny hamlet of four buildings with a cobbled court that dated from the seventeenth century. The stone walls of the buildings were two feet thick and the beams were a foot square, hand-hewn. Workers here had milled grain in the age of Elizabeth and the grain storage room had become the main living room. It had been remodeled in 1730, and it later became the residence of artist Etienne Drian. It was the first and only house the Windsors ever owned together.

The twenty acres were partly enclosed by ancient walls and the Duke saw the garden as "a chaos of cabbages and chickens" with some fruitless old trees and a few rose-covered wire hoops. "It was the chance for the first time in my life to create a garden of my own."

Wallis gave the house itself a sophisticated rusticity. There were no bathrooms and Wallis put one in for every bedroom. She added a modern kitchen, a swimming pool and a cabana. The main building had ten rooms, including a formal dining room, a sitting room, a small library, a thirty-five-foot drawing room, two master suites plus service rooms. To get from the Duke's room to the Duchess', one went across the hall and up a small flight of stairs. Her bedroom was a long, low-beamed room in pink and light-green, and his had the feeling of a loft, littered with golf books, an autographed picture of Arnold Palmer, old 78 rpm records of *Carousel,* sheet music from *Gypsy,* stacks of old magazine articles and newspaper clippings, one of which read: CRISIS THAT ROCKED EMPIRE.

Cattle stalls were converted into guest rooms and the barn made into a museum of the Duke's kingly past. Pipe banners of the Seaforth Highlanders were hung on the walls, and drums of the Grenadier and Welsh Guards served as tables. There he kept his commissions in the Royal Navy and Army, trophies from pig-sticking and steeplechase contests, a specimen of every button used by the British Army during World War I, a curving razor-sharp Gurkha kukri, a thermometer from the top of the Empire State Building, a medal struck when he first visited the United States in 1919, a bronze statuette of a hunter, the mugs for his coronation in 1937, three golf balls mounted in silver representing "three accidental occasions on which I made a hole-in-one," and a commemorative mug for Neville Chamberlain when he returned from Munich, on which was printed: PEACE IN OUR TIME.

"This table might interest you," the Duke told a guest on a guided tour of his museum. It was Chippendale, delicately carved, covered with framed photographs of royal ancestors. On it was a small plaque which read:

> *On this table King Edward VIII*
> *signed the instrument of abdication*
> *at* 10:30 A.M. *December 11, 1936.*

Starting with dirty, naked walls, the Duchess had imbued The Mill with an informal coziness, making generous use of colorful Italian pottery, comfortable divans and chairs, fireplaces of beautiful stone, flame and yellow curtains, padded banquettes big enough to seat a dozen people, ceramic fruit scattered as ashtrays and paintings everywhere of flowers, fruits and vegetables.

Wallis had a penchant for abstract art which the Duke did not share. Once she bought a painting and had it hung in the hallway. The Duke saw it and turned it upside down. Later that afternoon the Duchess asked him if he had seen anything new in the house.

"No, not really," he answered.

"It's right in front of you," she said. "It's that painting."

"Oh, and it's an abstract," he commented. "But it's upside down."

"That's how much you know about it," she replied with some irritation.

"Really?" he answered. "Take it off the wall and look at the signature."[16]

After looking at the signature and at her husband, Wallis returned the painting to the artist.

Like the Paris house, this one also was filled with flowers. Everywhere, too, was a plethora of pillows with embroidered messages which emphasized the informality: "Never Explain—Never Complain," "Don't Look Now—Somebody May Be Gaining on You," "A Cat May Look at a King" and "Smile at the Poorest Tramp as You Would the Highest King."

The former king often looked like a tramp out here, but a happy one, working hard alongside three other gardeners to make a rock garden and transforming an overgrown French yard into an enchanting old English garden—a lavender hedge, a rose garden and herbaceous borders with giant delphiniums, all within view of the French doors of the house. In contrast to the geometrical formality of the French, an English garden stresses a random planting of grass and flowers. The Duke spent two years working intensely at it, begrudging any time he spent elsewhere.

"You would see him lugging those stones for the rock garden or flailing away with a scythe," an aide remembered.[17]

"There wasn't a thing here, nothing," emphasized the Duke proudly. "I put in every stone."

A garden was a mood, explained the Duke, quoting Rousseau, and the Duke's mood was intimacy. At The Fort he had drafted guests to help hack out huge laurel bushes, installing a tidy landscape of shrubs and flowers. In Nassau, he was the governor and it was improper to do his own gardening—there were prisoners for that. But he planned what he wanted—and after he left, the one thing that worried him was that someone would rearrange his garden.

Here at The Mill, he gradually filled the old walled garden with phlox and lupines, chrysanthemums and asters and roses of a dozen colors. His prize was the Duke of Windsor rose, which an English gardener had created and named for him. His bedroom had eight long windows, almost bringing the garden inside to him. Alongside the kitchen, the Duke made a cutting garden for his wife. In the course of time, he even built a series of small dams to break the flow of the stream and create waterfalls.

The Duke was happy at The Mill. Wallis described it as "his house." They spent weekends and holidays here. Harry Reasoner asked the Duchess what was so different about life at The Mill.

"It's very quiet here," she answered. "You never hear a sound."[18]

Their friend Mrs. Merriweather-Post had a plaque made for their garden which read:

> *The kiss of the sun for pardon,*
> *The song of the birds for mirth.*
> *One is nearer God's heart in a garden*
> *Than anywhere else on earth.*

For him, not her. For her, no place was as important as people. For him, there was only one person in his life. His ties with the royal family were torn. His loyal friends were few. She was his sun and moon.

"I found it touching," remembered a secretary, Dina Wells Hood. "He watched her every movement, responded to every inflection of her voice, was restless in her absence. He never made any attempt to conceal his feelings. More than once, I saw him take her impulsively in his arms and kiss her tenderly. He bought her exquisite jewelry. Nothing was too good for her.

"Sometimes she would call him from a distance, from the garden or another part of the house. Then he would leave whatever he was doing at once. You could hear his voice calling to her from afar, 'Coming, darling,' or 'Yes, sweetheart.'

"I have seen him, in the middle of a haircut in his dressing room, get up and run to his wife, leaving the startled hairdresser agape."[19]

One thing that made him impatient, and even angry, was a late tea. Once, though, he even forgot to be annoyed when he heard the Duchess sneeze. "He came running into the reception room. 'Dolly! Dolly! I do hope you aren't taking cold,' using his intimate name for her, the dimunitive of darling. He then went from room to room, closing windows, making sure there was a fire in the fireplace of every room where she was apt to go."[20]

Even in the last years of their marriage, if he went to bed before she did, the Duchess would come to her room and often find a single white flower on her pillow.

Something else that channeled his energy at this time was his autobiography. It was something creative and specific and provided him with a new purpose. Wallis continued to accept invitations to dinners and parties but the Duke now had an excuse to stay home. "Can't you say 'No' sometime?" he would say to her.

They continued to make their annual visits to the United States in the spring for four months, and then regular trips to the Riviera and London (for him, mostly) and Biarritz.

It was in Biarritz that they met Jimmy Donahue. James P. Donahue was the son of their friend Jessie Woolworth Donahue of Palm Beach, New York and Southampton. She had the reputation of being a non-drinker, a nonsmoker and a great gambler. She could afford it. Mrs. Donahue was the daughter of Frank Woolworth, founder of the Woolworth dime store fortune of 600 stores and $78 million. In 1950, the year Jimmy first met the Windsors, he had inherited $15 million. He was then thirty-five years old, gay, debonair, handsome. Wallis was almost twenty years older, but they were kindred spirits.

As a young man, Donahue had dropped out of the exclusive Choate School in Connecticut and soon found himself tagged by the press as the Playboy of Park Avenue. His charming, genial father had been a backer of Florenz Ziegfeld, and young Jimmy similarly plunged into show business. He got a short-lived role as a dancer in *Hot and Bothered* in 1933, took on assorted jobs as assistant stage manager to learn the business, and then became a producer of such quick flops as *Transatlantic Rhythm*. A number of showgirls were associated with his name, but never seriously or for long.

The press found it more interesting that Jimmy went along on the honeymoon of his favorite first cousin, Barbara Hutton, another Woolworth heir. That was a round-the-world wedding trip with Georgian Prince Alexis Mdivani. He also went along on Barbara Hutton's honeymoon with her second husband, Count Kurt Haugwitz-Reventlow of Denmark, when they visited Italy in 1935. Reporters observed that Jimmy acted as unofficial bodyguard, carrying a pistol under his coat. In Italy he created a tumult when young fascists were holding a street celebration of Italy's invasion of Ethiopia by shouting from a balcony in Venice, "Viva Ethiopia!" He was quickly ushered over the border to France.

He piloted civil air patrol planes in the early years of World War II, spent a short time as a private in the Army and later bought the Vanderbilt mansion on a 108-acre estate in Old Brookville, Long Island. There he had frequent parties for "all the beautiful people," as he called them. If the Folies Bergère was in town, he would invite the whole show to entertain his guests. His chef was the best that money could buy.

Donahue was everything the Duke was not. The Duke was a ripe audience for his wife's wit, but Jimmy generated his own. The Duke was highly organized, punctual about appointments and responsibilities; Jimmy was completely carefree, did almost everything on whim. The Duke was a pinchpenny; Jimmy was profligate. The Duke was precise in all habits; Jimmy was an impulsive man who believed that if you made a gesture, you must make a grand gesture.

The Duke enjoyed Jimmy; Wallis loved him.

She had lived all these years with a man who absolutely idolized her. Her whole life had been dedicated to him, and she had no complaint. Their life had moved in predictable patterns and she had enjoyed the social status and the changing scenes. But she was now in her mid-fifties. She had just heard about the death of her first husband, and it made her ponder her mortality.

Besides that, even as a girl, she was the one among all her friends who was always first in reaching for something more, something different.

Jimmy was very different. What he offered was what she wanted most: fantasy. To make her patterned life more exciting she wanted the unexpected, the unpredictable. An unceasing diet of adoration can be wearing. The cocoon was tight and she had a need to break out. Now that the Duke had increasingly tied himself down with his book, and she refused to stay home, she needed an escort.

Jimmy was perfect. He entertained her the way she had entertained the Duke. "He makes me laugh, he always makes me laugh," she told a friend. Above all, he supplied fantasy. If it was a cloudy day, he might say, "There are clouds up there, let's get the clouds away by doing something with sunshine in it," or, "Let's go somewhere where there are no clouds." If the Duke was with them and mentioned that they couldn't do that because somebody was coming to dinner, Jimmy was apt to say, "All right, let's prepare a wonderful dinner for him, but let's not be there."

The Duchess loved that. It was marvelous being the audience rather than the performer. More than that, she discovered that she and Donahue sparked each other. They both had the same kind of wit, the same kind of gaiety, the same kind of imagination.

If she was a perfectionist, he was more so. She matched the color of her placemats and china to the color of her cut flowers, but Jimmy grew flowers to match the colors of the rooms in which they would appear. Wallis collected Meissen, but Jimmy would pay $17,000 for a single piece of porcelain and had a wider range of expertise.

Donahue not only was a spirited conversationalist, but also was fluent in a half-dozen languages. He could not only play the whole score of *Tosca* on the piano, but sing it in French. Despite his playboy image, which he deserved, his friends also knew him as serious and loyal. He was almost always "up," but a close few knew his "down" side, his deeply disturbed feeling that everybody loved him only for his money. Since he sat on top of the Social Register he was little impressed by the outer show of people. He "adored" the Duchess because she was so "natural." She had a nickname for him and he reveled in it; she called him "Bunny."

Jimmy was also a "safe" escort. He was a homosexual.

This was no secret. He was not a blatant, overt homosexual. He did not simper or preen. But there was no question about it, everyone in their set knew. Donahue, however, also liked being with bright, pretty women.

She found his attention flattering. He didn't simply send her a dozen roses, he would send five dozen. Instead of a violinist to serenade her at dinner, he would have a whole orchestra follow them wherever they went. He was lavish with his gifts. When they were visiting a museum and she admired a painting, he was overheard saying, "Shall I buy it for you for Christmas?" She simply laughed and answered, "I'd rather have all the Woolworth stores in Boston."[21]

Some friends felt Donahue was acting the role in the refrain of the song "I Danced With the Boy Who Danced With the Girl Who Danced With the Prince of Wales." In that sense, it was something similar to Aly Khan's conquest of Lady Furness. Others who knew Donahue well claimed it was much more than that. It was true, he felt himself riding with history, and in an international spotlight. But Wallis had captured him in the same way that her attentive charm had captured so many other men.

James Donahue had his own needs. His $15 million and Woolworth background gave him international entree, but his homosexuality remained a trauma for him. He sensed the public smirking. It partly explained his much-publicized earlier encounters with showgirls. A mutual friend even insisted he was bisexual. Wallis gave him her sensitive and affectionate understanding, perhaps even a greater feeling of self-confidence. If he wanted to feel more masculine than he was, perhaps she was able to make him feel it. She had had much practice in that.

In any event, Jimmy Donahue soon became much more than an escort; he became, in effect, almost a part of the family. Hostesses were soon made aware that when they invited the Duke and Duchess, they should also invite Donahue. Elsa Maxwell later claimed to have a number of telegrams from the Duchess specifying this.

Friends noted carefully that Donahue was highly respectful of the Duke at all times. In his lavish way, he insisted on picking up all the checks and many of the bills. He also gave the Duke several expensive gifts such as gold cufflinks with sapphires.

"The Duke was very tolerant about it," claimed one of his closest friends, "maybe too tolerant. He was a jealous man even when there was no cause for jealousy. He was jealous of anyone who shared any of her time."[22]

Jimmy and Wallis were both "night people" who enjoyed staying up until the early hours of the morning. Wallis had not had much of this kind of company for a long time. When Doc Holden visited the Windsors years before and spent much of the night sitting up with Wallis talking, the Duke made it a point of coming down in his bathrobe almost every half-hour. Since Jimmy's company stretched out for years, it is difficult to imagine the range and boundary of the Duke's feelings. There are those, however, who insist that the Duke enjoyed Jimmy as much as Wallis did.

At the beginning of this unusual situation, the Duchess went alone to New York in the winter of 1950. The Duke had business about his book in France. The press pounced on the separation. This was the first time they had traveled apart except for his trips to England. Headlines used the word "rift." Was this the beginning of the end of the romance of the century? New York reporters observed Wallis and Jimmy Donahue as a steady duet. Elsa Maxwell publicly cautioned the Duchess on the importance of "appearance" and "discretion." This was the first crack in their friendship.

Elsa Maxwell disguised herself as a fortuneteller at a party given by Mrs. Millicent Hearst. When Wallis entered the dark room, she said, "Tell me the worst. I can take it."

Elsa Maxwell answered in a foreign accent, "O, there is no worst, lady, because your husband loves you. All will be well if you return his love. If you do not, I see trouble. Big trouble."[23]

When the Duke arrived at the New York dock about ten days later, Wallis had been waiting almost an hour for him at the gangplank in the cold wind. They were both much more demonstrative than usual in their public show of affection, hugging and kissing many times. To the reporters' queries of a rift, they looked at each other and laughed.

The Duchess was hospitalized in 1951 for an undisclosed operation. During the recovery period she stayed on in New York while the Duke waited at a friend's home on Long Island. She had persuaded him to go there because she said she knew how much he wanted to play golf. The doctor delayed her departure from New York, and she was reported to be attending parties with Jimmy. The Duke became increasingly restless. One of the other guests overheard him telling her over the phone, "And I want you down here by Friday, no later." It was the first time this friend ever had heard the Duke being so commanding and peremptory to the Duchess.

The three seemed to travel everywhere together. Jimmy's mother was their hostess in Palm Beach. They even traveled throughout Europe together. Occasionally, the three would arrive at a party and the Duke would go home alone soon afterward. When the Duke was too tired to go at all, the Duchess often tried to get a mutual friend to join her and Jimmy as a chaperone. When a friend once would not go with them, she was indignant.

They were all in New York in February 1952, when the Duke's brother King George died. The Duke went alone to the funeral. Royal circles buzzed with stories of Queen Elizabeth's bitterness. The unwanted kingship, she felt, had shortened her husband's life. She would never forgive the Duke.

The Duke knew his sister-in-law's feelings well, and was not much concerned. What did bother him, as always, was Wallis. He blamed himself for the renewed spate of rumors. He traced many of their problems to the rain of royal indignities heaped on his wife. He blamed himself for not having the foresight to insist on her proper status before his abdication. He knew how simply it could all be settled. The new Queen Elizabeth was his favorite niece and she had publicly proclaimed him as her favorite uncle. All she had to do was to invite the Duke and Duchess of Windsor to her coronation. The whole social atmosphere would suddenly clear. Establishment doors would open. Perhaps they might even move back to England, back where he belonged. He would be happy anywhere with Wallis, but he could never be completely happy away from his native land.

The young, unsure new Queen Elizabeth consulted her advisers. The advisers consulted the government. The government said no.

The Duke had told Wallis often, "We must not go anywhere that we can't enter by the front door."

They watched the coronation on television with a small group of friends. Both made frequent comments about the young queen, praising her poise and dignity. The Duke remarked how the coronation ritual with costumes and jewelry so much better fit a young, pretty woman than a man. He pointed out the way the Queen sat with her hands crossed in front of her, giving a feeling of humility that was most difficult for a man to portray.

But when the crown was put on Elizabeth's head, the Duke turned toward his wife, brushed his hands across his eyes in a gesture a man uses to fight back tears.

Still Margaret Thompson Biddle felt that their behavior then was enormously poised. "They are big, generous, natural people."

Their generosity stopped at the point of forgiveness. "Would you see your family if they wouldn't see your wife?" the Duke asked an interviewer.[24]

The Duke's mother died the following year, and he went back for the funeral. He had had cold words about her, but he kept a large portrait of her in his drawing room and smaller framed pictures throughout the house. He had had so little love from his parents, but _what he did get he got from her. She saw herself as a queen first, a mother second. She did what her son could never do; she put her duty above her emotions. At his abdication, her sympathy was not with him but with her second son, who would become king.

She had given David her genes and her heritage, but not her intimacy and seldom enough love.

Jimmy Donahue was no longer always in regular attendance, although his appearance was never surprising. Once the Duchess went alone to a fancy-dress ball given by Elsa Maxwell at the Champs Elysées Restaurant in Paris. Jimmy Donahue was already there and the two were photographed. The reporter noted that the Duchess did not stay long and was escorted home by Mr. Donahue. Donahue was also with the Windsors in 1954 on a Mediterranean cruise, and again made the news when some thieves stole six of his sports jackets, a golden rosary, his passport and $2,000 in cash.

Society watchers noted that Jimmy's appearance with the Windsors became less frequent. When he was with them his adoration of the Duchess seemed unabated and her interest in him likewise unflagging. Something, though, had happened, and friends wondered what it was. Their best reasoning was that the Duke had made a stand. Friends quickly came into the breach to invite the Windsors without Jimmy. Elsa Maxwell made a point of having a photographer at one of her parties take a picture of the Duke and Duchess together dancing, and smiling.

It was in March 1955 that society columnist Cholly Knickerbocker reported:

The great friendship of the Duchess of Windsor for James Donahue, heir to the Woolworth nickel-and-dime store fortune and a cousin of Barbara Hutton, has long been a conversation piece in society. For the last two years there is no question that the witty and carefree Jimmy enjoyed the position of No. 1 favorite at the all-millionaires' court of the former King of England and his American Duchess. Whether in New York or Europe, an evening rarely went by that the Duke and Duchess and Mr. Donahue were not seen together.

They carried European waters ensemble, and Jimmy and his mother, the kindly and generous Jessie Woolworth Donahue, were often hosts to the ducal pair—but now the great friendship seems to have cooled, and society doesn't know what to make of it. For the last few weeks the Windsors and Donahue have failed to appear anywhere together, and even though the Duke went to Palm Beach alone, Jimmy and the Duchess have not made a single night spot together, a steady occurrence until a few weeks ago.

When I spoke to him, Jimmy explained that he was still on very good terms with the Duke and Duchess, but that he was "tired of all those large dinner parties," and that's why he kept away from it all. But it's not only the large affairs that Donahue is avoiding; he's not appearing at the Windsors' small gatherings either.

Perhaps the gaiety was gone, perhaps the unexpected had become predictable, perhaps the charm was no longer there. Or perhaps she discovered that the parallel lines of her life had bent and clashed, that her love for the Duke was more enduring and deeper than she had articulated even to herself, and that her choice was clear.

Donahue had lasted a long time, almost five years. Whatever had been there no longer existed. For all her great imagination, Wallis Windsor was also a pragmatic woman. She surely knew that the situation was untenable. Despite his gallantry and understanding and great manners, the Duke had his own limits of tolerance.

Donahue disappeared from the headlines, gave large sums to charities, hospitals and the Metropolitan Opera. He confided to his best friends how much he missed Wallis, but he almost never spoke of the Duke. Once, though, he almost belligerently insisted to a small group of friends that the Duke was not a homosexual. Jimmy and the Windsors seldom saw each other in later years, although Jimmy once had a big party for them at his Long Island home. He still traveled with an entourage, still impulsively chartered planes for foreign countries. But friends noted a growing depression. He talked more of his father, who had committed suicide. Then one day he was found dead of acute alcoholic and barbiturate intoxication.

It had been a strange interval for the Duke and Duchess. Afterward they seemed to wipe it out of their minds. Friends never again recalled any conversation about Donahue. Their lives once more regained the familiar pattern. The fantasy was finished.

42

"I am well aware that there are still some people in the world who go on hoping our marriage will break up. And to them I say, 'Give up hope,' because David and I are happy . . . And that's the way it will continue to be."

At The Mill some years later Wallis said to an old friend, "You think I destroyed him, don't you? Why don't you tell me?"[1]

Guilt for each other was something they would feel as long as they lived. They buried it as deeply as they could but it often seemed to surface during periods of stress. Still, when asked how they would like to spend the rest of their lives, the Duke quickly answered, "Together."

To the never-ending question as to whether he had had any regrets about the abdication, his stock answer was "Not for a single second."

That is hard to believe. It is true that no known friend of his has ever been quoted as ever remembering the Duke expressing any such feeling. He had been bred to contain such complaints. But surely, in their life of leisure and elegance, there were also long stretches of emptiness, the sense of waste. Wallis had had the lifetime job of replacing the British Empire, all the pressing appointments and those red leather dispatch boxes arriving by special courier. It was a herculean job and she had succeeded beyond measure. She had approximated for him the comfortable outer shell of life, framed with the reassuring feeling of habit.

"I've never had a dull moment with the Duchess," he said often, and with emphasis.[2]

They knew that the whole world was jealous of what they had done and what they had, and that some people even had prayed for the failure of the marriage. This knowledge tied them even more tightly together. Commenting on this, a friend said, "What's wrong with a woman depending on a man, and a man depending on a woman?"[3] In the early part of their marriage, his dependence on her was greater than hers on him; as the years passed their dependence became more mutual.

Etta Wanger, who was a generation younger, once told the Duchess that her husband Harry was not only her lover but her friend. "That's the way David and I are."[4] Though the Duchess was the power and force in their house, the Duke was still the hub of it.

The ebullient Etta, who was as natural as the Duchess, recalled a gay deception she and Wallis had played on some luncheon guests, saying, "That's a great act; you could have played it at the Palace."[5] She was, of course, referring to the Palace Theater in New York. But she, the Duchess and the Duke suddenly realized what had been said and broke into laughter. Later, when Wallis referred to her husband as His Royal Highness, Etta again started laughing.

"What's so funny now?" asked the Duchess.

"Well, that's what my mother used to call my father when he was reluctant to take out the garbage."

The Duchess' laugh was now as loud as Etta's. "Well, I sometimes have trouble getting him to do things too," she said.[6]

One of Etta's memories which typified the tone of the Windsors' life at the time concerned a miniature jukebox they had in the sitting room between their bedrooms. A gift from a friend, it was unused because they didn't seem to know how to operate it. Etta bought a batch of records and she and the Duchess finally got it to work. The first record came on very very loud. She and the Duchess started improvising a dance to a song called "Winchester Cathedral," when the Duke rushed out of his room wearing an old bathrobe.

"I thought you'd come out looking like Douglas Fairbanks, Jr.," Etta told him, still dancing.

The Duke went back to his room, quickly returned looking like Douglas Fairbanks, Jr.,[7] then started dancing with each of them, one after another.

"They really enjoyed each other," Etta said afterward. "It was a good marriage."[8]

"I have a responsibility, a great one, to give him twenty-four hours of my day, because of what he gave up for me," the Duchess told a friend.[9]

"I needed her all those years," the Duke said. "I love her and need her now. I always will."[10]

When they reached their sixties in the mid-1950s, some friends expected Wallis to slow down and the Duke to retire to his initialed velvet slippers. The Duke more willingly would have done this, but the Duchess "was always so gay, so gay, and she never wanted to stop—whatever it was."

Her fun sometimes had a frenzy to it. In Palm Beach perhaps it was linked to Helena Rubinstein's slogan, "Triumph Over Time." The resort had become a popular stop for the jet set. Here was the place of therapeutic sunshine and ever-present parties where the rich and famous hoped that time really would stop.

This meant maintaining a pulsating social life, accepting all interesting invitations. Wallis often repeated that she had married a saint, but even the saint felt impelled to occasionally protest, "Must we see these people again?" and "Can't you sometimes say 'No'?"

"No" was not a word that featured largely in Wallis' vocabulary.

There no longer seemed to be a Paris set or a New York set or a Newport set—they were all merged somehow into an international set, jetting from place to place with the seasons and the sun.

Wallis was not quite part of the swinging group, although she tried hard. She kept up with the styles, the music, the dances, the gossip, the books. She had more energy than many of the younger women, and her looks belied her years. If anybody triumphed over time, she did. Perhaps she did it better at Palm Beach than in Paris because she suddenly felt free of the French formality. The frenzy entered the picture only because she was a woman in her sixties. The difficulty in "swinging" also came from the fact that she had a status above and beyond the international set. When she arrived at the end of the social season in Palm Beach, her presence there simply extended the season.

She knew her social power and enjoyed it, and used it. The five square miles of Palm Beach had grown gradually into one of the pleasure places of the world. The chic shops of Worth Avenue were as eye-filling as any anywhere. The jewelry and gowns at the Palm Beach charity balls could have financed a full-scale war against poverty. The exclusivity of the Everglades Club maintained almost a sacrosanct quality. When Wallis and the Duke first arrived there, Palm Beach had not yet felt the incursion of the poor millionaires, but still belonged to the super-rich as well as to the transient remaining royalty of the world.

Wallis was Her Royal Highness here. Despite all her protests, this had much meaning for her. It is one thing for an ordinary socialite to swing loose at a party, but when a Royal Highness does it, it has an electrifying effect.

Once at a Palm Beach party a heavy rain cracked through the plastic roof over the courtyard. The band and guests crowded to the sides and the party looked wet and dead. The Duchess saved the day by going upstairs, changing into a black dress, parting her hair in the middle, putting a rose in it, then coming down to do "a really flashing flamenco dance."

"She takes over like a storm," a Palm Beach newspaper said of her.

"Nickey and Bunny Du Pont warmed up their guests in their colorful villa on the ocean . . . with a parade of beautiful people from all over the world arriving to play with the Duke and Duchess of Windsor," wrote Lorelle Hearst in the Palm Beach *Daily News*. "Susie Gardner in a knock-out apple green crepe gown BELTING out a song with a good lusty bang. Doc Holden did his 'I'll Be Down to Get You in a Taxi Honey' song and dance which he had been doing at parties for many years. However, the *pièce de résistance* was when the Duchess asked Dysie Davie to do a dance. Dysie turned to the orchestra and said, 'Just play "St. Louis Blues": give it to me in a low-down beat.' She did a one-woman show of jazz ballet that was a phantasmagoria . . ."[11]

The Duke also liked to let loose. The Duchess told him not to dance the twist in public because she felt it was undignified for him and, besides, he had a bad back. But he was in the swing and mood of it at another Palm Beach party and told Susie Gardner, "Come on, let's get behind a post so the Duchess won't see us."[12] He later complained that as soon as he had learned how to dance the twist, "it went out of style."

At the end of one season Suzy Knickerbocker wrote: "Everyone in Palm Beach is saying that it is hard to remember when the Duchess of Windsor has ever looked so marvelous. She's a smash in everything she wears, be it her flowered paper dress or the pale blue caftan from Balenciaga she turned up in at Ruth and Joe Tankoos' party for her and the Duke at the Colony Hotel. Why, more people were staring at the Duchess than were casing Shalimar, the belly dancer . . . The

Windsors almost always leave a party by midnight or earlier but they stayed at l'affaire Tankoos until one o'clock dancing and laughing and eating crabmeat and artichokes, chicken chipolata, pureed broccoli a la Duchesse de Windsor and gateau Normande."[13]

Discussing the Duchess at such parties, a friend said, "She just seems to float into a room."[14] Not only did she have the grace and ease of a woman twenty years younger, but the wit was always there. Sitting on the terrace one evening with some other women, they saw the Duke and a small group of men heading for a clump of bushes. "I don't know why they do that. They've got perfectly good bathrooms in the house. And they're led by my husband, the greatest pee-er of them all."[15] When the Duke first applied for a driving license in Palm Beach, he puzzled what to write for "Occupation" and finally wrote "None." His friend Lord Dudley, however, scratched that out and wrote "Peer of the Realm."

The Wallis wit revealed itself in another favorite anecdote about a cosmetic shop on Worth Avenue run by a friend of hers. The shop owner sent Wallis a box of a new powder called "Duchess of York." The Windsors referred very privately to the Queen Mother as "the dowdy Duchess." And when she appeared on television in their presence, one of them was heard to say, "Here comes the Blimp." Thanking her friend for the Duchess of York powder, Wallis answered, "And you know where I'll put it."[16]

Much has been said of the Duchess' lack of meanness and how much she prefers saying good things about people, but there are human exceptions. Elsa Schiaparelli gave a dinner for the Windsors at her unique town house on the Rue de Berri. As the Duchess walked into the studio living room, she startled the assembled guests into utter silence by commenting to the Duke, "The woman in this painting looks just like your mother."[17] The face in the painting was tight and bitter.

Usually, she was much more adroit. At a dinner in their honor in Mexico City, the Duchess checked the guest list, as she always did, and noted the name of Clare Boothe Luce. For some time there had been little love lost between the two women. The Duchess had someone find out whether Mrs. Luce was scheduled to make a speech. She was. The Duchess then learned exactly when the speech was scheduled and exactly where Mrs. Luce would sit. Just before the speech was to begin, the Duchess stood up in the dining room and commented loud enough to be heard, "It's very warm in here. Do you have a veranda?" Everyone knew, of course, that it was much hotter outside. "Then I think I'll excuse myself and go out for a breath of air," she said and allowed a young man to accompany her grand exit.[18]

Her problems with Elsa Maxwell were more complex and longer lasting.

For years they had been friends. Miss Maxwell had climaxed the relationship by giving a spectacular New York affair called the Duchess of Windsor Ball for more than 1,200 internationally prominent guests with the Duke and Duchess doing a special Windsor waltz.

The estrangement began when brash Miss Maxwell had the effrontery to advise the Duchess on "discretion" in her personal affairs. The rift grew and Elsa Maxwell eventually wrote: "I no longer see the Duchess of Windsor. She has become so completely engrossed in herself and in her pursuit of pleasure that she neither knows nor cares what others are thinking or feeling. Had she been more conscientious about her position in history, she would not have to search so constantly for excitement and amusement. She would have found peace within herself. . . . It's my considered opinion that many of the things she has done in this search, largely because of the high-handed, selfish way in which she has done them, have contributed to her final frustration—the fact that the Windsors' prestige is not what it was—what it used to be."[19]

It was a nasty attack and the Duchess' answer was silent dignity. But, when Wallis was informed that Elsa Maxwell planned to have a ball with four duchesses from different countries, Wallis answered, "It would take four ordinary duchesses to make one Duchess of Windsor." And when Miss Maxwell took a hundred guests on a cruise off the coast of Greece, Wallis was quoted as calling it "Elsa's Zoo." Wallis protested, "I didn't call it a zoo. I merely said that no boat has carried a crew of so many people since Noah's Ark."[20]

Elsa counterattacked at the April-in-Paris Ball in New York. The Duke and Duchess were guests of honor, but Miss Maxwell managed to garner all the attention of the press. Besides having at her table the governor of New York and the mayor of New York City, Marilyn Monroe arrived wearing a backless gown with a plunging neckline. "Naturally, when Marilyn came in," Miss Maxwell later reminisced, "all the attention was focused on our table; and there was nearly a stampede."[21] A newspaper story read: ELSA OUTDOES THE DUCHESS.[22]

Describing the feud, Art Buchwald wrote, "The Quai d'Orsay and the British Embassy have already been notified, and while the American Embassy has made no effort to interfere, despite the fact that Miss Maxwell is an American citizen, State Department officials are keeping a close watch on the situation."[23]

Finally the two women reached a semblance of peace, but the truce did not temper Miss Maxwell for long. She still felt it necessary to say to Wallis, "Another thing, Duchess, is that you never listen to anyone." Some time later the Duchess attended Miss Maxwell's birthday party in Paris, sitting between two gentlemen commonly classified as "intellectual." As she stood up to leave, she said, "Elsa says I never listen, but I have listened tonight."

Elsa's quick comment was "Duchess, did you learn anything?"

"And she went away laughing," remembered Miss Maxwell.[24]

When the feud again exploded, it was the Duchess who made the final peace overture at a party to which they both had been invited. The thin, tiny woman walked over to the short fat one, held out her hand and said, "Elsa, I am so very glad to see you."

"She has G-U-T-S," said Miss Maxwell, admiringly now.[25] "The Duchess, let me say, is a remarkable woman. In these last years, it seems to me, she has grown sweeter; completely lost all of what I used to think as a driving nervousness. The Duchess and I always have fun together, her delightful sense of humor meeting mine head on. When I quarreled with ex-King Farouk of Egypt, who was suing me for five million francs, just before going to court I received a package from the Duchess containing two little frogs, one jade, one carnelian. 'These frogs and I are on your side.' I keep these frogs with me, believing somehow that they bring me luck."[26]

"The Duchess is generous and brave," she added. "She cared for the Duke when he had a bad case of shingles a few years ago—an agonizing ailment. Her care of him would be a lesson to most modern wives."[27]

The Duchess gave a farewell party for Elsa in Paris, where she smilingly made a short speech about "my old—and new—friend."

"I played the piano like mad," Elsa remembered, "and the Duke, sitting beside me, sang all his favorite songs, interpolating with barber shop chords."

The Maxwell affair was only a curious ripple in the Windsor

household, a highly publicized matter of small moment. The royal family was an ingrained part of the friction of their lives. The initial gesture here came with the unveiling of the plaque in memory of Queen Mary. This was not a royal marriage or a coronation where the Duke's absence could be excused and explained. The royal family and the establishment had no option on the unveiling. The Duke's presence was compulsory or the public might angrily react against the government. Since he would not come without his wife, their decision was forced. They had to invite her. It was the first palace invitation sent directly to the Duchess, the first official royal recognition of her after thirty years of ostracism. The irony was that Queen Mary had become the catalyst for the Duke's official forgiveness, she who had been the most unforgiving.

A group photograph marked the event. This was neither a time to smile nor a time for triumph. The ceremony was simple and their visit short. According to *Burke's Peerage*, the Duchess of Windsor was still junior to twenty-nine other duchesses.

At Queen Mary's funeral, the *Express* had editorialized, "It is the deep and earnest desire of the nation that he [the Duke] . . . should make his home in this, the land that gave him birth."[28] Of his several dozen trips to England the Duchess had accompanied him on six. Queen Elizabeth had lunched with him alone twice and had tea with him once. The same friendly *Express* added later, "Never is he permitted to feel at home here. Seldom is a welcoming hand extended to him. The strong emotions had faded long ago from the public mind —but apparently in the little world of pomp and protocol they are still bitterly remembered." An organization called The Octavians had spent fruitless years pleading the Duke's cause, asking only that the Duke be invited to return in recognition for past services, and that the Duchess not be "relegated to the background."

Despite all friendly efforts and despite the new mood, the invitation never came.

The royal attitude again cooled. The official expectation still was that the Windsors would discreetly leave Paris whenever the Queen made a state visit to France, as she did in 1957. The Windsors were due to return at that time but extended their stay in the United States "to avoid causing her any embarrassment."

The Duke never got over his exile. Reminiscing with a friend who had just come from England, the Duke asked if an old oak tree was still standing in the Windsor Park. The friend was embarrassed; there were so many trees in the Windsor Park. But still, he answered that the old oak was still there. The Duke sighed with relief, then told his friend how often he had played and picnicked under that old oak. France had been officially generous, properly discreet and protective, but no matter how long they lived there, the Windsors always felt themselves outside looking in. How could they be part of a country when they couldn't understand the language well enough to laugh at its jokes?

At one of their rented houses, the Duke went to introduce himself to the gardener and said, *"C'est moi qui suis le Duc de Windsor"* ("I am the Duke of Windsor"). Responded the gardener, *"Je m'excuse. Je ne comprends pas l'anglais"* ("Pardon me. I don't understand English").[29] The Duke often told this story on himself. The Duchess had her own problems with her "kitchen French." She called it her "sex problem," because she often confused the genders of masculine and feminine nouns.

Nor did they have many French friends. The upper crust of French aristocracy had ignored them for years. The Windsors never forgot the slight. A friend once asked them, "If you dislike France so much, why stay? Even if you can't go back to England, what about the United States?"

"Can't do it," growled the Duke. "Taxes."[30]

The Windsors were two of the few people in the world who didn't pay taxes to any government. Their royal allowance was tax-free in England and the French gave them a diplomatic status, exempting them entirely from taxes. Although the Duchess was an American, she was also a British citizen by marriage living abroad, and similarly exempt.

So they remained royal nomads and their old friends became fewer. They had reached the age of funerals. Their Palm Beach host Robert Young committed suicide. Lord Dudley died, and they made their only return trip to Nassau to see him while he was still alive. The Duke went to London for the memorial service for Fruity Metcalfe, best man at his wedding. Wallis heard that Ernest Simpson was dying in London and she sent him a bouquet of yellow and amber chrysanthemums with a white card that read, "From the Duchess of Windsor."

The Duke never drank before 7:00 P.M. After that he occasionally made up for lost time. They were on a transatlantic crossing, and he

472

had had too much to drink and was having difficulty negotiating the steps between the decks. A passenger saw him and rushed over to help him. The Duchess, who was standing there, grabbed her arm. "Don't help him," she said. "What do you mean?" said the other. "He'll fall." The Duchess' face was strained and she answered, "No, he'll manage. But don't help him."[31] Then the other woman suddenly understood. It would have battered his pride if a woman had offered him help.

Wallis understood the range of his weakness and the depth of his pride. She could be his anchor and his buffer, and she was, but she could not always sit at the center of his soul. She could tell him what to do, and he did it, but she had to leave him some of his inner life to move as he willed within his own limits. Even in a social world of triviality he had to have his own sense of integrity, his own small area of decision and action. If he did not, then he would only be a shell of himself, or a vassal of hers and this would utterly disintegrate the delicate balance between them.

In 1964 doctors discovered the Duke had an aneurysm, a balloonlike blister the size of a small cantaloupe on an artery that threatened to burst and kill him. The swollen section needed to be cut away and replaced by four inches of knitted Dacron tubing. The surgeon specializing in that operation was Dr. Michael DeBakey in Houston and they went there. Before they wheeled the Duke into surgery he kissed her. A great many friends such as Marlene Dietrich faulted Wallis for journeying with him by train instead of insisting that they fly. Nobody knew better Wallis' abnormal fear of flying, and the decision was just as likely the Duke's as hers. They did fly back and Wallis sat still and frozen in her seat until the Duke leaned over and said, "Let the pilot fly the plane."

Winston Churchill died in 1965, while the Duke was embarking for a trip to England. They had not been close in those final years. Earlier, a mutual friend had informed the Duke about Churchill's worsening condition and the Duke had answered, "He's eighty-seven, isn't he? I haven't seen him for a number of years."[32]

There were those who criticized the Duke for not flying to Churchill's funeral. Again, the Duchess would not fly and he did not want her to make the ship crossing without him. As always, there was still the question of protocol, the embarrassment of royalty at their presence. Then, too, the reconciliation between the Duke and

Churchill had been more of a patch-up than a heartfelt forgiveness. Each had his own residue of irritation with what the other had done in earlier years. One of the Duchess' last memories of Winston Churchill was at the gambling casino in Monte Carlo when he told her, "Better not sit next to me tonight; I haven't been very lucky."

The Duke's own stays in hospitals were now more frequent. The effects of age set in swiftly soon after he was seventy. He was operated on three times in London for a detached retina. The young queen visited her uncle in the hospital after one of those operations. Whenever the Duke was hospitalized the Duchess always slept in an adjoining room, so that she could be with him constantly. Always a great newspaper reader, she now read at least six a day, from England, the United States and France. She would read them thoroughly, even the ads, and then give him a rundown of what was happening in the world. "Here's the news," she would say, and a friend who was there remarked that her summary was astonishingly complete. The Duke would then interpolate and explain the significance of some items. In earlier years he had read to her, not only from newspapers but from magazines and books. He had the kind of memory that could recall all the French presidents, in their proper order. He used this retentiveness to supplement his reading. It surprised him when their friend Princesse de Polignac could not immediately remember the name of the French president who fell out of a train and ran along the train tracks in his pajamas.

The Duchess herself had been astonishingly healthy through the years. She had had her appendix removed and a facial scar eliminated; a recurrent stomach ulcer usually kept in remission. The major cancer surgery had been completely successful.

Somehow she also had miraculously appeared to defeat age. The one whisper that had never stopped was that she had had face lifts. The initial persuasion supposedly came from a friend who used the argument "You take great pains with your clothes. You have your own hairdresser. You strive to look as nice as possible. You wouldn't think of going around in a wrinkled suit. What is there any different about having your face lifted?"[33]

A prominent plastic surgeon, Dr. Daniel Shorell, whose patients had included Madame Chiang Kai-shek and Zsa Zsa Gabor, was bluntly asked if he had performed the operation on the Duchess. "Let us say I know her very well," he answered. "Beyond that, I don't think I'd like to go." He admitted that the patient was not "a member of the royal family by lineage." He also explained that he had operated to "reduce redundancy of the neck, and to improve the jowls."[34] During one operation, her prominent facial mole also disappeared.

The Duchess has denied having any face lifts and so has Dr. Erno Laszlo, who has been the guardian of her skin for twenty-five years. Laszlo, whose other clients included Greta Garbo, firmly believes in the soap and water treatment, but his soap costs ten dollars a cake. Those who have talked to her masseuse confide that the Duchess' skin, all over, even at seventy-seven was incredibly beautiful, white and very delicate. A beauty expert insisted that basic to her skin beauty were certain uplift massage treatments. Another added that her firm, square-cut jaw played a large part in preventing fat bulges, which make the ordinary chin sag.

Whatever the truth, the result was clear. Even close to the age of eighty, she looked at least ten years younger. But age was not her favorite subject. On a trip to Baltimore, when a friend remarked that he had a photograph of the two of them taken before 1912, she bristled at the mention of the date. When another friend later told her that she brought regards from a man in Baltimore, the Duchess asked, "Who?" Then, when she was told, simply said, "Oh, yes."[35] That ended that conversation. The past was yesterday and yesterday was dead.

The world still followed the Windsors wherever they went, but the headlines were smaller. Their names were still the most wanted names to head the charity balls. Whether they were in Biarritz or Baden-Baden, Palm Beach or Newport, New York or New Orleans, their presence was the automatic highlight at any party. In New Orleans, at the Mardi Gras, the Duchess curtsied and the Duke gave a deep bow to the play-acting king and queen of Mardi Gras. An observer commented, "They've got class."[36] The photograph became the Picture of the Week in *Life* magazine, but Wallis had only a single query, "Will it be seen in England?"[37]

They gradually cut out certain stops on their annual pilgrimage, searching for a more permanent place in the sun. Spain always had delighted them. They knew the Franco family well, and the Duke often had gone hunting with the Spanish dictator. They also had many friends among Spanish aristocrats. Life there seemed simple and unstrained. They acquired more than three acres in Marbella, a resort area on the southern coast, and decided to build a house without guest rooms. Wallis hired a Rumanian architect whom she had known in China and who then lived in Hammamet, Tunisia.

The problem with Marbella was the time it took to get there. Wallis still hated to fly and the train journey from Paris took three fatiguing days. In addition, they found it difficult to adjust to the late dining hours in Spain and did not want to impose their habits on their friends. They finally and reluctantly abandoned the idea of a home there.

The Duchess meanwhile had written her memoirs. Like all memoirs, they were most interesting for the things they did not say. Cleveland Amory, who had been hired to help write the book, finally left, saying that he could not and would not write a book that would make the Duchess look like Rebecca of Sunnybrook Farm.

It was only human that the incredible togetherness of their marriage would show occasional signs of strain. The Duke had a hair-trigger temper, but almost never exercised it on Wallis. The Duchess was renowned for her self-control, and only rarely did her anger explode. There were exceptions. At teatime, he sat, as always, at his own table drinking his usual big cup of tea and milk with biscuits. As he got older, his hands were shakier. "Be careful, darling, don't spill your tea," she would tell him. Once, when a dog collided with his table and his tea spilled, the Duchess was angry. "Now see what you've done!"[38] He meekly apologized, explaining about the dog. Once, when she was busy and he came to her with his cup of tea, she brusquely told him, "Take your tea in the other room."[39]

While visiting friends years earlier the Duchess got so furious with the Duke that she slammed the door behind her and rushed toward the elevator. The friend, as host, ran after her to mollify her. Just as he reached her, she whirled around and hit him hard in the stomach. Then, when she saw who it was, she apologized, "Oh, excuse me, Charles, I thought it was the Duke."[40]

The known existence of such rare incidents merely adds reality to myth. There are very few Rebeccas of Sunnybrook Farm. And what marriages made in what heaven are utterly free of the caustic comment, the flickers of hate?

They presented the more expected public image at the premiere of a movie about the Duke's life. It was called *A King's Story.* Jack Le Vien, who produced it, recalled the filming of the part where the

Duchess refers to the Duke as "the most desirable bachelor in the history of mankind."

"The Duke was sitting next to her, and when she said it, he looked down shyly."[41]

When the Duke filmed the abdication speech there were a dozen technicians on the set, together with the Duchess. Before he was done Le Vien remembered that everyone on the set was wiping away tears, including the Duchess. "At that time he seemed more royal than I've ever seen him," said Le Vien.[42]

During this brief time he was no longer the meek husband; now, once again, he was the king. After he filmed the abdication scene, the Windsors discussed it as they seldom had.

"But I had made up my mind already, before you left," he told her.

"I didn't know that," she said, "you didn't tell me."

"I didn't tell anybody," he replied, a small note of triumph in his voice. "But I knew it—here." He pointed to his head.[43]

A King's Story was an extremely moving film, evoking the era as well as the man. At the end of the premiere showing, the Duke kissed his wife tenderly and then told Le Vien, "Jack, I cried all the way through." The Duchess' quiet comment was "You see how much he gave up."[44]

"I gave up very little for what I received," he answered.[45]

A technician who had worked on the film afterward said that a photograph had been removed near the end of the film. It was a picture of the rather ramshackle house in Pennsylvania where the Duchess was born. The Duchess had requested its removal. The film was his pride and she wanted nothing in it to shame her.

A few friends thought she sometimes mocked him too much, but it was usually gentle, and often witty. When Yul Brynner starred in *The King and I* on Broadway, he dined with the Duke and Duchess. The Duchess afterward told Leonard Lyons, "Tonight I danced with two Kings, although only one is working at it."[46]

Some relatives faulted Wallis for her actions during Aunt Bessie's final days. Aunt Bessie reached the venerable age of 100, and there was a family birthday party. Bessie had been a substitute mother to Wallis, the one confidante on whom Wallis could always depend to come when called. Wallis arranged to pay for the champagne and birthday cake, but she did not come to the party. The cake had a hundred candles on it and photographers wanted a picture. As brash as ever, Aunt Bessie said, "What do you want me to do—go out and climb a tree? I'll be glad to do it."

Several months later, Aunt Bessie died. Wallis was in a New York hospital having a bunion removed and she sent the Duke to represent her at the funeral, asking a cousin, "Please take care of the Duke as he's not used to being alone with the family."[47] Relatives criticized Wallis for not visiting her dying aunt before she had her foot operation. They also noted that another cousin had come to the funeral even though she had fallen and broken her collarbone the previous day and was in considerable pain. The Duchess, they said, could have either postponed her operation or else hobbled in on a cane.

It was a family matter, kept quiet, not aired in the press. But it became another cross the Duchess had to bear.

The Duke rode in the funeral procession with cousin Corinne and another cousin in a British Embassy limousine. The Duke sat on the jump seat. It had been a cold day, and the buxom elderly cousin Corinne informed the Duke of her need to stop at the nearest service station. The Duke transmitted the message to the driver, who informed him that it was a new highway and there were no stations nearby. Cousin Corinne said nothing but sat there grimly for a while longer. She next asked the Duke who owned the car. He told her that the British Embassy did. "Well," she declared, "unless you tell the driver to stop the car immediately, the British Embassy will be very unhappy about what will happen to the fancy upholstery in this car."[48] The Duke so informed the driver, who pulled over at an emergency stop. The roadside was completely bare of trees or shrubbery, but fortunately Corinne's servant was a big heavy woman who acted as a shield from the funeral cortege that stopped behind them.

If the Duke thought about it at all, he must have smiled at how amused Aunt Bessie would have been at the incident. He had liked Aunt Bessie very much. Like Wallis, she was a real person in his unreal world. The shape of that world somehow seemed stranger than ever to him now. Skirts were shorter, violence more explosive, hate uglier and young people less understandable. Good manners seemed to be disappearing along with dignity.

What he and Wallis had had throughout the years was truly exceptional. No marriage had been more opposed or more envied and it was truly remarkable that they had managed to keep the foundations of it firm and fresh. They had reached the time of their marriage where they almost had blended into a single human being. Her energy added vitality to him. They had the same outlook, liked the same people and the same things. Furthermore, they could now sense each other without words. A flicker of an eye, a shadow of a smile, a barely heard whisper all spoke volumes to each other.

Clare Boothe Luce remembered once in Paris when she and the Duke were discussing foreign affairs, the Duke suddenly picked up a handful of almonds from a silver dish and started peeling them, while he continued talking. When his dish was full of peeled white almonds, he motioned for a butler and instructed him to take the almonds to the Duchess. Looking at Mrs. Luce's surprise, he explained, "The Duchess loves fresh almonds, but peeling them breaks her nails."[49] As the butler delivered the almonds, the Duchess glanced up at the Duke quickly with a gay, grateful smile.

That was the secret of his marriage: he always felt as if he were a young man in love with a young girl.

Would children have changed anything? Perhaps. But then, he might have been jealous of them as he was jealous of anyone who took too much of her time. This included everything and everyone— except their dogs.

Behind the garden at The Mill, there was a series of small white stones, the graves of their dogs. For many years they had wiry, shaggy-coated cairn terriers, whom they called "little gangsters." A friend gave Wallis a tawny pug, saying that pugs were always the favorites of royalty. They soon had five of them. The Duke and Duchess insisted on feeding the dogs themselves to keep a sharp eye on a proper diet so they would not get fat.

Dining at the exclusive La Grenouille Restaurant in New York, the Duchess was not above taking her leftover steak back to the Waldorf in a doggy bag. Another time, in Palm Beach, when the press rumored that she had spent the day shopping for a million dollars' worth of jewels, the Duchess smilingly replied that she had been shopping, but for dog food. In any final analysis, her dogs were more important to her than her jewels.

When Wallis went to a pug dog show in London, she confided, "The Duke was terrified when he knew I was coming here because he knows I like them so much. He is afraid I will buy a houseful."[50]

"She liked the idea of buying a bitch, but I advised her not to," said Stanley Dangerfield. "She agreed. She said, 'I suppose it would not be wise to upset my old boys.' "[51] They talked to their pugs as if they were children, and they loved them as much. One of the most typical photographs of the Duke and Duchess during their yearly travels showed each of them carrying a pug under an arm. When one died, they went into mourning.

The only exercise Wallis ever took was to walk her dogs in the Bois. "I'm very lazy," she explained. Besides walking the dogs, she claimed her only other exercise was "moving the ashtray an inch."

Once one of the dogs impulsively decided to relieve himself on the rug at The Mill. The Duke was furious. In his thin, high-pitched voice, he yelled, "Stop it . . . Stop it . . ." A guest smiled and told him, "You may have been king of England, but even a king can't stop that once it's started."[52]

Dogs were an emotional outlet for Wallis, and she needed one. She was not the kind of woman who could go to an empty beach and scream and scream to the wind and come home relieved and relaxed. Relaxing was the most difficult thing of all for her. She was always so conscious of appearance and perfection, never a hair out of place, never a wrinkle in her clothes. If she could have let her hair loose, or her skirt rumple, or if she could have yelled more often, it would have helped so much. As it was, she was a woman full of private fears.

One of them was a fear of going anywhere alone, particularly in New York City. No matter where she went, people would stare at her, and she would freeze. When this happened, she need someone to hold on to tightly. This was especially true in an elevator. The people had not forgotten, and never would. As Wallis once told a close friend, with real envy, "You and your husband can go to Atlantic City anytime you want and have all kinds of fun. We can't."[53]

She was once early for an appointment at the St. Regis Hotel and when her friend arrived, she rushed to him and said, "I'm so glad you came early. If you hadn't, I'd just have to sit here alone, and it would be terrible."[54] Even in the highly sophisticated St. Regis, a haven of celebrities, the lobby was in silence as people stared at them.

One thing she did enjoy doing in New York just before returning to France was to shop in a supermarket. Some of the staples she always selected were angel food cake mix, corn muffin mix, canned corn, canned black cherries and laundry detergent.

The Duke's prime enjoyment was to get in his game of golf on every possible day. He freely described himself as "a hacker" with a handicap of eighteen. He said he was always happy to break ninety, but that didn't happen often. His best round, he said, was a seventy-five in Biarritz.

"I cannot say that I agree with Bernard Shaw that golf is a wonderful walk, spoiled by a little white ball," he said. "I love hitting that little white ball. Walking for the sake of walking bores me." Golf was such a passion with him that his first question on arrival at Palm Beach usually was "Is the golf pro waiting?"[55] He would make the appointment in advance so there was no time wasted.

It was during a golf game when a young man said to him, "Say, weren't you a king or something?"

"Yes, I was," he answered, standing a little taller.[56]

To a woman at a party, he remarked, "You know I was crowned king."

"Jesus, I didn't know that," she said.[57]

There was one unforgettable irreverence. For all his friendliness, the Duke was very specific about the privacy of his person. He did not like to be touched. (Some psychologists insist that this indicates a lack of early love, a fear of emotional involvement.) Even his best friends didn't shake his hand, unless the Duke first offered his. But an old friend, standing behind him at a party had an absolutely irresistible impulse, and she goosed him. He turned around and stared at her in complete horror.

"I felt terribly embarrassed afterward," she said, "and I promptly went over to Hammacher Schlemmer the next day and bought him a gift—a set of gardening tools."[58]

Many called the Duke's life an empty life, a waste. The Duchess finally rebutted in anger. She said her husband had been punished all these years "like a small boy who gets a spanking every day of his life for a single transgression." She discussed his unparalleled knowledge, his training in state affairs shunted away in a minor appointment during World War II. She blamed the royal family and the British establishment for refusing to put his many talents to use and giving him a job of proper responsibility.

The first British press reaction was the bristling: HOW DARE SHE?

British Conservative MP Charles Curran was quick to comment: "What use has he made of this knowledge, this training, this experience? The answer is: nothing. . . .

"Instead of waiting for Britain to employ him, why does he not employ himself? Why hover uneasily around the Throne that he gave up?

"For he might have done anything. He is rich, healthy, childless. The cares of money weigh on him no more than the cares of parenthood. When he abdicated, he was in his prime. He could have put aside his title and qualified for a profession. He could have become a don, a doctor, a lawyer. He could have gone into business; or bought a newspaper; or turned farmer; or taken charge of a social settlement.

"If he felt in exile from power, he could have sought to gain it across the Atlantic. He could have become a naturalized American and entered politics—stood for the Senate or tried to be Mayor of Miami.

"He could have turned patron. But while he might have done anything, he has dedicated himself to nothing. He has spent a quarter of a century treading the social treadmill and traveling to and fro, like an animated luggage label."

Curran went on to say that the Duke might be "a member of P. G. Wodehouse's Drone's Club, an aging Bertie Wooster. His life is a vacuum—a vacuum, de luxe, mink-lined. He has no job, no profession, no occupation. He is not even an eccentric. His life is blameless, harmless, pointless, useless.

"But the Duchess complains that he is persecuted. It is rather like ringing up the Anti-Noise League to complain about the last trumpet."[59]

It was cruel, but was it truth?

Some of it was. It was his life. Many felt the options were his. And yet, were they, really? He was badly limited by his past and by his dignity. There was always the echo of something his father had said, "My dear boy, you must always remember who you are."[60] He didn't have a talent for science or the mind for business. A king cannot be a car salesman. He had been trained for one thing only, and once you have been on the mountaintop, you discover there are not many other mountains. Curran begs the question. The main blame still belongs to the government that trained him and failed to use that training. He would have been a first-rate special ambassador to the United States, a satisfaction for himself as well as his country. He applied for that job, or anything comparable, with a persistence bordering on desperation. He wanted to work. He wanted to serve. It was the British establishment who most firmly decided the way of his life.

Once he accepted that decision, he adjusted to it. He was not an ambitious man. He had worked hard, giving the best years of his life in service to the British Empire, on a grueling schedule of world travel and ceremonials, becoming the most popular Prince of Wales in British history. He felt he had earned what money he had. He felt he had earned his leisure. He had the one thing he most wanted— Wallis. The social scene was her preference, not his. Now he had reached the age of simplicities—his golf and garden could content him. What seemed like a waste to some was pleasure to him.

When their good friend Diana Vreeland said to him, "You were always my golden Prince of Wales,"[61] he still looked shy, but pleased.

The Duke showed a map of the British Empire on the wall of his home to reporter Robert Meusel, and said, angrily, "Look what happened to the British Empire." Meusel answered, "Well, why didn't you stay and try to keep it?" The Duke was silent for a minute before replying, "It wasn't possible."

Normally, when displeased, he would simply grunt. Once, though, he exploded with rare venom. An intimate friend wondered whether he ultimately planned to return his British medals and swords and flags and plaques to the British government. "I don't care about the British Government," he said, almost biting his words, "or about the British."[62]

"A memory is only as good as the good memories," Wallis liked to say, quoting her Aunt Bessie. She herself added the postscript, "Be merry and wise."

She and the Duke still worked their giant jigsaw puzzles many nights, and often took a dinner tray to eat in front of the TV. But Wallis still showed strong flashes of her incredible reserve of energy and drive.

In her seventies, the Duchess of Windsor could still be photographed dancing the "hully gully" and the "jerk." While she often had been described as "smiling grimly" and saying, "No comment," she now spoke more freely on more issues. She said her motto was to work as hard as you play, laugh as hard as you cry and put everything you've got into everything. She started a pattern-making business, which was not overly successful, but which she enjoyed. She became a governor of the American Hospital in Paris. Washington *Post* editorial writer Meg Greenfield saw her at the Colony Club, marveled at her grace and energy and said, "With that kind of drive, you could cure cancer."[63]

She was outspoken about the "best-dressed list," calling it "phony" because the judges never saw the people they were judging. And when she was asked by a Boston *Globe* reporter for her opinion on "hot pants," she lifted up her skirt to the thigh and there they were, hot pants designed by Givenchy. The Duke, though, afterward told an interviewer that "We're a little past the age of being with it,"[64] and the Duchess added, "We even spent Easter in bed."[65]

But the balls and parties in their honor did not diminish. On April 4, 1970, President and Mrs. Richard Nixon gave them a swinging party at the White House, returning the hospitality the Windsors had shown them four years earlier in Paris. The 106 guests included Cabinet members, golf champions, business tycoons, astronauts, entertainers and members of the social elite. The menu included *Le Saumon Froid Windsor,* a mousse of sole and shrimp molded in the form of a royal crest, surrounded by cold salmon, and a strawberry dessert called *Le Soufflé Duchesse.*

Bobby Short sang some of the Windsors' favorite tunes while the seventy-five-year-old Duke tapped to the beat with his cane. "I used to be a great dancer," he told Short, "but now I'm arthritic."[66]

In response to Nixon's champagne toast, the Duke said, "I have had the good fortune to have had a wonderful American girl consent to marry me and have thirty years of loving care and devotion and companionship—something I have cherished above all else."

And it was true. In Palm Beach Doc Holden had three pictures of his dearest friend: the first as the young Prince of Wales, the second as the middle-aged King, and the third a recent picture of the Duke. On that the Duke had inscribed: "The last forty years have been the best. E."[67]

The Duchess felt the same. Once when complimented on how highly the Duke spoke of her at a party, the Duchess answered, "Now you see why I fell in love with him."[68]

Later when John Barkham asked, "Sir, if you had to do it all over again, would you do it?" The Duke's voice was firm and strong when he replied, "Yes, I would do it again."[69]

43

"I TOLD HIM to stop smoking all those cigarettes," said the Duchess. "We had some friends who had died of throat cancer. He said he started smoking a lot when he was traveling around as Prince of Wales making so many speeches. He was always nervous about making speeches and that's why he smoked so much. He did cut down. He started smoking half-cigarettes in a holder. But I guess it still added up; it was still too much."[1]

His throat cancer had been diagnosed, but the decision was against an operation. Instead, they treated it with cobalt radiation, and it went into remission. It was only after a hernia operation, early in 1972, that the cancer cells seemed to reactivate.

He was a stoic about death as he was about life. What concerned him most about his death was his wife. He did not want death to separate them.

He had bought two plots at Green Mount Cemetery in Baltimore and there was even speculation that the city had offered to build a heroic mausoleum for them. They had decided to be buried in Baltimore because the Duke feared that the British would refuse to bury his wife alongside him—if he died first. His angry feeling, too, was that if the British would not properly receive his wife in her lifetime, then they should not receive her after her death. It became a subject of much royal discussion. Finally, they agreed that he and the Duchess should be buried in royal ground in England. Instead of St. George's Cemetery, where so many previous kings had been buried, they selected Frogmore, on the grounds of Windsor Castle, alongside George, the Duke of Kent, the brother he loved best. Close by was the mausoleum of Queen Victoria and Prince Albert. That done, the Duke then sold his plots in the Baltimore cemetery.*

His remaining worry was the health of his wife. Close friends long ago had hoped that he would die before her, since she was the stronger and the less dependent. By the early months of 1972 in France, the Duke was prepared for his fate. He knew how much Wallis loved life, and he had left her well provided to enjoy it—and he wanted her to. Even toward the end, he was more concerned with her health than with his own. The pain was often intense but he said little so as not to worry her. Whenever she was with him, he often rallied so much so as to seem almost well. But the ravages of his illness became more and more visible. The final sign was the day he could no longer walk his dogs.

"I'm convinced that the Duchess did not let herself know that the Duke was dying," insisted one of her close friends, who was with her some of that time. "I think the shock was too much and she just refused to accept it."[2]

How could she accept his death when he had been so much the reason for her life? To accept his dying would have meant accepting her own. This she could not yet do. She had spent her lifetime building up a façade of control and she would keep it intact.

It was different from accepting his abdication. That she did not understand. She understood this, but she did not want to. Her memory would often slip away and now she let it slip away more easily. She wanted only the good memories. Death was not beautiful to La Belle Jolie because she still wanted more out of life. She always wanted more.

If Wallis seemed to refuse to accept the fact that her husband was dying, the same seemed true of the royal family. Sam White, the distinguished Paris correspondent for the *Evening Standard,* discussed this with a royal family spokesman, who said, "You know he's dying, I know he's dying. But WE don't know he's dying."[3]

Mutual friends now increased efforts to effect a full reconciliation between the Windsors and the royal family. They emphasized that this would not only fulfill the Duke's dearest wish but it would also eliminate unnecessary embarrassment and misunderstandings after-

* Of the thirty-nine monarchs since William the Conqueror, only five are buried in foreign soil: in France, William I, Henry II, Richard I and James II; in Germany, George I (who was born there).

ward. It would be a simple, generous gesture to recognize Wallis as "Her Royal Highness."

Queen Elizabeth had not seen her uncle for five years. Her state visit to France that May had been long announced. It was expected, as always, that the Duke and Duchess would not be in the city at the time. But when Winston Guest visited the Duke, he knew he was dying. En route home to New York, he stopped in London to see Lord Mountbatten, told him about the Duke and asked him to tell the Queen immediately. It was then, and only then, that the Queen rearranged her royal schedule to include a visit to her uncle. She managed a twenty-minute visit after the races, and just before attending a public reception. That evening she was due at a big ball.

The Duke supposedly had a blood transfusion earlier that morning to give him the added strength to be dressed and put in a chair to receive his niece. He insisted that all the tubes be detached from his body so he could receive her in dignity. One intravenous tube could not be removed, but he kept it covered. She was his niece, but she was also the Queen, and it was a question of manners and high style and courage. It was a massive effort. He could not come down to her and so it was she who came to him. The small, thin man now seemed so much smaller, so much thinner. He weighed only ninety-six pounds. It was difficult for him to talk. His mind and memory were alert, and his manners impeccable. He tried to make their meeting as painless as possible for her.

As she left his room, the Queen must have been startled by the four-foot-high portrait of the Duke in the resplendent robes of the Order of the Garter. It was almost identical to a similar portrait of the Duke when he was Prince of Wales, except that the head on this one was of a man in his fifties. Painted at the insistence of the Duchess, it was a portrait of a king who might have been. Prince Philip had come with the Queen, and so had Prince Charles. Wallis acted as hostess with all her expected grace and dignity. There was no banter this time, no small jokes. The air was polite and proper.

Neither the Queen nor the Duchess ever have reported the gist of their short conversation. At the gate, however, a photographer recorded the Duchess in her curtsy to the Queen, making a valiant attempt at a pleasant smile.

As soon as the Queen left, the Duke was quickly put back into his bed, and never again left it. The Duchess then slept in the adjoining sitting room, between their bedrooms, so she could always be available.

There was no way of knowing then just how much longer the Duke would live. Susie Gardner, who had been ever-present, finally had to leave and said good-by to her old friend.

"Sorry, Susie," he said to her, "sorry I had to be so sick while you were here. I always look forward to your visits so much."

"I cried on that plane all the way home," recalled Mrs. Arthur Gardner.[4]

The Duchess hardly left his room after that.

Two days later, he was dead.

As previously arranged, the public announcement came from Buckingham Palace.

"It is announced with deep regret that His Royal Highness, the Duke of Windsor, has died at his home in Paris at 2:25 A.M., Sunday, May 28, 1972."

The Duchess herself was in a controlled kind of daze. She did not weep. Someone said she sat as if she had been crushed. She seemed to refuse to accept his death just as she had refused to accept his dying. If she was his life, he was her world. They had seldom been separated for more than a few days. She had made his life the purpose of her own. She had protected him, nursed him, watched what he wore and how much he drank, worried about his diet. They were the closest companions, tied always by the Windsor knot of history.

How she would miss this man! His love had been pure and unquenchable. It was like waking up every morning and knowing that the sun was out. How can a woman ever feel old when she looks into her husband's eyes and sees herself as young as he sees her? To this man, she was perfection. He saw her as no one else ever did, or ever would. Now she would only have a mirror, and now she would get old.

Sunday in the nearby Bois brought the usual crowds for a promenade. A group of perhaps a hundred stood at the police barriers in front of the giant black gates of their home topped with golden spikes and the monogram "ER." A sign outside said in French that all those who wished to express their condolences could go to the British Embassy the next morning and sign the book. It was not a crowd of the grieving, but of the curious. The former king had been a myth to them, an occasional headline. Now they primarily wanted to know whether the Queen would come. Seeing the crowd at the gate, a German sports car stopped and the driver asked if this was the racetrack entrance.

Within five hundred yards of the gate, there were six soccer matches going on as well as a softball game between Harry's Bar and a rival team. The Duke would have liked that. Some old men were playing boule and there was racing, as usual, at nearby Longchamps.

One of the first and few to enter past the police to express his personal condolences to the Duchess the next day was former King Umberto of Italy. Several years earlier he had dined with the Duke and Duchess at Le Club in New York, and the Duke had lifted his drink and toasted him wryly, "Here's to us two kings."[5]

The French coroner came and went. The undertaker arrived to arrange for a temporary coffin. Madame Betty Zeldon-Rust, who ran the local beauty parlor for dogs, said of the Duke and his dogs, "He was so fond of them, he practically did all the trimming himself."[6]

An English neighbor arrived to leave her note of sympathy, saying, "Some of us were very hard on him when he abdicated."[7] Among others calling at the house to express sympathy were Alexandre, the Duchess' hairdresser, and French foreign minister Maurice Schumann. Schumann had been the only French journalist at the Windsors' wedding. The president of the French National Assembly arrived. Masses of flowers were delivered. More people with more notes. Cars came from the British Embassy. Someone who saw his body said, "It is like it always is in death. He looks younger, not so haggard. He had been a good-looking man."[8]

Then there were batches of telegrams from friends, who remembered how they had once cried for him. Prime Minister Heath wired, "In all he did he sought to make the monarchy less remote and more in tune with the needs and aspiration of his time." The Queen of England added: "I am so grieved to hear of the death of my uncle . . . I know that my people will always remember him with gratitude and great affection and that his service to them in peace and war will never be forgotten. . . . I am so glad that I was able to see him in Paris ten days ago."

She also invited the Duchess to stay with her at Buckingham Palace during the funeral.

In its original resolution expressing its condolences, the House of Commons omitted all mention of the Duchess. The oversight was caught and corrected in time, but the incredible thing was that it happened at all.

Wallis now put herself in the hands of others.

The Duke's body was flown by a Royal Air Force plane to England,

and met by his nephew, the son of his favorite brother, George, the Duke of Kent. The Duchess did not accompany the body. Her doctors had decided she should not.

He had specified years before that he did not want a state ceremony, only a private funeral. He would lie in state for two days at St. George's Chapel in Windsor, when the public could file past and pay its respects. The private service at Frogmore would then be limited to family and a few friends.

The story circulated in high social circles that Prince Philip had said to the Queen, "Now is the perfect time to have the short ceremony which will officially make the Duchess someone who can be addressed as 'Your Royal Highness.'"

"I couldn't do that to her now," the Queen reportedly answered. "If I did that to her now, she would have every right to spit in my face."[9]

The Duchess arrived in the Queen's comfortable private plane on Friday, with a few friends and staff. She was most charming and polite to everyone, but her mind often wandered and there were times when she knew neither where she was nor where she was going. Lord Mountbatten was there to meet her. He had been with the Windsors on the *Nahlin* cruise, but not at the wedding. He escorted the Duchess directly to Buckingham Palace. Her suite of rooms on the first floor overlooking the mall was usually reserved for visiting heads of state.

Shortly after her arrival, the Queen came to see her and told her to consider the palace her home, and if she wanted anything at all, she only had to ask. If she wanted to see the Queen, the Queen would come. If she didn't want to see the Queen, or anyone else in the family, they would understand. Whatever she wanted, they would do. That day and evening, the Queen lunched and dined with her. The charming Prince Charles, who joined them, called her Aunt Wallis and said that he hoped he would be as good a Prince of Wales as his Uncle David had been.

Her doctor had made himself a buffer to ensure the Duchess more quiet, but quiet may not have been what she wanted. She would soon have more than enough of that. The Queen had assigned her own butler and her lady-in-waiting to the Duchess, and Wallis' dear friend Lady Dudley was always with her. Meals had thoughtfully been prepared with the Duchess' ulcer diet in mind.

Such was her dignity and composure that a servant afterward said admiringly, "She could teach something to some of our royals."[10]

There was some question that the Queen might cancel the Trooping of the Colors, the celebration of her official birthday that Saturday. She decided to convert the Trooping into a memorial for her uncle. Riding sidesaddle and wearing a black armband on the left sleeve of her crimson uniform jacket, the Queen led an escort of the mounted Household Guards from the palace to the Horse Guards Parade Grounds.

The ceremony began with a roll of black-draped drums, a minute's silence, and the playing of a bagpipe lament, "Flowers of the Forest." Prince Charles later told Wallis that he had burst into tears when he heard the piper's lament. From a window of the palace, the Duchess watched the beginning of the ceremony and a photographer caught her haunted look of utter sadness.

It was all too late. If he could have been with her, in the same suite, at this same window any time within the previous three decades, how it would have changed the mood and tone of his life. Why did they have to wait until his death to make this gesture to her?

Directly after the Trooping of the Colors, the Queen again came to visit the Duchess. Memorial ceremonies were scheduled at Windsor Castle the next day, Sunday. The Queen could see that the strained Duchess was almost at the end of her emotional tether. There were still no tears. She had never cried even once throughout all the services of the last three days. The Queen suggested that perhaps the Duchess might want to stay home that Sunday and the Duchess gratefully agreed.

Saturday was the worst day of all for her. She was utterly tired. She took a walk in the garden. A few friends came. Lady Monckton remarked how impressive the Duke looked in his casket on the catafalque and suggested it might do her good to go and see it. She had not planned to do that. She had wanted to remember him as he was when he lived.

The procession of people outside of St. George's Chapel was sometimes more than a mile long. It included a Highlander in kilts; Lord Boothby; twenty-two American Girl Scouts in uniform; the Soviet ambassador; women carrying shopping bags coming straight from the shops; the high commissioners from Bangladesh and Botswana; whole families, including babies; the secretary for Northern Ireland. Some were silent and staring and some were crying.

One woman broke down and exclaimed, "Good-by . . . good-by . . ." Winston Churchill's widow was there, the Baroness Spencer-Churchill, and so was sixteen-year-old Carol Palmer, who said, "I'm here out of sheer respect. Anyone who gives up so much for the woman he loves is fantastic."[11]

The Queen and Prince Philip and Princess Anne visited the chapel that afternoon. The Queen insisted there be no interruption in the public homage. As the public slowly moved around the catafalque, the three stood a few yards away, their heads bowed in six minutes of silence.

The Duchess came to the catafalque after the people had gone, just before the coffin was taken to the nearby Albert Memorial Chapel. She came with Lord Mountbatten and the Prince of Wales. She carefully examined the flowers around the casket, then stood alone in front of her husband, a pale, frail tiny figure in black. Her body began swaying with emotion when Lord Mountbatten quietly took her arm as she turned away. To Mountbatten and the Prince, she kept repeating, "Thirty-five years . . . thirty-five years . . ."[12] That day would have been their thirty-fifth wedding anniversary.

The private funeral service on Monday began at St. George's Chapel after the great bell in the thirteenth-century tower had tolled for an hour. The Queen sat closest to the altar and the Duchess sat next to her. The only king present was the Duke's cousin, sixty-eight-year-old Olav of Norway; Wallis knew him; he had dined at her home on several occasions. The Duke's only surviving brother, the Duke of Gloucester, was ill at home.

The coffin was draped with the Duke's personal standard that had hung in their home in Paris. On top lay a small cross of white Easter lilies from the Duchess, selected by the gardener at Windsor Castle. The Archbishop of Canterbury, Dr. Michael Ramsey, gave the blessing.

Inscribed on the plate of the coffin lid:

"H.R.H. the Prince Edward Albert Christian George Andrew Patrick David, Duke of Windsor. Born 1894. Died 1972. King Edward VIII 20th January–11th December 1936."

As the Archbishop recited all the honors awarded to the Duke, the Duchess was moved, and later told a friend, "They don't give honors like that any more."[13]

Red tunicked Welsh guardsmen had carried in the coffin from the nearby Albert Memorial Chapel, and the choir sang "I Am the Resurrection and the Life." At the end of the service the state trumpeters sounded post and reveille. Then the Duchess, for a few poignant moments, again stood motionless before the coffin, her head bowed.

"It was very strange," remembered a friend who was there. "The service was over and then all of us left for lunch, leaving the Duke's body alone with the four guards. Then, after lunch, the body was buried. It struck me as most bizarre."[14]

Bizarre was the proper word. The forty guests sat at four separate tables, and only a few of them were her friends. The rest were royal strangers and members of the establishment. These were the people who had frozen her out of British life and society these many years. These were the people who had shunned and denied him. Conversation had been the vibrant blood of her life but what could she say to the taciturn Prince Philip, who sat next to her? Words would not come. Nor could she force herself to eat. Her husband was dead and alone in that chapel and here they were all eating a hearty lunch before going to the grave. She felt ill. She wanted to leave.

As soon as the body was buried, she told the Queen that she had to go at once. The Queen asked her why.

"Because I want to go," she said.[15]

She had reached her breaking point. The Queen understood.

Her departure was hurriedly arranged. No member of the royal family went to see her off. There were only the lord chamberlain and the Queen's lady-in-waiting. A lady who blamed the Duchess for the abdication and resented the Duke for his decision confessed that she felt ashamed that the royal family did not see fit to be at the plane to say good-by to this woman whom they had treated so shabbily throughout the years.

In Sydney, Australia, the *Sun* declared, "The great love story has ended."[16]

They were wrong.

Nobody dies as long as people love and remember.

Epilogue

LONELINESS is not simply a matter of being alone; loneliness is the feeling that nobody else truly cares what happens to you.

After the abdication, the Windsors had learned who their friends really were. Only a handful dared show up for their marriage. Age gradually cut down their best friends, and most of Wallis' close family. Now, when the Duke died, there was still another falling-away of those who had stayed because of him, not her. Her final circle was small and tight.

"I am very lonely now," she told a friend. "I miss him very, very much."[1]

The void was enormous. They had filled each other's lives so completely that it was suddenly as if half the gears of a watch were gone. "I have nobody to explain things to me now, as he always did," she said.[2]

There would never again be anybody to worry about her as he had. She had planned the movements of her life around him and his movements were always directed to be where she was. "Darling, are you there?" he would call, as soon as he returned from golf. Or, even more intimately, "Dolly . . . Dolly . . . where are you? . . . WHERE ARE YOU? . . .

That was over. She still had her staff of seventeen including John Utter, the Duke's private secretary, who had worked for the U.S. State Department. One gossip sheet even dreamed up the idea that she and Utter would soon marry. Sidney Johnson stayed on. She still had her butler, her secretary, her maid and the others. She also still had her house in the Bois, which belonged to the French government. Immediately after the Duke's death, a number of people had filed with the government to gain possession of that house, but the government publicly announced that the Duchess could stay as long as she wanted. She originally had paid a peppercorn fee in rent because the Windsors had paid the great cost of redecorating. Now the rent was made more equitable to the government.

She kept his room intact, almost in the same way Queen Victoria had maintained her dead husband's room for the rest of her life. Wallis had left the Duke's toilet articles as he had wanted them, his twenty-three pictures of her just as he had seen them. A friend insisted that, every night, before going to her own bed, she entered the Duke's room and said, "Goodnight, David."[3]

After a husband's death, executors often appear with long, gloomy faces to alert the widow to the need for a belt-tightening budget. There was none of this with the Duchess. The executors informed her she would not have to change her style of living one whit.

Her closest friends estimated that the Duke had left her a minimum of several million dollars, well invested, and possibly as much as $10 million. Her jewels represented another small fortune. She furthermore decided to sell The Mill. She could hardly bear to go back there. She could still hear him saying, "I put in every stone." She had wanted a million dollars for it, but finally sold it for much less. There is even good reason for believing that the Queen continued the royal allowance that had been annually granted to the Duke, an estimated $75,000 a year.

Money was no longer a worry, if it ever had been. But it no longer had much meaning either. Almost eighty now, she had no urge to travel. Clothes no longer had the importance they once had. At that age, she said, one doesn't buy much any more of anything.

She made a short, sentimental journey to Biarritz, where she and the Duke had spent so many summers. The director of the Palace Hotel had put up a plaque naming his famous guests, with the Duke's heading the list. Here was where they had their first highly publicized rendezvous before going on the *Nahlin* cruise. Here they searched for the small bistros, and here, possibly, is where they first fully found each other.

It was sad now to hear her say, "My dogs are such great company for me now. Things are very different for Black Diamond, too, and I had to close the Duke's room to keep him out of it."[4]

The Duke's other pug, James, died soon after his master. He simply stopped eating and pined away. The Duke himself always had fed James his whole wheat biscuits.

Being the woman she was, it became impossible for her to remain solitary for long. Four months after the Duke's death, she began appearing more frequently at private dinner parties around Paris. Her invariable companion was a twenty-six-year-old Parisian named Claude Roland. Her choice was considered tactful, since anyone older would have caused unnecessary speculation.

It was, somehow, no longer the same. Friends worried that her memory was getting poor. A friend defended her, saying, "Of course her memory isn't what it was. Whose is?" When she had guests for dinner, they now made sure they left earlier than they might have, so that she might rest earlier. She always had had difficulty sleeping, and now it was worse. She always ate little, and now seemed to eat even less. Friends felt she was fading away.

Security became an obsession with her. Besides her spiked fence and guarded gate and an electronic system at all windows, she kept the Duke's pistol on her night table and hired a former French paratrooper to patrol her grounds. She also had a special phone to the police stationed at the corner. Since she slept little, she checked often to make sure everybody was awake and alert.

She designed the cream-colored Welsh marble stone for her husband's grave under an old plane tree. More often now, she confided to friends, "You know, I've got a little place of my own, right next to him."[5] Her inscription would read: "Wallis, Duchess of Windsor."

She gradually seemed to lose interest in the social scene. Her chef informed her that he had received a number of offers, some of them from her friends, but that he still wanted to stay if she wanted him. She said she did. Asked by someone why he stayed, the chef said, "Why should I leave? I learn so much from her every day."

She still sat straight in her chair. She still spent each morning with a make-up man, and then a hairdresser. The few friends who came to dinner found her absolutely marvelous from nine to eleven in the evening. Afterward she seemed to slip away from them.

Then, one day, she found it painful to walk, finally stayed in bed. It took ten days before the doctors decided to X-ray, and then discovered that she had fractured her hip. One of the special nurses at the hospital was told that her patient was very senile and would have to be carefully watched. "She was very confused. She would ask the

496

same question forty times and still not seem to understand the answer. We attached a button to her nightdress to turn off the light, but she just couldn't find it, as hard as she tried. They had to put sideboards on her bed because she kept trying to climb out at night. I remember her saying once that if it wasn't for her, Elizabeth wouldn't have been queen."

It took time, but the hip healed. Her walk no longer had the grace it once did, but she still walked tall, and with dignity. Once again, gradually, she emerged from the shadows of her sadness. When a friend, Edmund Bory, came to visit, she remembered that he, too, had fractured his hip, and she greeted him with "Hip, hip hooray!"[6]

It may have amused her that Patrick Montague-Smith, editor of the new edition of *Debrett's, the Guide to the British Peerage* flatly asserted that the British Parliament had acted unconstitutionally and illegally in withholding from her the title of "Her Royal Higness." In the preface to the 1972 edition of *Debrett's* Montague-Smith wrote, "We know now that the exclusion of the Duchess from the title or style of H.R.H. resulted from advice tendered by Ministers in Britain and various countries of the Commonwealth."

It somehow seemed unimportant now, almost trivial. The satisfaction of such homage, and the need for it, was gone. More important was the question of whether or not the house in the Bois with all the rooms and all the servants was really too big for her. She talked increasingly of an alternative suite in a hotel. Her closest friends advised her against it. After the ambiance of a big house and grounds and greenhouses, an apartment would be confining, not just for her but for her pugs, Black Diamond and Gin-Seng. The pugs were a telling argument. She truly had nobody else now for whom she felt any greater love.

She even talked about leaving her money to foundations for animals.

Such was her recuperative bounce that she soon once again sparkled, her wit sharp. Even on her most despondent days, she always looked as if she had stepped out of a bandbox, every hair perfectly in place. When she made an entrance in the evening, it was in the style of a grand entrance.

A dinner guest of the Duchess, Mrs. Gilbert Miller, described what the meal was like at her home without her, when she was ill upstairs. "Without her, it was like eating in a restaurant. With her, it was something festive. She had the secret of sparkle."[7]

Once again she was ready for parties, dinners, balls.

"Why don't we go somewhere tonight?" she said during a visit to Cap Ferrat. "I haven't been anywhere. How about Monte Carlo?" Then she added in a quiet aside, "I love poker. I think it's a marvelous game. And I like chemin de fer, but I don't gamble much. I always think what I could buy with the money I lose. I hate to lose!"[8]

She had lost much in life, but she had won much more. She might have been queen of England. Or she could have been the woman behind the King, the most important woman in England, and perhaps in the world. In effect, she might have ruled the social force behind the British Empire.

On the final line, what was it that she had won? In history, it was only a footnote, but in the romantic story of the ages, she had a whole niche of her own. When in history had a king given up his throne for the woman he loved? Soon there would be no more kings and no more thrones. If there was still room for romance in the changing world, then hers would be unique.

On the table in her dressing room, centered among several photographs of her David, was a framed message from him on his royal stationery:

My friend, with thee to live alone
Methinks were better than to own
A crown, a scepter, and a throne.

Acknowledgments

A BOOK IS MANY PEOPLE.

My gratitude, first, to the Duchess of Windsor, who talked to me so freely and frankly even though she knew that this would be an unauthorized biography over which she would have no control.

I am equally grateful to Lord Brownlow, one of Edward VIII's closest friends, the only one to whom he entrusted the care of his future wife on her flight to France during the abdication—Lord Brownlow was most generous of his time and his invaluable memories; Lady Monckton, whose husband was the King's most intimate counsel and liaison during the crisis, was similarly generous of her time, as well as her permission to quote from her husband's diaries; the Duchess' oldest friend, Mrs. Wolcott Blair, whose friendship dates from the Baltimore schoolgirl days, could not have been more gracious or more cooperative. This is also particularly true of Diana Vreeland, former editor of *Vogue* and *Harper's Bazaar,* whose assistance was invaluable; Mrs. Arthur Gardner, Lady Dudley, Mrs. Cordelia Robertson, Mrs. Eleanor Miles, Mrs. Elizabeth Schiller Morgan, Edmund Bory, Mrs. Gilbert Miller, David Metcalfe, Princesse de Polignac, Madame Schiaparelli, Mrs. Graham Mattison, Baron Cabrol, Mrs. C. Z. Guest, all of whom are close friends of the Duchess and all of whom were most helpful. Particular thanks are due to my friend Jack Le Vien, producer of *A King's Story.*

A special note of gratitude to Etta Wanger, not only a friend and admirer of the Duchess but a writer who understood my needs. My thanks also to Nancy Adler for introducing me to her, and for helping me in other ways.

Mrs. Lelia Noyes Lucas, near Front Royal, Virginia, the closest living relative of the Duchess, has my deep appreciation for her cooperation, and so do Craig and Helen Livingston, and Mrs. Bessie Pomeroy.

I am also thankful to the many people in Baltimore who were so willing to search their letters and their memories, Headmaster George S. Nevens, Jr., and, especially, Mrs. Robert B. Wagner, alumnae secretary, of Old-fields School and the scattered surviving classmates of Wallis Warfield, including Mrs. Augustine Janeway, Mrs. Harold Kersten, Mrs. Katherine Poole, Mrs. John Tennant, Mrs. Isaac Granger, Mrs. Joseph Hazell.

Bill Boucher III in Baltimore deserves singular mention because the title of this book is his suggestion. His wife, Annie, has my deep gratitude for her varied and vital assistance in arranging appointments and confirming facts. Dr. Edgar and Phoebe Berman also considerably eased my research in the Baltimore area.

Earl Pruce, the librarian at the Baltimore *News American,* was particularly invaluable to me, his assistance being above and beyond the call of duty. I am thankful to Thomas J. White, Jr., the executive editor of the *News American,* his secretary Olga Tilman, and Price Day, the editor of the Baltimore *Sun,* for their willing cooperation.

The Maryland Historical Society staff also deserve my appreciation, and I am indebted to its noted genealogist, William Marye.

In the Washington area, Paul and Shirley Green, as always, helped me research a wide range of material, as well as pictures. Paul was also invaluable in interviewing several people for me in both Washington and Paris. I am grateful also to Robert Wolfe, head of the Captured Records Branch of the National Archives, and his assistant John Mendelsohn, who was so patient with me. I also thank Arnold Price of the Central Slavic Division of the Library of Congress, and Ronald Swerczek, the Diplomatic Branch chief in charge of the State Department files. My thanks, too, to my friends Ben Bradlee, the executive editor of the Washington *Post,* and Meg Greenfield, on the Editorial Board. My dear friend Mrs. Nellie Myers, helped by Tom Miller, spent much time for me digging into local records. My thanks, also, to Joseph Borkin, Frank Waldrop, George Williams, and Kay Halle.

In Palm Beach, besides the pivotal help from Mrs. Gardner, I am most appreciative to Milton "Doc" Holden, one of the Duke's oldest and closest friends, for sharing his memories with me. I am thankful also to Christopher Dunphy and Irvin Larner. An added note of appreciation to Lois Wilson, librarian of the Palm Beach *Post-Times,* whose help continued long after I left the area; Elizabeth Crow, librarian of the Palm Beach *Daily News,* and Ellen Robinson.

In the Bahamas, my thanks first to Bill Kalis, director of the Bahamas News Bureau, and Steve Libby, whose assistance was constant and indispensable. Mrs. Greta Moxley, the Duke's former secretary, was also a great help. The single major source of necessary information came from Sir Etienne Dupuch, publisher of the Nassau *Daily Tribune.* He was unstinting of his time and assistance. I am also grateful to the *Tribune* editors Eileen and Roger Carron and to Mrs. Doris Bullard, who was so patient in finding facts I needed.

In Nassau, I also thank Sir Barkley Ormerod and Lady Ormerod, at whose home the Duke and Duchess lived for a time, Sir Harold and Lady Christie, Lady Solomon, Sir Roland Symonette, Mr. and Mrs. Leslie Higgs, and, again, Lady Dudley, so gracious a lady and a hostess. Lady Dudley was with the Duchess during the Duke's final days and accompanied her to the funeral in England. Her husband was one of the Duke's closest friends.

There's a long list of names of people in England and France who were most valuable to me. In London, Mrs. Ann Ebner, once again, followed up on my research in the Public Records Office, and so did my niece Katherine Pastel. Historian and biographer Allen Andrews and his wife, Joyce, helped much out of the wisdom of their background and experience. So did Howard and Gabrielle Byrne, Michael and Jo Wybrow, David Golding, Herbert Mayes, Vincent Korda and Robert Meusel. Fred Waller, the librarian at the London *Evening Standard*, deserves special mention for all the time and information he gave me. V. J. Hale, who had been butler to the Duke and Duchess, provided many interesting sidelights. At the Wiener Library Institute of Contemporary History, my thanks to Janet Langmaid, Mrs. Gita Johnson and Anthony Stoll.

People in Paris to whom I am deeply obliged include Aline Mosby, who has so expertly reported on the Duchess for so long, and similarly Sam White of the London *Evening Standard* and Hebé Dorsey, society editor of the Paris *Tribune*. Peggy Sunde of the *Tribune* was also most cooperative, and so was Julia Clemenceau, who helped me with my interview appointments. My thanks, too, to John Utter, the Duchess' assistant, Herbert Bigelow and my dear and old friend David Karr for smoothing many roads. My personal appreciation to my friend Mrs. Nina Wallace for all her gracious help and kindness.

I must also mention Mlle. Monique Bonneton, Mrs. Betty Grafstein, Charles Sultner, Lisa, Mrs. Chambers, among many others.

In New York, my good friends Marvin Sleeper, Ed Cunningham, Stan Swinton and Andrew A. Rooney all helped, as they always have, when I needed them; so did Mr. and Mrs. John McAllister, Mrs. Gloria Schiff, Lewis Ufland, Ed Antrobus, Gretchen Katz, William Henry Sheppard, Ed Plaut, Jane Bradford, Millie Gardner, Neil A. Grauer, Sidney Shore, Irving and Ida Epton, Ruth Tropin, Esme Fink, Dr. Murray Krim, Charles Ochsenreiter, Peggy Wiener and Joseph Willen.

I am grateful to my old friend Mark Senigo, promotion director of *The New York Times*; James Patterson, assistant managing editor of the New

York *Daily News*, and Joe McCarthy, librarian of the New York *Daily News*; Nat Glasser of the National Headline Service; Arnold Fox, librarian of the Associated Press; Kay Hartley, librarian of the Columbia Broadcasting System; and my dear friend Olga Barbi, senior editor at *Newsweek*.

To Tom Deegan, Billy Baldwin, Alfred Katz, Alan Searle, Susan McCarthy and her father, Joe, L. M. Davies, William H. Sheppard, my added appreciation for their help. My thanks, too, to Mrs. Marilyn Brown, deputy clerk of the Circuit Court of Fauquier County in Warrenton, Virginia; F. W. Roberts, director of the Humanities Research Center at the University of Texas, and Jeanette Green, who helped research files there for me; Isabel Hamilton of the Nassau Public Library and Elsa Resnick of the Great Neck Library; Mrs. Robert Shenton, assistant to the director of the Arthur and Elizabeth Schlesinger Library on the History of Women in America at Radcliffe College; Mrs. Eleanor G. Horan, curator of the Edward R. Murrow Collection at Tufts University; Christine Bevan at the British Information Service; and Timothy Beard at the Genealogical Room of the New York Public Library.

I thank Tiana Toumayan for translating those French articles for me; Joanny V. Lang for copying all those documents; Eve Brown Schimpf for her helpful background; and Margaret W. Littlefield for providing me with that gold mine of newspaper clippings.

I am fortunate to have the full and constant cooperation of the Oyster Bay Public Library and its director, J. Peter Johnson. Mrs. Christine Lane, as always, has made it her personal project to search throughout the state library system for anything I need, even material I have not requested but which turns out to be most valuable. Also helpful have been staff members Gene McGrath, Laura Lucchesi, Annette Macedonio, Kenneth Weil and Jane Schwamberger.

I do not know what I would do without Mrs. Mari Walker, who has transcribed my tapes and translated my notes for so many of my books. She is indispensable.

To Sophie Sorkin, copy chief, my thanks for her wisdom and her good humor; to Gail Greene, for her extracurricular contributions; to Jean Smith for the actual copy editing; to Louise Fisher for preparing the final manuscript; to Eve Metz for her superb taste in the design of this book.

My old and dear friends Harriett and John Weaver kept me well supplied with a variety of information; Len Slater gave me some important background; Bob and Edna Brigham supplied some very useful contacts; and my friend and neighbor Irma Remsen helped in a variety of ways.

I must also thank Madame Felipe Espil in Argentina for giving me some most valuable background on her husband.

Betty Copithorne supplied her usual excellent editorial comments, and

I am also thankful to her husband, Bill, for his help. To my dear friends Ruth and Larry Hall, who come whenever I call them—and I have called them often—once again, my deep, deep thanks. To my one and only sister, Naomi Van Clair, who came many times and spent many hours proofing and checking the manuscript, and to her husband, Stanley, and my nieces Joyce and Audrey, who helped her, I give them my love.

I want to thank Michael Korda, who suggested the idea of my doing this book, and I particularly want to thank Peter Schwed, for his warm and constant encouragement, and Dick Snyder, for his strong support. My editor and my friend Phyllis Grann—who helped birth my only novel for another publisher years before—helped shape the form and content of this book in many pivotal ways. My agent and friend Sterling Lord helped keep it alive, and Dick Kaplan, executive editor of the *Ladies' Home Journal*, must assume the ultimate responsibility for its rebirth.

Finally, my three grown children—Maury, Betsy and Tina—have helped in every phase of this book, from research to footnotes, and my dear wife, Marjorie Jean, with the patience of Job, as always has been my first reader and editor, and an integral part of this book, as she is part of my life.

Picture Credits

Grateful acknowledgment is made to the following for permission to use these photographs.

Page 97 TOP LEFT, UPI; TOP RIGHT, from the files of the Baltimore *News American;* CENTER and BOTTOM, UPI

Page 98 Courtesy of the New York Public Library Picture Collection

Page 99 TOP LEFT and TOP RIGHT, UPI; BOTTOM, Popperfoto from Pictorial Parade

Page 100 TOP LEFT, UPI; TOP RIGHT and CENTER RIGHT, courtesy of Oldfields School; BOTTOM RIGHT, UPI

Page 101 Photo by Central Press from Pictorial Parade

Page 102 TOP and BOTTOM, UPI

Page 103 TOP, photo by Bigelow from UPI; BOTTOM, New York *Daily News*

Page 104 TOP LEFT, courtesy of the U.S. Naval Academy Museum; TOP RIGHT, courtesy of the New York Public Library Picture Collection; BOTTOM, UPI photo from *McCall's* magazine

Page 105 TOP and BOTTOM, courtesy of the New York Public Library Picture Collection

Page 106 LEFT, UPI; RIGHT, photo by Bigelow from UPI

Page 107 LEFT, courtesy of the New York Public Library Picture Collection; RIGHT, King Features Syndicate

Page 108 TOP and BOTTOM, Popperfoto

Page 109 TOP LEFT, UPI; TOP RIGHT, Wide World Photos; BOTTOM, UPI

Page 110 TOP, Popperfoto; BOTTOM, UPI

Page 111 TOP LEFT, Pictorial Parade; TOP RIGHT, Wide World Photos; BOTTOM, UPI

Page 112 TOP, courtesy of the New York Public Library Picture Collection; BOTTOM, UPI

Page 113 TOP, courtesy of the New York Public Library Picture Collection; BOTTOM, UPI

Page 114 LEFT and BOTTOM RIGHT, courtesy of the New York Public Library Picture Collection; TOP RIGHT, UPI

Page 115 Pictorial Parade

Page 116 TOP, New York *Daily News;* BOTTOM, Popperfoto

Page 117 TOP, UPI; BOTTOM, Popperfoto

Page 118 TOP, courtesy of John D. Le Vien; CENTER, courtesy of Herbert Bigelow; BOTTOM, UPI

Page 119 TOP, CENTER RIGHT and BOTTOM, courtesy of Herbert Bigelow; CENTER LEFT, UPI

Page 120 TOP and BOTTOM, Popperfoto; CENTER, UPI

Page 121 TOP and BOTTOM, UPI

Page 122 TOP, UPI; BOTTOM, New York *Daily News*

Page 123 TOP, Pictorial Parade; BOTTOM, UPI

Page 124 TOP and BOTTOM, UPI

Page 125 TOP, A.F.P. photo from Pictorial Parade; BOTTOM, courtesy of the New York Public Library Picture Collection

Page 126 TOP, London *Daily Express* photo from Pictorial Parade; BOTTOM, New York *Daily News*

Page 127 TOP, Wide World Photos; BOTTOM, UPI

Page 128 UPI

Bibliography

In reviewing my book *Jennie: The Life of Lady Randolph Churchill*, historian Martin Gilbert—the author of the official multi-volume biography of Winston Churchill—aptly said that to be a biographer one must be both a detective and a dramatist. There is, however, a vast difference between being "a detective" on a woman such as Jennie, who has long been a part of history, and on the Duchess of Windsor, who is very much alive at the time of this research and writing.

With Jennie it was mostly a matter of finding trunks full of letters and documents in attics and archives. There were few alive who knew her well, although I was fortunate to talk to her third husband shortly before he died. With the Duchess, still highly vibrant, the emphasis is on interviews with a large number of people who form different mosaics in her life. However, in view of her vibrancy, there is reluctance on the part of many to be quoted. In the notes, therefore, I have been forced to respect their wishes and describe these sources under the classification of "Personal interview." Anyone I quote in this way was an intimate part of the scene described.

There is, of course, still a considerable amount of "detective" work in establishing such seemingly simple things as the time of her parents' marriage and her own birth date, all the specifics and maneuverings of the abdication crisis, the details of the Nazi kidnap plot in Spain, the Oakes murder in the Bahamas, among many other things. For this, there were the invaluable resources of archives and documents, particularly the Public Records Office in London, the British Museum and the Institute of Contemporary History; the captured German documents in the Library of Congress and the National Archives; as well as the files of a great many newspapers and periodicals in all parts of the world.

Even more important were the diaries of such people as Lord Monckton, Harold Nicolson, Geoffrey Dawson, among many others, as well as the memoirs of both the Duke and the Duchess. In both the latter cases, they were even more interesting for their omissions.

As for the other books which have been most helpful, the following is a selected bibliography.

Airlie, Countess of, *Thatched with Gold*. London. Hutchinson. 1962

Allen, Frederick Lewis, *The Big Change*. New York. Harper. 1952

Andrews, Allen, *Quotations for Speakers and Writers*. London. Newnes Books. 1969

Annual Register. London. St. Martins Press. 1936

Annual Register. London. St. Martins Press. 1937

Arlington, L. C., and William Lewisohn, *In Search of Old Peking*. New York. Paragon. 1967

Attlee, Clement R., *As It Happened*. New York. Viking. 1954

Baldwin, Hanson, and Shepard Stone, eds., *We Saw It Happen*. New York. Simon and Schuster. 1938

Balsan, Consuelo Vanderbilt, *The Glitter and the Gold*. New York. Harper. 1952

Beaton, Cecil, *The Wandering Years*. Boston. Little, Brown. 1961

Beaverbrook, Lord, *The Abdication of King Edward VIII*. Ed. A. J. P. Taylor. New York. Atheneum. 1966

Beirne, Francis F., *The Amiable Baltimoreans*. New York. Dutton. 1951

Benson, E. J., *Queen Victoria*. London. Longmans, Green. 1935

Birkenhead, Frederick Winston, *Walter Monckton*. London. Weidenfeld and Nicolson. 1969.

Bocca, Geoffrey, *The Woman Who Would Be Queen*. New York. Rinehart. 1954

Bolitho, Hector, *King Edward VIII*. Philadelphia. Lippincott. 1937

Bove, Charles F., *Paris Surgeon's Story*. Boston. Little, Brown. 1956

Bredon, Juliet, *Peking*. Shanghai. Kelly & Walsh. 1922

Bridge, Ann, *Peking Picnic*. London. Chatto & Windus. 1967

Brody, Iles, *Gone With the Windsors*. Philadelphia. John C. Winston. 1953

Churchill, Randolph S., *Lord Derby*. London. Heinemann. 1960

——, *Twenty One Years*. Boston. Houghton Mifflin. 1965

Churchill, Winston S., *The Gathering Storm* (Vol. I, *Second World War*). Boston. Houghton Mifflin. 1948

——, *Marlborough: His Life and Times*. London. Harrap. 1936

——, *Their Finest Hour* (Vol. II, *Second World War*). Boston. Houghton Mifflin. 1949

Considine, Robert B., *It's All News to Me*. New York. Meredith Press. 1967

Cooper, Diana, *The Light of Common Day*. Boston. Houghton Mifflin.
1959

Crawford, Marion, *The Little Princesses*. New York. Harcourt Brace. 1950

De Gramont, Sanche, *The French: Portrait of a People*. New York. Putnam. 1965

Dennis, Geoffrey, *Coronation Commentary*. New York. Dodd, Mead. 1937

Dodd, William E., Jr., and Martha Dodd, eds., *Ambassador Dodd's Diary 1933-38*. New York. Harcourt Brace. 1941

Dupuch, Sir Etienne, *Tribune Story*. London. Ernest Benn. 1967

Eden, Anthony, *Memoirs: Facing the Dictators*. Boston. Houghton Mifflin.
1962

Ensor, R. C. K., *England 1870-1914*. London. Oxford University Press.
1936

Fei-Shi, *Guide to Peking*. Peking, 1924

Flanner, Janet, *American in Paris*. New York. Simon and Schuster. 1940

Fremantle, Anne, *Three-Cornered Heart*. New York. Viking. 1970

Gibbs, Sir Philip, *Ordeal in England*. New York. Doubleday, Doran. 1937

Gordon, Elizabeth, *Days of Now and Then*. Philadelphia. Dorrance. 1945

Graham-Murray, James, *The Sword and Umbrella*. Isle of Man. Times
Press. 1964

Graves, Robert, and Allen Hodge, *The Long Weekend*. New York. Norton. 1963

Guedella, Philip, *The Hundredth Year*. New York. Doubleday, Doran.
1939

Gunther, John, *Inside Europe*. New York. Harper. 1938

Hagen, Lewis, ed. and trans., *The Schellenberg Memoirs*. London.
Deutsch. 1956

Halle, Kay, ed., *The Grand Original: Portraits of Randolph Churchill by
His Friends*. Boston. Houghton Mifflin. 1971

Hesse, Fritz, *Hitler and the English*. London. Wingate. 1954

Hibbert, Christopher, *Edward: The Uncrowned King*. London. St. Martins. 1972

Hoffmann, Heinrich, *Hitler Was My Friend*. London. Burke. 1955

Hood, Dina Wells, *Working for the Windsors*. London. Wingate. 1957

Horne, Alistair, *To Lose a Battle*. Boston. Little, Brown. 1969

Horst, P., *Photographs of a Decade*. Ed. George Davis. Locust Valley, N.Y.
J. J. Augustin. 1944

Houts, Marshall, *King's X*. New York. Morrow. 1972

Inglis, Brian, *Abdication*. New York. Macmillan. 1966

Jardine, Robert, *At Long Last*. Culver City, Calif. Murray & Gee. 1943

Jones, Thomas, *A Diary With Letters, 1931-1950*. London. Oxford University Press. 1954

Kavaler, Lucy, *The Astors*. New York. Dodd, Mead. 1966

Laird, Dorothy, *Queen Elizabeth*. London. Hodder. 1966

Leighton, Isabel, ed., *The Aspirin Age 1919–1941*. New York. Simon and Schuster, 1949

Leslie, Sir Shane, *Long Shadows*. London. John Murray. 1966

Lockhart, Aileene, *Cosmo Gordon Lang*. New York. Macmillan. 1949

Marcuse, Jacques, *The Peking Papers*. New York. Dutton. 1967

Martin, Kingsley, *The Magic of Monarchy*. New York. Knopf. 1937

Marwick, Arthur, *Britain in the Century of Total War*. Boston. Little, Brown. 1968

Maryland Writers Program, *Maryland*. New York. Oxford University Press. 1940

Maxwell, Elsa, *The Celebrity Circus*. London. W. H. Allen. 1964

——, *R.S.V.P.* Boston. Little, Brown. 1954

McElwee, William, *Britain's Locust Years, 1918–1940*. London. Faber & Faber. 1962

Minney, R. J., ed., *The Private Papers of Hore-Belisha*. Garden City, N.Y. Doubleday. 1961

Mitford, Jessica, *Daughters and Rebels*. Boston. Houghton Mifflin. 1960

Moore, George, *Letters to Lady Cunard 1895–1933*. London. Rupert-Hart Davis. 1957

Muggeridge, Malcolm, *The Sun Never Sets*. New York. Random House. 1940

Murder of Sir Harry Oakes, The. Nassau. The Nassau Daily Tribune. 1959

Ney, John, *Palm Beach*. Boston. Little, Brown. 1966

Nicolson, Sir Harold, *Diaries & Letters, 1930–1939*. Vol. I. Ed. Nigel Nicolson. New York. Atheneum. 1966

——, *King George V*. Garden City, N.Y. Doubleday. 1953

O'Connor, Harvey, *The Astors*. New York. Knopf. 1941

Perrott, Roy, *The Aristocrats*. New York. Macmillan. 1968

Pope-Hennessy, James, *Queen Mary, 1857–1953*. New York. Knopf. 1960

Raymond, John, ed., *The Baldwin Age*. London. Eyre & Spottiswoode. 1961

Ribbentrop, Joachim von, *The Ribbentrop Memoirs*. London. Weidenfeld and Nicolson. 1954

St. Johns, Adela Rogers. *The Honeycomb*. Garden City, N.Y. Doubleday. 1969

Sampson, Anthony, *Anatomy of Britain Today*. New York. Harper & Row. 1965

Schmidt, Paul, *Hitler's Interpreter*. Ed. H. E. Steed. New York. Macmillan. 1951

Shirer, William L., *Berlin Diary*. New York. Knopf. 1941

——, *The Collapse of the Third Republic*. New York. Simon and Schuster. 1969

——, *The Rise and Fall of the Third Reich*. New York. Simon and Schuster. 1960

Sitwell, Osbert, *Escape With Me!* London. Macmillan. 1949

Slater, Leonard, *Aly*. New York. Random House. 1964

Speer, Albert, *Inside the Third Reich*. New York. Macmillan. 1970

Stevenson, Frances, *Lloyd George*. Ed. A. J. P. Taylor. New York. Harper & Row. 1971

Sullivan, Mark, *Our Times, The War Begins*. New York. Scribner. 1932

——, *Our Times, Over Here*. New York. Scribner. 1933

——, *Our Times, The Twenties*. New York. Scribner. 1935

Sulzberger, C. L., *A Long Row of Candles*. New York. Macmillan. 1969

Sykes, Christopher, *Nancy, The Life of Lady Astor*. New York. Harper & Row, 1972

Taylor, A. J. P., *Beaverbrook*. New York. Simon and Schuster. 1972

——, *English History*. London. Oxford University Press. 1965

Templewood, Viscount (Sir Samuel Hoare), *Nine Troubled Years*. London. Collins. 1954

The Times, A History of, Volume IV. London. The Times. 1954

Vanderbilt, Gloria, and Lady Furness, *Double Exposure*. London. Frederic Muller. 1959

Virginia Writers Project, *Virginia, A Guide to the Old Dominion*. New York. Oxford University Press. 1940

Wilson, Edwina, *Her Name Was Wallis Warfield*. New York. Dutton. 1936

Windsor, Duchess of, *The Heart Has Its Reasons*. New York. McKay. 1956

Windsor, Duke of, *The Crown and The People*. New York. Funk & Wagnalls. 1954

——, *A King's Story*. New York. Putnam. 1947

——, *Windsor Revisited*. Boston. Houghton Mifflin. 1960

Wrench, Evelyn, *Geoffrey Dawson and Our Times*. London. Hutchinson. 1955

Young, G. M., *Stanley Baldwin*. London. Rupert Hart-Davis. 1952

Young, Kenneth, *Churchill and Beaverbrook*. London. Eyre & Spottiswoode. 1966

Yule, Henry, *The Book of Ser Marco Polo, the Venetian, Concerning the Kingdoms and Marvels of the East*, 2 vols. New York. Scribner. 1926

Yutang, Lin, *Imperial Peking*. New York. Crown. 1961

Sources

Full publication information for each book cited is given in the Bibliography.

CHAPTER 1

1. Baltimore *Evening Sun*, December 4, 1936.
2. Harry Wright Newman, New York *Herald Tribune*, December 13, 1936; Rosalie Fellows Bailey, New York *Daily News*, December 2, 1936.
3. Personal interview. Mr. Marye is the genealogist for the Maryland Society, Colonial Dames of America, and Chapter No. 1, Colonial Dames of America of Baltimore. Together with Francis Culver, librarian of the Maryland Historical Society of Baltimore, Marye compiled a detailed account of Wallis' genealogy, published in *Southern Spectator* in 1937. Other sources: Joshua Dorsey Warfield, *The Warfields of Maryland* (Baltimore: Daily Record Co., 1898); Harry Wright Newman, *Anne Arundel Gentry* (Annapolis, 1970), Vol. 1, pp. 345–473.
4. London *Sunday Chronicle*, December 7, 1936.
5. Marye and Culver, *op. cit.*; George William Montague, *History & Genealogy of Montague Family of America descended from Richard Montague of Hadley, Massachusetts and Peter Montague of Lancaster Co., Virginia* (Amherst, Mass.: Press of J. E. Williams, 1886).
6. Baltimore *Sun*, January 19, 1885.
7. Washington *Herald*, December 9, 1936.
8. Nellie W. Jones, *A School for Bishops: A History of the Church of St. Michael and All Angels* (Baltimore City, 1952).
9. Baltimore *American*, June 21, 1896.
10. Baltimore *News*, July 6, 1896.
11. Baltimore *American*, July 5, 1896.
12. Baltimore *News*, September 28, 1896.
13. Elizabeth Gordon Biddle Gordon, *Days of Now and Then*.
14. Interview with former Anne Kinsolving, Baltimore *Sun*, June 23, 1973.

15. Duchess of Windsor, *The Heart Has Its Reasons*, p. 5.

CHAPTER 2

1. S. Davies Warfield, *The Passing of Carroll Island* (privately printed, 1917).
2. Bocca, *The Woman Who Would Be Queen*, p. 21.
3. Baltimore *News-Post*, February 4, 1957.
4. *Ibid.*
5. *Ibid.*
6. Gordon.
7. Baltimore *News-Post*, February 8, 1957.
8. Charles F. Bove, *Paris Surgeon's Story*.
9. Windsor, *The Heart Has Its Reasons*
10. Personal interview.
11. New York *Evening Journal*, February 6, 1937.
12. *Ibid.*
13. *Ibid.*
14. Windsor, *The Heart Has Its Reasons*, p. 30.
15. *Ibid.*, p. 22.
16. Personal interview.
17. *Ibid.*
18. Personal interview.
19. Personal interview.
20. Baltimore *Sun*, June 24, 1973.
21. Excerpts from letters by Mary Kirk (Radcliffe College, Schlesinger library on the History of Women in America [A-149]).
22. *Ibid.*
23. *Ibid.*
24. Lucie Lee Kinsolving in *Oldfields in the Teens*, Oldfields Centennial Diary.
25. Personal interview.
26. Baltimore *News-Post*, October 1, 1936.
27. New York *Evening Journal*, undated clipping.
28. Personal interview.
29. Personal interview.
30. Personal interview.
31. Windsor, *The Heart Has Its Reasons*, p. 33.
32. Oldfields Centennial Diary.
33. Benedick, Act II, Scene iii; quoted in *The New York Times*, June 3, 1937. Source described as wife of a naval officer.
34. Oldfields Centennial Diary.
35. Framed document in files of Oldfields School.

CHAPTER 3

1. Mark Sullivan, *Our Times, The War Begins*, p. 18.
2. *Ibid.*
3. *Ibid.*
4. Sullivan, *Our Times, Over Here*, p. 49 note.
5. Oldfields Centennial Diary.
6. Personal interview.
7. *The Sunday People*, London, April 29, 1973.
8. Baltimore *News-Post*, December 19, 1936.
9. Personal interview.
10. Personal interview.
11. *The Sunday People, op. cit.*
12. *Ibid.*
13. *Ibid.*
14. Personal interview.
15. Francis F. Beirne, *The Amiable Baltimoreans*, p. 285.
16. Windsor, *The Heart Has Its Reasons*, p. 40.
17. Beirne, p. 109.
18. *Ibid.*
19. New York *Evening Journal*, December 4, 1936.
20. Beirne, p. 119.

21. Baltimore *Sun*, December 8, 1936.
22. Beirne, p. 297.
23. Baltimore *Sun*, December 8, 1936.
24. Baltimore *News-Post*, February 8, 1957.
25. Baltimore *News-Post*, November 21, 1936.
26. Baltimore *News-Post*, September 30, 1936.
27. Sullivan, *Our Times, Over Here*, p. 39.
28. Harold Begbie, London *Daily Chronicle*, August 5, 1914.
29. Iles Brody, *Gone With the Windsors*, p. 65.
30. Windsor, *The Heart Has Its Reasons*.

CHAPTER 4

1. Harold Nicolson, *King George V*, p. 53.
2. James Pope-Hennessy, *Queen Mary*, p. 292.
3. *Ibid.*, p. 291.
4. *Ibid.*, p. 293.
5. New York *Evening Post*, January 22, 1936.
6. Pope-Hennessy.
7. Countess of Airlie, *Thatched with Gold*, p. 113.
8. *Ibid.*, p. 112.
9. Randolph S. Churchill, *Lord Derby*, p. 159.
10. Nicolson, *King George V*.
11. Duke of Windsor, *Windsor Revisited*, p. 33.
12. *Ibid.*
13. Duke of Windsor, *A King's Story*, pp. 27–28.
14. Christopher Hibbert, *Edward, The Uncrowned King*, p. 1.
15. Windsor, *A King's Story*, p. 59.

16. *Ibid.*, p. 60.
17. Anthony Gibbs, *The New Yorker*, October 3, 1941.
18. *Ibid.*
19. *The New York Times*, May 29, 1972.
20. Winston S. Churchill, *Marlborough: His Life and Times*.
21. New York *Evening Post*, January 22, 1936.
22. Personal interview.
23. Windsor, *A King's Story*, p. 69.
24. *The New Yorker*, October 3, 1941.
25. *Ibid.*
26. Kingsley Martin, *The Magic of Monarchy*, p. 15.
27. Windsor, *A King's Story*, p. 79.
28. Nicolson, *King George V*, p. 147.
29. Windsor, *A King's Story*, p. 81.
30. *Ibid.*, p. 97.
31. Windsor, *Windsor Revisited*, p. 101.
32. *Ibid.*, p. 77.
33. Windsor, *A King's Story*, p. 88.
34. *Ibid.*, p. 106.
35. *The New Yorker*, October 3, 1931.
36. Windsor, *A King's Story*, p. 97
37. Windsor, *Windsor Revisited*, p. 80.
38. Inglis, *Abdication*, p. 12.
39. *Ibid.*, p. 13.
40. *Ibid.*, p. 13.
41. *Ibid.*, p. 13.
42. Philip Guedella, *The Hundredth Year*, p. 23.
43. De Witt McKenzie, Associated Press article, October 27, 1936.

CHAPTER 5

1. Windsor, *The Heart Has Its Reasons*, p. 46.

2. U.S. Naval Academy yearbook, "Lucky Bag," class of 1910.
3. Personal interview.
4. Personal interview.
5. Baltimore *News-Post*, October 1, 1936.
6. Baltimore *News*, September 16, 1916.
7. Baltimore *American*, May 26, 1946.

CHAPTER 6

1. Windsor, *The Heart Has Its Reasons*, p. 51.
2. Washington *Herald*, November 14, 1936.
3. Millay, Edna St. Vincent, *A Few Figs From Thistles* (1922).
4. London *Daily Express*, March 12, 1958.

CHAPTER 7

1. Personal interview.
2. Personal interview.
3. Washington *Post*, November 26, 1942.
4. Personal interview.
5. Personal interview.
6. Windsor, *The Heart Has Its Reasons*, p. 86.
7. Personal interview.
8. Personal interview.
9. Personal interview.
10. Personal interview.
11. Personal interview.
12. Personal interview.

CHAPTER 8

1. Personal interview.
2. Personal interview.
3. Personal interview.

4. Henry Yule, *The Book of Ser Marco Polo*.
5. Windsor, *The Heart Has Its Reasons*, p. 106.
6. *Ibid.*
7. *Ibid.*
8. Cecil Beaton, *The Wandering Years*, p. 307.
9. Personal interview.
10. *Ibid.*

CHAPTER 9

1. Personal interview.
2. Personal interview.
3. Baltimore *News-Post*, December 28, 1936.
4. Baltimore *American*, May 26, 1946.
5. Baltimore *News*, October 28, 1927.
6. Personal interview.
7. June 15, 1924.
8. Associated Press article, October 17, 1936.

CHAPTER 10

1. Associated Press article, October 17, 1936.
2. Windsor, *The Heart Has Its Reasons*, p. 127.
3. *Ibid.*
4. *Ibid.*
5. Gloria Vanderbilt and Lady Furness, *Double Exposure*, p. 274.
6. *Ibid.*, p. 274.
7. *Ibid.*
8. Windsor, *The Heart Has Its Reasons*.
9. Bocca, *The Woman Who Would Be Queen*, p. 107.
10. Vanderbilt and Furness, p. 275.
11. *Ibid.*
12. Slater, *Aly*, p. 88.

CHAPTER 11

1. *The New York Times*, May 29, 1972.
2. Windsor, *A King's Story*, p. 134.
3. Windsor, *Windsor Revisited*, p. 116.
4. *Ibid.*, p. 101.
5. Airlie, p. 145.
6. *The New Yorker*, October 3, 1931.
7. Windsor, *A King's Story*, p. 144.
8. *Ibid.*, p. 134.
9. *The New York Times*, January 14, 1970.
10. *Ibid.*
11. Isabel Leighton, *The Aspirin Age*, p. 370.
12. *The New York Times*, December 11, 1936.
13. *The New York Times*, May 29, 1972.
14. Inglis, *Abdication*, p. 23.
15. Nicolson, *King George V*, p. 366.
16. Frederick Winston Birkenhead, *Walter Monckton*, p. 124.
17. Windsor, *A King's Story*, p. 203.
18. *The New York Times*, May 29, 1972.
19. *News Review*, December 10, 1936.
20. Brody, p. 115.
21. Baltimore *American*, October 14, 1934.
22. Personal interview.
23. Personal interview.
24. Vanderbilt and Furness, pp. 177-178.
25. Personal interview.
26. Personal interview.
27. Slater, *Aly*, pp. 87-88.
28. *Ibid.*
29. *Ibid.*
30. Personal interview.

CHAPTER 12

1. Ferdinand Kuhn, "Britain: A Story of Old Age," in Hanson Baldwin and Shepard Stone, eds., *We Saw It Happen*, p. 169.
2. *Ibid.*, p. 174.
3. A. J. P. Taylor, *English History*, pp. 298-299.
4. *Ibid.*, p. 285.
5. Hector Bolitho, *King Edward VIII*.
6. Airlie, p. 178.
7. Windsor, *The Heart Has Its Reasons*.
8. Kirk letters, *op. cit.*
9. *Ibid.*
10. Edwina Wilson, *Her Name Was Wallis Warfield*, p. 86.
11. Vanderbilt and Furness, p. 275.
12. Windsor, *The Heart Has Its Reasons*, p. 163.
13. *Ibid.*, p. 164.
14. Diana Cooper, *The Light of Common Day*, pp. 159-160.
15. Windsor, *The Heart Has Its Reasons*.
16. Personal interview.
17. *Ibid.*
18. Vanderbilt and Furness, p. 291.
19. London *Daily Herald*, March 16, 1959.
20. Vanderbilt and Furness, p. 294.
21. New York *Sunday News*, September 20, 1936.
22. Slater, *Aly*, pp. 86-87.
23. Personal interview.
24. Windsor, *The Heart Has Its Reasons*, p. 183.

CHAPTER 13

1. Personal interview.
2. *Ibid.*
3. Personal interview.

4. Vanderbilt and Furness, p. 295.
5. Ibid., pp. 296–297.
6. Ibid., p. 297.
7. Ibid., p. 298.
8. Time magazine, Dec. 14, 1936.
9. Personal interview.
10. Personal interview.
11. Liberty magazine, January 23, 1937.
12. Personal interview.
13. Baltimore American, March 11, 1951.
14. Personal interview.
15. Personal interview.
16. Bocca, The Woman Who Would Be Queen, p. 98.
17. Airlie, p. 200.
18. Ibid.
19. Baltimore News-Post, August 10, 1934.
20. Baltimore News-Post, August 15, 1934.
21. New York Sunday News, September 20, 1936.
22. New York Evening Post, October 4, 1938.
23. Baltimore American, October 14, 1934.
24. Windsor, The Heart Has Its Reasons, p. 191.
25. June 18, 1935. National Archives, Washington, D.C.
26. Windsor, The Heart Has Its Reasons.
27. Airlie, p. 197.
28. London Observer Review, June 24, 1973.
29. Personal interview.
30. Viscount Templewood, Nine Troubled Years, p. 216.
31. Time magazine, November 9, 1936.
32. Personal interview.
33. Cooper, p. 159.
34. Harold Nicolson, Diaries & Letters, 1930–1939, p. 232.

35. Ibid., p. 238.
36. Ibid., p. 258.
37. Windsor, The Heart Has Its Reasons, p. 212.

CHAPTER 14

1. Duke of Windsor, The Crown and The People, pp. 1–2.
2. Taylor, English History, p. 398.
3. Time magazine, November 23, 1936.
4. Inglis, Abdication, p. 45, quoting Lord Boothby and Walter Elliott, Minister of Agriculture, who overheard it.
5. March 1, 1936, BBC.
6. Inglis, Abdication, p. 148.
7. John Gunther, Inside Europe, p. 232.
8. Ibid., p. 230.
9. Windsor, The Heart Has Its Reasons, p. 216.
10. Ibid., p. 217.
11. Nicolson, Diaries & Letters, pp. 261–262.
12. G. M. Young, Stanley Baldwin, p. 233.
13. Anne Fremantle, Three-Cornered Heart, p. 223.
14. Nicolson, Diaries & Letters, p. 263.
15. Ibid., p. 255.
16. Birkenhead, p. 157.
17. Washington Post, September 20, 1936.
18. The New York Times, October 3, 1936.
19. Personal interview.
20. Personal interview.
21. Birkenhead, p. 128.
22. Time magazine, October 5, 1936.
23. Cooper, pp. 173–174.
24. Ibid., p. 174.
25. Cavalcade, August 15, 1936.

26. Windsor, *The Heart Has Its Reasons*, p. 221.
27. Cooper, p. 180.
28. Windsor, *A King's Story*, p. 309.
29. Cooper, p. 183.
30. New York *Sunday News*, September 20, 1936.
31. *Ibid.*
32. *Ibid.*
33. *Ibid.*
34. Helen Worden, New York *World Telegram*, December 10, 1936.
35. Personal interview.

CHAPTER 15

1. Nicolson, *Diaries & Letters*, p. 246.
2. *Time* magazine, November 7, 1936.
3. Airlie, p. 199.
4. Windsor, *A King's Story*.
5. Beaton, p. 308.
6. *Time* magazine, November 2, 1936.
7. Airlie, pp. 197–198.
8. *Ibid.*, p. 198.
9. *Ibid.*
10. *Time* magazine, October 5, 1936.
11. *Ibid.*
12. Beaton, p. 301.
13. London *Observer Review*, June 24, 1973.
14. Beaton, p. 301.
15. *Ibid.*
16. *Ibid.*
17. *Ibid.*, p. 302.
18. *Ibid.*
19. *Ibid.*

CHAPTER 16

1. Brody, p. 199.
2. David Hume, *History of England*, New York, Harper, 1880.

3. Birkenhead, p. 125.
4. *Ibid.*, p. 126.
5. *Ibid.*, p. 157.
6. *Ibid.*
7. Nicolson, *Diaries & Letters*, p. 269.
8. *Ibid.*, p. 275.
9. Birkenhead, p. 129.
10. *Ibid.*, p. 127.
11. *A History of The Times*, Vol. 4, p. 602.
12. *Literary Digest*, May 29, 1937.
13. Birkenhead, pp. 129–130.
14. Lord Beaverbrook, *The Abdication of King Edward VIII*, p. 130.
15. Inglis, p. 179.
16. Beaton, p. 305.
17. Inglis, p. 74.
18. Gunther, p. 262.
19. *Ibid.*
20. *Ibid.*, p. 233.
21. Inglis, p. 130.
22. Gunther, p. 266.
23. Young, p. 51.
24. Inglis, p. 73.
25. Churchill, *The Gathering Storm*, p. 216.
26. Inglis, p. 72.
27. Thomas Jones, *A Diary With Letters, 1931–1950*, p. 69.
28. May 3, 1935.
29. Young, p. 234.
30. Windsor, *A King's Story*, p. 319.
31. *Ibid.*, p. 320.
32. Inglis, p. 69.
33. *The New York Times*, October 20, 1936.
34. Lord Rothermere quoted in New York *Evening Journal* editorial, December 14, 1936.
35. Walter Winchell column, undated clipping 1936.
36. New York *Daily News* editorial, undated clipping.
37. Letter dated October 15, 1936,

signed BRITANNICUS IN PARTI-
BUS INFIDELIUM, in Evelyn
Wrench, *Geoffrey Dawson and
Our Times*, p. 339.
38. *Ibid.*
39. *Ibid.*, p. 342.
40. Inglis, p. 151.
41. J. G. Lockhart, *Cosmo Gordon
Lang*, p. 106.
42. *Ibid.*, p. 398.

CHAPTER 17

1. Anonymous Irish poet, in Inglis,
p. 168.
2. Personal interview.
3. Hearst correspondent Thomas
Watson, quoted in *Time* magazine, November 9, 1936.
4. Jack Beall, New York *Herald
Tribune*, quoted in *ibid.*
5. W. F. Leysmith, *The New York
Times.*
6. *The New York Times*, October
28, 1936.
7. *Ibid.*
8. *Ibid.*
9. *Ibid.*

CHAPTER 18

1. *Time* magazine, November 2,
1936.
2. *Ibid.*
3. Inglis, p. 192.
4. *Ibid.*, p. 193.
5. *A History of The Times*, p. 598.
6. *The Times* of London, editorial,
December 3, 1936.
7. Templewood, p. 223.
8. Wrench, p. 343.
9. Airlie, p. 201.
10. *Ibid.*, p. 200.
11. *Ibid.*
12. *Ibid.*
13. Personal interview.

14. Personal interview.
15. New York *Daily News*, November 17, 1936.
16. Fritz Hesse, *Hitler and the English.*
17. *Ibid.*
18. Cooper, p. 216.
19. Nicolson, *Diaries & Letters*, p.
276.
20. Wrench, p. 344.
21. Beaton, p. 301.
22. Templewood, pp. 218–219.
23. *Ibid.*, p. 219.
24. *The New York Times*, November 19, 1936.
25. Wrench, p. 345.
26. *The Times* of London, November 29, 1955.
27. Beaverbrook, p. 99.
28. *The Times* of London, November 29, 1955.
29. *Ibid.*
30. Inglis, *Abdication*, p. 210.
31. Birkenhead, p. 126.
32. *Ibid.*
33. Windsor, *The Heart Has Its
Reasons*, p. 236.
34. *Ibid.*
35. Personal interview.

CHAPTER 19

1. Windsor, *A King's Story*, p. 330.
2. Birkenhead, p. 134.
3. Inglis, *Abdication*, p. 212.
4. Windsor, *A King's Story*, p. 333.
5. *Ibid.*
6. Pope-Hennessy, pp. 574–575.
7. Airlie, p. 200.
8. *Ibid.*
9. Pope-Hennessy, p. 575.
10. Clement R. Attlee, *As It Happened*, p. 123.
11. Nicolson, *Diaries & Letters*, pp.
279–280.

12. *News-Week,* November 26, 1936.
13. *Ibid.*
14. *Ibid.*
15. *Ibid.*
16. *Ibid.*
17. Fremantle, p. 178.
18. Windsor, *The Heart Has Its Reasons,* p. 240.
19. Windsor, *A King's Story,* p. 290.
20. Birkenhead, p. 137.
21. Inglis, p. 267.
22. Windsor, *A King's Story,* p. 343.
23. *Ibid.*
24. *The Sunday Times* of London, April 24, 1966.
25. Inglis, p. 181.
26. *Ibid.,* p. 184.
27. Beaverbrook, p. 55.
28. *Ibid.,* p. 34.
29. *Ibid.,* p. 35.
30. *Ibid.*
31. *Ibid.*
32. *Ibid.,* p. 57.
33. Nicolson, *Diaries & Letters,* p. 280.
34. Article by Margaret Case Harriman, in Leighton, p. 378.
35. *Ibid.*
36. Marion Crawford, *The Little Princesses,* p. 72.
37. *Ibid.,* p. 80.
38. Leighton, p. 378.
39. Windsor, *A King's Story,* p. 346.
40. Nicolson, *Diaries & Letters,* p. 280.
41. *Ibid.*
42. Wrench, p. 346.
43. *Ibid.,* p. 347.
44. Leighton, p. 379.
45. Birkenhead, p. 126.

CHAPTER 20

1. *The New York Times,* December 4, 1936.
2. Washington *Post,* October 24, 1936.
3. *Ibid.*
4. *Time* magazine, November 16, 1936.
5. New York *Evening Journal,* December 11, 1936.
6. New York *Herald Tribune,* November 28, 1936.
7. *Ibid.*
8. *Ibid.*
9. Washington *Star,* December 16, 1936.
10. *Ibid.*
11. Washington *Star,* December 19, 1932.
12. *Ibid.*
13. Personal interview.
14. *The New York Times,* December 8, 1936.
15. Baltimore *News-Post,* December 9, 1936.
16. Christopher Sykes, *Nancy, The Life of Lady Astor,* p. 376.
17. Nicolson, *Diaries & Letters,* p. 396–397.
18. *Ibid.*
19. *The New York Times,* December 16, 1936.
20. Windsor, *The Heart Has Its Reasons.*
21. Wrench, p. 347.
22. *Ibid.*
23. Birkenhead, p. 140.
24. *Ibid.,* p. 136.
25. C. L. Sulzberger, *The New York Times,* May 31, 1972.
26. Inglis.
27. Personal interview.
28. *Ibid.*
29. Beaverbrook, p. 70.
30. *Time* magazine, December 7, 1936.
31. *Ibid.*
32. Wrench, p. 349.
33. December 10, 1936.

34. Leighton, p. 379–380.
35. December 10, 1936.
36. Inglis, *Abdication*, p. 277.
37. *Ibid.*
38. Washington *Star*, December 16, 1936.
39. *Ibid.*
40. *Ibid.*
41. Washington *Star*, December 23, 1936
42. Washington *Star*, December 17, 1936
43. *Ibid.*
44. *Ibid.*
45. Washington *Star*, December 17, 1936.
46. *Ibid.*
47. *Ibid.*
48. *Ibid.*
49. Newbold Noyes, Washington *Evening Star*, undated clipping.
50. *Ibid.*
51. Windsor, *The Heart Has Its Reasons*.
52. Wrench, p. 349.
53. Young, p. 238.
54. Windsor, *A King's Story*, p. 359.
55. Personal interview.
56. *Ibid.*

CHAPTER 21

1. Personal interview.
2. *Ibid.*
3. *Ibid.*
4. *Ibid.*
5. *Ibid.*
6. *Ibid.*
7. Washington *Herald*, December 5, 1936.
8. Personal interview.
9. *Ibid.*
10. Beaverbrook, p. 78.
11. Personal interview.
12. *Ibid.*

13. *The New York Times*, December 7, 1936.
14. *Ibid.*
15. Personal interview.
16. *Ibid.*
17. *The New York Times*, December 7, 1936.

CHAPTER 22

1. Windsor, *A King's Story*, p. 361.
2. Young, p. 242
3. Inglis, p. 303.
4. Kenneth Young, *Churchill and Beaverbrook*, p. 123.
5. Churchill, *The Gathering Storm*, p. 218.
6. Pope-Hennessy, p. 577.
7. Birkenhead, p. 142.
8. *Ibid.*
9. Beaverbrook, p. 78 note, quoting from Lloyd George papers.
10. *Ibid.*, p. 73.
11. *The New York Times*, December 7, 1936.
12. *The New York Times*, December 5, 1936.
13. London *Daily Herald*, December 6, 1936.
14. New York *Evening Journal*, December 7, 1936.
15. Washington *Herald*, December 5, 1936.
16. New York *Post*, December 4, 1936.
17. *Time* magazine, December 14, 1936.
18. *Time* magazine, November 16, 1936.
19. Jessica Mitford, *Daughters and Rebels*.
20. *Ibid.*
21. Birkenhead, p. 144.
22. Inglis, *Abdication*, p. 323.

CHAPTER 23

1. Martin, p. 111.
2. Interview by Clare Boothe Luce, *McCall's*, August 1966.
3. Lockhart, pp. 398–399.
4. *Ibid.*
5. *Ibid.*, p. 401.
6. Fremantle, p. 178.
7. *Ibid.*
8. Beaverbrook, p. 77.
9. Personal interview.
10. Personal interview.
11. Birkenhead, p. 145.
12. *Ibid.*
13. Nicolson, *Diaries & Letters*, p. 282.
14. *Ibid.*, pp. 282–283.
15. *The New York Times*, December 6, 1936.
16. *Literary Digest*, December 12, 1936.
17. *Ibid.*
18. *Ibid.*
19. *Ibid.*
20. *Ibid.*
21. *Ibid.*
22. Beaverbrook, p. 80.
23. *Ibid.*
24. Birkenhead, p. 144.
25. *Ibid.*
26. New York *Evening Post*, December 4, 1936.
27. *The Sunday People*, London, May 6, 1973.
28. Personal interview.
29. Beaverbrook, *Abdication of King Edward VIII.*
30. Washington *Herald*, December 8, 1936.
31. New York *Evening Post*, December 9, 1936.
32. *The New York Times*, December 6, 1936.
33. *Ibid.*
34. *Time* magazine, November 30, 1936.
35. Birkenhead, p. 145.
36. *Ibid.*, p. 146.
37. *Ibid.*
38. *Ibid.*, p. 145.
39. Washington *Herald*, December 7, 1936.
40. *The Times* of London, December 3, 1936, editorial.
41. Personal interview.
42. Washington *Herald*, December 8, 1936.
43. Windsor, *The Heart Has Its Reasons.*
44. Martin, p. 111.
45. Nicolson, *Diaries & Letters*, p. 282.
46. Inglis, p. 337.
47. Nicolson, *Diaries & Letters*, p. 284.
48. Beaverbrook, p. 109.
49. *Ibid.*
50. Nicolson, *Diaries & Letters*, p. 282.
51. Personal interview.
52. *Ibid.*
53. Personal interview.
54. *The New York Times*, December 9, 1936.
55. *The Times* of London, December 6, 1936.
56. Tom Driberg review of *History of The Times*, quoted in Inglis, p. 350.
57. Wrench, p. 351.
58. Personal interview.
59. *Ibid.*
60. From statement written by Goddard in July 1951, in Beaverbrook, p. 119.
61. Personal interview.
62. Beaverbrook, p. 119.
63. Birkenhead, p. 147.
64. Young, p. 243.
65. *Ibid.*

66. Inglis, p. 356.
67. Birkenhead, p. 149.
68. Personal interview.
69. *Ibid.*
70. *Ibid.*

CHAPTER 24

1. Personal interview.
2. Nicolson, *Diaries & Letters*, pp. 283–284.
3. Birkenhead, p. 150.
4. Windsor, *A King's Story*, p. 402.
5. *The New York Times Magazine*, January 22, 1939.
6. New York *World Telegram*, December 10, 1936.
7. Birkenhead, p. 150.
8. Windsor, *A King's Story*, p. 406.
9. *Ibid.*
10. New York *Evening Post*, December 4, 1936.
11. Nicolson, *Diaries & Letters*, pp. 285–286.
12. Personal interview.
13. Birkenhead, p. 148.
14. Personal interview.
15. Birkenhead, p. 151.
16. *Ibid.*, p. 152.
17. *Ibid.*
18. *Ibid.*, p. 151.
19. Inglis, p. 365.
20. Randolph Churchill, *American Weekly*.
21. *Ibid.*
22. Birkenhead, p. 152.
23. *Ibid.*
24. Personal interview.
25. Personal interview.
26. Birkenhead, p. 153.
27. *Ibid.*
28. London *Daily Telegraph*, May 29, 1972.
29. Birkenhead, p. 154.

30. *Ibid.*
31. Young, p. 241.
32. Inglis, *Abdication*, p. 369.

CHAPTER 25

1. Edna Livingston, New York *Evening Journal*, December 12, 1936.
2. London *Daily Express*, September 4, 1956.
3. New York *Evening Journal*, December 12, 1936.
4. New York *American*, December 9, 1936.
5. *The New York Times*, December 11, 1936.
6. Philip Gibbs, *Ordeal in England*, p. 96.
7. Dorothy Laird, *Queen Elizabeth*, p. 154.
8. *The New York Times*, December 26, 1936.
9. December 11, 1936, Department of State file, National Archives, Washington, D.C., 841.001, VIII/77.
10. *The New York Times*, December 11, 1936.

CHAPTER 26

1. Admiral Fisher, in Templewood, p. 223.
2. Beaverbrook, p. 109.
3. *The New York Times*, editorial.
4. *American Weekly*, December 9, 1956.
5. Lockhart, p. 405.
6. *Ibid.*
7. *Ibid.*
8. *Ibid.*
9. Inglis, p. 397.

10. Lockhart, p. 406. The original quatrain was written by Gerald Bulleth, with a different final line. Inglis, p. 384.
11. Washington *Herald*, December 26, 1936.
12. *The New York Times*, December 16, 1936.
13. *Ibid.*
14. Personal interview.

CHAPTER 27

1. *Time* magazine, December 14, 1936.
2. Baltimore *News-Post*, December 18, 1936.
3. New York *Herald Tribune*, December 21, 1936.
4. Brody, p. 240.
5. New York *Evening Journal*, December 29, 1936.
6. *The New York Times*, February 6, 1937.
7. Elsa Maxwell, *R.S.V.P.*, p. 310.
8. Baltimore *News-Post*, December 11, 1936.
9. *Time and Tide*, reprinted by New York *American*, December 11, 1936.
10. Vanderbilt and Furness, p. 276.
11. *Ibid.*
12. *The New York Times*, September 19, 1949.
13. New York *Sunday News*, December 11, 1966.
14. *American Weekly*, December 9, 1956.
15. Frances Stevenson, *Lloyd George*, p. 326–327.

CHAPTER 28

1. Brody, p. 237.
2. Personal interview.
3. Personal interview.

4. *The New York Times*, March 12, 1937.
5. Washington *Post*, May 5, 1937.
6. *Ibid.*
7. *Ibid.*
8. Personal interview.
9. Beaton, p. 305.
10. *Ibid.*
11. *Ibid.*, p. 306.
12. *Ibid.*
13. *The New York Times*, May 3, 1937.

CHAPTER 29

1. Windsor, *The Heart Has Its Reasons*, p. 288.
2. CBS *Person to Person* with Edward R. Murrow, September 28, 1956.
3. Beaton, p. 305.
4. New York *American*, June 3, 1936.
5. Personal interview.
6. Havelock Ellis, Washington *Herald*, December 16, 1936.
7. Personal interview.
8. Jardine, *At Long Last*, p. 54.
9. New York *Journal American*, June 3, 1962.
10. Beaton, p. 309.
11. Undated clipping.
12. Personal interview.
13. New York *Daily Mirror*, December 4, 1937.
14. Joy Miller, *Today's Women*, AGYS News Features, June 6, 1962.
15. Baltimore *American*, June 3, 1962.
16. *Burke's Peerage*, September 1, 1967.
17. New York *American*, June 3, 1936.
18. Birkenhead, p. 166.

19. *Ibid.*
20. Beaton, p. 307.
21. New York *Herald Tribune*, May 24, 1972.
22. Toledo *Times*, June 2, 1967.
23. Jardine, p. 72.
24. *Ibid.*
25. *Ibid.*
26. *Ibid.*, p. 73.
27. *Ibid.*
28. Beaton, p. 310.
29. *Ibid.*
30. *The New York Times*, June 3, 1936.
31. *Ibid.*
32. Toledo *Times*, June 2, 1967.
33. *Ibid.*
34. Jardine, p. 85.
35. *Ibid.*
36. Personal interview.
37. *The Times* of London, May 29, 1972.
38. Birkenhead, p. 166.
39. Jardine, p. 88.
40. *Ibid.*, p. 91.
41. *Ibid.*
42. Personal interview.
43. *The Literary Digest*, No. 14, 1936.
44. Birkenhead, p. 162.

CHAPTER 30

1. New York *Journal American*, June 3, 1962.
2. New York *Herald Tribune*, December 13, 1936.
3. Allen Andrews, *Quotations for Speakers and Writers*, p. 288.
4. *This Week*, November 25, 1956.
5. Windsor, *Windsor Revisited*, p. 198.
6. *The Literary Digest*, May 29, 1937.
7. Nicolson, *Diaries & Letters*, p. 286.

8. Birkenhead, p. 161.
9. Baltimore *Evening Sun*, June 3, 1937.
10. London *Evening Standard*, June 11, 1937.
11. *American Weekly*, November 11, 1936.
12. *This Week*, November 25, 1956.

CHAPTER 31

1. Winston Churchill, *Step by Step*, New York, Putnam, 1939, p. 137.
2. *The New York Times*, November 4, 1937.
3. Birkenhead, p. 168.
4. Windsor, *The Heart Has Its Reasons.*
5. *Documents on German Foreign Policy* [hereinafter DGFP], London, Her Majesty's Stationery Office, 1962, pp. 1024–1025. Telegram (?) on previous page missing.
6. Ribbentrop, Joachim von, *Ribbentrop Memoirs*, p. 61.
7. James Graham-Murray, *The Sword and Umbrella*, p. 125.
8. *Ibid.*, p. 162.
9. London *Daily Express*, October 30, 1962.
10. *The Times* of London, October 24, 1937.
11. William L. Shirer, *Berlin Diary*, p. 88.
12. Paul Schmidt, *Hitler's Interpreter*, p. 74.
13. London *Daily Express*, August 15, 1958.
14. *Ibid.*
15. Schmidt, p. 75.
16. Windsor, *The Heart Has Its Reasons*, p. 300.
17. *Ibid.*

CHAPTER 32

1. Birkenhead, p. 169.
2. Philadelphia *Inquirer*, undated clipping.
3. Manchester *Guardian*, November 12, 1936.
4. New York *Herald Tribune*, October 28, 1937.
5. November 2, 1937, Department of State memorandum of conversations, confidential file, National Archives, Washington, D.C., FW033.4111.

CHAPTER 33

1. Personal interview.
2. *Ibid.*
3. *Ibid.*
4. *The New York Times*, November 20, 1937.
5. *Ibid.*
6. Maxwell, *R.S.V.P.*, p. 300.
7. Birkenhead, p. 168.
8. *Ibid.*
9. Personal interview.
10. Nicolson, *Diaries & Letters*, p. 351.
11. *The Sunday People*, London, April 29, 1973.
12. Birkenhead, p. 169.
13. *The New York Times*, January 25, 1939.
14. Maxwell, *R.S.V.P.*, p. 301.
15. *The New York Times*, May 9, 1939.
16. Adela Rogers St. Johns, *The Honeycomb*, pp. 531–532.
17. Birkenhead, p. 170.

CHAPTER 34

1. Windsor, *The Heart Has Its Reasons*, p. 316.
2. Birkenhead, p. 172.

3. *Ibid.*
4. R. J. Minney, *The Private Papers of Hore-Belisha*, p. 238.
5. House of Commons, March 23, 1933.
6. Alistair Horne, *To Lose a Battle*, p. 116.
7. *Ibid.*, p. 118.
8. Report by Gordon Waterfield, in *ibid*, p. 112.
9. Quoting Simone de Beauvoir in *ibid.*, pp. 102–103.
10. *Ibid.*, p. 103.
11. Baltimore *American*, December 24, 1939.
12. Horne, p. 107.
13. *Ibid.*, p. 393.
14. *Ibid.*
15. *Ibid.*
16. *Ibid.*

CHAPTER 35

1. Lewis Hagen, *The Schellenberg Memoirs*, pp. 129–130.
2. *Ibid.*, p. 130.
3. *Ibid.*, p. 131.
4. *Ibid.*
5. London *Daily Express*, undated clipping.
6. DGFP, No. 2051, June 23, 1940, p. 2.
7. DGFP, No. 1, June 24, 1940, p. 9.
8. Windsor, *The Heart Has Its Reasons*.
9. DGFP, No. 2182, July 2, 1940, p. 97.
10. Public Record Office, London, Cable Reference F.O. 371, 24249, 556, Cable No. 479, July 4, 1940.
11. Cable No. 369, July 4, 1940.
12. Cable No. 1447, July 9, 1940.
13. DGFP, No. 2298, July 9, 1940, p. 187.

14. DGFP, Most Urgent, No. 1023, July 11, 1940, p. 187.
15. Ibid.
16. DGFP, Most Urgent, No. 2331, July 12, 1940, p. 199.
17. DGFP, No. 2558, July 13, 1940, p. 199.
18. Hagen, p. 138.
19. Cable No. 164, July 20, 1940.
20. DGFP, Top Secret, No. 2384, July 16, 1940, p. 223.
21. Ibid.
22. DGFP, No. 2474, July 23, 1940, p. 227.
23. DGFP, Urgent, Strictly Confidential, No. 2495, July 25, 1940, p. 290.
24. Hagen, p. 139.
25. DGFP, Most Urgent, Top Secret, No. 2520, July 26, 1940, pp. 317–318.
26. Washington Post, August 1, 1940.
27. Ibid.
28. Cable No. 1373, July 17, 1940.
29. Cleveland Press, undated clipping.
30. Cable No. 439, July 18, 1940.
31. Hagen, p. 138.
32. Ibid., p. 139.
33. Birkenhead, p. 180.
34. DGFP, Most Urgent, No. 808, August 2, 1940, p. 401.
35. Cable No. 478, July 24, 1940.
36. Ibid.
37. Cable No. 485, July 26, 1940.
38. DGFP, Most Urgent, Top Secret, No. 2663, August 3, 1940, p. 409.
39. DGFP, Most Urgent, Top Secret, No. 2598, July 31, 1940, p. 377.
40. DGFP, p. 398. Number on previous page, which is missing.

CHAPTER 36

1. The New York Times, August 19, 1940.
2. The New York Times, August 8, 1940.
3. The New York Times, August 9, 1940.
4. Baltimore News-Post, January 6, 1938.
5. The New York Times, August 9, 1940.
6. Ibid.
7. Ibid.
8. Ibid.
9. Ibid.
10. The New York Times, August 17, 1940.
11. Ibid.
12. Personal interview.
13. Life magazine, December 23, 1940.
14. Ibid.
15. Public Record Office, F.O. 371-24249-556, August 24, 1940.
16. Life magazine, December 23, 1940.
17. Ibid.
18. Ibid.
19. Leighton, p. 365.
20. Personal interview.
21. Leighton, p. 366.
22. Personal interview.
23. United Press International, Nassau, September 5, 1940.
24. Ibid.
25. Personal interview.
26. Ibid.
27. Ibid.
28. Ibid.
29. Ibid.
30. Ibid.
31. Ibid.
32. Ibid.
33. Life magazine, December 23, 1940.

34. *Ibid.*
35. *The New York Times,* August 24, 1940.
36. United Press International, Nassau, September 5, 1940.

CHAPTER 37

1. *The New York Times,* April 19, 1941.
2. *The New York Times,* September 26, 1941.
3. Personal interview.
4. Personal interview.
5. St. Johns, p. 466.
6. Baltimore *News-Post,* October 7, 1937.
7. Baltimore *News-Post,* October 10, 1941.
8. Baltimore *American,* October 12, 1941.
9. Baltimore *News-Post,* undated.
10. *Ibid.*
11. Baltimore *Sun,* October 14, 1941.
12. Baltimore *American,* October 12, 1941.
13. Baltimore *Sun,* October 14, 1941.
14. *Ibid.*
15. Baltimore *Sun,* October 13, 1955.
16. Baltimore *Sun,* October 14, 1941.
17. New York *Post,* undated.
18. Associated Press Features Service, October 14, 1936.

CHAPTER 38

1. Personal interview.
2. *Ibid.*
3. *Ibid.*
4. *Ibid.*
5. *Ibid.*
6. *Ibid.*
7. New York *Post,* June 5, 1943.
8. *Life* magazine, December 23, 1940.

9. *Ibid.*
10. Personal interview.
11. *Ibid.*
12. *Ibid.*
13. Personal interview.

CHAPTER 39

1. Personal interview.
2. *Ibid.*
3. *Life* magazine, December 23, 1940.
4. Personal interview.

CHAPTER 40

1. Elsa Maxwell, *The New York Times,* May 29, 1972.
2. Personal interview.
3. Maxwell, *R.S.V.P.,* p. 301.
4. Leonard Lyons, London *Sunday Express,* December 2, 1962.
5. New York *Daily Mirror,* December 8, 1946.
6. Personal interview.
7. London *Evening Standard,* December 13, 1946.
8. Personal interview.
9. Inez Robb, New York *Daily Mirror,* December 8, 1946.
10. *The New York Times,* December 11, 1947.
11. *Parade* magazine, August 20, 1967.
12. *Women's Wear Daily,* March 17, 1967.
13. *Time* magazine, April 8, 1966.
14. Boston *Sunday Globe,* June 6, 1971.
15. Helen Wordon, *American Mercury,* June 1944.
16. Personal interview.
17. *Ibid.*
18. *Ibid.*

19. *Ibid.*
20. "The Londoner's Diary," quoted in *The New York Times*, September 3, 1947.
21. Personal interview.
22. *Esquire*, January 1973.
23. Personal interview.
24. *Esquire*, January 1973.
25. Leonard Lyons, London *Sunday Express*, December 2, 1962.
26. Brody, p. 4.

CHAPTER 41

1. *Women's Wear Daily*, May 21, 1968.
2. Personal interview.
3. New York *Post*, June 3, 1972.
4. Personal interview.
5. *Ibid.*
6. *Ibid.*
7. *Vogue*, April 1, 1964.
8. London *Sunday Dispatch*, March 12, 1939.
9. Personal interview.
10. *Ibid.*
11. London *Daily Mail*, February 27, 1957.
12. Personal interview.
13. *The Sunday People*, London, May 13, 1973.
14. Considine, *It's All News to Me*, p. 321.
15. Personal interview.
16. Personal interview.
17. Baltimore *Evening Sun*, September 3, 1971.
18. Harry Reasoner, *Sixty Minutes*, CBS Television Network, February 4, 1969.
19. Dina Hood, *Working for the Windsors*.
20. *Family Weekly*, June 3, 1962.
21. Personal interview.
22. *Ibid.*

23. Maxwell, *R.S.V.P.*, p. 308.
24. Considine, p. 323.

CHAPTER 42

1. Personal interview.
2. Washington *Post*, May 24, 1967.
3. Personal interview.
4. *Ibid.*
5. *Ibid.*
6. *Ibid.*
7. *Ibid.*
8. *Ibid.*
9. *Ibid.*
10. London *Daily Express*, June 3, 1957.
11. Lorelle Hearst, Palm Beach *Daily News*, April 18, 1966.
12. Personal interview.
13. Suzy Knickerbocker, Palm Beach *Post*, April 6, 1967.
14. Personal interview.
15. *Ibid.*
16. *Ibid.*
17. *Ibid.*
18. *Ibid.*
19. *American Weekly*, December 18, 1955.
20. London *Evening Standard*, undated clipping.
21. London *Daily Telegraph*, September 3, 1957.
22. *American Weekly*, December 1, 1957.
23. Washington *Post*, July 7, 1954.
24. *American Weekly*, December 5, 1954.
25. Art Buchwald column, June 11, 1954.
26. New York *Herald Tribune*, December 1, 1957.
27. Elsa Maxwell column, undated clipping, Palm Beach.
28. London *Daily Express*, undated clipping.

29. Personal interview.
30. *Ibid.*
31. *Ibid.*
32. *Ibid.*
33. New York *Daily News*, February 3, 1941.
34. London *Daily Mail*, June 19, 1961.
35. Personal interview.
36. *Ibid.*
37. *Ibid.*
38. *Ibid.*
39. *Ibid.*
40. *Ibid.*
41. *Ibid.*
42. *Ibid.*
43. *Ibid.*
44. *Ibid.*
45. *Ibid.*
46. London *Sunday Express*, December 2, 1962.
47. Personal interview.
48. *Ibid.*
49. *McCall's*, August 1966.
50. London *Evening Standard*, May 7, 1956.
51. *Ibid.*
52. Personal interview.
53. *Ibid.*
54. *Ibid.*
55. Personal interview.
56. *Ibid.*
57. *Ibid.*
58. *Ibid.*
59. London *Sunday Dispatch*, January 22, 1961.
60. Washington *Post*, January 14, 1970.
61. *Ibid.*
62. *Ibid.*
63. *Ibid.*
64. *The New York Times*, January 14, 1970.
65. Washington *Post*, January 21, 1970.
66. Frances Levine, Associated Press, April 5, 1970.
67. Personal interview.
68. *Ibid.*
69. London *Sunday Express*, December 2, 1962.

CHAPTER 43

1. London *Sunday Express*, December 2, 1962.
2. *Ibid.*
3. London *Evening Standard*, May 30, 1972.
4. Personal interview.
5. *Ibid.*
6. London *Daily Mail*, May 29, 1972.
7. *Ibid.*
8. *Ibid.*
9. Personal interview.
10. *Ibid.*
11. Reuters, London, June 3, 1972.
12. London *Sunday Express*, June 4, 1972.
13. Personal interview.
14. *Ibid.*
15. *Ibid.*
16. London *Daily Express*, May 29, 1972.

EPILOGUE

1. Personal interview.
2. *Ibid.*
3. Charles Murphy, *Time* magazine, November 19, 1973.
4. Personal interview.
5. *Ibid.*
6. Personal interview.
7. *Ibid.*
8. *Ibid.*

(*continued from copyright page*)

Andre Deutsch Ltd. for material from *The Labyrinth* (published in Great Britain as *The Schellenberg Memoirs*) by Walter Schellenberg, trans. by Lewis Hagen, copyright © 1956 by Harper & Row, Publishers, Inc.

Rupert Hart-Davis for material from *The Light of Common Day* by Lady Diana Cooper, copyright © 1959 by Rupert Hart-Davis.

Blake Higgs for lyrics from "Love Alone" by Blake Higgs.

David Higham Associates Ltd. for material from *Geoffrey Dawson and Our Times* by Sir Evelyn Wrench, published by Hutchinson & Company Ltd., copyright © 1955 by Sir Evelyn Wrench.

Little, Brown and Company and George Weidenfeld and Nicolson Ltd. for material from *The Wandering Years* by Cecil Beaton, copyright © 1961 by Cecil Beaton.

Macmillan Publishing Company, Inc., and Hodder and Stoughton Ltd. for material from *Abdication* by Brian Inglis, copyright © 1966 by Brian Inglis.

Newbold Noyes for articles by Newbold Noyes, © 1936 by The Evening Star Newspaper Company.

George Weidenfeld and Nicolson Limited for material from *Walter Monckton: The Life of the Viscount of Brenchley* by Frederick Winston Furneaux Smith, Second Earl of Birkenhead.

Index

[Page numbers in *italics* indicate photographs.]

531

Harding, Warren G., 64, 67, 74
Hardinge, Alexander, 168, 191–92,
  195, 211, 212–14, 216, 228,
  235, 286, 288, 367
Harmsworth, Esmond, 158, 221,
  239, 283
Harriman, Margaret Case, 405
Haugwitz-Reventlow, Count Kurt,
  of Denmark, 457
Hawke, Sir John, 200, 201, 202
Hayden, Sterling, 422
Hayes, Helen, 231
Hearst, Lorelle, 467
Hearst, Mrs. Millicent, 460
Hearst, William Randolph, 203
Heath, Edward, 489
Henry II, King of England, 209,
  486n
Henry VIII, King of England,
  197, 209
Herbert, A. P., 198, 265
Herbert, Michael, 132
Herrick, Myron T., 42
Hesse, Rudolf, 155, 348
Hesse, Fritz, 206–207
Higgs, Blake, 397
Hitler, Adolf, 120, 135, 136, 155,
  175, 191, 206, 207, 207n,
  234, 341, 355, 363, 365,
  368
  and air bombardment of
  England, 392–93
  and Windsors, 343–49, 351–52,
  377–80, 387
Hoare, Sir Samuel, 157, 168, 191,
  204, 210, 222–23, 379, 380
Hodgson, T. J., 258
Hoesch, Dr. Leopold von, 155,
  206–207, 344
Holden, Milton W. (Doc), 205–
  206, 425, 459, 467, 484
Holland, 374
Holloway, Stanley, 313
Homer (Greek poet), 173
Hood, Dina Wells, 455
Hopkins, Miriam, 268

Hore-Belisha, Leslie, 369
Houston, David F., 35
Houts, Marshall, 430–31
Hoyningen-Huene, Baron Oswald
  von, 391–92, 431
Hunter, George, 188, 290
Hunter, Kitty, 188, 208, 290
Hutton, Barbara, 456–57, 462

India, 255
Ironside, Sir Edmund, 368
Isle of Man, 16
Italy, 135, 166, 171, 182, 191, 207,
  341, 376
Ives, Mrs. Ernest L. "Buffie," 140

James I, King of England, 164
James II, King of England, 209,
  486n
Janeway, Mrs. Augustine, 30
Japan, 135–36, 341
Jardine, Robert, 119, 324, 329–30,
  331–33, 334–35, 339
Jenks, Sir Maurice, 186, 191
Jerome, Jennie, see Churchill,
  Lady Randolph
Johnson, Jack, 34
Johnson, Sidney, 439, 494
Jones, Tom, 224, 234, 254
Josephine, wife of Napoleon
  Bonaparte, 209
Justinian I, Byzantine emperor,
  209

Kemal Ataturk, 174, 175, 182, 348,
  351
Kennedy, Buttercup, 202
Kent, Duchess of, 179, 326
Kent, Duke of (Duke of Windsor's
  brother George), 151, 179,
  295, 321, 423, 485, 490
Kerr-Smiley, Maud, 130
Kerr, Walter, 383
Kersten, Mrs. Harold, 30–31
Keyser, Irvine, 36–37
Khan, Aga, 144, 250